I've Always Loved
Older Women...

I've Always Loved Older Women...

Stories for a Memoir

HOWARD C. BARKER

To order additional copies of this book, contact:
Xlibris
1-888-795-4274
www.Xlibris.com
Orders@Xlibris.com
748343

Contents

To my patient and tolerant family, with love,
My wife, Madeleine,
Our children, Thomas, India, and Mia,
And our grandchildren,
Christopher, Patrick, and Pearl.

AUTHOR'S NOTE

DURING MY SEVENTY-YEAR career as a set designer in theater, motion pictures, and television, I have been privileged to meet and work with many famous and near-famous personalities. Many of their names as well as some of their pictures appear in this book. However, this does not indicate personal nor intimate relationships. It simply means that I've enjoyed meeting and/or working with them, some only briefly, but I have admired them all.

Some other individuals' names in this memoir may have been changed. However, all my relationships, with my family and friends, have been warm, without rancor, and all of them have taught me a lot about life.

As my brilliant writing teacher, Mary Carroll Moore, said to her class of would-be authors,

"If you happen to be a famous movie star, a great athlete, or an American war hero, everyone will want to read your memoir. If you're not, you'd better write a very good book."

To me, writing a memoir is like visiting a half-remembered country, picking up souvenirs. Let me share these souvenirs with you.

CHAPTER I

A LITTLE ANCIENT HISTORY

Mississippi, 1893–1919

VELMA BISHOP, THE daughter of Sara and Stanhope Bishop, was born in Wayne County, near the small town of Hiwannee, Mississippi. Velma had two sisters, Amber and Clyde, and seven brothers–Bernard, Chester, Raymond, Ledger, Collin, Grady, and Howard–who made up the rest of the Bishop family. The Bishops were of Scotch-Irish and English heritage, with the exception of one exotic touch–an ancestor from Austria, whose name escapes me.

In the 1800s, the Bishops were not a huge family, and in those days, not all offspring survived. When I was a child, both Bernard and Chester had already passed away, but those who were living told me and my brother stories about our ancestors. I learned that in the latter part of the century, the Bishop family settled in the small town of Hattiesburg, Mississippi. Some of the grown-ups married and had children, some stayed home and supported the family, and most of the young ones went to school. After graduating, young Velma became a schoolteacher herself.

Clarence Waldorf Barker was a U.S. Army corporal in the cavalry during World War I. Born in Fort Wayne, Indiana, and a Yankee far from home, Corporal Barker was stationed at Camp Shelby, near Hattiesburg. After being introduced to Velma Bishop at a Methodist church spring social, the young soldier rode his horse to and fro between the camp and her home to court the young lady. In 1918, they were married in the family living room with her mother, brothers, and sister, a few relatives and friends attending. A yellowed newspaper clipping typically described their wedding, with details of the bride's dress, the flowers, and the guests, as well as mentioning that Clarence's father, C. C. Barker, had made the long train trip from Ohio for the wedding.

A marriage which came as a surprise to the many friends of the young couple was that of Miss Velma Bishop and Sergeant Clarence Waldorf Barker, of Fort Wayne, Ind., which occurred on Christmas Eve at the home of the bride's mother, Mrs. S. E. Bishop, on North Main street. The single ring ceremony was used, with the Rev. Paul D. Hardin, pastor of the Main Street Methodist Church, officiating.

The parlor was made beautiful with Yuletide decorations, cut flowers and two large United States flags.

Although a quiet marriage, with only the immediate relatives of the bride, and Sergeant Pope, of Camp Shelby, friend of the bridegroom, in attendance, it was beautiful in its extreme simplicity.

The bride was attractive in a suit of Pekin blue, with silver gray accessories and corsage bouquet of Killarney roses and ferns.

The marriage is of much interest in this city, where the family of the bride is well known and where she has resided since early girlhood. She has made a host of friends by her sweet disposition and charming personality. After graduating from the Hattiesburg high school several years ago, she attended the Mississippi Normal College and for the past few years has been classed as a most efficient public school teacher.

The bridegroom comes from a prominent Indiana family. He has been stationed at Camp Shelby since September, soon after which time dated the beginning of the romance which ended in the pretty marriage of Christmas Eve.

The young couple left immediately for a bridal trip to Sergeant Barker's home. They expect to return to Hattiesburg about January 5, where they will be at home to their friends.

This was the newspaper clipping about the wedding of my parents in 1918.

Nine months later, the happy couple's first baby, Courtland Bishop Barker, was born in the post hospital at Camp Shelby. As he was the only baby born in the camp during World War I, the U.S. Army presented him a silver cup, engraved with "Courtland Bishop Barker. September 10, 1919."

My mother, Velma Bishop Barker, c. 1920.

My father, Clarence Waldorf Barker, c. 1922.

My grandfather, Cortland Clarence Barker, c. 1900.

My father with his parents and sister Helen.

CHAPTER 2

REDUS STREET

Hattiesburg, Mississippi, 1924–1928

I DREW MY first breath on May 14, 1924, at the Forest County General Hospital in Hattiesburg–no more unique than the birth of any other baby except, of course, to my parents. I was christened Howard Clarence Barker, after my mother's brother Howard Bishop, and my father, Clarence Waldorf, generally known as C. W. Barker. By that time, World War I was history, and my father had been honorably discharged. Unlike Bishop, I was not presented with a silver cup by the U.S. Army, a fact that didn't actually bother me until I was older.

The Barker family lived in a small wooden bungalow on Redus Street, a dead-end graveled road that branched off North Main Street, almost at the edge of town. Redus Street may have been given its name because a family named Red owned the house directly opposite its entrance. Forgive me, but I don't remember much before I was four years old, but I do remember a little boy named Basil Red was invited to my fourth birthday party. I think Basil had red hair too.

I also remember our two-bedroom house was so modest, it didn't have a proper bathroom. It did have running water in the kitchen sink, and as far back as I can recall, we had baths in galvanized washtubs of water warmed on a wood-burning kitchen stove. We attended to our "other bathroom business" in an outhouse, more acceptably referred to as a water closet or privy, in the backyard. I can remember Mama unbuttoning my rompers for me to trot out to our "two-holer."

I also remember the day I was four years old, I watched my father chop down a tall slender tree out in the woods at the end of the street where we lived. He trimmed off the small limbs, and then he put the tree trunk on his shoulder and started back toward our house.

"Why'dja cut that tree down, Daddy?" I asked.

"Just you follow me," he answered, "and you'll see."

I followed him home and watched him dig a hole in our front yard, set the tree trunk up in it, and then pack the dirt in firmly around it.

"Are we gonna have a tree growing right in the middle of our yard?" I asked.

"No, son, it's just a sapling. With its roots cut off, it wouldn't grow anyway."

"Then what is it for?" I insisted.

"It's for your birthday party this afternoon," he said. "And you can help me finish it."

Then he wrapped it from top to bottom with bands of pink and green crepe paper. It looked like a giant candy cane. Actually, I really didn't help. I mostly just handed him the rest of the pink and green streamers, one by one, and watched him attach about ten or twelve of them to the top of the pole.

"It's called a maypole," he said. "Where I lived up north, children whose birthday came in May had maypoles for their parties. You are supposed to sing and dance around the maypole and weave the streamers in and out all the way from the top to the bottom."

That afternoon at my birthday party, the children loved the maypole, but we didn't sing and dance and weave the streamers. We all ran wildly around and around the pole, laughing and jumping up and down. It was lots of fun, but lots of the streamers ended up scattered on the ground. My brother, Bishop, gathered the streamers, tied them end to end, and stretched them all around the yard.

We played games like blind man's bluff, pin the tail on the donkey, musical chairs, and hide-and-go-seek. If Bishop or I won a game, we weren't allowed to have the prize. Our mother insisted we give the prizes to the children who came in second and third place because they were our guests.

Mama had made a birthday cake, but after I blew out the candles, she wouldn't let us eat any of it. Mysteriously, the vanilla icing had turned green, and she was afraid it might be poison. She gave us an extra serving of ice cream from Daddy's hand-cranked freezer. Later, she discovered she had used food coloring in the icing instead of vanilla extract. Anyhow, my birthday party was a huge success, and we left the maypole standing where it was for a week.

One Saturday morning Daddy and Uncle Grady, Mama's brother, decided to make some wine out of the cherries from the wild cherry tree growing in our side yard. They spread an old tarpaulin under the tree, and Daddy climbed the tree, shaking cherries off the limbs. A flock of blue jays busily eating the overripe cherries squawked wildly at Daddy for ruining their lunch. Some of the jays were actually drunk from eating too many overripe cherries and were falling down into the cherries on the tarp bellow.

Uncle Grady, called the "cherry gatherer" by Daddy, filled several buckets of cherries, which he and Daddy carried into the kitchen to squeeze out the juice. When there was enough juice to fill a dozen bottles, they corked the bottles and put them on the top shelf in the kitchen pantry to ferment. Mama was fuming about the whole thing, but she didn't want to spoil their fun, so she just kept quiet.

A few nights later, Bishop and I heard loud noises coming from the pantry.

"I think it's the cherry juice fermenting," my brother said during the loud popping of the corks leaving the bottles, the rap as they struck the ceiling, and then the slight thud as each cork hit the floor.

Our parents didn't wake up, but I guess it was Daddy who cleaned up the mess. My brother and I laughed ourselves to sleep for at least a week. Of course, we never tasted the wine.

Another Saturday, Daddy handed a few pennies to Bishop and me and told us to follow him outside. The Gulf and Ship Island Railroad train tracks were situated right next to our small house, and as he led us across the yard, we could hear a train whistling in the distance.

"Clarence!" our mama called out from the front porch. "I hear a train a-comin'. You be careful with the children out there in the yard."

"All right, Velma," Daddy answered. "I'm being careful!" Daddy told us, "Hurry up now. Put your pennies on the tracks and hightail it back to our yard!"

A short time later, the steam engine passed, pulling a long line of freight cars.

"Won't the engine ruin our pennies, Daddy?" Bishop asked.

"You'll see," Daddy answered, and as soon as the last car, the caboose, passed by, he led us back to the tracks.

Only two pennies were still there, but they were no longer round. They were two perfect ovals, and Abraham Lincoln's head was stretched out twice as long as it was before the train had rolled over them.

"Well, look at that," he said. "You can't buy lollipops with them, but you surely have yourselves a couple of good souvenirs."

Bishop's and my eyes were glued to the coppers in our hands as the freight train's shrill whistle sounded from away down the track.

***

Small airplane shows were popular in the late 1920s. People flocked to empty pastures all around the country to be thrilled by the races, the stunt-flying, and, once in a while, the displays of daredevil copilots' wing-walking. My father took our family to an air show, and we joined a huge crowd standing at the edge of a flat empty field near Hattiesburg. Single-engine monoplanes and biplanes were taking to the air, one after another. Their pilots in the open cockpits looked like Charles Lindbergh, the idol of children and adults in those days. Wearing leather helmets and goggles and long white silk scarves like Lindy's blowing in the wind, the pilots put their planes through maneuvers that took our breaths away. The small planes rose high in the sky, loop-de-looping and then falling into tailspins, ending in barrel rolls and landing on the freshly mowed grass.

I remember when the show came to an abrupt halt. We were watching a monoplane coming in for a landing, and the little plane was flying too low over a power line at the edge of the field. Suddenly, its wheels got caught in the line. Like a fly caught in a spider's web, it hung there for just a moment. Then it flipped over and fell to the ground, flat on its back. As spectators hurried across the field to the spot where the plane lay, my father gathered our family together and quickly led us back to our car and opened the doors for us.

Daddy spoke quietly to us. "We're going home now."

"I wonder what happened to the pilot," Bishop said.

"I wonder too," I said to my mother. "What do you think?"

"I don't know," Mama said. "We're going home now."

I didn't say anything.

CHAPTER 3

BEYOND THE CORNFIELD

Hattiesburg, 1928

GRANDMOTHER–THAT IS, our mother's mother–lived in a white clapboard house too, but it was much bigger than ours and was situated at the end of her cornfield that separated her property from ours. Grandmother was in her early seventies, which, in her day, was quite old. Grandmother's hair was gray, and she wore it in a bun on the top of her head. Her given name was Sarah, but she was "Miss Sally" to her relatives, "Mama" to her eight adult children, and, as far as I remember, "Gramma" to all her many other grandchildren. However, to Bishop and me, she was always Grandmother.

Our grandmother presided over her home on its thirteen acres of land, its pear orchard, and its cows, pigs, and chickens with a quiet dignity. Our maternal grandfather had passed away before my brother and I were born, so we never knew him. But four of their offspring still lived in the family home. Our uncles Collin, Ledger, and Grady were mature bachelors, and Aunt Amber was their mature unmarried sister.

My three uncles, who still lived in the family home, were quite different. I remember Uncle Ledger as being a handsome man with coal-black hair, black eyebrows, and dark brown eyes. But because he was almost blind, he had little education and could not go work in the outside world. He couldn't read the daily newspaper, but he managed to plow the fields, plant and harvest the crops, and take care of the animals. Uncle Ledger could even find the time to help his sister, our aunt Amber, with the housework and cooking and still had a good sense of humor.

Uncle Grady, being the youngest of the three uncles, still shared his mother's bedroom for lack of space. He was only beginning to turn gray, but he always kept a bottle of Aunt Clyde's special hair "tonic" in his washstand. I guess he thought it kept him looking smart to the customers at Mathews Hardware Store, where he worked as a clerk and all-around helper.

Aunt Amber was another story. As she put it, besides doing the housework, she "slaved for all of them without a thank-you or a penny for all my efforts." As far as I remember, nobody ever went into Aunt Amber's room except me. I was always curious, and the day I slipped in, I found stacks and stacks of newspapers all over the place. I was very surprised, but I knew she could be a little odd at times. She had a sharp sense of humor and loved my brother and me without reservation. We loved her too, but then we loved them all. Children don't judge the ones they love.

Uncle Collin had a real-estate office on Main Street in downtown Hattiesburg. He sold pieces of property for people for a fee and owned some himself. His properties included a number of wooden shacks in the "bottoms," an area across the railroad tracks called the "Gravel Line." The shacks were inhabited by the descendants of slaves, who lived sort of hand-to-mouth. Sometimes my uncle took me with him to the bottoms to collect pitiful sums of money from his renters. It upset me when he called them "sorry no-goods" and threatened to evict them if they didn't pay. More than one renter would let out a friendly giggle and say, "Mista Bishop, you know I'd pay the rent money if I had it, but right now, I jes' don't. You gonna get it next week—God's trouf." Uncle Collin was basically a good man, and he never evicted anyone.

There was one person living in a shack owned by Uncle Collin who never had to pay him at all. Arilla Lincoln worked in her backyard with a wood fire heating a large black iron pot of water to fill her galvanized washtub. She scrubbed everything by hand and hung it out to dry on her clothesline. She ironed every piece of laundry with the old-fashioned flat irons heated on top of a bucket of red-hot charcoal. It was harder work than the electric irons used by most everyone, but the results were just as good if not better.   Once a week, Arilla left her shack and climbed the long slope behind Grandmother's house with a bundle of freshly washed finished laundry balanced on the top of her head. No matter if the bundle was big, it was always balanced on the top of her head.

I happened to be in the car with Uncle Collin one time when he dropped off a few extra pieces of laundry to Arilla. We walked around her shack and found her and her little daughter, Rosalie, "doing the clothes" in the backyard. Arilla was ironing, and Rosalie was gathering clothespins from the ground and putting them into a bucket. While Uncle Collin talked to Arilla, her daughter backed away from us. We didn't say hello. We just stood and looked at each other. When our eyes met, there was a moment before we looked down and waited while our grown-ups finished talking.

The next time I saw Rosalie, she was probably going on six, and I was too. She was following Arilla up the slope behind Grandmother's house. They were both carrying bundles of laundry on top of their heads–Rosalie's bundle much smaller than her mother's, of course. When I looked at Rosalie, her eyes met mine. We smiled at each other but only for a moment. That was in the early spring of 1930.

CHAPTER 4

GRANDMOTHER'S HOUSE

Bishop's Lane, Hattiesburg, 1928

THE NAME BISHOP'S Lane may not be official for the graveled road that led to my grandmother's house and thirteen acres, but everybody as far as I knew had called it that anyway. There was an orchard of pear trees, open farmland, a fenced-in garden, pasture as well as livestock barns, and a two-car garage.

Our grandmother's house, like ours on Redus Street, was clapboard with a four-posted front porch. Inside, there was a living room and four bedrooms off a center hall. The dining room and kitchen were at the end of the hall near a good-sized back porch. The kitchen stove was an enormous black iron range that had to be fired up by split logs each and every day. There was also a small kerosene stove near the window, but it was mostly used for cooking quick breakfasts for two of my uncles who worked downtown.

My nine-year-old brother and I were as close as two brothers born five years apart can be, but he and his friends spent more time together than he and I did, so my mother often let me run up through the cornfield to our grandmother's house to visit her. I was allowed to go by myself because even though I was only four and thought it was far away, it was probably no more than a quarter of a mile. I loved running through the rows of corn and feeling the leaves on the cornstalks flapping me as I passed them. I liked taking different routes up to Grandmother's house to make it more of an adventure. I enjoyed visiting my grandmother. I usually found her sitting by a window in her bedroom and sewing.

"Here, Baby, thread this needle for me," she would say with a soft chuckle. "These tired old eyes aren't as good as they used to be. Come to think of it, my glasses are kinda tired too."

After visiting with Grandmother for a little while, I would slip into Uncle Collin's room. I always loved to smell the bar of Cashmere Bouquet soap on Uncle Collin's washstand. Going through his clothes closet, I discovered an odd-looking black felt hat with no brim. It was made of black felt and had a long white ostrich feather sewn flat on the top. Next to the hat was a long sword in a silver scabbard. My uncle had never shown the sword to me, but once I had heard him talking about being a Shriner. I didn't know what that really meant, so I looked to see what I could find in his dresser drawers. Once, I found a pistol–a big revolver. I didn't dare touch it, so I just closed the drawer and slipped out of the room to go and look for my Uncle Ledger.

I went out back, and when I didn't find him, I decided to climb the fig tree. I didn't like the taste of the figs, so I climbed higher. Somehow my foot slipped, and I fell. I was surprised because I had always thought I was a pretty good climber. I must have hit the ground face-first because when I rubbed my nose, there was blood on my hand, and then it was dripping on my shirt.

"Uncle Ledger!" I yelled. "Uncle Ledger-r-r!"

My uncle suddenly appeared and scooped me up from the ground.

"Uncle Ledger, my nose," I said and tried to tell him what happened.

He took a towel off the old iron hand pump, wet it with cold pump water, and put it to my nose. "I'm takin' you home to your mama." And he did, as quickly as he could, holding the wet towel to my nose and humming.

"It's all right. It's all right," he said quietly. Then he scooped me up and carried me home through the cornfield, sort of singing all the way–"It's all right, Baby. Everything's all right." And when he put me in Mama's arms, I knew everything would indeed be all right.

Uncle Ledger working, standing in front of the
barn, with a few neighbors visiting.

One Saturday morning, as I ran through the corn, I suddenly came upon a wide-open space. The entire area was filled with thick green vines and what looked like hundreds of watermelons. I could not believe my eyes. So I ran on up to the house, calling Uncle Ledger. When I told him about the unbelievable thing I had seen, he seemed to be quite surprised.

"I think we should go and have a look," he said.

I led him back to the watermelon patch, and he suggested we pick one and taste it. Then he split it open with his big pocket knife, and we each ate a large piece. It was delicious. It was a long time after that when I realized how smart my uncle had been, planting his watermelon patch in the center of his cornfield. It was his way of keeping it a secret from the neighborhood poachers.

Another time, when I went up to Grandmother's house, I was surprised to see her huge hog that usually was stuffing himself at the trough of slops from the kitchen was now hanging upside down by his hind legs from a wooden rack in the middle of the backyard. Several black men were standing around, watching. Uncle Ledger seemed to be in charge.

"Hey, keep the child back!" my uncle shouted as a big black man I had never seen before was holding an ax as he moved closer to the hog.

All of a sudden, the big man swung the ax at the hog and hit him on the head. The hog gave a horrible squeal, and the man swung the axe again, hitting the hog's neck. The hog jerked wildly back and forth, with blood spurting in all directions from his neck. I was terrified. As the man swung the ax a third time, the hog flinched quietly and then was still. I backed away from the spectacle and then turned and ran toward the cornfield.

"Baby!" Uncle Ledger shouted. "Baby, come back here to Uncle Ledger!"

But I was already running fast on my way home, my feet hardly touching the ground.

"Mama, Mama!" I called as loud as l could.

Mama came out of the house and met me at the backyard gate. She picked me up and held me close, trying to understand what I was telling her about the violent event until I finally calmed down.

That night, I must have awakened the rest of the family as they found me standing up in bed over Bishop, pounding him with a pillow.

"That's the way they killed him!" I was yelling. "Blood all over the place. The big man kept on hitting him in the neck, and then the hog stopped movin'."

I must have had a nightmare in my sleep, but I never remembered anything about that night. I also never saw another hog killing again.

CHAPTER 5

HOME SWEET HOME

Hattiesburg, 1929–1930

T HAT SUMMER, WE built a new house way out near the college on the other side of town–where all the nice neighborhoods are. I don't mean "we" built it. I mean our parents had it built. Although the Great Depression was in full swing, they had dreamed, planned, and borrowed money from the bank to have a lovely home built for us. Daddy having a steady job probably made it possible.

One Sunday afternoon the whole Barker family piled into the Chevy, and Daddy drove us out to Twenty-Fifth Avenue, where our new house was being built. We walked into the framework of the first room. I'll never forget the smell of the wood shavings on the floor between the studding. Bishop and I loved piling them up and lying in them and scattering them again.

"This will be the living room," said Daddy, "and you are now looking at the first finished wall." Then he pointed to an archway. "Next, we have the studs for the dining room," Daddy said as Mama walked on into what would become her kitchen.

We followed her and found her looking at an open space in the studding.

"The sink will go under this window," said Mama, "and a new gas stove over on this wall."

"Of course, Velma," Daddy agreed and said, "Next, where the center hall will be, there'll be enough room for the whole family to sit and listen to radio programs. Off the hall, there'll be a bedroom for us", he said to Mama, "and next to it the room for the boys."

I walked on a little ways down the hall studding. "Hey, everybody!" I called out. "Come look at what I found."

I was staring into a small finished room. It had pink tiled walls and a white toilet bowl like the one I'd seen one time in the hall outside Daddy's office. Next to the toilet bowl in the pink room, there was a sink, not as big as the one in our kitchen, and on the other wall, there was something that looked like . . . I don't know what, maybe a kind of a white boat you could sit in. Mama, Daddy, and Bishop were looking over my shoulder.

"This is going to be our bathroom, and that's the bathtub, Howard," Daddy said. "Better than our tin washtubs, don't you think? I suppose you boys have never seen one."

"I have," Bishop said. "But only in other people's houses."

My family walked on with Daddy, who was explaining something about a sun room, but I just stood and kept staring at the big bathtub.

***

The first winter in our new house brought chilly evenings, with our family sitting around a gas heater in the center hall, listening to the radio programs, comedy shows like *Lum and Abner*, *Fibber McGee*, and *Molly, Amos, and Andy*, dramas like *One Man's Family*, and the broadcasts of "The World News" with Lowell Thomas. What made our floor-model radio so special was that the carved wooden grill in the lower front was from a design made by our own father. I don't think our friends ever believed us when we told them he had won the first prize with his sketch of two birds and branches in a contest.

There was no garage where we used to live on Redus Street, but one was built in the backyard with a driveway out to Twenty-Fifth Avenue, and in the early spring, Daddy built a pen for the new cow and a coop in the pen for chickens. Mama said she'd feed the chickens, but "feeding and milking a cow was man's work." So when Daddy bought the cow, Daddy milked the cow. He didn't seem to mind. Sitting on a low stool, he squeezed the cow's teats exactly the right way to fill the milk pail. If I was there watching him, my father would aim at a passing chicken and squirt the milk at her. He never missed. The squawking chicken would scurry back to the flock, pecking for bits of grain around the cow's feeding trough. Daddy's talent for dousing chickens with milk impressed me almost as much as his talents with the telephone and the typewriter in his office downtown at the Hattiesburg Chamber of Commerce. I didn't know exactly what his work was, but when Bishop and I visited him, we would often find him at his desk talking on the telephone and typing. Back in those days, the phone's mouthpiece and receiver were separate, so our father would talk into the mouthpiece with the receiver propped on his shoulder and type with both hands. He still had to think of what he was writing about and carry on a business conversation at the same time. I thought Daddy was pretty smart.

Another thing about life in our new home was different from life back on Redus Street. On Twenty-Fifth Avenue, we had pets. Besides Bishop's dog that he named Queenie, I had a cat, Juicy Fruit. I called her that because she licked my fingers after I had put a couple of sticks of Juicy Fruit gum in my mouth. That surprised me, but I guess she really liked the taste. When you have a cat, sooner or later, you have kittens, and before long, we had two or three litters of cats, and it was about that time my brother had his tenth birthday party.

It was sometime before Halloween, but we thought it would be fun to decorate the living room with orange and black crepe-paper streamers. Mama served the kids orangeade and decorated his birthday cake with orange icing and black jelly beans, with ten black candles on his birthday cake. Our parents didn't know Bishop and I had planned to turn our thirteen black cats loose inside for the Halloween party, but when the kids started chasing the young cats around the room and catching them, all heck broke loose. It took the better part of an hour to get them herded into the sun room and quiet down their yowls. It was a lot longer than that before our parents found homes for all but one. That one was Juicy Fruit. Juicy had not been invited to the birthday party.

Bishop and I under a magnolia tree.

My big brother, Bishop, on the left and myself on
the right, possibly two years old, c. 1926.

My father, my mother, Bishop, and me.

Grandfather, Father, Bishop, and me.

My grandfather, my father, Bishop, and me.

This was our first and only train trip to visit our grandfather on my father's side, Courtland Clarence Barker, who lived in Ohio. He was our only living grandparent. We must have visited a botanical garden there. This is me, Bishop, my mother, and my grandfather.

CHAPTER 6

THE RUDE AWAKENING

25th Avenue, Hattiesburg, Summer 1929

A SWEET-LOOKING LITTLE girl named Peetie Dougal lived two doors away from my house. Peetie was the only child in my neighborhood near my age, maybe five or six. We had been playing on the see-saw in her backyard for a little while, and I couldn't help noticing when she went up on the seesaw, her underpants showed. I truly don't know who decided it, but after we got off the seesaw and hid behind the doghouse, we heard her mother calling.

"Peetie! Peetie Dougal!" Mrs. Dougal shouted. "Peetie, you and Howard come inside, you hear me? This minute!"

I knew we were in trouble–the "If you show me yours, I'll show you mine" kind of trouble. Peetie pulled up her panties, and I pushed my doololly back inside the placket of my short pants. As Peetie and I slunk out from the behind the doghouse, Mrs. Dougal was looking out the kitchen window.

"Right this minute!" she said, staring at us as we dragged our feet toward the back door.

Then Mrs. Dougal stood holding the door open and looking at us. We followed her inside.

"What on earth were you doing hiding out there in back of the doghouse?" she demanded the minute we faced her in the kitchen.

"We were just playing, Mama," Peetie said.

I looked at the floor and didn't say anything.

"Howard, you go right home," her mother said through her clenched teeth and glared at me. "You can't play with Peetie anymore if this is how you behave."

"Yessum, Mrs. Dougal," I said and backed out the door.

The walk home seemed the longest half a block I'd ever walked. I opened our back door as quietly as I could. My mother came to meet me.

"Why are you home so early?" she asked when I came in.

"Oh . . . we were through playing," I said as innocently as I knew how.

"You never come home from playing until it's practically dark," she said. "Why don't you tell me the real reason you came home so early?"

"We were just through playing," I insisted.

"Howard . . ." Her voice was stern.

"Mama, you don't want me to tell you . . . Really, Mama, you don't." I was fighting back the tears.

"Howard," she said. Her mouth was set in a tight-lipped line.

I started to cry.

"Howard, tell me what happened."

"We were just playing doctor," I blubbered. "That's all."

"That's all?" my mother said, raising her voice. "That's all? 'Playing doctor'? Howard! I happen to know what that means. Aren't you ashamed? Answer me!"

"Uh, I guess so," I said. "I, uh . . . Yes, ma'am."

My mother said nothing more. She turned and left me standing alone in the room. Then I heard our phone ring and my mother say, "Oh, hello, Mary. I'm glad you called. Yes, he did . . ."

That's all I heard, but I was sure Peetie's mother had phoned mine with her version of the shocking information.

It was almost a month before I was allowed to play with Peetie again.

CHAPTER 7

I REMEMBER MAMA

Hattiesburg, late 1929

I WAS STANDING in front of the toilet bowl, holding my doololly tightly between my fingers to stop the red pee from coming out. At first, I could not move. Then my eyes darted around the bathroom, the sour taste of panic rising in my throat. In my panic, our pink tiled walls seemed to turn into the wooden walls inside the dark privy at our old house on Redus Street. It was as if Mama didn't come right then, she wouldn't see my red pee down in the mess below of the privy and she couldn't help me.

"Mama!" I called out. "Mama, come quick!"

My mother didn't answer. She must not have heard me.

"Mama!" I shouted. "I peed, and it came out red. Mama, come quick!"

My mother rushed into the bathroom, and she stared at the pink water in the bowl. I wanted her to do something, but she just looked scared. I was six years old, and I was scared too.

"What's wrong with me?" I whimpered. I let go of my doololly, and the rest of my pee went into the toilet bowl. It was still red.

"Clarence!" my mother called to my father. "Clarence, come in here, quick!"

My father came to the door, dressed for work and holding his hat.

My mother pointed into the toilet. "Look, Clarence," she said.

My father came in and touched my shoulder.

"What's wrong with me, Daddy?" I asked.

"I don't know, son, but you're going to be all right. I promise," he said and hugged me. "We'll call Dr. Thames. He'll fix you up. Velma, call the doctor right away. Don't flush the toilet."

We all went into the kitchen to sit and wait. When Dr. Thames arrived, my parents took him into the bathroom to show him what had happened. I stayed in the kitchen.

"Howard has already had measles," I heard my mother say. "And whooping cough. But nothing like this, ever."

"It looks like Howard may have a kidney infection," Dr. Thames said as they came back into the kitchen. "Possibly Bright's disease. We need to do some tests."

I was too scared to ask what it all meant.

He patted my hand. "Now don't you worry, son. We'll take good care of you." He opened his black leather bag and took out a thermometer. "Just keep this under your tongue a minute for me, all right?"

I looked up at him and nodded. His glasses were reflecting the light over the kitchen sink, but I could see his eyes as he squinted at the thermometer.

"A hundred and three," he said. "Into bed with you, young man."

I liked the doctor. He called me "young man."

My mother made up the bed in the sun porch, and my father watched as she covered me with blankets. The sun porch was warm, but I was cold, even in my flannel pajamas.

"Now you be good, Howard, you hear?" my father said and hugged me, just like he did every morning. Then he hugged my mother. "Velma, I'll call you from the office."

I heard Queenie, our dog, outside barking as my father started his car.

When he came home from work that night, my father brought me a candy bar–a Baby Ruth. He sat down on the bed with me while I ate it. It was the last solid food I ate for a while. In the days that followed, I was not allowed to get out of bed, even to go to the bathroom. I had to use a bedpan. My mother made the thin soup for me the doctor had ordered. I had to suck it through a bent glass straw because I could not sit upright. It wasn't easy for me to lie on my back day in and day out. Maybe it was Bright's disease, but actually, I never learned what I was suffering from.

The only thing good about being sick was being in the sun porch. It was early spring and still chilly outside, but with the sun shining through the windows all day, it made the room bright and warm. The sun porch was close enough to the kitchen for me to listen to my mother singing as she worked, and I knew she would take good care of me. Every day Mama made the simple nourishing food I was allowed by Dr. Thames. Bishop, my elder brother, would sometimes come in and sit on the bed to play games with me, but I didn't always feel like playing.

Some days, as I lay in bed, my fever would go up, and I'd have chills. Even though I was under the blankets, my feet would be cold. Then my mother would wrap the electric iron in a towel and put it under the blanket next to my feet to keep them warm. One day the phone rang, and my mother went to answer it.

"What are you driving at?" I heard her say, and I wondered how a person could be driving a car and talking to my mother at the same time. As I was listening to the sound of her voice, my feet were starting to get hot.

"Mama!" I called.

She kept talking. She didn't hear me.

"Mama!" I called again. "My feet are getting awful hot."

"I'm on the phone," my mother answered from the hall. "What is it, baby?"

I didn't like being called "Baby," so I didn't answer. But after a few minutes, I called out again.

"My feet are getting too hot!" I yelled. "Mama, come in here–hurry!"

"Just a minute, Baby, just a minute."

I couldn't move, so I pulled my feet up as far as I could away from the iron. The blanket began to smell like one of the fireplaces in my grandmother's house. The smell got stronger and stronger. Suddenly, I saw smoke coming out from under the covers.

"MAMA!" I yelled. "THE BED'S ON FIRE!"

Finally, my mother came running.

"OH MY LORD!" she screamed.

She flung back the covers and snatched the iron off the bed. No flames were there, but the towel around the iron was scorched brown and smoking.

"Oh lord! Oh, Baby, I'm sorry."

I started crying, and she hugged me tight. Then she started crying too and pushed her hair off her forehead like she always does when she's upset.

"I'm so sorry," she said, sobbing and hugging me. "It's all right, Baby. It'll be all right."

I knew it would be because Mama was there. That night, she slept in my bed with me. Sometime that night, I woke up. I heard Mama crying, and then I touched her hand.

"What's the matter, Mama?" I whispered. "Why are you crying?"

"I want my mama," she said. "I miss my mama." Then she wept softly.

I don't remember if I hugged her–I hope I did–before I went to sleep again.

There were days when Uncle Collin would drop by with a friend from downtown, like Mr. Wilson, who promised to share some stock in his oil well with me if I would do some of my artwork for him. Then I'd cut out small paper animals with scissors. That was about all I could do while I was lying in bed. He liked the cutouts and folded them up and put them one by one into his vest pockets. Sometimes I got as much as fifty cents, but I never got any stock in his oil wells.

My Aunt Margaret came to see me after a trip to New Orleans with Uncle Gordon to see the Mardi Gras parades. They brought me an amazing gift–a Spanish gaucho costume to wear for fun. I was so excited and wanted to put it on.

"Mama," I said, "Can I put it on? Right now! Please! Pu-leeze!"

"No, Howard, you're still sick. You know that. Daddy and I will ask Dr. Thames when you can put it on."

Then Mama put the sombrero on my head. I shook it, and the red cotton balls around the brim wiggle-waggled. Everybody laughed.

The next day, Dr. Thames had me sitting up in bed, and he said I could try standing. Mama and Daddy slipped the Spanish pants on me and stood closer. But as soon as my feet touched the floor, I fell flat on my face. My parents lifted me up and led me around the room. Soon, I was walking a little better, but it was easy to see that the Spanish outfit was too big.

"Don't you worry, son," Daddy said. "You'll grow into it–"

"Yes, you will," Mama interrupted. "You'll be wearing it before you know it. I promise!"

Nothing stopped me from looking forward to the day I'd grow into it. It wasn't long before I was outside playing again, riding our pony and whispering into her ear, "Just you wait 'til Halloween, Dolly. You'll see."

Actually, I did wear my Spanish outfit the next Halloween and every Halloween until I outgrew it. But I've never forgotten it and the special feeling that came over me each and every time I did.

CHAPTER 8

LIFE WITH FATHER

25th Avenue, Hattiesburg, Spring 1929

BISHOP AND I had a bit of bad luck the day we got into an argument about the car, Daddy's Chevrolet. We had seen our father working since early morning on the car, crawling in and out from under it with odd-looking metal parts, tools, and rags, stuff we had never seen before. Finally finished, he wiped the grease off his hands and went inside to lie down to take a rest.

At the advanced age of eleven, Bishop decided he was old enough to drive the Chevy. I told him he was wrong and followed him out the car.

"I'm not really going to drive it," he said. "I'm just gonna back it up the driveway and then drive it forward to the garage."

"You do, and I'll tell on you," I threatened him. "Daddy will be mad as a hornet."

"I know how to shift gears," my brother bragged. "I've seen Daddy do it a million times. And besides, he told me I could."

"I don't believe you," I said.

Bishop opened the car's door and climbed into the driver's seat. "See?" He laughed and put the key in the ignition.

"I still don't believe you," I said and climbed in beside him.

He put his foot on the clutch, switched on the key, and started the motor. I turned it off. He switched it on again and pulled the gear shift into reverse. I was furious. As the car moved slowly backward, I grabbed the key and turned off the motor.

"Don't do that!" Bishop said loudly, pushing my hand away and turning the key on.

The motor coughed and then started. With threats and accusations and a tangle of arms, we repeated the childish routine, on and off, on again and off again, the motor coughing and sputtering, gears shifting, the car backing up and then stopping again—until a mighty explosion shook the car. The ominous silence that followed was broken by my father's angry voice.

"STOP!" he shouted. "What are you doing?!"

He ran from the house, wrenched the car door open, and literally dragged us both out onto the driveway. Holding the two of us by our shirt collars with one hand, he pulled off his leather belt with the other, and he started swinging and slapping it across our backsides. We were in shock and yelled bloody murder.

"CLARENCE!" our mother shouted from the side door of the house. "STOP! Stop it this minute! You are killing them!"

Daddy let us go and looked ashamed. We were in shock. He had never laid a hand on us before. We slunk over to Mama. Daddy put his belt back on and walked over to us. He was dejected.

"I'm sorry," he said quietly. "That was the new muffler I'd put on. I guess I'll just have to buy another one."

A few days later, when my father came home from work, he told my brother and me he had a surprise for us. Like all kids, we were excited.

"Daddy, Daddy, wha'dja bring us?" we shouted as he stood in the doorway with his hands behind his back.

"Guess which hand," he said.

Speaking at the same time, one of us said, "Right hand," and the other said, "Left hand."

He brought both his closed hands out in front of us. "Guess again," he said.

I saw something small and white sticking out of his fist. I was puzzled. "A salt shaker," I guessed.

Daddy laughed and opened both his hands. In each hand, he held a little white mouse! We couldn't believe our eyes.

"Look, Mama," I said.

Our mother was standing behind us. She didn't look too happy.

"It's a pair," Daddy said, smiling. "When they grow up, they can have baby mice. Then you will have a family."

Mama was not smiling.

I named my mouse Jackie, and Bishop called his mouse Jill. The following day, Daddy made a house for them out of the old wood crate Mama's piano had come in. He made two levels inside, with ramps for our pet mice to run up and down on. Then he covered the open front with window screening so we could watch our pets scamper around. Daddy also made a little door on the ground floor of their house for us to set dishes of food and water inside for them.

Jackie and Jill were smart mice and settled into their new home immediately. They must have been an extremely affectionate couple because in a short time, we found a nest of tiny pink baby mice. Soon, the babies were covered with downy white fur, and they matured quickly. It wasn't long until the babies grew up and Jackie and Jill became grandparents.

Within months, we had three or four generations of white mice scampering from floor to floor. Jackie had grown larger as he aged, and Jill was now a full-bodied matron. Who knows how many pet mice we could have had, but for a strange and violent occurrence. One summer night the whole Barker family was awakened by horrible sounds of high-pitched shrieks and squeals coming from the garage. It was frightening. My father went out to see what was going on. In less than a minute, he came back in and closed the door quickly.

"Skunk," Daddy said.

Even with the door closed, we smelled a powerful stench and could hear the squeals of the mice.

"Bishop, where's your baseball bat?"

"Here, Daddy," Bishop answered, "Right here behind the door."

My father grabbed the bat and ran back outside. Then we heard him hitting the bat against the mouse house. For a moment, all was quiet, and then we heard a dull thud. The pungent scent of the skunk followed my father as he came back inside.

"That's the end of that skunk," my father said.

The next morning, everything became clear. The skunk had pushed his way through the feeding door and was attacking the mice. My father propped the door open and beat the back of the box. The alarmed skunk ran out, and my father conked him on the head.

Now we saw the tragic scene: dead mice were everywhere. Jill was dead, lying among her dead children and grandchildren. Jackie was still alive, crouching with a few survivors, but my brave pet was overwhelmed by the ordeal. He and the rest of the mice died within days. That was the end of the white mice saga.

For a short time, we had a baby alligator. Bishop had ordered it from a nature magazine. The alligator was only seven or eight inches long, and it arrived in a cardboard tube with directions for feeding. My father made a home for it, a large open wooden box with a bowl of water surrounded by sand. We pushed small bits of raw liver into the little alligator's mouth and waited to see it grow, but alligators are slow growers. Before getting any larger, the unfortunate reptile mysteriously disappeared. My guess is that our cat ate it. The baby alligator was replaced by two small turtles my brother had caught in a creek near our house. Eventually, we turned them loose back in the creek.

It is a moot point whether the old adage about black cats and bad luck is true or not, but our series of bad-luck events with pets seemed to continue. Bishop's sweet dog, Queenie, was struck by a hit-and-run car in front of our house. My brother saw it happen and was inconsolable. He cried, mostly at night, for three days. It took him several years before he acquired another dog.

My cat Juicy Fruit disappeared one day, and didn't come that night nor the rest of the week.

Bishop and I looked all around the neighborhood without success, and on the weekend, our father went with us to search in the nearby woods. At some point, we heard a "meow" coming from above us. Looking up, we saw Juicy crouched out at the end of a limb of a tall pine tree. Each of us called her, and she meowed, but she literally couldn't turn around on the narrow branch to go back to the trunk of the tree. No amount of calling her name would coax her to try.

"I have an idea," Daddy said. "You boys keep talking to Juicy while I go back to the house for something to help her down." A few minutes later, he returned with a blanket and a fishing pole. "Now, you keep on talking nicely to her, and the three of us will hold the spread-open blanket under her. I will try to push her off the limb, and when she falls on the blanket, we'll catch her."

After a few tries, Daddy pushed Juicy off the limb, and down she came, but as soon as she hit the blanket, she sprang up, leaped off it, and ran like lighting into the woods. We called and called her, but she was gone. I think after being trapped on that limb, probably for days, with nothing to eat or drink, the poor cat was terrified. It was getting dark, and we knew we couldn't find her.

"We'll look for her in the morning," Daddy said. "Let's go on home."

For the next week, we searched the woods wherever we thought Juicy might be, but she was nowhere to be found. Weeks went by, and I would often go to the woods to look for her. One day I heard a meow. Then, a few yards away, there was Juicy Fruit. I called her and walked toward her. She meowed again, but when I came closer to her, she turned and ran away into the bushes. I never saw my cat again.

Even in the late 1920s, many of the roads in Mississippi were still unpaved. When my father took the family on car trips, you could count on at least one or two flat tires per trip. While Daddy jacked up the car and took off the tire to patch up the inner tube, Mama would spread a tablecloth (usually a clean sheet) under the trees by the side of the road. Then she'd lay out the food, and we'd have a picnic. Mother prepared all kinds of sandwiches for picnics along the way. She made chicken salad sandwiches, tuna fish salad sandwiches, and ham sandwiches. Sometimes she made pineapple sandwiches and banana sandwiches on white bread with her homemade mayonnaise. We loved the sandwiches, but my favorite thing was her deviled eggs. I can still taste them.

Usually, Daddy would have just a cup of cold lemonade from the thermos and put the fixed tire back on so we could get on our way. Then he'd have a sandwich in one hand and steer the car with the other while he was driving. Like his cow-milking trick and the telephone-typewriter feat, this impressed me too. My brother and I were too young at the time to judge our father's musical talents, but while he was driving, he'd often burst happily into song. My favorite was about "the big rock-candy mountain." I freely admit I may have improvised some of the following lyrics:

I'm headin' for a land that's far away, beside the crystal fountain
To a land that's free, so come with me, we'll go and see
The big rock-candy mountain
Oh, the buzzin' of the bees and the cigarette trees, the soda-water fountain
Where there's lemonade springs and the bluebird sings
In the big rock-candy mountains

On our fishing trips to Gulfport and Biloxi, beach towns on the coast of the Gulf of Mexico, there were no big rock-candy mountains, and we didn't stay in hotels with soda-water fountains. Actually, there were only a few hotels in the coastal towns, and they were expensive, so we stayed in tourist camps. These camps were clusters of little wooden cabins with one or two small rooms, furnished with beds and cots and modest facilities.

On one trip with the Edgar family, friends who lived down the street from us, I awoke to the sound of muffled adult voices. I heard my mother waking my brother lying in the cot next to mine.

"Shhh, Bishop, don't wake up the baby," she whispered, holding a flashlight near him.

"Why?" I heard Bishop whisper.

"He's too young," my mother answered him with a whisper. She and my father were moving about quietly in the semidarkness.

"Too young for what?" I said out loud and sat upright on my cot. "I'm not asleep."

"The men are going fishing," my mother answered. "Now go back to sleep."

"Is Bishop going?" I asked.

"Yes, but he's older than you, and they're going out in the gulf in a rowboat," she said. "And it's going to be real chilly."

"I don't care. I want to go!" I wailed. "I'm not too young. I'm five years old!"

"I'll take care of him, Velma," my father said quietly. "Let him go with us."

In order not to wake up the entire camp with my bawling, my mother gave in. I was allowed to go.

It was still dark as the rowboat eased out into the Gulf of Mexico, but the two kerosene lanterns lit up the faces of my father and Mr. Edgar, my ten-year-old brother, and eleven-year-old Frank Jr. I didn't feel like a baby anymore. The gentle waves were lapping at the sides of the tiny boat, and the smell of the salt water was new and exciting to me. It may have been chilly, but I was thrilled to be out with the adults. Mr. Edgar and my father took turns rowing in silence.

By the time we were a few hundred yards out from shore, the sky was beginning to change from black to a deep grayish blue. A few clouds tinged with pink hung over us, and I could see we were all alone in a vast expanse of calm dark water. Mr. Edgar dropped a small anchor over the side of the boat, and the chain rattled until it hit bottom. He and my father baited hooks and threw their lines out into the water and waited for the fish to bite. They also baited lines for Frank Jr. and Bishop. They didn't bait a line for me, but I didn't mind. I was in a boat out in the Gulf, where I wanted to be, and I was happy.

On the distant horizon, where the night sky met the sea, a tiny glow appeared. I watched it become a thin curved sliver of orange light rising out of the water. As the heavens turned pink, the sliver of light got bigger and bigger, and within minutes, it swelled into a gigantic fiery ball floating upward in the bright blue bowl of the sky. The fiery ball was the morning sun, lighting up the entire Gulf of Mexico! My heart was beating so hard, I could almost hear it. The only word I can use to describe what happened that morning is probably the modern generation's favorite–*Awesome*!

***

I remember an earlier trip to the Gulf Coast. I must have been no more than three or four. Our family was on an excursion to Ship Island, a tourist destination some miles out from the mainland's beaches. The boat carried no more than a hundred people and was primarily for deep-sea fishing, but it had a recreation area serving food, and there was a small combo that played for dancing in the evening.

Perhaps my parents were brushing up their foxtrot when I edged out onto the dance floor to see what was going on. But by the time I had made my way to the middle of the dancers, I was lost in a forest of legs. All I could see all around me were grown-ups' knees and feet moving in time with the 1920s jazz. I didn't know which way to turn or where to go, and I must have panicked. I sat down on the floor and started to cry. At that moment, my father appeared, picked me up, and carried me off the floor and upstairs to the top deck.

"It's all right, Baby," my father said. "We'll just sit on the bench over here under the lights."

I didn't mind being called "Baby." I nestled close to my father and looked up at a million stars glittering in the night sky. The music drifted up from below, and the strings of lights overhead cast a soft glow on couples who were enjoying the warm evening breeze. The boat under us was gently rocking.

My father tried to light a cigarette, but the wind blew out his matches. I watched him put his unlit cigarette into his vest pocket and carefully take the empty Camel package apart. Then he flattened the silver foil inner wrapping on the bench, and with his penknife, he cut out a small bird, its wings outstretched as if it were in flight.

"What kind of bird is it, Daddy?" I asked.

He sat quietly for a moment. "A bluebird, son," he said, putting his knife away. "Yes, I'd say it's a bluebird." Then he held it up in the palm of his hand and let the wind take it out of his fingers.

We watched the tiny silver bird shining in the lights above us as it flew away and disappeared into the darkness.

CHAPTER 9

THE SATIN DOLL

Hattiesburg, 1930

ONE BRIGHT SPRING day, on his way to his office downtown, my father was driving my mother and me over to visit Aunt Margaret and Uncle Gordon. I was sitting in the back seat of the Chevy, but I could hear everything they were saying.

"My nerves are just a mess," Mama said. "I don't know why I can't just take it easy like you do." My mother was a sweet, beautiful woman, but she was a little high-strung.

"You have to take it easy, Velma," Daddy said. "You worry enough for both of us. Besides, there's not all that much to worry about. I still have my job. We have a car, plenty to eat, and we're up to date on the loan payments."

"I know, Clarence, but I worry. There's always something. You know, like today. When Miz Butler asked me to come over, she said to bring the baby."

Mama lowered her voice, but I could still make out what she was saying. At six, I was small for my age. In those days, little children were often considered delicate, and their parents kept a close eye on them, especially in winter, when the flu was going around. My uncles and aunts still called me "Baby," and my mother said I was "sensitive."

"You know how I feel about taking the child inside that house."

"Yes, I know, Velma, but Gordon's TB is in remission. He's been home from the sanitarium now for over a year. I don't think it'll flare up again."

"Maybe not, but how about germs? No telling how long they can last. Miz Butler always wants to hug and kiss Howard. She could infect him."

They were quiet for a little while.

"Velma, why do you and all your family call Gordon's wife Miz Butler? You know that's not her name. It's Margaret. She's been married to your brother for years. Her last name is Bishop, same as all your folks."

"Well, she was married to a Mr. Butler from New Orleans. You know that."

"But they were divorced years ago. Before Gordon ever met her," Daddy said. "Why don't you just call her Margaret?"

"Sometimes I do," Mama said. "To her face, I do."

They were quiet again until we reached Aunt Margaret's. Daddy stopped to let us out. The lawn smelled freshly mowed, the shrubbery was neatly trimmed, and the roses in front of the house smelled spicy sweet.

"Y'all have a nice time now, you hear?" Daddy said to us as we got out. "I'll pick you up at noon and drive you home."

"If you can't leave the office, telephone me," Mama said. "I expect Miz Butler can—oh, all right, Margaret. It just doesn't sound right. That's all."

Daddy laughed and drove away.

"And remember, don't touch anything," my mother ordered me when we got to the door.

Now I was worried. How could we go in and sit down and not touch anything?

Aunt Margaret opened the door and welcomed us. "My goodness gracious, Howard, you must have grown two whole inches since I last saw you," she said.

Mama was right. Aunt Margaret bent down and hugged me tight. It was like pressing my face into two soft sofa pillows. I guess I was stiff as a board.

"You are such a sweet boy," she said and kissed me. "Would you like some lemonade and cookies?"

That sounded nice, but when I looked up at my mother, she was frowning.

"Say no, thank you, Howard," she said. "Howard just had breakfast. He might get cramps."

"No, thank you, Aunt Margaret," I said.

"Well, maybe later, Sugar," she said. "You just tell me if you do. You want to run outside and play?"

I looked at my mother.

"I think it's best if Howard stays inside, Margaret," Mama said. "Now, Howard, don't you go 'round touching things. I don't want you to go 'round messing up your Aunt Margaret's nice house."

"Yessum, I won't," I said. I knew what she meant.

"Oh, he couldn't hurt a thing," said Aunt Margaret. "Velma, can I get you some coffee?"

"No, thank you, Margaret. I've already had my coffee at home. By the way, where is Gordon?"

"He's gone to the store for me. I expect he'll be back before long."

I moved away very slowly as Mama and Aunt Margaret started talking about the weather. I never did understand why grown-ups were always interested in how hot or how cool it was. Right now, the weather was warm, and I had already started to wear my short pants. All my friends had been wearing short pants since April, but my mother didn't let me stop wearing my knickers and long socks until May.

"I don't want you to catch your death of cold," Mama had said. "Spring weather is so changeable."

I examined the whatnot shelf in the corner. The little china figurines were so pretty–young men and young ladies standing close together, some of them in dance poses and some sitting on little benches and kissing. Next to them, there was a mermaid sitting on a rock. She had long brown hair falling over her shoulders and covering her bosom. I looked closer to see if her nipples were showing. They weren't. I looked back to see if Mama and Aunt Margaret were paying any attention to me. They didn't notice me when I left the parlor. In the dining room, I was surprised to see Aunt Margaret had the same picture over the buffet that we had in our dining room at home, the picture of the pretty lady lying by a beautiful lake of blue water. A little girl is standing next to her, bending over and looking at her. The lady is wearing a thin white dress with a gold scarf tied around her waist, but the little girl is as naked as a jaybird.

"The original is by Maxwell Parish," Mama had told me. "I believe it is called a classic."

I went on into the kitchen and sat down at the table for a minute. The enamel tabletop was cool. It felt good when I put my cheek down on it. Then I remembered what Mama had said about germs everywhere and not to touch anything. I took a spoonful of sugar from the sugar bowl anyway and put it in my mouth. It tasted sweeter than the sugar at home.

From the kitchen, I went out onto the back porch. It was screened in, and there was a trunk and some boxes full of newspapers out there. A box of milk bottles by the back door, a mop, and a broom were about all there was. Then I went through a door into a little hallway and past several closed doors. I could still hear my mother and Aunt Margaret talking but couldn't hear what they were saying. I had never been anywhere in Aunt Margaret and Uncle Gordon's house before except the living room, which they always referred to as the parlor.

I was a little excited snooping around. Through one door, I could see into a room that had a nice set of furniture. Except for a stack of newspapers on a bench at the foot of the bed, everything was so neat, it looked like it almost wasn't being used at all. But then I saw two pairs of bedroom slippers, and I figured it must be Uncle Gordon and Aunt Margaret's bedroom. The next door was to the bathroom. I didn't have to pee, so I didn't go in.

The last door at the end of the hall was a little bit open. The shades were pulled down, but there was just enough light for me to see that it was a bedroom. There was a sweet perfume-y smell. Now I could hear Mama and Aunt Margaret talking. I stood real still and listened.

"Gordon is well now, Velma. You and Clarence ought to bring the boys over and have supper with us sometime. It gets kind of lonely here in this small town, with all my folks way down there in New Orleans."

"Well, Margaret, we'll certainly plan to do that," Mama said. "I just don't know where the time goes, but real soon."

When they kept on talking, I looked around the room. There were pretty draperies the color of pink roses, and they matched the spread on the big bed. There was a bunch of fancy little pillows near the headboard. I figured I was probably in the guest room. In the middle of the pillows was the most beautiful thing I had ever seen in my life. It was a doll, not like any other doll I had ever seen, not like the baby doll Peetie played with. This doll looked like a beautiful lady, and she was tall, half as tall as I was. She was dressed in a shiny green satin dress, real long and full, spread out all around her. It had ruffles, and it was trimmed with lots of black lace. She had real hair, all wavy, with two long curls hanging down on one shoulder, and it was as black as Mama's velvet dress hanging in her closet at home. The doll's face was pale, almost white, but she had pink cheeks and shiny red lips. There was a little black spot near her mouth. I had never seen a spot like that on a real person before, but it looked sort of good on her. I reached across the bed, and I touched it ever so gently.

What I liked most of all was her eyes. They were blue, and her eyelids were a smudgy purple. She had long black eyelashes that made her look kind of sleepy, but she was definitely awake. I moved close to the bed. The lady doll's arms were open wide, and it looked like she was waiting to hug somebody. I crawled up onto the bed and lay down next to her.

Even though I could still hear Mama's voice in the living room, it didn't stop me from touching the doll's dress. I lifted her ruffled skirt very slowly and looked underneath. She was wearing black high-heeled shoes and white stockings and long lacy underpants. I folded her skirt back and looked at her for a long time. I didn't know exactly what was happening to me, but I climbed up and lay down on her. It felt so good, I buried my face in her hair. It smelled like roses, and I wished I could stay there forever.

"Howard, where are you?"

I heard my mother's voice coming from the parlor across the hall. I didn't answer her.

"Where are you?" she said. "We ought to be going soon."

I jumped up. "I'm coming, Mama!" I called back to her.

I got off the bed as fast as I could, and when I reached the door, I looked back and saw the lady doll's dress was pulled up over her head. I ran back and fixed her dress the way it had been when I found her. Then I leaned over and kissed her right on her lips.

"Bye-bye," I whispered and ran back down the hall to the back porch and through the kitchen and dining room.

"What have you been doing, Howard?" my mother asked when I came into the parlor, where she and Aunt Margaret were still sitting. "I hope you weren't meddling in things that don't concern you."

"No, ma'am," I said. "I was just looking at some funny papers in the back room."

"Oh my goodness," said Aunt Margaret. "I've been meaning to go through those newspapers and get rid of them. Did you find anything you liked, Howard?"

"Yessum, Aunt Margaret, I did."

Just then, Uncle Gordon came in the front door, and Mama stood up.

"Y'all don't have to leave so soon, do you, Velma?" Uncle Gordon asked. "Don't rush off now. Hello, Howard. How you come on?" Uncle Gordon asked me.

"Just fine, sir," I said. I was never quite sure what to say to Uncle Gordon, but he just chuckled a little and put a two-bit piece into my hand.

"Buy yourself some candy, son, you hear?" he said and winked at me.

"Clarence will be picking us up any minute, Gordon," Mama said. She lifted the lace curtain at the front window and looked out. "We'll visit next time." She took the coin from me and wrapped it in her handkerchief. "I'll just keep it in my pocketbook, Howard, so you won't lose it."

"Yes, ma'am," I said.

"I believe that's Clarence's car pulling up outside now," she said. She sounded relieved. "I'll call you soon, Margaret. Come on, Howard. Let's go."

I followed her as Uncle Gordon opened the front door for us. I stole a quick look into the little hall. Through the open door of the bedroom, I could see the lady doll lying among the pillows. Her eyes were half closed, and she was looking straight at me.

"Y'all come back soon, you hear?" Aunt Margaret called as we went out to my father's car.

"You be sweet, Howard."

"Yessum!" I called back. "Thank you, ma'am."

CHAPTER 10

GYPSIES

Hattiesburg, 1930

OUR HOUSE ON Twenty-Fifth Avenue backed onto the woods, but I never ventured any farther than a nearby creek where I used to catch minnows and tadpoles or tiny baby turtles for our goldfish tank. Sometimes my brother and I built ramshackle "clubhouses" out of branches and pine straw but close to home and in the daytime. We were free to roam the woods around us, and if we sometimes learned something surprising and forbidden in our adventures, it was just another one of the steps we may have to take as we were on our way to becoming adults. Other than trying to smoke hand-rolled cigarettes made of dried chrysanthemum leaves, no scary things ever took place in our woods until one morning Bishop and his friends decided to explore them farther.

"Can I go too?" I asked and started to follow them.

"No," my brother, Bishop, said. "You stay home this time," he said firmly.

I was puzzled. I worshipped my brother, who was five years older than me. "Why?" I begged. "Why can't I come with y'all?"

"You just can't," he insisted. "You're too young."

"Aw, let him come on with us," his friend Emmett said. "He might learn something. He's old enough to learn about it."

I was all ears, so I tagged along. "What is it I'm old enough to learn about?" I asked Emmett.

As we walked down the dirt road, he told me that grown-up men and women parked cars in the woods at night and did it.

"Did what?" I asked.

"I'll tell you later," Emmett said.

So I followed the older boys into the woods. It was a hot summer day, but as soon as we got deep into the shade of the trees, it was cool, and the birds were singing. Then the road turned into nothing but car tracks winding through the scrubby bushes.

"Hey, y'all," one of the boys said, pointing at the ground. "I found one."

We gathered around. What he had found looked like a small deflated balloon. A little farther on, we found some more of them, but they were long, not round or in bright colors like regular balloons. I had never seen anything like them before.

"What are all those things?" I asked.

"They're called merry widows," Emmett said.

I didn't understand what he meant, but Emmett was twelve, and he must know what he was talking about. I didn't ask any more questions. I just stood and watched while the boys picked up some twigs and started counting the messy rubber things.

"There's a lot of 'em," Emmett said. "This lovers' lane sure must be a busy place at night–with so many grown-ups doing it."

Then they all laughed and raked the merry widows into a pile. It made me a little sick at my stomach.

As we walked farther into the woods, we came to a small clearing where there were three or four ratty-looking tents and a bunch of gypsies sitting around a campfire. If I saw a gypsy woman on the street in our town, I would know it by the way she was dressed–like the gypsies in picture books, long colorful skirts and carrying baskets, trying to sell odd stuff. Here in the woods, all the women wore the same kind of colorful clothes, with flowered scarves on their heads and lots of beads and jewelry. Some of the men had bandanas, and they all had earrings in their ears.

When the gypsies saw us, the men scowled and spit into the fire. There was a big black pot on the hot coals, and one of the gypsy women was stirring what was cooking. She turned and looked at us and stopped stirring.

"Hey, boys!" she shouted. "Want to make zig-zig?"

Another woman scratched her palm with her forefinger and giggled. "Want to make pinchy-pinchy?"

Then the whole band of gypsies laughed loudly. The older boys in our group looked embarrassed and didn't answer. My brother took my hand, and all of us turned and hightailed it back down the road and out of the woods.

On the way home, Emmet walked next to me. That was when he told me that if grown-ups did it in bed together at night and didn't want to have a baby, the man had to put a merry widow on his doolally. I didn't understand exactly what Emmett meant, but I decided not to ask any more questions.

One day, not long after that, I was meddling around in my parents' bedroom. I saw my father's vest hanging on the back of a rocking chair and had a peek into his pockets. In one, I found a little gold-paper-wrapped packet. I opened it and took out a small rolled-up rubber thing. When I unrolled it, I had a new merry widow in my hands. I knew it was something I shouldn't be seeing in my father and mother's bedroom. I felt guilty for snooping and a little bit scared. I rolled it up carefully and put it back in the little gold packet and slipped the packet back into my father's vest pocket. Then I hightailed it down the hall and out the back door.

I believe most children, even when they're too young to know what the word for "it" is, have a natural curiosity. I didn't have had a word for "it" when I was a child, but I had that curiosity too. So after I heard secret words older kids were talking about, I took a small piece of paper and wrote what they sounded like to me. Then I folded the paper up and hid it where I knew nobody would ever find it: an iron grating in the foundation of our house. A couple of years later, I retrieved the hidden scrap of paper. By that time, I had learned the right way to spell the naughty words, but I certainly didn't want the incriminating evidence to be found by anyone. So just to be on the safe side, I tore the scrap of paper up into little pieces and threw them away.

CHAPTER II

SCHOOL DAYS, SCHOOL DAYS

Hattiesburg, 1929–1932

Dear old golden rule days
Reading and writing and arithmetic taught
to the tune of a hickory stick
You were my queen in calico, I was your bashful, barefoot beau
And you wrote on my slate, "I love you, Joe"
when we were just a couple of kids

UNLESS YOU ARE as old as I am, you probably haven't heard that old song. Well, my name isn't Joe, and we didn't write on slates in 1929. But because my mother had been a schoolteacher, by the time I was five, I could count from one to a hundred and say my ABCs. I could read *Baby Ray Has Three Chicks* and write a little, so at the age of five, I was allowed to enter the first grade a year early. Even though I was told my classmates were all six years old, it didn't occur to me that that would be a problem. But eventually, it turned out to be.

On the first day of school, a pretty little girl walked into the classroom. She was the prettiest in the classroom. In fact, she was the prettiest little girl I had ever seen. Olive Johnson had a heart-shaped face, sky-blue eyes, and lips as red as cherries. Her hair was the color of corn silk. She was wearing a short cotton dress, apple green, with matching green pantaloons. Of course, Olive was six, and I was still five. I didn't speak to her because I was too shy.

I must have gotten to know Olive well enough to get over my shyness and be friends because many adult years later, I dreamed of little Olive Johnson. In my dream, we were both still children, and she was wearing the same green dress and pantaloons she had worn back in our school days. I was holding her little face in my hands and kissing her right on her lips. It felt so good. When I woke up the next morning, I remembered the dream, and I still felt good.

Just before entering the second grade, I saw a pretty little girl riding a big red tricycle on the sidewalk in front of a house near ours. She must have been new to the neighborhood because I had never seen her before. As she pedaled slowly up and down the sidewalk, she saw me and tilted her head sideways as she smiled at me, and each time she turned her tricycle around, her little dress slipped up a little higher.

Maybe she wasn't as pretty as Olive Johnson, but I was six and not as shy as I had been when I was five, so I waved my hand to her and said, "You've got a pretty red tricycle."

"Hello, fresh!" she said. "Where do you live?"

"I live down the street," I said, "in the brick house. Next to the vacant lot."

"My name's Janet Fisher. We just moved here." Then as she pedaled slowly away from me, she looked back over her shoulder and smiled again. "See you in school!" she shouted.

Janet had long dark curly hair, luscious lips, and very white teeth, and I wanted to hug her. Maybe it was just fascination or "puppy love." Whatever it was, she made an indelible impression on me. To this day, I can still see Janet on her tricycle and remember her luscious lips. Strangely enough, I don't remember seeing Janet again. She must have gone to another school.

Well, never mind. In the third grade, I was in love with Mary Sloan Hawkins. Mary Sloan sat at the desk in front of mine, and her long honey-colored corkscrew curls just about drove me crazy. That may sound a bit too exaggerating for a seven-and-a-half-year-old. But I think all the boys in my class were in love with Mary Sloan. She seemed to favor just one boy–Donat Green. Who could blame her? Everybody liked Donat. He was popular with girls and boys alike. Taller than all of us, he had golden hair, the whitest teeth, and dark brown eyes. Donat was also the smartest student in the class.

"I'm planning to give Mary Sloan a box of chocolates for Valentine's," Donat told me one day. Valentine's Day was approaching. "You know the kind of chocolates I mean, the kind that come in a red heart-shaped box."

I was desperately jealous, but suddenly, I had an idea. "Donat," I said. "Why don't you let me go half with you? Then both of us could give Mary Sloan the box of Valentine candy."

Donat looked at me, hesitating a moment.

"Please," I begged. "I'll pay my share. Just let me know much, okay?"

I could hardly believe it, but he agreed. I was ecstatic and saved every nickel I could scrape together, and the day before Valentine's, I had enough. I gave my money to Donat, and he bought the heart-shaped box of chocolates.

On Valentine's Day, all the children in class made valentines and traded them with one another. I made a special one for Mary Sloan, and inside, I printed the words "Will you be my Valentine?" I gave it to her at recess. She didn't make a valentine for me, but she gave me a heavenly smile. After school that afternoon, Donat and I walked with Mary Sloan outside and gave her our box of chocolates. She tossed her golden corkscrew curls, gave Donat a heavenly smile, and sweetly thanked both of us. Then we sat on the school's steps and shared the candy. It was a great Valentine's Day, and I was filled with love.

***

In fourth grade, I fell in love with my teacher, Miss Fountain. Since I was only seven years old, I suppose "in love" is an exaggeration. But as far as I am concerned, my feelings for Miss Fountain were serious. I loved my parents, but that was different. I also loved my brother, but I wouldn't have said so.

Miss Fountain was another story. I just wanted to be near her, close to her—all the time. That wasn't easy. There were all those other children in the class. They may have loved her too but not like I did. I did everything I could to please her. I was quiet. I paid attention. I tried to do whatever we were supposed to do as well as I could. I smiled when she looked at me, and when she smiled back, I was filled with joy.

Miss Fountain was a large woman—not fat, just large. (Of course, to an eight-year-old, almost all grown-ups are large.) Miss Fountain was just right. She had beautiful blue eyes and high cheekbones. She had full red lips and a wide smile. When she smiled, her teeth were beautiful too.

"Howard," she asked me one day, "what do you think makes you want to draw pictures all the time?"

"I don't know, Miss Fountain," I said after I found my voice. "I just like to draw."

"Well, I think you are very talented. Maybe when you grow up, you'll become an artist."

I felt my face flushing.

"But, Howard, for now, let's wait until we have our art period," she would say, smiling gently. "Let's try to think now about our arithmetic, all right?"

"Yes, Miss Fountain," I answered. My face must have turned a brighter shade of red.

I was jealous when Miss Fountain spoke to other children. If she complimented them, I could hardly stand it. I would look down at my desk and sulk. If she noticed me, she would walk down to my desk. I didn't dare look up at her.

"Is something wrong, Howard?' she would ask.

"No, Miss Fountain," I would say. "I was just thinking."

"Or maybe daydreaming?" she would say.

"Maybe," I answered and raised my eyes to meet hers.

She smiled.

"I guess so," I answered.

Of course, she was right. I'm afraid I did a lot of daydreaming in those days. I daydreamed about walking with Miss Fountain in fields of flowers, on sandy beaches, even on the town's streets. She would always be holding my hand. Sometimes I felt like I was tall, like she was, and it didn't feel strange at all. We talked, and she laughed at a lot at things I would say, even if I didn't know what I was saying. It didn't matter. In my daydreams, I was with her, and I was happy.

I came into class one morning after having been kept at home a couple of days with a cold and a sore throat. As small children usually do, all my classmates were talking and laughing.

"All right, class, let's quiet down now," Miss Fountain said. "We have a lot to do before we leave, you know."

I wondered what she meant, but as the students quieted down, I paid attention.

"Do you all have your suitcases packed?" Miss Fountain said. "Did you remember to put in a warm sweater and a jacket too? It's still warm here, but Switzerland is in the mountains called the Alps, and it can get pretty cold there."

The children were all excited and saying, "Yes!" and "I've got mine!" I was puzzled and wondered what was happening.

"What about warm pajamas and your toothbrush?" Miss Fountain went on. "Do you all have a cap and a scarf?"

"I do, I do!" they answered.

"You know, you all will like the food in Switzerland because we had Swiss cheese sandwiches yesterday for lunch when we planned our trip. All right, get your things together. The bus is waiting."

That was when I panicked. My heart climbed up toward my neck. Tears flooded my eyes and rolled down my cheeks. "My mother won't let me go," I said, and a loud sob slipped out of my mouth. "She won't let me." Then I started blubbering.

The classroom fell silent. Miss Fountain came over to me and touched my shoulder.

"Howard," she said softly. "Don't be upset. There's no need to cry. We aren't really going to Switzerland. We had a geography lesson yesterday, and we planned to go on an imaginary visit to a foreign country."

I hope I smiled when Miss Fountain patted my hand. Anyway, I stopped crying.

That afternoon, at the end of class, when I was leaving, I slowed down my walk when I came to Miss Fountain's desk.

"Howard," she said, "wait a minute." She was putting papers away. "Before going home, do you think you would have time for me to show you something?"

I looked around as the other children were leaving the classroom. "Yes," I said. "I guess so."

"All right," she said with a wide smile. "Good. Then let's go."

I followed Miss Fountain into the hall and out the front door of the school. We walked together toward the teachers' parking lot.

"Is your mother expecting you at home right after school?" she asked. "I mean, she won't worry if you're a few minutes late, will she?"

I was puzzled by her questions. "I don't think so," I said. "Sometimes I stop on the way home to play."

"I want to show you something in my room in the dorm," she said and opened the door of her car, a little blue Ford coupe. I had often seen her get into it after school. "Hop in. I want you to help me drive."

I had no idea what she meant.

As she started the car, she turned to me with another big smile. "When I put the car into gear, sometimes the shift jumps out, and I have to hold it with my right hand and steer with my left."

"But how can I help you drive?" I asked.

"I want you to hold the shift in place for me."

What she said sounded as if it was the most natural thing in the world for a little boy to be holding the gear shift in place while a grown-up drove a car, but I didn't say anything.

"Now with you in the car, holding the gear shift, I can hold the steering wheel with both hands."

She put the car into first and pulled slowly away. I held onto the knob at the top of the stick tightly until Miss Fountain suddenly covered my hands with hers and pushed the stick into second gear. Her touch sent a small feeling of warmth through me, and I smiled happily.

"Am I doing all right?" I asked.

"You're doing just fine," she answered. "Now here we go, into third. Hold on tight."

We soon pulled up in front of the teachers' dormitory.

"I'll take over now, dear," she said. "Thank you so much. You've been a big help."

I think that's what she said, but mainly, I just heard her call me "dear." I was feeling a little scared, but when she took my hand as we went up the steps, I was sure everything was all right.

Miss Fountain's room was large and comfortable looking. There was a bed with a pretty spread on it and a table next to it with a lamp and a stack of books. There was also a desk with a lamp and more books, a dresser, and a large chest of drawers.

"This is where I live, Howard," she said. "How do you like it?"

"It's nice," I said, not knowing what else to say.

Miss Fountain then went to the dresser and took a package from the bottom drawer. I watched as she unwrapped a stack of small plates and placed them carefully in neat rows on the bed. There were at least a dozen, all different, some with flowers, some with fruits, some with butterflies and intricate patterns.

"Do you like them?" Miss Fountain asked.

"Yes, I do," I said. "They are nice. I mean, they are beautiful."

"I'm glad you like them. I painted them myself. I like to paint china," she said, smiling. "I want you to have one. Pick any one you like."

I couldn't believe what she had said. "I don't know if I should. I don't think—"

"It's all right," she said. "Go on, choose one. Any one you want."

I looked at the plates, and I wanted to say I liked them all, but I knew she meant for me to have just one. "I think if it's all right, I would like the fruit one." The little plate had a border of pears and leaves painted in delicate colors.

"That's a good choice. I like that one too. You can use it when you eat pears or any fruit. When you do, you can remember me. I will certainly remember you."

At first, I didn't understand. To remember her as if she would no longer be there was unimaginable. Then I suddenly realized Miss Fountain would not always be my teacher. Not being in her class after I move on to another grade had never occurred to me. But then I also realized I would never forget my beautiful fourth grade teacher for as long as I lived.

"Now we must go," Miss Fountain said. "Your mother must wonder why you're not home yet, so I will drive you home."

"Do I get to hold the gear shift again?"

"Yes, my dear," Miss Fountain said. "Yes, you can, and I'll be depending on you."

CHAPTER 12

STORM CLOUDS

Hattiesburg, early November 1932

BISHOP AND I were finishing our breakfast in the kitchen–cereal with sliced bananas. Everything had been pleasant enough until my mother and father had "words."

"Clarence, are you plumb crazy? You must be out of your mind, taking that boy squirrel hunting on a day like this!"

My mother's voice was a little loud. My father didn't answer her question, and he didn't reply to her accusation either.

"Don't you realize you could catch your death of cold? We're all a little run down, and you know there's the flu going around."

My father stopped rubbing his rifle with an oil rag. He laid it on the floor next to his chair. "Now, Velma, calm down," he said quietly. "I've heard all about the flu. Don't take on so. It's only November. It's not so cold."

My brother and I pretended we weren't paying any attention to our parents' squabbling.

"It probably won't rain anyhow," my father said. He sounded a little hopeful.

"It's drizzling already," Mama said. "It'll probably be pouring by noon." She pushed her hair back off her forehead. She always did that when she was upset.

"Well, if it does, we'll just head on back home," my father said.

That seemed to settle it. He and Bishop went squirrel hunting.

***

They didn't come back until after dark, and they were soaking wet to the skin. Their teeth were chattering, and their lips were blue. My mother didn't say much, but she had that "I told you so" look on her face.

"I've got some hot soup for you," she said, trying to sound nice. "You're freezin'. Get out of those wet clothes right now. You never should have gone." she went on, "You could catch your death–"

"I promised him, Velma," my father said. "I couldn't go back on my promise."

"Galavantin' all over creation," my mother spoke to no one in particular. "Chasin' squirrels!"

"We weren't galavanting all over creation." Daddy acknowledged her remarks.

"Yeah, Mama," Bishop chimed in. "An' we weren't chasin' squirrels. We were huntin' them, but we jus' didn't get any."

"Never mind. It's almost November," Mama said. "The cold goes right through you." She put Bishop into a hot tub and wrapped a blanket around my father. "We all ought to go straight to bed right after supper."

And we did–the whole family.

By the next morning, Bishop had chills and fever. My mother covered him with extra blankets and put the electric iron wrapped in a towel to his feet like she had done for me the year before. By noon, his temperature had risen to 103 degrees. Dr. Thames came and confirmed her fears. Bishop had the flu. Mother called my father at his office at the Chamber of Commerce.

"Well, Mamie, if he's too busy to talk, you just tell him to come right home," she said into the phone. "His child has the flu. No, the eldest one. Howard is fine. I'm feeling a little achy myself though."

Two days later, my mother came down with the flu too. Dr. Thames was called again. He held her hand gently as he took her pulse.

"Now, Velma, we can't have you sick like this. Don't forget to take your aspirin on time regularly, and you must drink lots of liquids. Soup, juice, tea, water, anything." He smiled, but his eyes stayed serious. "And you must rest. Rest, rest, rest. That's the best thing for you."

Watching the gentle doctor as he talked to my mother, I was thinking if his beard had not been neatly trimmed, Dr. Thames could have passed for Santa Claus. Almost as if he had been reading my mind, he turned to me.

"Son, you know Christmas is just around the corner. Have you thought about what you would like Santy Claus to bring you for Christmas if you've been a good boy?"

"The Bluebird," I answered. "I'm hopin'."

"The bluebird?" he asked. "What's the bluebird? Some kind of kite, maybe?"

"No, sir," I answered. "The Bluebird is a genuine authentic model of Sir Malcolm Campbell's famous racin' car. It's the fastest drivin' car in the world. It's streamlined!"

I could have gone on and on about The Bluebird, but perhaps the slight wave of Dr. Thames's hand stopped me.

"I hope Santy does bring you The Bluebird, Howard," he said. "But you know, sometimes he just can't remember everything for everybody."

One of my friends had told me that your mother and father put your presents under the tree at Christmas. At first, I refused to accept such a notion. I had clung as tightly to my convictions about Santa as I had about the Easter Bunny, and I had put my basket out the night before Easter next to my brother's. Bishop was five years older than me, and he still did it. The next morning, our baskets were filled with brightly colored eggs. Hoping my friend was wrong, I wrote my letter to Santa and wasn't disappointed. So this year, even if I had my doubts about Santa, I had no intention of giving up my plan to ask Santa for The Bluebird.

Dr. Thames was putting his stethoscope away in his black leather bag when my father came home from his office. He walked the doctor out to his car and asked for his opinion.

"I think we had better put both Bishop and his mother into the hospital," I heard the doctor say, "and as soon as we can."

That afternoon, Daddy took them to the hospital. It was strange being in the house alone, even for an hour or two. It seemed so empty without my mother. I just kind of played by myself until he came back.

I don't remember whether my father had brought me into his and my mother's room during the night or if I had just crept into their bed with him while he was asleep. Anyway, I woke up there with him the next morning, warm and quiet and feeling good, not alone. I was wearing my flannel pajamas, but my father was in his long johns. I'll never forget that because the first thing I saw was his shoulder and arm lying on the blue woolen blanket, right next to my nose. His familiar sweet-sour smell hung faintly around the edge of the covers. Then I noticed he was shaking.

"What's the matter, Daddy?" I asked.

"I've got a chill, son," he said. "Guess I'm getting a touch of the flu too."

Then I saw he was wet with sweat. I knew he was sick. He took a deep breath and stood up. He pulled his pants on quickly, but he was still shaking, even after he was dressed.

"I think I'd better have Dr. Thames take a look at me," he said. "Get your clothes on, son. I'll leave you over with Aunt Amber."

Aunt Amber was my favorite aunt. She was a maiden lady and wouldn't tell anybody her age. She and the last three of her unmarried brothers still lived in their mother's house. Our grandmother had died only a year earlier at the age of seventy-four. (In those days, seventy-four was old.)

After my father warmed up the Chevrolet, I ran out and got in. The ride to Grandmother's house on the other side of town did not take long, but now, in the car, my father was quiet.

"Do you think Mama and Bishop will be out of the hospital soon, Daddy?" I asked.

"I surely do hope so, son," he said. "Yes. I expect so."

When we pulled up in front of Grandmother's porch, Aunt Amber was standing in the open front door.

"Amber, I woke up feeling terrible!" Daddy shouted over the noise of the car's motor. "I want you to take care of Howard while I go see Dr. Thames. After that, I'll stop by the hospital to look in on Velma and Bishop."

"How are they?" Aunt Amber shouted back.

"Velma's worse," he said. Then as he opened the door for me, he said, "I'll pick Howard up later."

I ran up the steps as he drove away.

When my father didn't come back that evening for me, my aunt told me Dr. Thames had put my father into the hospital too. She said I would be staying there with her and my uncles for a few days.

"It's the best way, you know," Aunt Amber told me. "When folks get the flu, they have to rest, and the hospital is the best place for them. It's so clean and nice there, and the nurses wait on you hand and foot." She hugged me and laughed a little. "We'll have a good ol' time. I'll take care of you 'til your mama and daddy and Bishop get well. You can help me feed the chickens, and Ledger needs you when he milks the cows. You can go downtown with Collin to his office and to the Merchant's Café for pie and ice cream."

"What about school, Aunt Amber?" I asked.

"Well, we'll see," she said. "Maybe you'll just stay out of school a few days 'til we get things all straightened out. You have to watch out too and not get yourself sick like the others."

My temperature had started to rise during the night and not gone down at all the next morning. I was kept in bed in Grandmother's old room.

"We can't take any chances, Amber," I heard Uncle Collin telling her. "You know this house is no place for a child with the flu. A wood fire just heats up one side of you while the other side freezes. We should have put in gas a long time ago. Would have too if Mama had allowed it. She hated change. The boy will get better care in the hospital."

"Better care! I'd like to know what better care he'll get than from his own flesh and blood!" Aunt Amber fumed.

"You know what I mean," Uncle Collin said, stopping her, "and you know I'm right."

"Lord have mercy," Aunt Amber said, with the back of her hand over her mouth. "Then the whole family will be in the hospital at the same time!"

"Hush up, Amber," Uncle Collin said, putting an end to the discussion.

Things got "straightened out" immediately. I was put into the hospital that afternoon. In the examination room, I was undressed and put into an odd-looking hospital gown. Then I was placed on a cot with wheels and was examined by a smiling doctor with a thermometer and some other things I'd never seen before. When he was finished, a very fat nurse in a white uniform smiled at me too and took off her white cloth belt, which she put around both me and the rolling cot.

"Just so you won't roll off," she said with a little laugh. "Now off we go to your hotel room."

From then on, I was cared for with all the treatment available for the raging flu epidemic moving across the Southern United States: plenty of water, aspirin, and lots of other liquids to bring down my temperature, with complete bed rest.

CHAPTER 13

THE FUNNY PAPERS

Hattiesburg, November 1932

I N THE HOSPITAL, I was diagnosed with influenza, but I must not have been seriously ill because I was sent home within a week. Well, not home exactly. Uncle Collin decided to take me to Uncle Raymond and Aunt Maggie's house. Aunt Amber did not approve of the arrangement and insisted on coming to the hospital with Uncle Collin to pick me up. She told me later it was just to make sure they gave me back my own clothes, but I think it was so she could make sure she could warn me about my Aunt Maggie.

"That woman is mean," Aunt Amber said.

Aunt Amber had never liked Uncle Raymond's wife and often referred to her as Maggie Chapman–her maiden name. She also blamed Aunt Maggie for real and questionable treatment foisted on his own family by Uncle Raymond. Uncle Collin was quiet as he drove us away from the hospital. I sat in Aunt Amber's lap while she complained.

"I don't see why I can't take care of the baby," she fumed. "I'm his mother's own sister. She is not even a member of the family."

"She is, by marriage," Uncle Collin corrected her.

"Raymond rues the day he married her, even if he won't admit it," replied my aunt.

"Amber, don't take on so," said Uncle Collin. "You don't know what you're talkin' about."

"Raymond stole practically every square foot of property any member of this family ever owned." Aunt Amber almost spat out the words. "And she put him up to it. I know that for a fact."

"Now, Amber, you hush up," he said, clearing his throat.

"You might as well have handed everything to him on a silver platter," Aunt Amber snapped. "Grady is too weak to protect his rights, and poor Ledger is as good as blind."

It was just a few miles from the hospital to Uncle Raymond's, but those were spent in a silence broken only by Uncle Collin's throat-clearing. (The family referred to it as Collin's catarrh.)

"I'll wait in the car," Aunt Amber said when we got to Uncle Raymond's house. "And don't you worry now," she whispered as she hugged me goodbye. "You won't be there long. If I had my way, you'd never set foot in that house."

But set foot, I did, and I was given a small room at the end of the hall to sleep in. It was actually a sewing room, but there was a daybed in it and a dresser where I could put my things. All I had were the clothes I had worn to the hospital. There were no toys to play with because when my father had dropped me off at Grandmother's house, my toys had all been left behind at home.

Uncle Raymond and Aunt Maggie were gentle and kind to me, but I'm afraid I didn't return their affection. I was much too intimidated by Aunt Amber's preconditioning. Within a week, I was quickly enrolled in an elementary school nearby, and even though the weather was razor-sharp cold, I was allowed to walk to and from classes. My new classmates were friendly enough, but I was shy, and it was strange being in unfamiliar surroundings. Somehow I just could not get my mind on the things the teacher talked about. When she gave a spelling test, I could not remember which letters to use, and I was panicked. I had never cheated before in my life, but suddenly, it seemed so important to be perfect. So I cheated. When I thought nobody was looking, I opened my spelling book to the right page and placed it on the floor between my feet, where I could look down and see the answers. I was ashamed, but I cheated anyway.

I didn't like staying at Uncle Raymond and Aunt Maggie's house. It had a musty smell, different from our house. Their house smelled old. I mean, like houses do sometimes where only old people live. I had been there for about a week or two, and it must have been a Sunday because I was reading the funny papers back in the sewing room. I loved the funny papers–*Popeye, Toots and Casper, The Gumps, The Katzenjammer Kids*. I heard Aunt Maggie calling me.

"Howard, come here!" Aunt Maggie called to me from the living room.

"Yessum," I answered but not very loudly and kept on looking at the funnies.

"Howard!" After a minute or two, she called again in that singsong way. "Howard, your Uncle Collin is here!"

I left the funny papers on the floor and walked up the hall into the living room. I was surprised to see that Uncle Grady and Uncle Ledger had come with Uncle Collin. Aunt Maggie was sitting in her big rocking chair, and Uncle Raymond was standing next to her.

"Hey, baby," Uncle Grady said. "How you come on?"

"Just fine, sir," I said.

Uncle Ledger just smiled and winked at me, like he always did. Uncle Collin just cleared his throat. Everybody was there except Aunt Amber. I wondered, with everybody in our family there except my mother and daddy and Bishop, who were still in the hospital, where was Aunt Amber?

It was very quiet. Then Aunt Maggie held out her arms to me.

"Baby, come sit on Aunt Maggie's lap."

I didn't like being called "Baby," and I didn't want to sit on her lap. I had never been close to Aunt Maggie, but I did as I was told and climbed up into her lap. I didn't like her powdery old-lady smell.

"Baby, your mama died," Aunt Maggie said, just like that.

She tried to hold me close, but I pulled away. Uncle Raymond put his hand on my arm, but he didn't say anything. I looked around the room. It seemed a little too warm. Uncle Grady and Uncle Ledger didn't say anything either. Uncle Collin was looking out the window and clearing his throat over and over. Nobody was looking at me. Aunt Maggie held me and rocked slowly back and forth.

"Sweet child, would you like to come and live with Uncle Raymond and me?"

What was she talking about? Not fully understanding, I heard myself answering her. "No. I want to live with Daddy."

"Baby, your daddy died too," Aunt Maggie said, hugging me. "Oh, my precious."

I pulled away again from my aunt.

Uncle Raymond started to speak. He opened his mouth and drew in a deep breath, but nothing came out. His cheeks were wet. I had never seen him cry before. I guess he just didn't know how. Uncle Collin kept looking out the window, and Uncle Grady and Uncle Ledger just stood staring straight ahead. I tried to comprehend what Aunt Maggie had been saying. I knew she wouldn't tell me something that was not true. I knew I should try to believe her, but nothing was making sense.

"Bishop—where's Bishop?" I asked.

"Your brother's still in the hospital," said Uncle Collin. Just as he got the last word out, he went into an eruption of throat-clearing.

"Bishop is mighty sick, Baby," Aunt Maggie said. "But they think he'll be all right soon.

Stay with us, honey. We'll take real good care of you."

I was looking down at the floor. "I want to go home," I said. "Uncle Collin, I want to go home."

"Not today, son," Uncle Collin said. "Real soon, Baby, but not today. For the time being, you'll have to stay with Uncle Raymond and Aunt Maggie."

I felt like something was stopping up my throat. I did not cry. I don't know why, but for some reason, the tears just would not come.

"I want to go read the funny papers," I said. That was all I could say.

Aunt Maggie let go of me, and I got down from her lap. I left the room and walked straight through the house back to the sewing room. I sat down on the floor where I had left the funny papers: Barney Google, Tillie the Toiler, Little Orphan Annie—real people to me, real living people—even Flash Gordon and Tarzan. I could understand the funny papers. They were something I could believe. I kept thinking that all I had just heard was not so, that somebody would do something to make it just not so. I knew I had not been lied to, but I still could not believe what Aunt Maggie had told me. After a few minutes, she came into the sewing room.

"Baby, the funeral is tomorrow," Aunt Maggie said. (Did I stop reading? I don't know. I don't remember.)

"I don't want to go," I said.

"You want to see your mama and daddy for the last time, don't you?"

"No," I said without looking up.

I knew something about death. Just a few years earlier, I had seen my grandmother lying in her coffin at the funeral parlor. Then at Roseland Park, I had watched the coffin being lowered into the hole in the ground that was surrounded with mats of too-bright fake green grass. My cousin Howard Bishop Jr. ran across the graves in the plot next to our family's plot, and I was shocked. Everybody was crying. I knew then you had to feel sad, but I didn't cry.

"I don't want to see them . . . looking like Grandmother in her coffin," I said. "I'm not going."

Aunt Maggie didn't say anything else. She just turned and left the room.

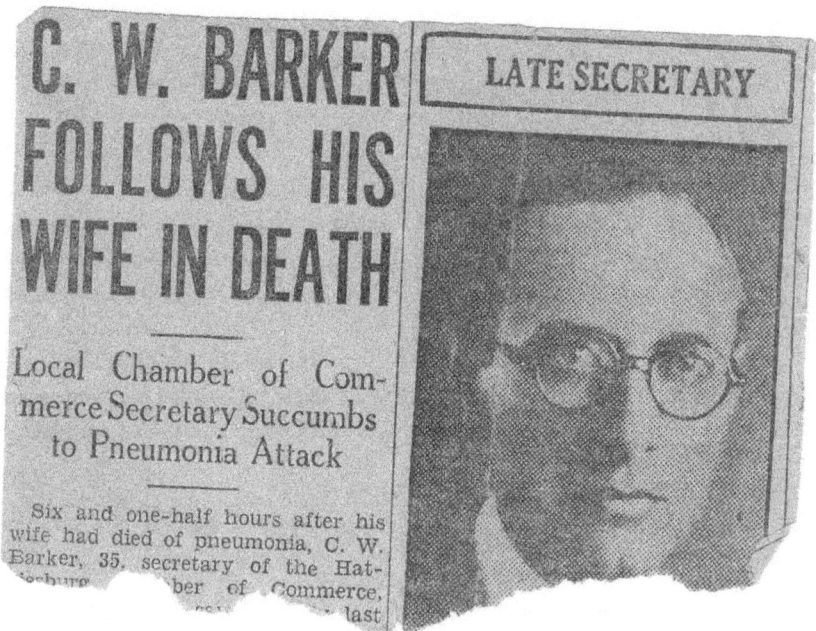

C. W. BARKER FOLLOWS HIS WIFE IN DEATH

LATE SECRETARY

Local Chamber of Commerce Secretary Succumbs to Pneumonia Attack

Six and one-half hours after his wife had died of pneumonia, C. W. Barker, 35, secretary of the Hat-tiesburg ber of Commerce, last

Obituary, unfortunately incomplete, of my father and mother's death (courtesy of the *Hattiesburg American*).

CHAPTER 14

THE BLUEBIRD

Hattiesburg, mid-December 1932

I DIDN'T GO to my mother and daddy's funeral. I did not go back to school either. Nor did I stay at Uncle Raymond and Aunt Maggie's. The following week, I was back at home, in my own house. How and why that decision was made, I'll never know, but I'm sure it was made with the hearts and not the minds of my uncles and Aunt Amber. From that day on, they were the ones who took care of Bishop and me.

"We have to be very careful when Bishop comes home from the hospital," Aunt Amber said to me one morning as we were sitting in the kitchen, eating cornflakes. "He nearly died too, you know," she said. "He just barely pulled through."

"Does he know about Mama and Daddy?" I asked.

"He thinks they're still in the hospital," said Aunt Amber. "The doctors said not to tell him the truth yet. They are afraid he will have a relapse from the shock."

The day Uncle Collin brought Bishop home, I could not help thinking how small he looked. He was also still a little weak from the pneumonia. His four and a half years on me seemed to have just disappeared, and in a way, we were just alike.

December dragged on, wet and cold. Bishop was not allowed to play outside. He busied himself with his airplane models and his erector set. Then sometimes he would dismantle what he had made and start all over again, assembling the miniature metal girders and geometric pieces into new and different designs. He didn't talk much. It seemed to me he did a lot of thinking. I started back to my old school again, but the afternoons were endless.

"Do you think Mama and Daddy will be home for Christmas?" Bishop asked me one day.

But when I said, "I don't know," to his question, my stomach felt all fluttery. "Wait a minute," I said. "I'll be right back."

Bishop looked up at me.

"I have to go to the bathroom," I said. It was just a little lie, so I stayed in the bathroom a few minutes, hoping he would forget what he had asked me.

"What can I tell him?" I whispered to Aunt Amber in the kitchen. "He wants to know if I think they'll be home for Christmas." I looked into her eyes for an answer.

She covered her mouth with the back of her hand. Then she spoke very softly. "I don't know," she said, shaking her head. "Try to change the subject. We can't tell him yet. He's not well enough. We have to wait 'til he's a little stronger."

More than once, Bishop asked me if I thought our parents would be out of the hospital and be home for Christmas. Each time, when I avoided answering him in one way or another, I felt he sensed something was wrong, but he never continued the conversation. Just as I didn't want to lose my belief in Santa Claus, I think Bishop didn't want to lose his belief that our parents would be all right and come home for Christmas. Then one day he simply stopped asking.

Christmas was only four days away when Uncle Collin brought the tree home for us. Bishop and I took all the boxes of decorations down from the top shelf in the hall closet and unpacked them. We put the strings of colored lights on first and then the balls and the tinsel and lastly the icicles. When we finished, it was beautiful. To children, no matter whether they are tall or short, thickly laden with ornaments and tinsel or not, with a star or an angel or nothing at all on top, I am sure to those who have decorated them, every Christmas tree is the most beautiful tree in the world.

I wrote my letter to Santa Claus, as I had always done. Bishop encouraged me to do it. He even helped me with the spelling, but he didn't write one himself. When my letter was finished and folded in an envelope, I placed it on a branch of the tree. I did ask for The Bluebird, even though I was sure it was a lost cause. Even if Santa didn't exist, I was sure none of our troubled relatives would have the presence of mind to try to locate such a special toy. But I did hope.

On Christmas morning, when Bishop and I woke up, it was still dark outside. We got out of bed and went into the living room. The tree lights were on and glowing in the dark. Under the tree, there were presents wrapped in colored paper, and on one branch, not wrapped, was The Bluebird! It was there! My Bluebird, at least a foot long! Sleek and gleaming, it was the most beautiful blue I had ever seen. If it could have been possible, I would have truly believed in Santa Claus again, and for a moment, I almost did. Holding that racing car, playing with it, even just sitting and looking at it gave me a feeling of warm contentment. I don't remember if Bishop got what he wanted, but I know what he did not get. Nobody could have given it to him. He didn't mention our parents again. And neither did I.

***

One Sunday early in January, I was playing with The Bluebird in the living room when Uncle Collin came by in his Buick.

"We'll go out for a drive," he said.

A ride in Uncle Collin's car was a treat, but somehow I was sure something was going to happen because Uncle Grady was with him. I took The Bluebird out to the car and climbed in. There was just enough room for three in my uncle's car. We rode up there and looked out the small back window and watched the road roll out behind us. For a while, no one said anything. The only sound besides that of the motor was Uncle Collin clearing his throat. Finally, he spoke.

"Bishop, your mama and daddy died in the hospital," Uncle Collin said very gently.

It was very quiet in the car.

My brother didn't say anything. Then he started sniffling. After a minute or two, he whispered something that sounded like "I know."

"We didn't want to tell you before," said Uncle Grady. He sounded all choked up. "The doctors were mighty worried about you. But now that you're well, we needed to tell you."

Bishop cried very softly for a while. Then he was silent. He looked so small between Uncle Collin and Uncle Grady. Neither of my uncles said anything else. I remembered I had The Bluebird with me. There was just enough space between the back window and me to roll it back and forth. By this time, we were way out in the country, but Uncle Collin kept on driving. Now the only sound was the noise from the Buick's motor. I stopped playing with The Bluebird and looked out the back window again. The road just kept on rolling out from under us and disappearing in the distance.

Deep in the South, where I came from, it was traditional to wear a carnation on Mother's Day. If your mother was living, you wore a red carnation, and if she wasn't, you wore a white one. Aunt Amber made sure Bishop and I wore white carnations pinned to our shirts, just over our hearts, when we went to church that Sunday. Ever since then, when I smell carnations, the scent, something like cloves, takes me back to that Mother's Day. Although I refused to go to my parents' funeral, I've been to others through the years, and funeral flowers always seem to be redolent of carnations, those spicy, sweet carnations. I still love the smell.

CHAPTER 15

CHILDHOOD DAYS

Hattiesburg, 1933

SPRINGTIME IN THE South came early. Flowers were already in bloom, and Aunt Amber had already started her campaign for Uncle Collin to buy a pony for Bishop and me.

"Shetland ponies might be expensive, but I bet a regular pony won't cost too much," she said. "It can be a kind of early birthday present for the baby–I mean, for Howard. He doesn't like us to keep on calling him Baby, you know. He's getting a little old for playing cowboys and Indians on those stick horses Bishop made out of old broom handles. He'll be nine soon and old enough. A pony could be a good distraction for Bishop too. He needs to get his mind off . . . things."

Aunt Amber was right. We loved the pony and named her Dolly. We rode her around the yard and in the open field behind our house. Bishop taught Dolly to jump across a small ditch at the bottom of the hill. With me sitting behind my brother, Dolly would gallop down the hill and leap over it like a real steeplechase horse. Dolly was an important addition to our life. Aunt Amber made sure my brother and I fed and watered the pony each day, and after riding her, we currycombed her all over before she was put out to graze.

When I rode Dolly by myself, I pretended to be a young Buffalo Bill. Then I'd give her two sugar cubes for a treat.

From reading the Sunday funnies, I also saw myself as Buck Rogers or Flash Gordon (preferably both at the same time). I would also have settled for being the young hero in *Terry and the Pirates*. Like Terry, I was fascinated with the Dragon Lady, a Chinese villainess who wore a long tight skirt split up the sides, revealing her thighs. She also wore a cut-off blouse that let you see the bottom half of her "titties" just below her nipples. The characters in the comic strip didn't seem to think that was naughty, but I did, and I liked it.

Children have a knack for inventing things to share with other kids, and Bishop and I were no exception. We had never been to an actual circus, but we had seen pictures and knew enough about them to make one in our backyard and to charge a few pennies for admission. We promised our little friends our circus would have "Prehistoric Monsters" (our baby alligator and Bishop's snapping turtles), a "Mysterious Sleeping Tiger" (my lazy cat), "Wild Black Panthers" (our litter of all-black kittens), plus "Jack, Special Guest Star Aerialist." I had trained Jackie, my pet white mouse, to hang by his front paws and swing on a little doll-sized trapeze.

We were doing pretty good business, maybe twenty or thirty cents, when Emmett Landry's mother found her son's puppies caged in a wooden box labeled "Unknown Wild Animals." She was furious. Without a word, she kicked in the thin bamboo bars and took the puppies back home, and that was the end of our business venture.

One day, not long afterward, Uncle Collin came with some bad news. Aunt Amber called my brother and me to come into the room for him to tell it to us himself. That was when he quietly told Bishop and me that we would have to move out of our home.

"There is no way for us to keep up with the loan payments," our uncle said.

I wondered how such a thing could happen. Bishop knew I didn't understand, and he tried to explain it to me.

"Daddy had been making the payments on the money the bank lent him to build our house. But now there is not enough money for our uncles to pay off the bank loan and all the other expenses."

"Don't worry," Uncle Collin assured us. "You boys are going to come and live with us in your grandmother's house. It'll be fine." He stopped to clear his throat, "Your pony will come too—"

"Dolly can live in the barn with the cow and the chickens," Aunt Amber said, interrupting him. "We'll have a good ol' time."

I was upset about having to leave our home, and though Bishop didn't say much, I knew he was upset too. There was nothing for us to do but accept the facts.

Aunt Amber supervised the entire moving, making sure all our belongings, every piece of furniture, every picture and bric-a-brac, and every light fixture was loaded into the huge moving van. Bishop and I were relieved when Dolly was shoved in too. We watched the truck as it pulled out of our driveway, with Dolly looking out over the tailgate.

CHAPTER 16

TO GRANDMOTHER'S HOUSE WE GO

North Main Street, Hattiesburg, 1933

THE OLD-FASHIONED WOOD-FRAMED house at the end of a graveled lane, a block off North Main Street was where Sarah (Miss Sally) Bishop and her husband, Stanhope Bishop, brought up their family of eleven children. It was not a four-columned mansion boasting Palladian windows with a balcony above a grand entrance, the kind you might see in romantic movies about the South. Grandmother's house was a one-story dwelling with a four-posted porch, built around 1900.

The front and back porch were connected by a long center hall. The house was simply furnished, with the exception of the living room, which was referred to as the parlor. The parlor's plush-covered Victorian furniture was beautifully stuffy and probably had been ordered from an early Sears-Roebuck catalog. There too was Grandmother's prized possession, a wind-up Edison Victrola with a small collection of thick one-sided records like Chic Sale's cornball monologues, Enrico Caruso's soaring tenor, and an unknown soprano singing, "There's a long, long trail a-winding to the land of my dreams . . ."

Before Bishop and I were moved into Grandmother's house, there had been no electricity. In the old days, old-fashioned kerosene lamps were lit at night, and in winter, warmth had to be coaxed from fireplaces. In the kitchen, there was a vintage wood-burning iron range and a sink with running water, but like our old Redus Street bungalow at the end of the cornfield, there was no bathroom. There was a two-holed outhouse, often referred to as the privy, not far from the back porch next to a large chinaberry tree, fun to climb by children and a source of hard green berries to load into homemade popguns. Each bedroom had a washstand, a small cabinet with a large pitcher and a wash bowl on it, and a towel rack. The cabinet door underneath concealed the "slop jar."

My brother and I had visited Grandmother Bishop many times, so we were very familiar with her house. At the time of Grandmother Bishop's death in 1927, all but four of her eleven children were out of her house, married with children of their own, or long dead. Aunt Amber and her unmarried brothers— Collin, Ledger, and Grady—were the only Bishop offspring still living in the family home.

When it became necessary for my brother and me to be moved there in the spring of 1933, we were surprised to see only one new thing. Electricity had been installed. That meant there were single light bulbs in pull-chain sockets hanging from the center of the ceiling in each room, a far cry from the ornamental light fixtures in our own house on Twenty-Fifth Avenue. Bits and pieces of our furniture found their way into the old-fashioned house, but the bulk of it—the living room, dining room, and bedroom sets—ended up stored in the barn with a myriad of other household items. Dolly, for better or worse, was now sharing the cow stall.

Uncle Grady, the youngest of our three uncles, was still a sales clerk at Mathews Hardware Store. His room (Grandmother's bedroom before she died) had enough space in it for another double bed, so Bishop and I became our uncle's roommates. He didn't seem to mind. There was an extra chest of drawers and a large chiffonier in the bedroom for our clothes and things. I liked the big clock on the mantle over the fireplace. Under the clock's face, there was a door with a glass window where you could see the pendulum swinging back and forth. I hid my silver dollar there inside. Nobody knew.

When it was time to go to bed, instead of my having to go to the outhouse, Uncle Grady would take me out to the front porch to pee. He and I would stand at the edge of the porch, looking at the night sky until I was ready to relieve myself. My uncle had a little trick to help me start.

"*Pish, pish, pi-i-ish,*" he would make the sounds through his teeth, and involuntarily, I would pee into the flowering lantana bushes growing around the porch.

I soon became fast friends with a youngster named Bobby Glenn, who lived nearby on Main Street. Bobby's thoughtful mother invited me to spend a couple of weeks at their house while things got "straightened out" in ours. Mr.

and Mrs. Glenn treated me like a member of the family, and I enjoyed having someone to play with who was my own age. I also enjoyed having showers with Bobby in a real bathroom again, and Bobby liked to come over to the old-fashioned house where I lived to play toy cars on the hard sand under Grandmother's house. Like many of the old Southern homes, it was built on brick pilings four feet high to let air circulate under the house to keep it cool in the hot summer months. Bobby also liked to see how far my pet chicken could fly when I tossed her up in the air from our back porch—all the way to the outhouse. But what Bobby liked best was to ride behind me on my and my brother's pony Dolly in the front of our house and down to the railroad tracks at the bottom of the pasture.

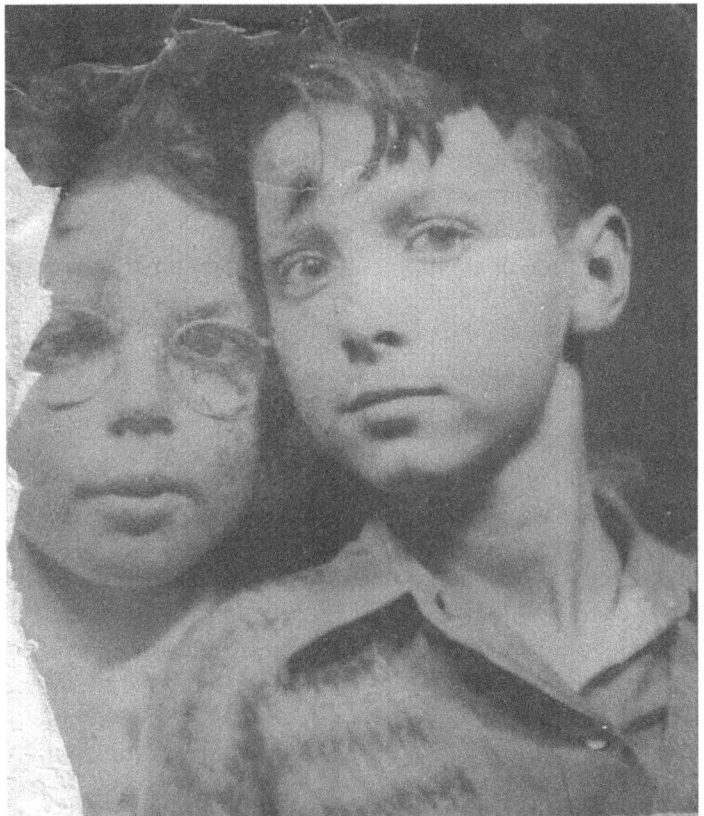

Me and Bobby Glenn at maybe ten years old.

Bishop and his new friend, Emmett Fairchild, were looking around a nearby city dump and found an abandoned wooden housing from a pickup truck. Somehow they got it into our pasture and created a "clubhouse" where they could hang out with their pals. Sometimes when it was unoccupied,

Bobby and I would sneak into it and play with our doolollies like we'd heard older boys do. (Nothing much happened.)

We had more fun hiding under the railroad trestle at the edge of the pasture when we heard a freight train approaching. As the train passed over us, we'd look up and see the sparks flying from the train's wheels. We had to hold our hands over our ears because the noise was so deafening.

***

My brother and I slowly adjusted to our new life. Bishop, still only thirteen, had dropped out of school after our parents died and now spent most of his days hunting and fishing. He became a loner and didn't let me follow him on his new "adventures." Bishop had a molasses-colored squirrel dog he called "Lasses" who followed my brother everywhere he went. Uncle Collin, our legal guardian, did not force my brother to conform, whether wisely or simply because he didn't know what else do. Bishop had to find his own salvation.

Uncle Ledger had the bedroom next to the back porch. He was actually my favorite uncle. He was a kind, gentle man who smiled a lot and always had time for Bishop and me. Uncle Ledger had suffered from poor eyesight all his life, and all he was able to do was tend to the cow and chickens and help Aunt Amber around the house. In the spring, he also planted the cornfield, and in the summer, he picked the ripened corn from the field. Uncle Ledger also knew how to choose the best tomatoes in his garden. Together, we would take out a salt shaker, pick a sun-warmed tomato, bite into it, and then shake a little salt on the juicy inside and eat it right there in the garden. Tomatoes never tasted so good at the dinner table. As I write this many years later, my mouth suddenly fills with the sweet taste of those tomatoes in Uncle Ledger's garden.

Aunt Amber was totally occupied during the day, seeing to "her boys" and all the other chores as the only woman the house fell heir to. She was sweet and always affectionate. Most days, she was cheerful, but nights were often a different story. Aunt Amber, bless her, was a troubled woman. Her nightly "sermons," when everybody else had gone to bed, were mostly aimed at Uncle Collin. As she walked up and down the dark hall, talking to whoever would listen, she would go through a long list, sobbing softly and moaning pitifully after each one.

"Those children need indoor plumbing," Aunt Amber would complain. "They're not used to living like heathens the way we do."

Uncle Collin, who usually ignored her, referred to her complaints as "preaching." Uncle Grady and Uncle Ledger tried to stay out of it. Aunt Amber's favorite "sermon" besides the lack of a proper bathroom was Uncle Collin's sorry woman. I didn't exactly know what she meant by sorry woman, but that was when Uncle Collin would open his door, go out in the hall to face his sister, and talk back to her.

"Hush up now, Amber," he would say. "No use ranting and raving this way. You just hush up and go back to bed." This had no effect on her.

"It's a sin," she would go on. "An out and out sin, the way you behave with Ledger, who's half blind, Grady, who's not normal, and me here, working our fingers to the bone trying to make a good home for Velma's children and you consorting with that sorry woman, driving her all over town in broad daylight for the whole world to see. You ought to be ashamed!"

"Hush up, Amber." Uncle Collin would raise his voice at his sister. "Stop all this preaching and go to bed!"

Most of the time, she would keep it up, moaning and crying. Uncle Grady usually didn't have much to say, but sometimes he too would go out in the hall. Bishop and I could hear every word.

"Amber"–he would parrot Uncle Collin–"You've got to hush up now. This isn't accomplishing anything. Go on back to your room."

I remember it was Uncle Ledger who kept quiet, but when it got like it was getting out of hand, he would come and take Aunt Amber's arm and quietly lead her to her room, where she would cry herself to sleep. Bishop and I were not used to this kind of behavior in grown-ups. We didn't know what to do, so we just kept quiet and tried to go back to sleep. The next morning, nobody spoke of what had happened the night before.

If all this sounds like Aunt Amber was a "weak sister," she wasn't. One night I was awakened by strange noises outside. The chickens were clucking loudly, and Dolly was kicking in her stall in the barn. I got up and saw Aunt Amber walking through the dark hall toward the back door. Slipping out into the hall, I followed her.

She turned and whispered, "Something's goin' on."

She opened the door quietly, and we listened for a moment. There was a rustling in the branches of the chinaberry tree.

"Howard!" Aunt Amber suddenly spoke loudly, loud enough for the intruder to hear. "Get me the gun!" Then softly, she said to me, "It's in Collin's dresser. He's not home."

Without a moment's hesitation, I ran down the hall to Uncle Collin's room. I grabbed his pistol and hurried back to my aunt. She took the pistol and opened the screen door very slowly. I watched her point it at the chinaberry tree and pull the trigger. The explosive noise almost deafened me. Then all was quiet.

"Might've just been a possum," Aunt Amber said and latched the screen door. "Here, put the gun back in Collin's drawer before he gets in. We'll go back to bed."

Neither Uncle Grady nor Bishop woke up. I guess Uncle Ledger hadn't heard anything either.

Life in Grandmother's house went on pretty much as usual. From time to time, Aunt Amber would walk in the hall at night "preaching," as Uncle Collin called it. She never ran out of complaints, but as his "sorry woman" slipped in importance, the need for a proper bathroom "for the children" became foremost. In the mornings, after Uncle Ledger made the coffee and Aunt Amber served breakfast, Uncle Collin drove into town, dropped Uncle Grady off at Mathews Hardware, and went to his office.

Eventually, Uncle Collin had a small area at the end of the back porch enclosed and bought a bathtub, a sink, and a toilet bowl. But the fixtures were never connected to the pipe that supplied the water. As the adults in the house had always done, we children made do with the bedroom washstands and the outhouse in the backyard.

On Saturdays, Uncle Collin would go to his office and do a little bookkeeping and wait for the people to come in to pay their paltry rent money. My uncle owned a row of unpainted two-room shacks down on the Gravel Line, a deserted railroad that served as the border of an area which had been known as "the quarters" since the shameful days of slavery.

When the renters of the miserable dwellings didn't show up, Uncle Collin would drive his car down to scold them and threaten to "throw them out." However, in spite of his warnings, he actually was a tenderhearted man, and he never did.

"Ooo-ee! Mista Bishop!" they'd say with a hearty laugh. "Now you know you don't mean that!" Then they would give him what little they had and promise to pay up "next time."

One of Uncle Collin's unpainted shacks down on the Gravel Line was occupied by a woman who did our family's laundry in exchange for the rent. Arilla was a quiet, dignified person who, in a different society, would have been called a lady. In the 1930s, south of the Mason–Dixon Line, that term was reserved for white women—well, if they indeed were ladies.

One afternoon my uncle took me by Arilla's house to leave some things for her to wash. We walked through the two neat rooms to the back porch to find Arilla ironing clothes. Arilla's little daughter, Rosalie, was helping her mother by stirring the black iron pot of dirty clothes that boiled over a wood fire in the backyard. Boiling the clothes was the first step in Arilla's process of washing, which went through soaking and scrubbing with Octagon soap on a washboard and ending up with line-drying and being ironed. Arilla's ironing was done with care on an old ironing board with one of her two irons heated to the "jus' right degree" over a bucket of red-hot coals nearby.

While Uncle Collin spoke to Arilla, I went out in the yard and stood near Rosalie and watched her as she stirred the pot. I think Rosalie and I were about the same age, but we were both too shy to speak. The most we could manage was a mere flicker of a smile at each other before my Uncle called me after he left the pillowcase full of used shirts and underwear with Arilla.

"I don't 'low nobody to tetch my irons and ironing board," Arilla had told me. "I inherited them from my mother, and they are the best."

Uncle Collin told me Arilla was known for the high quality of her washing and ironing and was able to make a fair amount of money from other white folks to keep up with her expenses.

Believe it or not, but I can remember seeing Arilla delivering the laundry, climbing the slope behind Grandmother's house with a huge bundle of wash wrapped in a sheet balanced on top of her head. A few steps behind her, Rosalie followed Arilla with a smaller bundle on her head like her mother.

Sometimes on Saturdays, when I went downtown with Uncle Collin, Uncle Ledger would dress up in a suit and tie and hat and ride with us. To me, he was the picture of a distinguished Southern gentleman. Even though his eyesight was very poor, he liked to stand on the sidewalk and chat with a few of his old cronies. Some of the men seemed to have nothing better to do than to pass the time of day talking about the weather, often chewing tobacco and spitting discreetly into the gutter between the parked cars. One of the best things on those Saturdays was when Uncle Collin would treat me to a snack at the Merchant's Café. I usually chose a piece of cherry pie. Warm cherry pie with a glass of cold milk was my favorite.

When Halloween came around that fall, it was different from the way we celebrate it nowadays. Back then, there was no such thing as "trick or treat" on Halloween and no sparing the tricks to get candy from your neighbors. Kids just roamed around after dark, turning lawn furniture upside down and then ringing doorbells and running or simply hiding the chairs in the next-door neighbors' shrubbery. Older kids, if they were strong or clever enough, sometimes managed to put the furniture on top of people's woodsheds or garages.

Some families gave small costume parties for younger children. I had grown into the Spanish suit Aunt Margaret had brought me from New Orleans, and riding Dolly, I felt I looked like a real gaucho. I can still hear the sound of Dolly's hooves crunching the gravel when I rode home up the lane in the moonlight. There were plenty of places I could ride Dolly–the pasture in front of Grandmother's house, the woods in the back of the pear orchard and cornfields–but the streets in town were off-limits.

Uncle Collin was obliged to drive me back and forth to Davis School, some distance from Grandmother's house. It was the first time I was back in elementary school regularly since my mother and father had died. I had missed four months, but I was put into the fifth grade anyway. It was another new experience for me to handle. One afternoon, when Uncle Collin picked me up after school, I opened the door to his Buick coupe, and there was a lady sitting in the seat next to him. I was surprised because I had never seen her before.

"Hello, Howard," the lady said and smiled. "There's enough room for you here next to me. You just squeeze in."

I was puzzled and, for a moment, didn't know what to do. But I had no choice, so I did as she suggested.

"My name is Martha Loftus," she said. "I guess you should call me Mrs. Loftus."

I slid in and tried not to touch her. She had a sweet smell of powder and perfume. I didn't know what to say, so I didn't speak. Uncle Collin kept clearing his throat as usual, but he didn't say anything either.

"How do you like your new school, dear?" Mrs. Loftus asked.

"Fine, ma'am," I said. "It's nice to meet you," I added in a small voice. I had been taught to say that whenever I was introduced to a grown-up.

"Thank you, honey," Mrs. Loftus said. "It's nice to meet you too. Do you like your new friends?"

"Yessum, I guess so," I said as politely as I could.

And that was all that was spoken until Uncle dropped me off at home and drove away. Mrs. Loftus seemed like a very nice person, but somehow I knew not to mention to Aunt Amber I had just met Uncle Collin's sorry woman.

In late December, the second Christmas since our mother and father had died was approaching, and it would be the first Christmas in Grandmother's house. Uncle Collin and Uncle Grady took Bishop and me out in the woods to find a Christmas tree. We picked out a holly. It was roundish, eight or nine feet tall, and loaded with red berries. It filled a large corner of the parlor, and we decorated it with ornaments and tinsel that we had brought with us from Twenty-Fifth Avenue. The finishing touch was the gossamer spun-glass blanket Uncle Grady had brought home from Matthews Hardware Store.

The night before Christmas, I put the Bluebird, my toy racing car, under the tree. It just seemed like the thing to do. Christmas Day, with a few presents after dinner and no "incidents," turned out to be fine. Two months later, the Christmas tree, with dead leaves falling off, was still standing. It seemed like nobody wanted to take it down.

CHAPTER 17

STORY TIME

Hattiesburg, Late Spring 1934

MY FIFTH GRADE teacher was Misss. Flora Auchmuty. She had a lovely aquiline face and a bright smile, and she wore a beautiful ring with a large turquoise stone. I remember she had a habit of twisting the ring around and around her finger as she talked. She had a very precise way of speaking and made everything sound interesting, like the story she told us about the time she had forgotten to take her toothbrush with her on a visit to a friend in the country.

"Well, naturally, I brush my teeth every day," she said, "so can you imagine what I did? I went outside and found a small twig. I chewed the end of it, and it made into a kind of brush. Then I brushed my teeth with it!" she said triumphantly.

The image of my teacher brushing her teeth with a twig stuck with me, but I don't recall anything she said about lessons. The main thing I remember about Miss Auchmuty was that I liked her very much, and I was sure she liked me.

My elementary school had an assembly hall with a stage where school pageants and small plays were put on several times a year. In our health pageant, I was to be a carrot. Dressed in my orange-and-green-crepe-paper costume, I waited with a group of agitated children in our classroom for our turn to go onstage. As our nervous chatter grew louder, Miss Auchmuty closed the door and, to calm us down, said she was going to tell us a story.

"It's about a man who had a milk-white face and blood-red hair," she said in a conspiring voice.

We grew quiet.

"Once upon a time, in a very large city, there was a department store where all kinds of things were sold. You could buy clothes–suits and dresses, coats and hats and shoes–for grown-ups and children and even things like toys and gifts of all kinds. You could buy furniture and sheets and towels and all the things you need to fill a house."

Now we children were listening intently.

"But what about the man with the milk-white face and the blood-red hair?" I asked.

"Shhh," she whispered. "The store was always filled with rich folks who had money to burn. They spent thousands of dollars on themselves and never gave a thought to all the people in the city who often didn't have enough to eat. The poorest were too proud to beg, but outside the big store, they would see rich people in all their fine clothes going in and out the revolving doors."

"But we want to hear about the man with the milk-white face and the blood-red hair," said a little girl who was standing next to me.

"Well," said Miss Auchmuty in hushed voice, "One day, a particularly cold day, a little boy and his sister decided to go inside the big store just to see what it looked like. So they slipped into the revolving doors behind a very rich man. They were dazzled to see all the wonderful things everywhere. There were many glass counters filled with beautiful handbags and glittering jewelry and gifts of all kinds."

"'Going up?' The children heard the elevator operator's voice. They started to go in, but his voice stopped them. 'Room for just one more,' he said. The little boy and his sister looked up at him as the elevator doors were closing. The operator had a milk-white face and blood-red hair! The little boy and his sister backed away from the door.

"Inside the elevator, it was crowded." Miss Auchmuty continued, "No one looked at anyone else. The elevator stopped at the second floor, and the doors slid open. A group of people pushed forward to get in." Miss Auchmuty's voice became deeper and more threatening. "'Room for just one more,' said the operator with the milk-white face and the blood-red hair, and he let just one person on. The same thing happened on the third and fourth floors."

We children were mesmerized. The health pageant on the stage in the assembly hall was forgotten.

"On each and every floor," Miss Auchmuty said, "all the way to the top of the big store, the man with the milk-white face and the blood-red hair grinned and said the same thing–'Room for just one more'–and he let on just one rich, greedy person. The elevator was now packed with people. As soon as the operator closed the doors on the top floor, there was a sound of metal snapping, and then suddenly, the elevator began to fall. Then faster, faster, and faster it fell! Before it hit the bottom, you could hear the man with the milk-white face and blood-red hair screaming. 'Sorr-ee, there's room for just . . . one . . . morrre!'"

Miss Auchmuty ended the story in guttural tones. My classmates and I were petrified.

"But what happened to all the rich, greedy people?" I asked as soon as I could speak.

"Why, my dear, they were all killed," Miss Auchmuty said simply in her normal sweet voice. "Now it's time for you all to go onstage."

So wearing my orange-and-green crepe-paper carrot-top hat, I got in line with a dozen other kids dressed as vegetables and fruits, and we marched into the assembly hall and onto the stage. I don't remember the health pageant, but I'll never forget the story and that day I fell in love with my teacher.

The last time I saw Miss Auchmuty was thirty-three years later, when I was in Hattiesburg with my wife and our two small children, visiting my brother and his family. Bishop was developing new neighborhoods in our hometown and had designed and built a lovely home for Miss Flora (I was old enough by then to use her first name) and her sister. Miss Flora had invited us to come to tea. Instead of tea, we sipped sherry and enjoyed genteel conversation with the two maiden ladies for hours. They were charming, and Miss Flora seemed to be very much as I had remembered her–vibrant, attractive, and still twisting the turquoise ring on her finger. How could I not still love her? I would have asked her to repeat the milk-white face and blood-red hair story, but just as well, it had slipped my mind.

CHAPTER 18

THE LONG HOT SUMMER

Hattiesburg, August 1935

T HE SUMMER OF 1935 was one of the hottest of my childhood– one hundred degrees Fahrenheit was not unusual. Electric fans, iced tea, and lemonade were the principal methods of keeping cool. Back then, air conditioning was not common in Mississippi. The Saenger Theater, the elegant Art Deco motion picture palace, was the coolest place in town. I don't know how the theater was cooled, but in my imagination, it could have been by a giant fan blowing over a huge block of ice somewhere out of sight. Whatever it was, it worked. Almost every Saturday morning, you could find me, either with my friend Bobby or alone, at the ten-o'clock picture show.

The Hattiesburg Saenger Theater.

Motion picture theaters in those days usually ran a newsreel before the feature followed by a cartoon. I liked Popeye the Sailor Man ("I fights to the finish 'cause I eats my spinach") and his girlfriend, Olive Oyl. But my favorite was a lovable little flapper named Betty Boop. I can still hear her sing,

> *I wanna be loved by you*
> *Just you and nobody else but you*
> *I wanna be loved by you alo-o-one*
> *Boop, boop-a-doop!*

Her tantalizing voice, sweet but a little naughty, is as clear now as it was then, over eighty years ago. When Betty Boop leaped from Max Fleischer's pen onto the movie screen in the early thirties, the "boop, boop-a-doop" girl's skirt was blowing up in the wind decades before Marilyn's over the subway grating in *The Seven-Year Itch*.

At such an early age, I was in love with Betty Boop.
But of course, that was just a child's fantasy.

After I saw the movie *Tarzan and His Mate* at the Saenger, all those comic book heroes and heroines I had idolized were forgotten. I just wanted to be like Tarzan, and I was determined to swing through the trees on vines the way Tarzan did. The next day, I found some ropes in the barn and slipped away into the woods beyond Uncle Ledger's cornfield. I climbed a couple of trees and rigged the ropes like the vines in the movie. Then in my "African jungle," I stripped down to my underpants and swung half naked through the trees. Nobody ever saw my awkward athletics (not even Bobby) or heard my pitiful "Ahh-eee-ahh!" calls, and all the animals within earshot must have been puzzled.

Fortunately, Bouie River was too far away from Grandmother's house for me to try the nude swimming scene in the movie. The underwater sequence of Johnny Weissmuller endlessly swimming after the exquisite Maureen O'Sullivan–Tarzan and Jane–took my breath away. That was long before the Hays Office put its collective feet down on nudity, on land or underwater.

Then when I saw *Gold Diggers of 1935*, with chorus girls singing and dancing in brief costumes, I decided to put on a show with singing and dancing myself. I recruited kids in my neighborhood and had rehearsals in Grandmother's parlor. I remember, clear as day, coaching them to raise their hands as they sang, "I'm shooting high, got my eyes on a star in the sky—shooting high!" I was sitting on one of Grandmother's Sears-Victorian chairs and holding a little girlfriend, Frances Hudson, on my lap like the leading man did in the movie. When I kissed her on her lips (wet, as I recall), I heard Aunt Amber's voice from the doorway where she stood watching.

"Lord have mercy," Aunt Amber said in shock. "If your grandmother saw that, she would turn over in her grave!"

We never performed the actual show.

One sizzling Saturday, mainly to cool off, I went alone to The Saenger to see a picture show, probably another Tarzan film or a Charlie Chan detective thriller. Sitting with my eyes glued to the screen, I was deeply involved in the movie when Frances Hudson found me in the last row of the theater.

"Howard, you've gotta come quick!" she said, pulling my arm. "Your house is on fire!"

We ran out through the lobby to the street. Believe it or not, there was a taxicab sitting there. I had never been in a taxi in my life, but we got in and slammed the door. I remember the rest of what happened as clearly as if it was in a movie itself.

"Sir," I said to the taxi driver, "I've gotta get home quick. My house is on fire! It's out on North Main Street. Please hurry!"

And just like in the movies, he did.

When he drove up the lane to the house, there was a fire truck and a huge crowd of people, but there was no house. There were only three brick chimneys surrounded by a mass of charred timbers and mounds of smoking ashes.

I don't remember paying the taxi driver—maybe I gave him what was left of my allowance—but when I heard Aunt Amber screaming, I jumped out, leaving Frances, and pushed my way through the crowd of people to get to my aunt.

"Ai-i-i-eeeee!" Aunt Amber was screaming in a high-pitched hysterical wail. "What are we going to do? What are we going to dooo?" she kept repeating.

I was terrified. Uncle Ledger and Uncle Grady were trying to console her, but she would have none of it. She pushed aside anybody who tried to comfort her and kept on crying, her eyes glued to what was left of our house.

Bishop, who had been out fishing, came through the crowd. He touched Aunt Amber for a moment and then started walking toward the remains of the house. Uncle Collin stopped him.

"Stay away from there," he said. "Some of those timbers are still hot."

"I just wanted to find my Indian-head penny collection," Bishop said. "My Indian arrowheads are in there with it."

"My silver dollar I hid in the mantle clock burned up too, Bishop," I managed to say.

"It's all gone," Uncle Collin said, clearing his throat. "Everything's gone."

Bishop turned and walked away. I watched him disappear among the people.

Paying no attention to the onlookers, Aunt Amber turned and grabbed her brother's arm. "You are going to rebuild this house, Collin!" she shouted. "Mark my words! You are going to rebuild this house! I am not setting foot off this property until you have rebuilt this house for us and for Velma's children!"

For once, Uncle Collin was speechless. I was scared, upset, and worried. If he could not have afforded the payments to save the home our parents had built, he could never afford to build a new house to replace this one either. Aunt Amber stood next to me by a scorched lantana bush in the front yard and wept.

As the crowd slowly dispersed, my uncles and I looked at the smoking ashes. Only three things had been saved—a large mahogany rocking chair (my parents' wedding present from Uncle Collin), a crocheted throw pillow made by my mother, and a red Chinese vase. All three were from our Twenty-Fifty Avenue home. Everything else was totally destroyed.

CHAPTER 19

FROM PILLAR TO POST

Hattiesburg, 1935 and 1936

AUNT AMBER STUCK to her word when she flat-out turned down Uncle Collin's plan to move us all into an empty house owned by Uncle Raymond. She simply refused to budge and put it to him clearly in no uncertain terms.

"It'll be a cold day in August before I'll be indebted to that scoundrel, even if he is my own kith and kin," she said. "Besides, it's on the other side of the tracks down past the train depot. It's not an area fit for the children to be raised in. We'll stay right here and live in the barn."

So Aunt Amber, Bishop, and I, along with Uncle Grady, "camped out" in the storage room next to the cow, the pony, and the chickens. Uncle Ledger went to live with a cousin in nearby Wayne County. Uncle Collin created a makeshift bedroom in the building downtown where he had his office. I later realized it was more convenient when Mrs. Loftus came to town for a visit.

I was invited again to my friend Bobby's house, but I stayed only a few days and then came "home." Although our future was unknown, Bishop and I were still together for better or for worse.

Bishop and I playing around. I may have been maybe eleven years old.

It wasn't all bad, living in the barn. Several beds and a few pieces of old furniture, among the things from our house on Twenty-Fifth Avenue, had been stored in the barn. Uncle Grady brought a kerosene stove from the store where he worked. He and Uncle Collin provided groceries. It was kind of fun until winter came, with its cold rain and winds. Our unheated "campsite" was no longer habitable. The day the outdoor hand-operated pump froze and our water supply disappeared, Aunt Amber had to give up.

We moved, after all, into Uncle Raymond's house down by the depot. It had the amenities, but it didn't prove to be an ideal solution. Within a few months, Uncle Grady surprised us with his sudden and unexpected marriage. He created a private apartment in half of the house and brought home his wife and her teenaged son. The son had some mental disabilities, and she herself turned out to be quite disagreeable. Unfortunately, all of us had to share the one bathroom.

After bearing it for six months, Aunt Amber decided it wasn't an acceptable arrangement. She convinced Uncle Collin to rent a furnished apartment for us. It was small but in a better part of town. Sadly, it was situated right next to a large cemetery and was somewhat depressing to all of us.

From there, we moved into the home of a pleasant couple who ran a dancing school. They rented us a large bedroom with a kitchenette, and we shared their bath. The Hyde School of Dance primarily taught ballroom dancing for people who felt a need to brush up on their technique. There were no nightclubs in our town, and mature couples used the school to socialize or to simply dance. Mr. and Mrs. Hyde, both good dancers, were the instructors. Their son Charles, a polite late teenager, and Merle Baggett, an effervescent high-school senior, rounded out the teaching staff. Merle was very sweet and attractive and an amazingly talented tap dancer. She taught a class for adolescent kids whose mothers were usually frustrated performers.

For a while, this turned out to be a fortuitous move. Elizabeth Ann Carter, a popular schoolmate of mine who lived across the street, invited me to my first dancing party. At thirteen, going on fourteen, I didn't know how to dance, but Mr. and Mrs. Hyde offered me free lessons, providing I would partner some of the ladies in their ballroom classes. Picture a skinny teenage boy pushing a heavyset older woman around the classroom while she sang along with the record player to popular tunes like "Harbor Lights."

"I hear those harrr-bor lights . . . You light our wa-a-ay, although we ma-a-ay . . . be parrrting . . ." she cooed in my ear as I whirled her around the dance floor.

My hefty partner was actually light on her feet. I secretly called her Jennie Twinkle-Toes. Incidentally, Elizabeth Ann's dancing party was delightful, and all those lessons paid off.

The Hydes were a nice couple, but after a time, they decided their son needed our room, and we had to move. Our next home was a room in a cozy boarding house where we stayed through the winter. Not so incidentally, it had been suggested by Jennie Twinkle-Toes, who lived there.

I remember saving up all my money to buy this
jacket. I thought I looked pretty smart.

***

In the spring, Aunt Amber found a better place for us—a bungalow on Main Street very close to the business section of town. Uncle Collin agreed he'd pay the rent until she could manage it herself. My courageous aunt had plans of turning it into her own boarding house, which she was able to do pretty quickly. In our sixth home in less than four years, I had my own room for the first time in my life, and so did Bishop. Uncle Grady, after a sudden split with his impossible wife, moved in with us. Now if he wanted to, he could actually walk to work.

The three extra bedrooms filled up quickly, and Aunt Amber was in business. She had managed to set up a dining arrangement in the wide hall and, with some inexpensive help, served lunch and dinner to her boarders and her own family. Things were really looking up for all of us!

Aunt Amber's home at 89 Main Street, Hattiesburg, Mississippi, with Uncle Collin's car parked out front.

An older Uncle Collin.

An older Uncle Ledger with my brother, Bishop, later in life.

A young Uncle Grady.

CHAPTER 20

THE PALMER METHOD

Hattiesburg, 1937

Hattiesburg High School
Hattiesburg, MS.
by
Donna Kirkland Woods
2002

O UR NEW HOME on Main Street was just three blocks down the street from the handsome old high school where my mother had graduated many years earlier. Now my brother and I were enrolled, Bishop in the eleventh grade and I in the seventh grade, in an added-on junior high school building.

I walked to school each morning with a tinge of excitement. Going from one classroom to another for different subjects taught by different teachers was a big change from elementary school. Getting to know older kids and having home rooms and morning assembly were new experiences. For me, assembly was unique and especially interesting. The junior high school principal, Mr. S. H. Blair, would greet the students and faculty and make announcements. Then he would lead us as we repeated the Pledge of Allegiance in unison. Next, led by a teacher at the piano, we students would sing one or two patriotic songs, "The Star-Spangled Banner" and/or "America the Beautiful." Afterward, we sang a couple more songs, such as "The Land of My Dreams" or "Love's Old Sweet Song," also sung to typed slides with lyrics projected onto a big white screen. Assembly always ended with a prayer by Mr. Blair. Refreshed or calmed down, we students would then go to our morning classrooms.

Specific memories of most of my teachers have faded away, and yet one teacher still stands out. My penmanship teacher, Miss Dozia McGowan, was not a pretty woman. In fact, she was exceedingly plain, or to be cruel, she was downright ugly, and like all female teachers in my school days, Miss McGowan was referred to as an old maid. However, she was very pleasant, and she took her job very seriously.

In the 1930s, the Palmer Method of handwriting was the prescribed form taught to children in our junior high school. Miss McGowan firmly demonstrated the Palmer Method with chalk on the blackboard. She expected her students to make every effort to emulate her beautiful, flowing script, and we tried to, with varying degrees of success. Our practice books were dutifully filled with pages of ovals and forward-slanted marks executed in groups and combinations. These shapes were supposed to be reflected in cursive handwriting. Miss McGowan's handwriting was as close to perfect as one could get. Holding her chalk or pen in the first three fingers of her right hand while lightly touching the writing surface with her fourth finger, pinkie extended, Miss McGowan produced beautiful penmanship in the Palmer Method. She fully expected her students to do the same.

Two major things made the Palmer Method difficult for seventh graders. The pens were wooden shafts with removable nibs, which Miss McGowan personally selected and distributed to us each day. Fountain pens were forbidden, and ball-point pens had not yet been invented. Each desk in the classroom had an inkwell containing black ink, and each student was responsible for keeping it filled to the proper level from a quart-sized bottle kept in the supplies cabinet. Black ink stains around the desk's inkwells were not uncommon.

One day Miss McGowan wasn't in the classroom when all the students took their seats. We started to horse around, passing notes, throwing spitballs, and acting foolish.

"Where's old Aunt Dozie?" somebody shouted, and all the kids started laughing. "Aunt Dozie, Aunt Dozie, where's ugly old Aunt Dozie?"

The cruel sing-song resounded throughout the classroom. Because the door was at the back of the room, no one had seen Miss McGowan enter. The students, row by row, became silent as the teacher passed them, walking slowly until she came to her desk. Then she turned and stood quietly looking at us. Finally, she spoke.

"I am disappointed in you," she said softly. "I'm very disappointed in you, in all of you." After a slow sweeping look around the room at our frozen faces, she walked to the blackboard and picked up a piece of chalk. "All right," she said as she began demonstrating the exercise for the day. "Now please take your pens . . ."

I felt deeply ashamed, ashamed of myself and ashamed of all the other students. As I dipped the tip of my pen into the inkwell, more than the point filled up. So did my heart. I will never forget Miss McGowan.

The Hattiesburg Public Library.

The special love I felt for another older woman was as memorable–in a different way. However, Miss Clyde Smith was not technically a teacher. She was the librarian in charge of The Hattiesburg Public Library.

Because the library was only half a block from our house, I spent a lot of my time in the ninth grade there–reading, meeting friends, and, although I didn't realize it, falling in love again. Miss Smith was a tall good-looking woman who took a warmhearted interest in me, now a gangly fourteen-year-old. Miss Smith guided me, advising me which books to read and telling me about their authors. I helped her by putting stacks of returned books back on the shelves, emptying waste baskets, and doing other small chores around the library. When Miss Smith learned I was a fledgling artist, she asked me if I would help her with a special project.

"I think a good librarian should encourage students to read more books," Miss Smith said with a smile. "Checking books out to young people and making sure they know when to return them is just a small part of my job. I think I have a good idea in mind to get students to read more."

She explained her project to me, and I knew I could handle the job. I started working with her every day after school.

With her supervision, I created a series of silhouetted city skylines on poster board, which we tacked up above the book stacks all around the entire reading room. Each time a student completed a book, a cutout of a colorful balloon with the youngster's name on it would be lifted, inch by inch, higher above the skyline. As each kid's balloon reached the top, his or her name would be a winner. There were second and third winners and more as long as the kids kept competing. Miss Smith's simple reading game worked. She stimulated many young minds that summer, turning students into new and enthusiastic readers.

The best part of my "job" was when Miss Smith would leave her front desk and come to my work table.

"Howard," she would say in a low voice, "I think it's time for a break. Let's go back to my office and have a dope."

My friendly librarian was not trying to seduce me with drugs. Back in the thirties, Coca-Colas were often called "dopes" because that most famous soft drink in the world was rumored to contain a smidgeon of cocaine. The rumor was proven unfounded, but the sobriquet stuck for quite some time.

For a few minutes, Miss Smith and I would be alone to enjoy our dopes, often with a cookie or a peanut-butter-and-cracker sandwich in the privacy of her cluttered office. Afterward, we would go back to our work, she cheerfully checking books in and out and I painting silhouettes of skyscrapers on poster board and cutting out balloons.

Eighty-plus years later, the memory of Miss Smith and the Coke comradeship we shared is locked away inside my heart.

My father was interested in photography, here I am with his camera

CHAPTER 21

WINK

Hattiesburg, 1940–41

S ENIOR HIGH SCHOOL days were good days for me. I made friends easily and liked my teachers. Beginning with the tenth grade, in addition to the required courses (English literature, math, biology, and civics), you automatically had to plan your elective courses, such as languages, with a student advisor. I had wanted to learn French–I don't know why, I guess it sounded romantic–but my student advisor, a very sweet but plain spinster named Miss Tunnel, strongly advised me to take Latin. (Miss Tunnel taught Latin.)

"Howard," she said firmly, "if you would like to take French or even Spanish, almost all languages have their roots in Latin." I took Latin.

At the innocent age of fifteen, my childhood fantasies of sweethearts blossomed into rampant, romantic (still innocent) attachments. Among them were perky Dot Reed (sweet and pretty) and winsome Betty Jean Cooksey (liked to cuddle). Sparkly Kitty McCaa (my first "fiancée") wore my ring for nearly a month. Mary Jane Eatman (you had to have a pack of Kools in your pocket) was exotic, and dates with gorgeous "Hungry" Ellen Robinson (always involved a food stop at the local drive-in). I loved them all!

Boys my age often made sure they knew when girls went to the picture show on Saturday so they could manage to sit with the girl they liked. We'd pair up and hold hands while watching the movie. Bolder guys put their arm on the back of the seat next to the girl they liked and, as soon as they dared, moved their arm down around her shoulder. If she didn't pull away, they'd go a little further.

Then there was Faith Garner. Faith and I had a relationship that was unusual between teenage boys and girls in those days: a friendship. Faith was a very pretty girl with red hair and sparkling eyes, and she was very intelligent. She had a great sense of humor and a redhead's high energy. We compared notes on each other's "affairs of the heart" and shared our hopes and dreams for the future. Why wasn't I in love with Faith? I don't know. We were very close, but the chemistry for romance just wasn't there. I guess you would say Faith and I were pals. Her answer to questions about our relationship was a grin and a sly wink.

One summer evening, after a movie—a sophisticated comedy at the Saenger—Faith and I wanted to prolong the mood, so we walked into the Forrest Hotel next door. Nine stories high, the Forrest was the only sophisticated thing in our three-story town. As we strolled casually through the lobby, I had a wild idea.

"Let's take the elevator up to the top floor," I suggested. "You want to?"

"Yeah," Faith answered, her eyes twinkling, and when no one was looking, we slipped into the elevator.

Feeling very adult, I pushed the top button, and the door closed. We watched the numbers 1 to 9 light up one by one, and when the door opened, I was relieved to see no one was there. We walked down the hall, and enjoying the lush feel of the carpeting under our feet, we read the room numbers on each door. At the end of the hall, there was a door with an EXIT sign over it. I opened it, and we looked out. It was the fire escape. With a conspiring look between us, we stepped outside. It never occurred to me that the emergency door could have locked behind us. I guess I was too excited by our little adventure to think about it.

The glittering stars in the night sky seemed to be a reflection of all the lights of the town and the houses in the neighborhoods beyond. It wasn't New York, but it was beautiful. We sat for the longest time and talked about what might happen in our lives. Faith hoped to be a writer, and I, from an early age, had planned to be a painter.

"You'll live in New York and have a fabulous studio in Greenwich Village," Faith said. "I've read that's where all the serious painters live."

Neither one of us had ever heard the proper way to pronounce the name of that mecca of artists, writers, and all sorts of avant-garde individualists.

"You'll become famous and live there too," I said. "I can illustrate all your stories when you get published in important magazines like *Colliers* and The *Saturday Evening Post*, even *Cosmopolitan*."

"Maybe I will," Faith said. "I sure hope so."

As we sat holding hands, looking at the stars, we were very serious about all of this, and we believed it was possible. It was a warm balmy night, but after a while, the iron slats of the fire escape started to chill our behinds. Thankfully, the door wasn't locked, so we were able to get back in and take the elevator to the ground floor—and to the reality of life in our small town.

"Will you design a dress for me?" Faith asked me one afternoon as we were walking home from school.

Surprised, I stopped and looked at her. "Design a dress for you?" I asked.

"Yeah," she said. "I know what I want it to look like. You're an artist. You can draw anything! If you can draw it, Mama can make it."

"But I don't know about patterns. You're crazy."

"Mama doesn't need a pattern. She makes a lot of my clothes. She can do it. So will you just draw the dress for me?"

"Okay . . . Yeah, I guess so," I said.

"I'd like it to be made out of sheer cotton in a soft green color, with a full skirt, puffed sleeves, and a tight midriff. That's where Mama can embroider 'Suivez-moi.'"

"Embroider what?" I asked.

"Suivez-moi," she said. "That means 'Follow me' in French. I got the idea in my French class."

"Suivez-moi. Follow me. Does that mean when you wear that dress, you want to be followed?"

"No, silly! It's just a fun thing. So, will you design the dress?" Her eyes were pleading.

"Oh . . . kaaay," I said, wishing I had taken French instead of Latin.

And that was the first dress I designed. Others followed. Half the girls in my junior class that year wanted me to design a dress for them. They didn't ask for a French phrase on it. (None of them wanted to be a copycat.) For a short time, I even considered the field of clothing design for a career. I made dozens of sketches of beautiful girls in glamorous gowns, probably inspired by those worn by movie stars in those sophisticated films. However, being a serious painter remained as my first choice.

This was Faith's 'Suivez Moi' dress along with
many more of my fashion designs.

Faith had a rampant imagination. We lived only a mile or so apart, but she would actually write letters to me, fantasizing about our two careers, our friends, and the social life in New York.

"Dear Howard," a letter from Faith would read, "Now that you're settled in your new apartment in Manhattan, I adore the name, Studio Noir. Sounds so decadent—it must be great for all your parties. Your roughs for my latest story, 'Tell Me the Way to Swendon,' are perfect. Loved them, but could you make Diedre just a little sexier when she's standing in the doorway waiting for Paul? You know, maybe with her robe slipping off her shoulder?"

I would answer her with my own fantasy letter. "Dear Faith, Hordes of celebrities attended the opening of my new exhibition. Orson and Nadine were there, Vivien and Larry, Noel, and tons of others. The reviews were brilliant! So sorry you and Bill couldn't make it."

Faith and I were just two high school kids with dreams of bright futures. After our graduation, she wrote in my yearbook next to her photo, "LOVE, Faith." Next to her name, she drew a winking eye with long lashes.

We went away to different colleges, and after Faith got her degree, she married her high school beau, Bill Woodruff. During the years I was away in the war, Faith wrote to me, not fantasies but real letters of encouragement, with real news about her life in our hometown.

After the war was over, I was actually living in New York, sharing a basement apartment (ironically in Greenwich Village). I continued to exchange letters with Faith about her marriage and children and about my work and occasional romances. Now and then, I would receive one of those delightful fantasy letters. It's a shame Faith couldn't follow her dream to become a writer. She would have been a brilliant one.

On my trips down South to see Aunt Amber and my brother, Bishop, I would always see Faith and her family, but as time passed and we grew older, we lost touch. Eventually, my dear old pal and I had a bittersweet reunion in a hometown restaurant at a lunch with a few old friends. Faith was there when my wife and I arrived. It was great to see her again, but unfortunately—and sadly—she could not see me. Faith was totally blind. However, her loss of sight had not dimmed her brilliance. She was, as she had always been, bright and witty, cheerful and funny, and in high spirits as we relived old times.

After lunch, when she heard me ask for the check, Faith said, "Well, if I had known you were paying, I would have ordered champagne!" I could have sworn I saw her wink.

Only one year older than me, Faith is still more than qualified to be in this memoir. My love for Faith is deep in my heart, where she will be forever young.

Faith Garner.

CHAPTER 22

HAPPY DAYS

Hattiesburg, 1939–1940

IN MY JUNIOR year of high school, my favorite teacher was Miss Ola Crossley, who taught eleventh grade English. Like almost all teachers those days in the South, she was unmarried, and of course, she was old. When you are sixteen, going on seventeen, anyone over thirty is old. But Miss Crossley was young in spirit. She was a slight birdlike lady and given to giggling easily. She made English literature fun, and all the kids liked her. I was especially pleased she directed the junior plays.

During summer vacation every year, Miss Crossley went to New York and saw Broadway shows. While there, she would stop by Samuel French Inc. and shop for plays for the high school drama department. I was always happy to see her when she returned and told the class about her visit to the big city. Miss Crossley was the only person I'd ever known close to the exciting world of the theater and art.

When Miss Crossley announced that the next stage production would be musical–the Gilbert and Sullivan operetta *HMS Pinafore*–I asked her if I could audition to be in the show.

"Of course, you can, Howard. Which role would you like to read for?" she asked me.

"I'd like to play an important part," I said.

Miss Crossley gave me a playbook and told me to read a passage where the leading man, Ralph Rackstraw, meets the leading lady.

"You can just speak the words to his love song until we have the singing audition," she said.

I read the young sailor's lines as clearly and loudly as I could. When I finished, I probably looked at Miss Crossley with hope in my eyes.

"Howard dear," she said in her sweet, musical voice, "I am so sorry to have to say you are not going play the romantic lead, Ralph Rackstraw, nor Sir Joseph Porter, the comic lead, either. But I would love you to be a sailor in the chorus."

"In the chorus?" I was disappointed. "But, Miss Crossley . . ."

"Don't fret," she said. "I have a part for you, mid-shipmate."

It was not a speaking part, but when the show went on, I happily sang my heart out along with the rest of the chorus.

For Miss Crossley's next production the following spring, I fared a little better. Although I had only just turned seventeen, Miss Crossley cast me as the old German pet shop owner in *Early to Bed*. It was a character part, a good one, and I wore a beard and age makeup. I had to use a German accent. I was still a kid in the eleventh grade at the time, but now the thought of what I looked and sounded like makes me shudder. However, being onstage in high school fed my desire to be in show business, and having an understanding teacher like Miss Crossley, who understood that desire, was my first step on the road to the life I wanted.

During the three years I was away from home in World War II, Miss Crossley wrote affectionate letters to me, sweet, newsy letters about school and the hometown. She always said she missed me and signed her letters "With love, Ola Crossley."

After the war, when I was living in New York, I got another letter from Miss Ola, as I now called her. "Howard dear," she wrote in June, "I will be visiting a friend in Long Island. I would love to see you. Call me." She gave me her friend's phone number, and to my good fortune, she was able to invite me for a long weekend. What a delight it was to see her again and, for the first time, on an adult basis! Her charm, wit, and love of life were all still bubbling. As we drank cocktails and socialized with her friends, Miss Ola casually lit a cigarette and smoked it with elegance.

"Miss Ola!" I said, my eyes opening widely, "*You're smoking?*"

"I always have, my darling," she said and giggled like a schoolgirl. "But of course, nobody in school ever knew!"

I loved Miss Ola.

CHAPTER 23

A HANDFUL OF STARS

Hattiesburg, 1941

NOW TO GET back to 1941 and those happy days in high school. "When you are a famous artist in New York, don't forget NTG." A beautiful girl named Bettie Cile Freeman wrote that next to her photo in my high school senior book. NTG stood for "Number Ten Green," the tenth hole on the golf course at the local golf course, and Bettie Cile was my first real sweetheart.

I recall the story
That night of love and glory
A night that left my heart romantic scars
We stood so near to heaven
That I reached clear to heaven
And gathered you a handful of stars

In the era of the big bands and pop music, we danced to that song. Ray Eberle sang it with Glenn Miller's orchestra. Whether it was a recording or on radio, a dance in the high school gym or in the back seat of a car, it was one of our favorite tunes for us to hold each other close, our cheeks stuck together with sweat, and to dream of love. I was a tall skinny sixteen-year-old with my share of pimples. I was hopelessly romantic, and like many other sixteen-year-olds, I had my fair number of those innocent and short-lived "love affairs." Then I met Bettie Cile Freeman.

Bettie Cile moved to Hattiesburg when I was in the eleventh grade. She was the new girl in town. She was very pretty. She had a heart-shaped face and a warm smile that turned easily into bubbling laughter. But often her eyes could be serious. I was smitten with Bettie Cile Freeman right away.

How do these things start? You meet maybe in class or in study hall or maybe just hanging around outside in front of the school after lunch. Teenage kids often got together at the movies on Saturdays, with the boy's arm draped over his girl's shoulders. One way or another, Bettie Cile and I got together.

Sweet remembered hours
When love began to flower
With moonlight through the trees like silver bars
And as the moon grew older
I looked across your shoulder
And gathered you a handful of stars

In Mississippi, driver's licenses were available to sixteen-year-olds, and one of my best friends, C. R. Domergue, was fortunate enough to have permissive parents who let him use the family car. Saturday nights would find us, Ceedy (CR Junior) in the driver's seat with his girlfriend, Wesa, and Snake (Albert Sladen) in the roomy back seat with his date and me, HB (the closest I ever got to a real nickname), and my date. Sometimes another of my best friends, Greasy (Sikes), and his date would share the back seat of the Packard instead of which one of us was "dateless" that evening. The four of us guys were as close as "The Four Musketeers."

Donna Kirkland Woods
2002

Beverly Drive-IN Theatre
Hattiesburg, MS
by
Donna Kirkland Woods

Usually, our date evenings started in the parking lot at the Beverly or the Whistlin' Pig drive-in, listening to big band music on the car radio and downing Cokes served on trays clamped to the car doors by the friendly "curb hops." Other teenage guys lucky enough to have the family car would also be there in the parking lot with their dates, and couples would stroll about from car to car, often smoking forbidden cigarettes, gabbing, and checking out who was with who. Then we would gather at some popular girl's house, like Peggy Turner's, dancing to records or at Mary Gene Hoffman's to sit on the front porch and nurse soft drinks provided by Mary Gene's parents. It was all fairly innocent, and lots of fun.

> *Sweet remembered hours*
> *When love began to flower*
> *With moonlight through the trees like silver bars*
> *And as the moon grew older*
> *I reached across your shoulder*
> *And gathered you a handful of stars*

Sometimes we went out to the Morrisons', whose home was on a lake surrounded by woods near the edge of town. I remember standing on the shore of the lake, and as we looked at the full moon's reflection in the dark water, we saw a small snake, a water moccasin, swimming near us. Moccasins can't bite if they are in the water, but when it wriggled closer to the bank near our feet, we quickly turned and walked back to the house. The sound of Sinatra's voice drifted out to us, and two teenage couples were cuddling on the chintz-covered wicker sofas on the veranda.

Mike's parents always welcomed young people and rolled up the living room rug for their dancing. Records of Harry James, Woody Herman, the Ink Spots, and Glenn Miller were stacked on the table near the record player, and young couples danced across the hardwood floor.

I placed my fingertips upon your lips
And stars fell in your eyes
Moonglow made a halo of your hair
Suddenly, you looked at me, and dreams began to rise
Oh, what things unspoken
Trembled in the air

There were other magical evenings, but the favorite spot for teenagers that summer was the country club near the edge of town, where we parked near the golf course after the club had closed. Listening to our favorite music on the car radios there in the dark, we held each other tight, kissing feverishly, and went as far as we dared. Some couples were rumored to be going "all the way" but only those who had been going steady for a long time and planned to get married.

Naturally, after all that smooching, our body heat rose and reached the boiling point. Then we would leave the cars, and our passions would be dampened by a hand-in-hand stroll on the dew-covered grass. We would chase fireflies, millions of them, rising and falling in the darkness, twinkling and glowing and rising up into the trees, competing with trillions of stars overhead.

Some nights, a full moon would light up the rolling hills, turning the golf course into a fairyland. After cooling off, we would walk dreamily back to the car for more frustrating hugging and kissing.

Our hearts were madly beating
And then our lips were meeting
And Venus seemed to melt right into Mars
Then while we stood caressing
Blue heaven sent a blessing
A shower of a handful of stars

On our radios, Frank Sinatra sang love songs like that until midnight, the witching hour when our dates had to be home. In the twelfth grade, I thought Bettie Cile and I were seriously in love. Well, we were—as much as possible. Who knew that graduating from high school meant a life change?

Young Betty Cile.

CHAPTER 24

SUMMER SOLSTICE

Hattiesburg, 1941

IN THE MONTH of June, my pals and I continued dating our girlfriends and searching for summer jobs. I landed one at thirteen years old, sweeping up and doing errands for the Roberts Brothers' Dental "Laboratory." It was a one-room business right next door to Uncle Collin's office. Doc Roberts and his brother, Bliss, created dental plates but spent most spare moments gazing at women's thighs in passing cars below their second-story windows. When Doc told me to "have a look," I was surprised at how many women drove with their skirts pulled up so high.

My next job was a step-up as assistant window decorator at Fine Brothers, Madison, just down Main Street from the Robert Brothers' Dental Laboratory. Fine Brothers, Madison was not actually a department store. The merchandise was primarily men's, women's, and children's clothing plus shoes and accessories. The owner, Mr. Nathan Fine, was a small elegantly dressed old man with the most meticulously complete comb-over I have ever seen. Every hair was plastered to his bald head so tightly, not one would be disturbed in a high wind. But he was a kind man, a respected member of the small Jewish community in Hattiesburg. I don't remember if there was a Mrs. Fine, but Mr. Fine's only son, Milton, was the affable, easygoing manager of the store.

My job in the "advertising" department was assistant to the advertising director, a friendly young man named Allen March. Each week, we stripped the two large show windows at the front of the store and installed new merchandise. I should call it "overly installed" because Mr. Fine's policy was to fill the windows with as much merchandise as possible, which I didn't agree with. Also, I didn't like him insisting we put price tags on each and every item in the windows.

In addition, we set up counter displays, and with assistance from salesladies, we dressed the mannequins standing about the store. Allen also put together ads for the *Hattiesburg American*, the local newspaper. The ads were as jumbled as the shop windows.

One morning I climbed a ladder to a storage balcony above the office I shared with Allen. There, in the semidarkness, I discovered dozens of unclothed mannequins. At seventeen and being surrounded by what appeared to be a score of naked women and men, if not in shock, I found I was delighted as my excitement rose just being among them. For a few moments, I hugged these beautiful people and kissed them on their painted lips. Suddenly then, feeling ridiculous, I turned away and climbed back down the ladder to resume my work assignments.

I think my experience with the mannequins in the dark up in the storage area may have given birth to a bold move. I wanted to propose an idea to Mr. Fine using mannequins, but I was afraid I'd be turned down. Because his son, Milton, was a young man, I chose to approach him instead.

"Milton, I need your help," I said to him. "I'm too scared to speak to your father about this."

Milton was puzzled. "What do you need?" was all he asked.

"I have a good idea for the display windows," I told him. "I know Mr. Fine might think I'm crazy and say no, but I think it will attract customers."

"I'll speak to him, but I think you should tell him yourself," Milton said. "I know he likes you."

After Milton talked to his father, the old man called me into his office.

"What is this I hear about you wanting to change our window display policy?" Mr. Fine asked, looking over his reading glasses.

"No, sir, I, uh . . . don't want to change your policy. I just want to design something different for the windows, something different from anything Hattiesburg has ever seen before."

Mr. Fine looked into my eyes, waiting for me to go on.

"Mr. Fine, I want to design elegant fashion windows," I said, looking straight back into his eyes. "Windows you would see on Fifth Avenue in New

York, and put them in Fine Brothers, Madison's for a week. That's what I want, Mr. Fine. Uh, that's all, sir."

The old man continued looking at me without speaking.

"I've seen some pictures in your trade magazines, and I think you will really like what I have in mind, sir."

He looked at me for a long minute. "All right, my boy," he said with a small smile. "But for only one week."

I explained my idea to Allen Crane, the head advertising director, and he approved. We cleared a work area in the hall outside our office and cut out New York City skylines from wallboard, each ten feet long. Painted black with small windows, they looked like the poster board silhouettes I had made for the book-reading club at the library. Next, we created terrace walls and painted them like brick parapets. We totally emptied all the merchandise out of Fine's shop windows and installed our set pieces.

Curious customers stopped to watch what we were doing. With help from the newly excited salesladies, I selected the evening gowns. While curious passersby gawked, I put the dresses on female mannequins in the windows, and Allen dressed male mannequins in tuxedos. We set up garden tables and chairs with cocktail and champagne glasses and added some big potted plants. Allen satisfied his theatrical ambitions, adding dramatic effects with special spotlights. It took a full day to complete my idea of a sophisticated party on a Manhattan penthouse terrace.

After the *Hattiesburg American*, the town's local newspaper, gave Fine's a write-up, many citizens stopped to take look at the windows, and Mr. Fine decided to let my work stay in another week. Maybe there had been an increase in business–I never knew. At the time, it meant something to me that people, especially my girlfriend, admired what I could do.

Bettie Cile and I kept on dating until that fall when we both went away to college, she to her second year at Mississippi State College for Women and I to Auburn University in Alabama. I never knew how my family could afford the tuition, but they did, and I was grateful. In retrospect, I would like to think perhaps I had turned over most of my salary from Fine Brothers to Aunt Amber to put away for college. I suppose Uncle Collin contributed a large part of the overall costs, but honestly, I don't remember. I do remember I wanted to "get away" from home and be, at least for a while, independent.

Auburn was only a few hours away, but it gave me a feeling of being on my own for the first time in my life. I majored in Art, but of course, that meant just a class or two in art and all the other required courses in the first year of college. I plunged into college life, met new friends, joined a fraternity, went to Saturday night dances, and learned how to drink–sometimes a bit too much.

I lived in a rented room within walking distance of school and stopped every morning for my favorite breakfast: toasted pound cake with a big glass of milk. My evening meal was at Mrs. Wagner's, my landlady's boarding house, where I became friends with her son, a student close to my age, named Lamar. Lamar loved jazz and dressed in the "zoot suit" style–long draped jackets with wider shoulders and pegged pants, which I had seen only in a movie or two. I was so impressed, I borrowed one of his sports jackets and a pair of his baggy pants to try to look like a "cool cat" for a trip home to visit my family. I hoped to impress my Hattiesburg friends. In retrospect, I believe I looked ridiculous.

Auburn was full of cute girls, and I dated several of them. The top of my list was Shannon Hayle, a luscious blonde from a town in Alabama. Shannon's home was far enough away from school for her to live in a dorm. Male students were not allowed in the girls' dorms, and I was still too inexperienced to try to slip into her room at night. Anyway, I really missed Bettie Cile, but what really turned me on was Shannon when she appeared one morning totally transformed. No longer a honey blonde, she was a stunning brunette (always my first choice in women). Her creamy complexion was enhanced by her new black hair. I was enchanted all over again.

CHAPTER 25

GOODBYE, BETTIE CILE

Mississippi, 1942–1943

BY 1943, WORLD War II was raging in Europe. I had heard news reports on the radio but only occasionally followed the details in the *Hattiesburg American*, our local newspaper. Fortunately, to teenagers like me, the horrors of war were still far away, and I had only vague thoughts about service in the military. However, at eighteen years of age, I was eligible for the draft, and for temporary deferment, I was obliged to join Auburn's ROTC, which was connected to the U.S. Field Artillery. That meant I'd automatically be inducted into the Army (Field Artillery) at the end of my first year of college. I had always fancied myself as a fun-loving sailor in white uniform, but that put an end to my plan to join the Navy when the time came.

In the year I was away at college and the two and a half years of military service, Bettie Cile fell in love with another young man, became engaged, and got married. With her husband, Dave Waite, she started a family and a career in radio talk shows on Hattiesburg's WDAM. My sweetly innocent high school romance with Bettie Cile was just that, and it was long over.

After I came home from the war, I left Mississippi and did what I had always dreamed of. I did make it to New York and pursued a career in the world of entertainment. I didn't become the famous artist Bettie Cile had written about in my high school yearbook, but I did get to be a professional set designer in New York in theater, television, and movies. And as she requested, I never forgot NTG.

Forty years later, after dealing with the highs and the lows of adulthood–career, marriage, divorce, bachelorhood, marriage with children, etc.–Bettie Cile and I were in touch again, mainly through Christmas cards and occasional visits to my hometown. Bettie Cile had participated in many creative and philanthropic activities, enough to fill volumes. Not long ago, I had mentioned to her I was writing a memoir. When I told her she wouldn't be in my book because it was primarily about my love for older women, she laughed.

"Why not?" she asked. "Have you forgotten? I'm a year older than you. Don't I qualify?"

"Okay." I said, "You're in!" delighted that she wanted to be in my memoir.

As a callow young man, I loved Bettie Cile in our school days, and now, at my advanced age, I realize the love I felt decades ago for her remains with me as a tender and enduring friendship.

Visiting with Betty Cile years later.

CHAPTER 26

YOU'RE IN THE ARMY NOW!

Fort Bragg, Florida, 1943–1944

I WAS INDUCTED into active service in the U.S. Army at Camp Shelby, the camp close to Hattiesburg, where my father, Clarence Barker, had been stationed in World War I.

"Welcome to Camp Shelby!" The army sergeant's shout woke me up. "Up 'n' at 'em, Sunshine!" he shouted again, this time at me, as he kicked the leg of my army cot. "You and the rest of you raw recruits line up for short arm inspection before you put on your uniform!" As soon as we were up and standing at the foot of our cots, he shouted once more, "ATTENTION!"

An army medical officer entered. The sergeant saluted and stood next to him.

"Drop your shorts!" the sergeant commanded.

"Okay, men, skin 'em back and milk 'em down!" shouted the med's assistant.

That's when I realized the inspection had nothing to do with our arms, short or long. One by one, we complied as the medical officer closely examined our exposed private parts and made quick notes on his clipboard. After he'd finished checking the two rows of young men, he spoke to the sergeant.

"NDD," he mumbled. When he saw our puzzled faces, he turned to us and explained his abbreviation. "No dripping dicks." He said with a smile. "There's no evidence of VD in any of you GIs," and left.

"At ease," the sergeant ordered. "Okay, privates, into your uniforms on the double! Chow in the mess hall in fifteen, followed by indoctrination!"

The first lesson I learned in the army? Obey orders and never ask questions. The second lesson: Army life is harder than civilian life. That first week was a confusing whirl of morning calisthenics, forced marches, rifle practice, and lectures.

There was one pleasant exception. On Saturday, forty-one other young GIs and I were taken in army trucks from Camp Shelby into Hattiesburg to attend a dance at the local USO. No longer a civilian, I jitterbugged with girls I did not know and learned how different it felt to be a private in the army instead of a civilian. I was surprised to find I had a good time.

My company was soon shipped by train to Fort Bragg in North Carolina for basic training in the Field Artillery. The day after we had unpacked our gear, we were loaded into trucks and ended up out in the piney woods on our first bivouac. We arrived in a furious thunderstorm, typical during summer months in most states south of the Mason–Dixon Line. Blinding sheets of rain were coming straight down from the sky. As Southerners would say, it was "raining cats and dogs." My brother Bishop, who sometimes liked to use Southern redneck expressions would have added, "It sounded like a cow pissing on a flat rock." Jagged bolts of lightning were snaking down from the scudding clouds. They looked as if they were coming closer. I was standing on top of a hill getting soaked. Thirty yards down the hill from me, a dozen soldiers, men from my company, were taking shelter under some trees. They were New Yorkers from the Bronx and Brooklyn and weren't aware of the danger of being near a tall tree in a thunderstorm. I probably looked like a complete fool to them as I stood out in the open, wet and exposed to bolts of lightning.

"Get away from those trees!" I yelled.

They could not hear me, so I jogged down to explain.

All of us were standing in rainwater almost ankle-deep. I remember a blinding white light, a deafening crack and a paralyzing shock—all in the same instant. Then nothing but blackness. *How strange . . . I can't see . . . I can't hear . . . I can't move . . . What is this? I have no feeling anywhere in my body . . . blackness . . . nothingness.* But my brain was working. Thoughts were racing through it so fast, I could hardly keep up with them. *Unconscious out here in the North Carolina woods . . . I must be dead . . . I'm not even in the war yet!*

Suddenly, I realized my eyes were open, but I could not move. I could see, but everything was blurry. I looked around. None of the other soldiers were moving either. *Dead too . . . All of us . . .* I tried to stand up. My legs wouldn't work. *Of course, they won't, you idiot. When you're dead, you can't move. And I'm dead . . .* I closed my eyes and lay there. I don't know for how long.

The first sound I heard was high-pitched sirens in the distance, screaming louder and louder as they came closer. I opened my eyes again, and near me, a man was twitching all over, and then another man started moving his legs as if he was running in slow motion. I struggled and managed to sit up.

Again, I tried to stand. No luck. I fell to my knees.

A large army van arrived on the scene, and the siren stopped. Two medics leaped out, took our pulses and carefully lifted us into sitting positions. I tried to stand up again but fell again. The medics loosened our field uniforms and examined our bodies. I could see several men had burns on their skin. The burn marks were shaped like jagged lightning bolts. A few of us were conscious now, others were not. Within minutes, the medics had lifted all of us up and moved us into the van.

In the field hospital, we were examined by army doctors and put to bed in a group ward. We were given liquids and more tests. We were told the lightning-shaped burn marks were thought to be caused by metal objects, such as knives or tools, in the clothes we were wearing. That was all we were told. Two days later, we were discharged and sent back to our units. We later learned some of the men were okay, but later, we heard that a few never regained consciousness.

***

Artillery Basic Training continued. The daily calisthenics, weapons training, forced marches in formation and KP (kitchen police duty, meaning mostly peeling potatoes and washing pots and pans) were made bearable by weekend passes to Fayetteville and USO dances. North Carolina girls were gorgeous.

Then came the high point of my military life so far: I saw my first live movie star!

With World War II raging in Europe, many show-business celebrities toured military bases in the United States and abroad to entertain the troops. From an early age, I loved going to the movies, and I had my share of crushes on the beautiful people starring in them. I had seen Betty Hutton in her first movie, *The Fleet's In*, and I was mad about her. Now Miss Hutton had arrived in Fort Bragg to do her show in the service club, and I was in the front row. Backed by a really hot, swinging band, the blonde bombshell was right there, live onstage, singing and dancing her way into my heart. She turned songs like "Can't Stop Talkin' About Him," "Murder, She Says," and "I'm Just a Square in the Social Circle" into a breathless, tongue-twisting tour de force. It was a great performance. The GIs loved her. So did I.

The tempestuous comedienne was quite young, only a couple of years older than me, but I was too shy to ask for her autograph after the show. Instead, I made a series of sketches of her performing and sent them to her at Paramount Film Studios, where she made her movies. Would you believe it? I got an eight-by-ten-inch photo in the mail, signed by Betty Hutton! My barracks buddies were impressed. I was incredulous. Talk about a crush. I was in love again. (Well, for a little while, I thought I was.)

***

Fort Bragg was probably like other wartime army posts across the United States: barracks, barracks, and barracks, GIs fall in, GIs fall out, roll call, calisthenics, marches, marches, marches, M1 rifle nomenclature, M1 rifle practice, and field maneuvers. In civilian life, whoever had any experience with field radio operation? But now I was learning the Morse Code: dit-da, da-dit, da-da-dit, dit-dit-da, etc. I wasn't particularly good at it, but I was classified as Field radio Operator, Forward Observer. I never knew what that meant.

I found out soon enough. Aunt Amber had written me that Bishop was home on leave and wanted to hear from me. I was surprised. My brother and I had not kept in close touch since he had volunteered for the Air Corps a few years before. I telephoned him immediately. When I proudly mentioned my classification–Field Radio Operator, Forward Observer–Bishop became silent for a moment. Then he shouted over the phone.

"Howard! You've got to get the hell out of there! You've got to ask for a transfer."

"Why?" I asked, puzzled by his reaction.

"In wartime," he answered, "a radio operator, forward observer, has a life expectancy of exactly eighteen minutes." He then told me to immediately apply for transfer to the Army Air Corps cadet training division. "There's a shortage of airplane pilots now, and they have to accept you. If you make it through training, you'll end up as a pilot and an officer. That's a helluva better life than being a private in the artillery. And besides," he said with a little laugh, "I'll have to salute you. You'll be a lieutenant, and I'm only a sergeant."

I was trying to take it all in and didn't know what to say.

"Pilot training is about eighteen months," he went on, "and chances are the war may not last long enough for you to be up for combat duty. Do it now! And let me hear from you."

I applied, and he was right. I was accepted, but neither of us anticipated what had happened to me in the Air Corps.

This is me as a new army recruit.

My brother, Bishop (maybe in his twenties?).

CHAPTER 27

INTO THE AIR, ARMY AIR CORPS . . .

Miami Beach, 1943

"**I**NTO THE AIR, let's go, men . . ." With these words sung loudly and lustily, I immediately felt on my first day as an Air Corps cadet that it was one of my happier days spent in all three branches of the army. Miami Beach was an amazing contrast to Fort Bragg. Marching in formation under palm trees to the parade field for early morning calisthenics was a joy, and I counted my lucky stars and silently thanked Bishop for rescuing me from the Field Artillery.

Cadets' barracks were actually groups of small rental apartments that were refurnished with army cots and metal lockers. Showers and toilets in each were barely adequate for the number men who used them. Basic Training in the Air Corps was pretty much the same as it was in the Field Artillery: listen, do what you're told, and don't ever disagree with a sergeant. The food was a bit better, but it was march, march, march in formation–wherever you went.

Anyway, the sound of the palm trees swaying around the hotels at night made up for a lot. It put me to sleep, and I actually learned the easy way to climb up the palm trees to reach the ripened coconuts from another cadet, locally born, who was one of my roommates. He also showed me the way to sneak from our morning march to the outdoor classes and spend half the day on the sunny beach.

Climbing a palm tree in Miami.

One evening we checked out a downtown club that featured a stripper, my first time seeing adult live entertainment. The gorgeous young brunette's movements and the accompanying pounding of the bass drum were thoroughly exciting to me–something of an innocent.

Miami Beach's charms all changed to quieter small-town ways when we finished basic training and were sent to the University of Florida in Gainesville, near the southern border of Georgia, for nine months of crammed college courses. Basically, all army protocol seemed to be missing, except we still had to wear uniforms. We behaved much the same as I had in my one year at Alabama Polytech in Auburn except for the drinking. It was against rules on campus.

Bill Ferguson and I became instant friends after we had met one morning at sick call. ("When I saw you, I knew you weren't sick either," he had said with a knowing grin.) We met girls at dances in town, and both he and I "settled down" with two of them. Bill had told me he was married, but that didn't keep him from sleeping with his local girlfriend. My girlfriend reminded me of the Dragon Lady in the old comic strip *Terry and the Pirates*. We were good together, doing the Lindy Hop, but that was as far as it got with her.

My brother Bishop was stationed at an Air Corps base in South Mississippi and surprised me by flying in one weekend to visit me. Not only was Bishop responsible for my being in his branch of the military, but he was interested in his "little" brother's life. Finally, we had something in common. We double-dated with a couple of girls I knew while he was there, and a good time was had by all.

Cadets received ten hours of actual flight training, learning to pilot small Piper Cubs with very patient instructors. They had to be. I don't believe any of us had ever been inside a Piper Cub before. In my logbook, my instructor's report read something like this: "Good student, tries hard, eager and enthusiastic but erratic."

At the end of nine months, I was still in the Air Corps and was shipped to a cadet classification center near San Antonio, Texas. There, I found myself sitting on a cot in a barracks full of other cadets, all of us sweating and waiting to be told what to do. Other than the flying field, it was like other military posts: headquarters buildings, equipment and utility buildings, barracks buildings, and thousands of men. After ubiquitous indoctrination and physical examinations, classification tests were given. I was classified as a Pilot-Navigator and not a Pilot. Even though I had learned to take off, soar, stall, bank, level, and land in a single-engine Piper Cub in Florida, my flight officer's evaluation in my logbook did say I was erratic. I was happy I had not "washed out," but my new classification was a confusing disappointment.

Bishop and I when he visited me in the army.

My brother, Bishop, in his uniform.

CHAPTER 28

SAN ANTONIO BLUES

Texas, 1944

"**P**ARDON ME, SIR. May I cut in?" I asked as I tapped the shoulder of a young lieutenant dancing with an incredibly beautiful girl in the middle of the dance floor.

They paused and looked at me. He didn't answer. The beautiful girl did.

"No, but thank you," she said pleasantly.

The girl looked straight at me with her beautiful dark eyes. In that one brief moment, I could see her face like a close-up in a movie. Her eyes were as dark as a night sky and just as unfathomable. I backed away. Where I come from, cutting in on the dance floor is an old Southern tradition. It's permitted without rancor, showing no disrespect. I figured that old tradition didn't exist in San Antonio—at least not at the Air Corps Cadet Center service club. They danced on, and I slunk away to the dry bar.

I watched them as they moved smoothly across the dance floor. He was holding her close the way we used to do at our high school proms. They were both laughing at the same time, a perfect couple. He was dark and handsome, and her long black hair fell around her shoulders as they swayed in time with the music. Her white silk blouse and tight-fitting black skirt didn't hide her beautiful body. I couldn't take my eyes off her. When the music ended, they hugged. There were other cadets dancing, but I paid little attention to them. I was thinking about myself. *What am I doing here?*

Now sitting alone with my watery Coke after being snubbed a beautiful girl, my ego took a nosedive. I stood and went back to watch the dancers. Then I saw her walking toward me–alone.

"Hello," she said and smiled. "My name is Andrea."

"My name is Howard," I said.

"Hello, Howard." She smiled again and held out her arms. "Would you like to dance now?"

Dancing with Andrea was like a stroll in a rose garden. We circled the floor, moving effortlessly as one, until I finally found my voice.

"I didn't mean to be rude, trying to cut in," I said. "Were you dancing with your boyfriend?"

"No, he's my cousin."

"The Lieutenant you were dancing with is your cousin?"

"Yes. He just got his wings. He's about to ship out, so I came from town to say goodbye."

Inside, I heaved a sigh of relief. "Andrea," I said, looking into her eyes, "I want another dance."

As I held her close, we moved together, and it was like we had always known each other–as if we had always been partners. No one cut in, and we danced all the rest of the afternoon. Of course, we talked, but I don't remember a lot of what we said. I do remember that Andrea told me her last name was Majalca, that she was born in Mexico and moved with her parents to San Antonio to go to school.

When the last dance ended and the orchestra stopped playing, we were still holding each other. Then following the other couples, we left the dance floor and walked out into the glare of the Texas sunshine. A bus was waiting outside the gates to take all the girls back to San Antonio. Andrea's cousin, the lieutenant, joined us as we walked. He hugged her and told her he'd write. Then he said goodbye. We shook hands, and he walked away, leaving us alone together. All around us, couples were hugging and kissing. Some were crying.

"I want to see you again," I said to Andrea.

"I can come again next Saturday," she said.

"Will you?" I said. "Please? Please come."

"I will. I promise. I'll be on the bus."

I hugged her. I hugged her hard. Then I kissed her. She kissed me back. We held each other until the bus driver honked his horn.

"All aboard" he yelled. "Come on, ladies. Kiss the boys goodbye."

A few days later, the reveille bugle call blasted over the loudspeakers, waking us up to an announcement.

"ATTENTION! ATTENTION, ALL CADET SQUADRONS! ATTENTION, ALL CADET SQUADRONS! ALL NONCOMMISSIONED OFFICERS WILL TAKE ROLL CALL DIRECTLY AFTER THE MORNING MEAL AND MARCH THEIR SQUADRONS TO THE PARADE FIELD WITHOUT DELAY! THAT'S TO THE PARADE FIELD WITHOUT DELAY!"

When that message came over the loudspeakers, speculation spread like a forest fire out of control in the mess hall, wild guesses were spit out between every bite we took. Apprehension flowed from table to table, and like every other cadet, I wondered what could be so important to interrupt the routine of the compulsory classes we were to attend each day. Soon enough, we found out.

Precisely at eight o'clock, the parade field was filled with young men standing at attention. Again, a voice over the loudspeaker system broke the silence.

"THIS IS YOUR PRESIDENT, FRANKLIN DELANO ROOSEVELT SPEAKING . . ." The voice, clear and strong, blasted from the loudspeakers positioned at intervals from one end of the field to the other, continued. "AS OF TODAY, ALL UNITED STATES AIR CORPS CADETS WHO HAVE NOT BEGUN PRE-FLIGHT TRAINING WILL NO LONGER BE MEMBERS OF THE AIR CORPS. AT THE CONVENIENCE OF THE GOVERNMENT, YOU WILL BE TRANSFERRED TO THE GROUND FORCES FOR THE REMAINDER OF THE CURRENT MILITARY ACTION IN THE UNITED STATES AND ABROAD."

I'm not sure if those were the actual words spoken by the president that day. There may have been more explaining why this drastic decision was necessary. If there were, I don't remember that either. But as unbelievable as the message from the president had been, it shattered my dreams of being a member of the elite club my brother had urged me to join. I wanted to be a pilot. I wanted to be a lieutenant. I wanted desperately to stay in the Air Corps.

I racked my brain, trying to think of somebody I could turn to. The only person who came to mind was the captain in command of my squadron. I asked for permission to speak to him, and after a half-hour wait, I was allowed to enter his office.

"Sir," I said as I saluted. "Cadet Howard Barker, sir."

"At ease, Cadet. What can I do for you?"

For a moment, I couldn't answer. What was I thinking? What could he do to counteract an order from the president of the United States?

"Sir," I spoke as clearly as I could. "Is there anything I can do to stay in the Air Corps? To continue being a cadet, I mean."

"No" was the captain's immediate answer.

He looked at me for what seemed like a long time. I shifted my weight from one foot to the other.

"We are at a very tough time in this war, Cadet," he spoke again. "Thousands of soldiers in the ground forces have been killed. Replacements are needed as soon as possible. Like many other young men, you are going to be transferred immediately to an infantry division and sent overseas. It's going to be very hard."

I didn't say anything.

"Tell me, Cadet, do you have any special skills?" His question puzzled me. Then he looked straight into my eyes. "Do you have any special talents?" He waited while I quickly searched my brain.

"Well, sir, I'm an artist," I said. "I can draw pictures, and I learned to paint signs in high school," I went on. "That's all they taught in the commercial art class. But I was pretty good at it."

The captain made a note on a pad.

"I was also in school plays, sir—and musical shows too. Does that count?"

"Not exactly," the captain said. "I doubt it, but what do I know about show business? I have an idea you might not make the best infantry soldier in the army." He slipped a sheet of Air Corps stationery into a typewriter on his desk. "I don't know if this will do you any good," he said as he pounded the keys. "But I am going to give you a letter of recommendation. Wherever you end up and get settled, request an interview with the Special Services Attachment in your division and show the commanding officer this letter. I don't know. It just may help you. That's all, Cadet. You're dismissed."

"Yes, sir," I stammered. "Thank you, sir. I really appreciate this very much."

"You are welcome, Cadet." He shook my hand as I came to attention and saluted. The captain smiled and saluted back. "Good luck, son," he said, and that was that.

The following Saturday, at the Service Club, Andrea danced only with me. I told her what had happened and that I'd be shipping out on Monday. We didn't say a lot to each other after that. We both knew there wasn't much hope for the future, so we just danced and held each other very closely. In my mind, I saw a picture of us alone together. God knows where or when that could be.

Like dreams fade away when you wake up in the morning, that picture faded as soon as the San Antonio transport bus arrived. Standing again with dozens of other lovesick couples at the gates, I held Andrea tightly. The pressure of her body against mine was creating a stirring I couldn't control. I didn't try. It was too sweet.

"Okay ladies!" called the bus driver. "It's time to go!"

Andrea and I kissed, long and hard, and we cried a little. She pulled away from me and waved goodbye as she climbed into the bus. I waved back. That was the last I saw of my beautiful Andrea Majalca.

CHAPTER 29

LOUISIANA LIMBERLOST

Early Summer 1944

TWO HOT, HUMID days and nights were spent sitting on a crowded troop train with an unknown number of other ex–Air Corps Cadets on a journey to God knows where. Talk was sporadic and without joy. The train ended up deep in the bowels of what's known as The Pelican State. I was in Camp Polk, Louisiana, back in the U.S. Army–not in the Field Artillery but in the dreaded Infantry–and once again, I found myself sitting on a cot in another stifling army barracks, waiting for orders.

A bunch of soldiers, asses dragging, came shuffling in. One young guy stopped and dropped his duffel bag on the cot next to mine. He was dirty, unshaven and looked exhausted.

"Hey," I said and stood up. "I'm Howard. We just got in from San Antonio."

"Hi," he said and looked at me. His eyes were bloodshot, but they were the bluest eyes I had ever seen. "My name is Dick. We just got in from the swamps."

"The swamps?" I asked as I watched him lay his rifle down next to his duffel bag.

"Maneuvers. Battle practice." He looked at me–almost blankly.

"How was it?" I asked.

"It was hell," he said, and that was the end of the conversation. He fell onto his cot and went to sleep.

"Welcome to the Infantry," I said to nobody in particular as I lay down on my cot.

Dick Besoyan and I got to know each other pretty quickly after that. It's easy to make friends in the military. Whoever sleeps next to you is likely to become a friend because you always need to bitch about things to somebody, especially if you find you have something in common. And Dick and I did. We found out we were the same age, and although we were from different parts of the country, we had grown up with similar likes and dislikes and similar aspirations and ambitions. He loved movies the same as I did. He was an amateur composer, and I was an amateur artist. He had grown up without a father, and I had grown up without a father or mother. So we found we were a pretty good match.

Once again, I was thrown into a whole new world, the U. S. Army–from Camp Shelby in Mississippi, where I had been inducted, to Fort Bragg, North Carolina, from basic training in the F   ield Artillery to Air Corps basic in Miami Beach and college classes at University of Florida to cadet classification in San Antonio, Texas. Now in Camp Polk, Louisiana, I was a private in the 8th Armored Infantry Division, starting basic training again for the third time.

Among other things, including more calisthenics, we had target practice with the M1 rifle and memorized its nomenclature. We had to negotiate punishing obstacle courses, forced marches, and combat maneuvers. We also were assigned the miserable KP duties. We never stopped, sometimes from early in the morning till after dark.

"I have a letter from my captain in the Air Corps," I said to Dick one day at rifle practice. "He told me to take it to the head officer in special services. It's a letter of recommendation. You want to come with me?"

"Why?" Dick asked.

"I think it's a good idea," I said.

The long and short of it was that after Maj. Henry Rothenberg, the officer in charge of the special services office, read the letter and interviewed us, he turned out to be a very nice guy.

"I can use a couple of soldiers like you two," he said. "You'll be attached to my command."

"Thank you, sir," Dick and I said at the same time. I silently thanked my air corps captain back in Texas.

Under Sgt. Adolf Bartke, who ran the office with the help of a young corporal named Domenic di Cairano (if I remember correctly), Dick and I were both assigned to the camp's weekly newspaper. Dick typed articles, and I drew pictures for cartoons dreamed up by a morose writer named Hal

Kanter. Another member on the staff was Pte. Mike Martiska, a talented sketch artist whose cartoons, featuring two nutty cleaning women called Brenda and Cobina, appeared in the newspaper. Dick also played piano in the club for soldier sing-alongs at the service club, and I alternated as a disc jockey. I also painted some pretty good signs in the camp's sign shop.

This was one of the signs I had designed in the special services.

I am on the far right, at work on a sign.

There were two Borscht Belt comedians, Jake Meyerson and Al Van Belle, and an aspiring young comic from Brooklyn named Ben Rodak. Chick Cain, who had been a professional crooner, completed the group. The entertainers did their acts in the service club at night, and all of us learned how to operate 16 mm motion-picture projectors to be able to show first-run movies from Hollywood.

Who would have thought–after my training as a Field Artillery Radio Operator, an Air Corps Pilot Cadet, and now an Infantry Rifleman–I would have a brief fling as an entertainer myself? Well, I did. I had met an actress who was visiting her brother, an officer at the camp. She also was a good dancer, and we decided to work up a routine to appear in shows at the service club. On our first performance at a dinner at the camp officers club, we thought we gave them a pretty good tango, but the applause was less than enthusiastic. Anyway, when my lovely partner left to go home to Ohio, it was the end of my dancing career in the army.

I am sure my brief connection with the entertainment world fed the fires of my fascination with the movies and show business. Dick and I had a good thing going with special services, but our days at Camp Polk were numbered.

In early fall 1944, the long hard months of training in the humid heat of Louisiana were over. The 8th Armored Division was scheduled to join the Allied troops in the ETO, the European Theater of Operations–in plainer words, the WAR. Major Rothenberg called a special meeting and made an announcement that struck our little group with abject fear.

"I'm sorry I've been ordered to inform you that you'll be reattached to your original infantry companies." He almost choked on his words.

It was out of Major Rothenberg's hands. We were now to be combat soldiers again. However, before dismissing us, he made another statement.

"I promise you, as soon as we get to England, I will do my best to get all of you back, reattached to my Special Services Department before we cross the channel to France."

His promise offered us a bit of comfort–and hope.

The winding route of the troop trains carrying the entire division ended in the railroad sidings of Camp Kilmer in New Jersey. After a week of processing–i.e., documentation, orientation, and physical examinations, including the ubiquitous "short arm"–we were given an overnight pass to say "so long" to the U.S.A.

I telephoned Ruth McCoy Harris, my mother's niece from Mississippi, a cousin I had not seen since I was a child. When I told her who I was and where I was, she couldn't believe it. She asked if I might be able to come out to Long Island for a visit.

"I sure would like to see you," I said. "But I can stay for only one night. It's our last pass before we go overseas."

I took a train from Pennsylvania Station to Manhasset and a taxi to Ruth's home in the village of Plandome. To me, it looked pretty grand from the outside. I rang the doorbell, and the door opened immediately.

"Welcome, welcome, welcome," Ruth said as she hugged me and led me inside.

Only in the movies had I ever seen an entry hall with a beautiful staircase to a second floor. There were two-story houses in the small town of Hattiesburg where I grew up but only where wealthy folks lived.

"It's so wonderful to see you again after all these years, and here you are, all grown up."

The living room was as elegant and inviting as a magazine spread in *House and Garden*. Even a warm fire was crackling in the fireplace. Being from modest circumstances, I was very impressed, but I was immediately made to feel at home. Russell, Ruth's husband, clapped me on the shoulder and shook my hand heartily. Cynthia, their beautiful twelve-year-old daughter, actually curtsied and smiled her welcome. They were a portrait of the perfect family I had been missing.

"Now, Howard, how about a drink before dinner?" Russell asked me.

"Thank you, sir," I answered. "That would be nice."

"Would you like a dry martini?"

"Uh, yes, sir," I mumbled.

"With an olive?"

"Yes, sir. Thank you. That will be fine, sir."

I had never had a dry martini, with or without an olive, and I suddenly felt very sophisticated. I nearly choked on my first swallow, but neither Ruth nor Russell seemed to notice. I was sure they were just being kind to their kid cousin in uniform. But I soon relaxed, and the rest of the evening was perfect.

I couldn't have realized it at the time, but the dinner with wine by candlelight, a good night's sleep in a downy bed, plus a loving farewell after breakfast from my rediscovered relatives must have given me the strength I would need to face what was to come.

CHAPTER 30

ACROSS THE NORTH ATLANTIC

Across to England, Winter 1944

THE CONVOY OF troop trucks came to a halt at the nameless docks in New Jersey. After a long wait for our turn, my company trudged up the gangplank of the *HMT Samaria*. I was surprised to find we were on an English ship. I was also surprised when the trip turned into a nightmare. Rough seas and mass attacks of sea sickness had most GIs throwing up over the railings. This probably was expected by the ship's crew, but it was an unknown experience for neophyte American soldiers.

The U.S. Army food was nothing to write home about, but the British hog swill we were given twice a day was an insult to the pathetic condition of our stomachs. Even in small amounts, it was impossible to keep down, and in spite of nausea, everybody was always hungry. I saw a guy I knew scurry out of the ship's kitchen, desperately hiding a head of cabbage under his fatigue jacket. Afraid of being caught, he looked furtively back and forth and then hid behind some garbage cans and began ravenously eating the raw cabbage leaves. Now nearly seventy years later, the poor GI's desperation is clearly etched in my brain.

Some British sailors took advantage of the pitiful food situation and started selling us forbidden sandwiches. This little black market was soon discovered by higher-ups and was immediately halted. Pity us!

The last straw was when Sergeant Bartke, who had been on guard duty outside the Officers' Mess on an upper deck, came to us with the news that scotch and red wine was being served to both British and American officers who were wolfing down sirloin steaks and tossed salads.

Mutiny was never an option. Down in our lower decks, we were too sick. As my buddy Dick had once said, "It was hell."

If the seas were rough in the daytime, they were rougher at night, making it impossible to sleep, head to toe in rocking canvas hammocks squeezed together far below decks, while officers were enjoying cabins above. We were never prepared for the rasping voice blasting over the ship's intercom each morning with "NOW HEAR THIS!" It was the signal for the daily drill for all personnel to get to their stations next to the lifeboats as quickly as possible. Then following the boat drill, all units assembled for an hour's instruction in English, French, and German about rules and regulations when we met the enemy on the continent.

On October 19, twelve days after the ship had left the docks of Jersey City, and what felt like a month at sea, we arrived in Southampton. While we waited for orders to disembark, one of the senior generals of the British army came on board the *Samaria* and greeted the men of the 8th Army over the PA system.

"Welcome to Great Britain." He began a speech in a clipped English accent I had only heard in movies. "I feel it is my obligation to tell you that you have never seen mud until you have seen the mud at your new training grounds in Tidworth."

He droned on and on until we were ordered to proceed to the gangplank to the docks, where a cheerful team of English Red Cross girls served coffee and doughnuts—a much warmer welcome than the general's.

The strangely quiet two-hour train ride through the quaint English landscape dotted with thatched-roofed cottages seemed like a journey back into a peaceful past. Arriving at Tidworth, our company unloaded and marched through a torrential downpour to Tidworth Barracks. The general did not lie. It was an amazing sight—the entire camp seemed to be floating on a sea of mud. However, we did receive a hot meal, the first edible food we'd had since we left the United States.

Truthfully, I don't remember all the day-to-day details of what happened during the next few weeks. However, I do recall that preparations for the move across the English Channel went forward with an urgency I had never known before. In addition to constant top-level staff conferences, there was an amazing amount of work for all personnel. Vehicles were brought from scattered ports and prepared for combat, all weapons were checked, artillery battalions tested cannon firing, tank battalions put the new "Shermans" through their paces, lectures were given on how to act in the event of capture by the enemy, and members of all medical detachments worked in nearby hospitals to learn the types of injuries they would soon be treating. The days passed quickly.

Somehow I found some downtime to sketch a bit. Though I drew a bit of my soldier mates, I was more inspired by the locals in Europe.

Major Rothenberg kept his promise. How he managed to do it, I'll never know, but one by one, the entire original Camp Polk Special Services staff (except for Hal Kanter) was back in SSO. Sergeant Bartke, Corporal Domenic, the comedians Jake, Al, and Ben, Chick the crooner, Mike the cartoonist, Dick, and I all returned to the fold. When that happened, I could not help but think about my Aunt Amber and one of her favorite sayings when she had a happy surprise: "Will wonders never cease?"

CHAPTER 31

THE LAST PASS

English Channel to France, 1944–1945

THE WEATHER OUTSIDE the mess hall looked miserable. A bone-chilling rain hadn't let up for days, and we were sick of slogging through the mud that engulfed the barracks. The exhausting combat maneuvers in the sodden English countryside were soon to be over, and we were given a weekend pass, the last hours of freedom we would have before crossing the channel to France and into action against the Germans.

"So, Howie, why don't we team up and head into London this weekend?" Jake said as we were finishing our last cup of coffee in the mess hall.

I flinched at the nickname Howie. I had never heard it before the army threw me into a company of New York GIs. "I don't know, Jake." I hesitated.

"We'll pick up some broads and get laid, okay?"

When Jake suggested "teaming up" with me on our weekend pass, I wasn't sure I wanted to or not. It was his Brooklyn bravado for us two GIs to approach easygoing girls and convince them to favor us with their bodies. As teenagers back home, kids like me parked with girls in moonlight-drenched cars, spending frustrating evenings of sweaty but innocent smooching. *Now I'm going into combat, maybe even to be killed. I've never gone far enough with a girl to win that badge of manhood.*

"Sounds good to me," I agreed.

As I lay in my bunk that night after lights out, scenes from the past year rolled through my mind's eye like scenes in a movie.

At first, there was artillery basic training in North Carolina, where I got knocked out by lightning in a thunderstorm, and my second basic training as an Air Corps cadet in Miami Beach, where tropical breezes lulled us to sleep at night, palm trees swaying like hula dancers in the moonlight. Even with the rules and regulations, the calisthenics, marching in formation, the months flew by, and yet the real war seemed even further away than it had in North Carolina. Then in San Antonio, after losing my chances to be a pilot, there was losing my girl, enduring my third basic training for the infantry in the hellish Louisiana swamps, and finally, the treacherous crossing over to England on the British military carrier ship.

Those scenes must have turned into dreams because I was abruptly awakened by the barrack lights going on and the sergeant's shout.

"All right, men, drop your cocks and grab your socks! Everybody out for chow in fifteen!"

Jake and I took an early train to London and hit Leicester Square just before noon. There was a bitter wind, but it wasn't freezing, and throngs of people filled the sidewalks. Clouds overhead could mean snow, but there was only a cold fog. London! This was my first time to be in a city abroad. Did I want to see Buckingham Palace, a museum or an art gallery, or Big Ben? (Did I even know Big Ben was a clock?) No, all I wanted to do was to live a little before crossing the channel into the war.

We walked and walked and looked at people—so many people, young and old. There were soldiers and civilians, men and women, families with children, couples and singles. There were also plenty of young women. They all seemed to be hurrying, so we hurried along with them.

Just ahead of us, two attractive girls ducked into an archway, so we ducked into the archway too. We followed them as they melted into a group of people going up a wide flight of stairs. On the first landing, there was an entrance to a busy cafeteria.

"Good place as any to start," Jake said and motioned me to go in. "Après vous, cher Alphonse," he said in his phony French accent.

Inside, we found ourselves in a line of people picking up lunch trays and moving along the glassed-in hot tables.

"A bit of lunch?" he crooned, now faking an English accent.

I laughed, and so did the same two girls in the line just ahead of us. Jake cleared his throat a little too loudly.

"Pardon me. Would you two young ladies care to join two lonely servicemen for lunch?" he asked them, his fake accent still intact.

They laughed.

"You aren't really English," one of them said. "You're Yanks."

"How did you guess?" he asked with a broad smile.

We followed the two girls to a table, and when they didn't object, we sat down. They were polite, quiet at first, but Jake pulled out all his old comedian tricks, telling jokes and pouring on the charm. One of the girls, Elsie, ate it up, and in no time, the four of us were talking and enjoying ourselves. Terrie, the pretty one, smiled a lot but was quiet. So was I.

After lunch, Elsie said she had to go back to work. Jake offered to walk with her. She accepted. Terrie said she'd planned to go to the cinema.

"I'd sure like to see a movie," I said. "Would you mind if I go with you? I'll treat."

She agreed. I was happy.

"So, Howie," Jake said, "Why don't we meet later, okay?"

"Okay, Jake. Where?"

"Right here, under the arch. Like at around six?"

"Sure. I'll see you then."

Inside the movie theater, Terrie and I were shrouded in the warm velvety darkness. There was a smell of humanity and moist clothing, yet it wasn't unpleasant. The film was just beginning, and as we looked for seats, I was back in high school.

On Saturdays at the movies, we used to make sure to find the girls we liked and sit next to them. If we were bold enough, we would slip an arm around the girl's shoulders, or if not, we would slowly take her hand and hold it until the movie was over. *But now I'm not in high school. I'm in London. It's wartime. I'm watching a movie with a pretty English girl I've just met.*

For a while, we were immersed in what was happening on the screen–I don't remember what it was about–but suddenly, it was interrupted by the words "AIR RAID ALERT" in red letters flashing over the scene. Then I was aware of the whine of sirens outside. I was alarmed and took Terrie's hand.

"What do we do?" I asked probably too loudly.

"What do you want to do?" Terrie asked.

"Is there a shelter anywhere near here?"

"I believe there is one," she answered, squeezing my hand. "Do you want to go?"

I looked around. A few people were getting up, putting on their coats, and walking slowly toward the exit.

"We can if you want to, but we will miss the rest of the movie," she calmly answered.

"Oh. Well . . ." was all I could say.

We went on watching the movie until it was over. Terrie didn't take her hand away from mine, even after the words "ALL CLEAR" faded out.

When the movie ended and began at the start again, we left the cinema, still holding hands, and walked along the river. Terrie told me it was the Thames. December was cold, but thin rays of sunshine sliced through the clouds, and the world looked a little brighter. We sat on a bench and talked about the raging war, the future, and ourselves and wondered what was going to happen to us. I had my arm around her shoulder and held her close.

It was nearly six o'clock and almost dark. Terrie said she had to be getting home—her parents would be worrying about her.

"It was so nice to meet you. I've enjoyed being with you," Terrie said. "Would you like to write to me, you know . . . keep in touch?"

"Yes," I answered. "And I would like to see you again."

"I would like that too." She turned to me. "When?"

"Terrie . . ." I stopped a moment. "I have to catch a train back to Tidworth. We're going to be shipped out to the continent first thing in the morning."

"What a shame. I am so sorry," Terrie said. "I could have shown you Buckingham Palace." Then with half a smile, she added, "From the outside, I mean."

"You said we could keep in touch. I'll write you," I said.

She took a pen and a scrap of paper from her small handbag.

Over her shoulder, I saw her address as she wrote, "Neasdon, SW." I read it aloud. "Where's that?"

"In Southwest London," she said. "I will be there when you come back."

"If I come back," I said and kissed her.

"See that you do," she said and kissed me back—harder.

We rose from the bench and hugged.

"So long, Terrie. Merry Christmas."

"Merry Christmas to you, Howard, wherever you may be."

I watched her as she turned and walked away.

By the time I got back to Leicester Square and found Jake waiting for me at the arched entrance, night had fallen, dark and cold, revealing another nightly blackout.

"How about a beer?" Jake said. "It'll loosen you up for the evening's festivities. Whaddaya say, old chappie?" Still the show-off—a little of Brooklyn and a bit of Cockney.

"Okay by me, old chappie," I agreed.

The pub was noisy, filled with people enjoying a Saturday night out. Londoners weren't letting the war dampen their spirits.

"Greetings, Yanks!" shouted the bartender. "How about a pint on the house? I've got a couple of cold ones next to the ice."

We thanked him, downed our pints, and hit the streets.

We soon found ourselves in Piccadilly Circus. In the blackout, there was just enough light glowing from the night sky to keep us from bumping into people–servicemen and civilians–walking in the chilly semidarkness. Cars and buses, headlights off, moved slowly through the streets. More than once, we heard a female voice–"Quickie in a cab for a pound?" We also heard air-raid sirens, but they weren't nearby.

At some point, we ducked through a black-curtained doorway and into a shop, a sort of pharmacy. When my eyes became adjusted to the lights inside, I noticed a girl wearing a leopard vest. She wasn't gorgeous, but she was pretty, and there was something about her that made me watch her as she moved through the aisles. She looked up and caught me looking at her. She gave me a little smile. I smiled back.

"Go for it," said Jake, and he gave me a shove.

I walked toward her. "Hello," I said.

"Hello, Yank. Are you looking for someone tonight?"

I was kind of taken aback, but I nodded.

"Well," she said, "it's getting late, almost eleven."

"Yeah, I know. Uh, yes, it is."

"I'm looking for a shack-up," she said simply. "At my flat. No quickie for me tonight."

"Me too," I managed to blurt out. "I mean, no quickie for me either."

"I'm Norah," she said. "A shack-up will be five pounds. What's your name?" She took my hand and led the way back through the shop to the entrance.

"My name's Howard." When I looked back, Jake was grinning and giving me the okay sign.

Norah and I walked arm in arm through the dark misty streets. I heard the sirens again in the distance. I wasn't sure what was happening. Well, I guess I was pretty sure, but I didn't know how it was going to happen. I knew I wanted this. It would be my first time. I wanted this before I went into the war across the channel. Maybe it would be my last time. Boy, talk about 'living in the moment.' This was it. I was scared.

As I followed Norah up the stairs to her flat, she looked back down at me and smiled. Now I noticed she was missing a tooth on one side. That kind of got to me. *Well*, I thought, *it's wartime. I guess the English don't have the best diets.*

"Just one more flight," she said.

She unlocked the door, and we went inside. We were in a tiny kitchen. *What do I do now?*

"Would you like a cup of tea?" she asked. "A bit nasty out tonight."

"Yes. Thank you. I would," I said. *What a relief!*

She lit a gas burner under a kettle. I looked through a door into a dimly lit bedroom. It was tidy. Pleasant. It was almost homey.

"I'll make us some toast and jam too," Norah said. "Aren't you a bit peckish?"

I didn't know what she meant by "peckish." "Yes, I guess so," I said. "Thank you."

She hummed softly as she prepared the tea, and I was beginning to feel more relaxed.

"We'll have it in here," she said, carrying the small tray into the bedroom.

There was a little lamp on the bedside table, and she placed the tray on the bed and sat down beside it.

"Sit down," she said, patting the bed next to her. "Isn't this cozy?"

Whatever she said or asked, I answered, "Yes," trying to be calm and nonchalant at the same time. Could she tell I was neither? When we finished our tea, Norah took the tray.

"Why don't you hop into bed?" she said as she left the room. "I'll be back in just a minute."

I took off my shoes and socks, then tore off my clothes. I retrieved a condom from my pants and crawled under the covers.

Norah, now naked, came back into the room, and in the soft lamplight, I could see she had a really nice body. She walked to the window and pulled the heavy draperies more tightly together.

"We have to make sure the light doesn't leak out into the street. Blackout, you know."

"Yes," I said. "Blackout."

She slipped into bed beside me. "Do you have something?" she asked and moved closer to me.

I was already erect. "Yes," I said. "It's already on."

She touched me, and after a moment, we moved together, and what happened after that was amazing. Considering I was completely inexperienced, it all seemed to come to me so naturally, so easily, so warm, so good. I moved slowly at first, and my heart started to throb. When I moved faster, my heart began pounding hard against my ribs, I thought it was going to burst. It didn't. It was so exciting. Norah was moving too. I just kept going, moving faster and faster. Then after a few minutes, it was all over. I laughed out loud. We didn't speak, just held each other close. *Mission accomplished!* I thought to myself. We fell asleep in each other's arms.

The next morning, when I awoke, Norah was in her tiny kitchen, humming and brewing tea.

"Good morning, Norah," I called in to her.

"Good morning, luv!" she called back. "Toast with your tea?"

When she came back in, she put the tea with one piece of toast with jam on the night table. Then she opened the curtains a little and looked out. She was wearing a robe now, sort of Chinese. In the thin morning light, I realized Norah might be a little older than I had thought. She turned to me and smiled and went into the kitchen. I ate the toast and drank my tea. It was like a caress to my empty stomach. I got up and stretched before reaching for my clothes. I was relaxed and comfortable in my naked body, so I dressed slowly and thought about the night before. *So that's what it's all about*, I thought. *I like it*. I folded six pounds and laid it on the little night table.

"I guess I'd better be going," I said as I walked into the kitchen.

"I've got Thursdays and Fridays open," Norah said and smiled. "If you like, you could be one of my regulars."

Suddenly, I felt flattered, and I didn't mind her missing tooth. After all, maybe she didn't know that I'd been a twenty-year-old virgin.

"I wish I could," I said. "But I can't. They're sending us over to France right away. This is my last pass. I'm really sorry."

"So am I," Norah said. "Well, I guess this is goodbye. Take care of yourself." She hugged me and gave me a quick kiss on the cheek.

"Goodbye, Norah," I said. "It was great."

She opened the door. I started down the stairs.

"Goodbye, Yank!" she called down to me from her doorway.

I stopped on the landing and looked up at her. "Thanks for everything!" I called back and hurried down the stairs, overwhelmed by the entire experience and grateful for her tenderness.

***

On the train ride back to Tidworth, bits and pieces of the last two days in London tumbled through my mind: the crowds in London's streets, being with Terrie in the movie theater, our walk by the river, her sweet goodbye kiss. My night with Norah was sweet too but in such a different way. My brain was in a sort of muddle.

When I reached the barracks, a lot was going on. We had orders to pack up and board the trucks. Men were emptying their lockers and packing their duffel bags. Jake was lying on his bunk next to mine. His duffel was already packed.

"Get your shit together, kid," he said. "We got a war to go to."

I didn't answer, but I started throwing my stuff on my bunk.

"So, Howie, how did it all go, pardner?" he asked. "I mean with the two broads."

"They weren't broads," I said.

Jake rolled his eyes and looked at the ceiling.

"Well, no matter. They were wonderful," I said. "I had a great time—with both of them." I got busy packing my duffel. "And yes, Jake, I got laid. How about you?"

"Elsie was a washout," Jake admitted. "But I picked up a pig later and got laid too. You got laid twice!"

He looked astounded, and I didn't explain the details. I looked across the barrack at Dick, who was sitting on his bunk, writing.

"You gonna tell your pal Dick all about your trip to London?" Jake asked.

Dick looked up, saluted us and went back to what he was doing.

"No, I don't think so," I said. "Unless he asks."

Jake and Al were already comparing notes of their weekend. When the load-up call came for us to leave for France, Sergeant Bartke and Corporal Cain led our Special Services group out to the trucks. Dick and I shouldered our duffel bags and walked out together. The rest of the group joined us. The temperature was dropping. The two-hour ride in the teeming rain to the Southampton docks was cold and miserable.

With the exception of orders shouted by "noncoms" and disgruntled complaining by the troops, company after company of the 8th Armored Division seemed to board the transport ships in silence. I was probably too scared to remember much about the crossing of the English Channel or how long it took, but I do remember it was cold and miserable.

Recently, looking through an old photo album, I found a snapshot of a couple of dozen soldiers grouped around a decorated Christmas tree in Tidworth Barracks. I don't know how the tree got there, and I don't remember the men in the photo. But there I am, smiling uncertainly, wondering what will happen to all of us when we find ourselves facing the enemy in a strange and frightening war.

Christmas with my troop in Tidworth Barracks, 1944.

CHAPTER 32

OVER THERE

France, January 1945

E ARLY IN THE morning on New Year's Day, the 8th Armored Division landed in Le Havre. No time was wasted getting us off the ship and onto the docks. Snow was falling. How could France be colder than England? Who knows? But it was.

"Fall in!" shouted an unknown sergeant, and our company joined other companies from the division.

This could have been the big SNAFU ("Situation Normal, All Fucked Up"), but actually, it went smoothly. Like sheep, soldiers were herded into the snow-covered troop trucks. The convoy pulled out and wound its way slowly through the ruined city. The streets were empty. No civilians were to be seen. The trucks sped up, bumping over the cobblestones. None of us knew where we were going. All we knew was that we were cold.

Hours passed. The hard wooden seats in the truck were rough on the ass, but everybody knew that bitching about it would just be wasted breath. As daylight faded into darkness, the snow let up, and the sky was clear. The countryside, blanketed in white, was lit up by a cold moon. The canvas tarp overhead was flapping in the icy wind, and we were shivering. The men had stopped talking and were huddling together, trying to get warm.

I was watching the road rolling out behind us, mile after mile, and the monotonous drone of the truck's motor began to make me sleepy. I was cold, but I must have fallen asleep and dreamed for a while. I was back in my hometown, dancing with my high school sweetheart at the senior prom in the high school gym–holding each other close, cheeks glued together with teenage sweat, "Moonlight Serenade," "Chattanooga Choo Choo," "Stardust," the orchestra playing the Glenn Miller arrangements, the beat of the music matching the beat of our hearts.

Something woke me up. I shook a shivering Dick.

"Where are we?" I asked him.

"Nobody knows," he answered.

We only knew our division was one of the ones pushing back the retreating Germans. Sooner or later, we would reach the front lines, and God only knows what would happen next.

Our training in the Special Services unit had included entertaining American combat troops by showing movies. Movies? At the front? It seemed a little ridiculous. Then I thought of our commander Major Rothenberg's final words before we landed in Le Havre.

"Even though Special Services personnel are not considered to be combatants, you are still under orders to carry your weapons at all times," he had explained. "If you should confront enemy troops in action, you must be ready to defend yourself and shoot if necessary."

Each of us carried our rifle and a belt of ammunition. Fortunately, the carbine was not as heavy as the regular infantry M1 rifles we had used in our months of training. But I had not gotten used to the idea of shooting anybody, even an enemy. My thoughts were interrupted by the convoy stopping suddenly.

"Piss call!" a voice called from somewhere up ahead.

Stiff from the cold, all of us stumbled and fell over one another climbing out of the truck. As far as I could see, the entire company was standing in the road peeing. The moon, still shining brightly, lit up the steaming yellow streams as they hit the snow. Although my bladder was aching, I was unable to relieve myself. I tried, but the freezing wind and the tension in my body wouldn't allow it. At the "load up" call, I climbed back into the truck and clamped my legs together in silence. The convoy rumbled on.

"GOD NEVER MEANT FOR US TO SUFFER LIKE THIS!" an angry voice shouted from the darkness. It was Mike Martiska, our cheerful cartoonist.

"SHUT THE HELL UP, MIKE!" someone shouted back, followed by a weak chorus of laughs from the rest of us.

As the hours passed, we tried to keep warm by huddling together, borrowing a little body heat from one another. I had never known such punishing cold. Finally, we pulled into a long winding snow-covered driveway and stopped in front of a huge chateau. In the moonlight, it looked like a small castle.

"All right, men, everybody out!" a noncom called. "Bring all your gear and go inside. Find a place to bed down."

I looked at my watch. It was two o'clock in the morning.

"We pull out in the morning at oh-six-hundred."

I stood in the shadow of the truck and peed. It was wonderful.

Inside the chateau, the moonlight shone through the windows of a cavernous entry hall. What looked like hundreds of GIs wrapped in blankets were already sleeping. There was no room for us, not a square foot of open space. With the rest of our company, Dick and I trudged up a wide flight of marble stairs to the second floor. Dozens of men from our convoy were searching the different rooms filled by more sleeping men, swaddled in their blankets. The rest of us climbed on up to the third floor and then on up to an attic.

Dick and I–with the last few cold, exhausted soldiers–found enough room to lie down. I went to a small window and looked out. Moonlight shone on falling snow. A few flakes blew in through a broken pane of glass and touched my face. It was almost pleasant. For a moment, I thought of home–not Grandmother's house, not all the other places my brother and I moved about with Aunt Amber. I thought about our house on Twenty-Fifth Avenue, the house Mother made into our beautiful home. The moment melted as quickly as the snowflakes on my cheek. I turned away from the window and looked at Dick. Each of us had only one blanket. Without speaking, we spread one blanket on the stone floor and lay down. We spent the rest of the short night huddled together under the other blanket like two lost children.

The morning after our arrival at the chateau, me in the middle
with Dick on the right and Mike Martiska on the left.

The next morning, while we were eating our cold field rations, we heard
the latest scuttlebutt: We were somewhere near Reims. The marble chateau
where we had slept had been commandeered by the U.S. Army from a
champagne baron who had collaborated with the enemy.

Scuttlebutt is a lot like gossip. It's usually based on fact, but by the time it
reaches you, it may not be factual. In the army, you tend to believe scuttlebutt
because it's all you have to hang onto as news of what's going on. Actually,
other than being constantly cold, not much had happened to us so far.

Late that night, we arrived at Thiaucourt, a rural town near the German border. Dick and I, with the men in our truck, were assigned quarters in a small inn. The owners, a French family, welcomed us warmly. What a difference a bowl of steaming soup can make! The daughter of the family, a smiling young woman, led us upstairs to our rooms.

"Bonne nuit," she said. "Dormez bien."

I had not taken French in high school—only Spanish and Latin—but I knew the word *merci* was French for "thank you," and I managed to blurt it out. A night's sleep in a real bed was even better than the bowl of soup. I felt almost human again. The feeling was short-lived.

We were awakened at daybreak, and the convoy moved out on another icy road covered with snow. It was hours later, and this time, when we stopped for a piss call, we learned that our division had caught up with the German forces on the run through Belgium and the Netherlands. We were not far behind them, but at this point, our Special Services unit had still not laid eyes on the enemy.

In Holland, the convoy stopped in a town called Maastricht, and for reasons unknown to us, our unit was ordered to unload and wait for another convoy. We were left standing in the freezing rain. The new convoy, a smaller one, arrived an hour later. We marched along the cobblestone street beside the line of troop trucks. Our duffel bags were already heavy before, but now, sodden with rain, they were almost unbearable.

"Troop, halt!" shouted the corporal leading the column. "Fall out! Okay, men, load up."

Mumbling to one another, we gathered behind an empty troop truck. Just as Dick and I were shoving our duffel bags onto it, a short convoy of American army vehicles passed by us. In the last one, an open jeep, a beautiful blonde woman wearing a GI raincoat and cap was standing up and waving to the soldiers. As we waved back, she saluted us, and I got a really close, good look at her before her jeep disappeared around a corner.

"I wonder who that was," I said as we climbed into the truck with the rest of the other guys.

"Who knows? Maybe a WAC officer?" Dick said.

"I don't think she was a WAC," I said. "There was something special about her."

The truck was packed, and we were wet and cold, but we were glad to be under a tarpaulin stretched overhead. The driver started the motor, and we pulled away with the other trucks in our new convoy.

"She was very beautiful," I said. "Even in the GI raincoat, she was beautiful enough to be one of those movie stars sent over to entertain the troops."

"Are you kidding?" Dick laughed at me. "Not a chance."

"I saw Betty Hutton once, in Fort Bragg. She was sensational!"

"Yeah, I'll bet. But that was back in the States. We're in a war over here, buddy. Maybe we haven't seen one German, but we've been lucky. I don't think you'll find many movie stars in these parts."

I didn't answer. *How would he know anyway?* It wasn't until many months later when I had learned the identity of the beautiful lady who saluted us that day.

Our convoy's seemingly endless push across Holland into Germany slowed down as we entered the outskirts of another town. The evening sky was losing light, it had stopping raining, and night was falling fast. The streets were deserted, and there were no lights anywhere. One by one, the trucks pulled into an empty lot behind an enormous building. In the moonlight, it looked like some kind of factory and appeared to be abandoned.

"Okay, men, this is your new home away from home!" the sergeant in charge called out as he passed along the line of trucks. "For a couple of days, anyway. Follow me."

GIs piled out of their trucks and crowded together behind him. He pushed open a large door on the side of the building and went inside.

"Holy shit!" we heard the sergeant yell. "Oh my god!" he shouted.

We followed him into the high-ceilinged chamber. He was gazing upward, pointing his field flashlight high above our heads. The beam revealed the ghastliest sight I've ever seen. At least a hundred bodies were hanging from pipes near the ceiling. It looked like there was nothing inside their clothes but skeletons. All of us stood in silent shock.

The beam of light moved across the hanging bodies and down rows of chains on pulleys against the wall. Hand over hand, the sergeant lowered a pipe down to eye level. His loud laughter broke the silence.

"Jesus, Mary, and Joseph," he said. "Look. It's not dead people."

The bodies hanging on the pipes were work clothes. The racks must have been pulled up on chains at the end of the day by the workers.

"Frigging German efficiency!" somebody yelled.

Before it got too dark to see, all the men found space to bed down for the night between the hunks of iron machinery. With a last look at the eerie spectacle above our heads, I closed my eyes and waited for sleep to come. Tired and still damp, I slept. I don't think I dreamed at all.

The chirping of birds and thin rays of winter sun told us it was morning. The men crawled from their blankets, and the clang of metal striking metal announced the arrival of the blessed chow wagon. When we went outside, the air was cold, but the smell of fresh hot coffee got us in line.

"Get your breakfast while it's hot!" shouted the cook. As he filled our metal cups with the steaming coffee with one hand, he tossed cardboard boxes of dry field rations with the other.

After our "hot" breakfast, we were given enough warm water to fill our steel helmets for what GIs call a "whore bath" if we felt like it. Some guys didn't feel like it. I did. The morning's quiet was suddenly shattered by a deafening explosion. Everyone froze. *Oh god! The WAR at last!* After a split second staring at one another, we all scattered, looking for cover. Petrified, we waited for a blast, but nothing happened. That was it. All was quiet. Within minutes, a jeep pulled in from the road.

"An enemy shell just hit and exploded a hundred yards from here!" the driver shouted. "Get your stuff and load up. We're retreating!"

Half an hour later, our convoy halted and waited for orders. The Germans had fired one last shell toward our position before they continued their retreat. Now they were on the run again, and our division was close behind them. Our trucks of noncombatants drove back far enough to be out of range of the enemy's cannon fire until further word came from headquarters.

From that moment on, however, our Special Services unit followed close behind the battalions.

Each week, members of our Special Services unit joined frontline companies and showed movies to the soldiers. Movies! How bizarre was that? The GIs watched movies in unimaginable "theaters"—deserted schools, churches, town halls, and an occasional bombed-out factory.

Every Monday each of us in S   pecial Services would load up a jeep with a 16 mm movie projector, a gas-driven generator, a movie screen—actually a ten-by-twelve-foot white tarp—and six new films from Hollywood. (The armed forces got to see new movies before they were released to the civilian public.) Then we'd head out to the front. Every night for a week, if the action quieted down, we'd show movies. Stars like Betty Grable, Rita Hayworth, and Alice Faye would sing and dance across the screen with their partners in first-run frothy musicals.

Sometimes I would get a message from a forward observer to lower the volume because we were too close to enemy artillery. The sound could give away our location. Whether the volume was low or, at times, full blast, the battle-weary men enjoyed a few hours of pleasure.

At the end of the week, when all six movies had been seen, we would head back to our base behind the front lines for a break—a washup, sometimes a shave—and pick up six new films for our next assignment. There was never very much free time. In what there was, Dick worked on a script for a musical comedy he called *At Your Service*. He hoped to see it staged for the soldiers of our division. He was clever enough to compose songs in his head without a piano and jot down music notes on a precious tablet he carried wherever we went.

"You told me you would like to be a writer," Dick said to me one day as I was reading some of his work. "Why don't you collaborate with me? It'll take me forever to get this finished alone."

I looked at him in surprise.

"I've told you all about it already, you know the story line," he went on. "I can give you some scenes to write. We could try it out."

I was surprised by his confidence in me, but I agreed right away. Dick was not exactly a great

vocalist, but he sang some of the songs he had written so I would know how they fit into the script.

"When we get back on the weekends from showing our movies," he said, "we can go over what we've done and kind of splice it together. Okay?"

Our partnership was formed. Whenever we got together to do our splicing, we often found we had written the same scenes, surprisingly similar, and sometimes almost identical lines of dialogue.

As the weeks passed, we both spent them with the troops near the front, showing often mindless movies under unbelievable conditions. Whenever I wondered why I was showing movies during a war instead of fighting it, I think of what my Air Corps captain said to me back in the San Antonio cadet center when he handed me his letter of recommendation: "I have an idea you might not make the best infantry soldier in the army."

Now, decades later, I think of something else. Not long ago, I read an article in *Esquire* magazine about the Kennedy family. It was titled 'What I've Learned.' "There is always inequity in life. Some men are killed in war, some are wounded, and some never leave the country. Some men are stationed in the Antarctic, and some are stationed in San Francisco. It's very hard, in military life or in personal life, to ensure complete equality. Life is unfair" (JFK, March 1962). To this day, I still find it bizarre that we were able, in the midst of combat, to show our movies to exhausted, but grateful fighting men.

As the 8th Armored Division pushed forward on its drive to the Rhine, there were casualties. The dead were collected, and the wounded were evacuated. Week after week, our battalions fought their way through towns and villages like Richelrath, Boisheim, Immendorf, Huckel Hoven, and Duken. If these names sound like places in bygone romantic operettas of Johann Strauss, Rudolf Friml, and Victor Herbert, it's because those operettas usually took place in "mittel Europan" towns. But that is where the similarity stops. The carnage of combat in World War II in no way mirrored those romantic antique operettas.

A light moment did occur one day. Somewhere in the Ruhr Valley, Dick "captured" one of the enemy. With his carbine poised (I don't know if it was even loaded), Dick marched into our base unit behind a young German soldier whose hands were clasped behind his head. The German looked both frightened and somewhat relieved, and so did Dick. The soldier was taken into custody and whisked away in a truck. I never knew what happened to him.

"So, Dick, tell us how you captured the Kraut," somebody said.

"I came around a corner of a house, and so did he. He threw up his hands before I could, and I managed to pull my gun off my shoulder and point it at him. That's how I captured him," Dick admitted with a shy grin. His act of "bravery" in the midst of conflict gave us a laugh. We needed one.

With battle action all around us, our unit continued to bring entertainment to troops as much as we could. Our slogan began to be "When the going gets tough, the 'tough' show movies."

CHAPTER 33

VE DAY

Germany, Spring 1945

DURING THE BITTER winter, my division, the 8th Armored, had been among those fighting their way through France, Belgium, and the Netherlands and finally into Germany. The end of military action was finally declared in the spring, and the war in Europe officially ended. Although there was enormous jubilation in the air, American and Allied forces were still at war in the Far East. Reliable scuttlebutt passed down information that the 8th could be deployed with other troops to the Pacific.

Shortly after VE Day, our battalion arrived in Gottingen, a beautiful university town in the Hartz Mountains of Germany. Gottingen had not been bombed, and its tree-lined streets were filled with females, young children, and very old men. All adult males and many teenagers were in what was left of the captured German army. It was surprising to find that civilians did not seem to be hostile. Either they weren't, or they were simply willing to make the best of the situation.

Major Rothenberg decided it was time for Special Services to do something really special for the troops in the area–a live show. Even if Dick's musical had been finished (which it wasn't), it was actually too ambitious to be produced quickly. Where would we find female leads who could sing musical comedy songs in English? And get chorus girls who could dance Broadway-styled routines? A simpler entertainment was what we needed. Special Services personnel put their collective heads together and came up with an idea: a musical "revue"–with songs and laughs–so the guys in the battalion could relax and let go of the tensions that had been building up during the months of combat.

Members of our SSO unit who had performing experience tossed plans about and came up with an opening number: a ballet takeoff of *Swan Lake*, with Chick Cane crooning to the ballerinas (GIs in tutus!). Jake, our star comedian, would need a sexy broad for his comedy routine. I was chosen to play the part.

"Why me?" I groaned. "Why can't somebody else be the sexy broad?"

"Because you're the prettiest," Sergeant Bartke said, smiling sweetly. "And you and Jake will have the eleven-o'clock number. In show biz, that's the best spot."

I was reluctant, but it was an order, and I had no choice.

The local opera house was commandeered for the show, and a very pleasant woman, the costume director for the Gottingen opera, became our civilian liaison. She organized a crew of backstage helpers and opened up the costume department for us to pick anything we'd need. Gisella decked me out in a gold lamé gown and a blonde wig. She made me up to look like a cartoon version of Marilyn Monroe. With the huge artificial boobs, I looked a little more like Jayne Mansfield.

After some days of hectic rehearsals, the curtain went up, with all seats filled. Our entire group from Special Services–wearing wigs, ballet tutus, and combat boots instead of toe shoes–pranced through the opening number. It was ridiculous, but the GIs loved us.

Our emcee, crooner Chick Cain, belted out a few songs. Jake and Al had dusted off their comedy routines, and Ben, our young comic from Brooklyn, did his solo act. All three got cheers.

Jake told more raunchy jokes and followed with his impression of Jack Benny's classic exasperated scanning of the audience. Cued by a drum roll, I sashayed onstage, rolling my eyes and batting my two-inch black paper eyelashes. I had no lines to speak, so I flirted lasciviously with smiles from my brightly painted oversized lips. I had refused to shave off my small moustache, but the smeared-on red lipstick totally covered it. The GIs guffawed every time Jake poked my big boobs, and I did bumps and grinds like the stripper I remembered from a Miami Beach nightclub when I was in the Air Corps. I kept time with the band's bass drum beats just like she had. We got a big hand.

If I remember correctly, our whole group sang "The Star-Spangled Banner," with the audience joining in for the finale. When we came out for our bows, I had taken off my lipstick and long black eyelashes. I threw the gold dress over my shoulder, ripped off the blonde wig, and got a huge applause.

We were a hit, if only for the one grand performance.

Late the next afternoon, Ben and I went out for a walk. The spring breeze was chilly, but the sun was still shining. The trees along the boulevard were showing tiny green buds. A couple of German girls, chattering to each other, giggled and smiled at us. American soldiers were under orders–"Do Not Fraternize"–but horny GIs were not following the rules. Ben and I followed the girls. Before long, they looked back over their shoulders. We walked a little faster. They slowed down, and we soon caught up with them.

"Wie gehts, Fräuleins," Ben said in his best Brooklyn Yiddish. "Spazieren mit uns."

The girls giggled again, and a stream of German was their answer.

"Ich bin Ben, und er ist Howard," Ben introduced us.

"Ich bin Gretchen," said the dark-haired girl. "Und sie ist Ilse."

By the time the sun went down, the four of us ended up exploring a deserted house. The owners must have left hurriedly because it was still fully furnished. The girls were agreeable, and soon, we were romping in adjoining bedrooms, I with the attractive brunette and Ben with Ilse, the zaftig blonde. Did we worry about the no-fraternizing edict? I guess not. The girls seemed to enjoy tumbling about in bed as much as we did, and before long, we were deep into action. This was my first time since the night with Norah in London five months ago. I was ready.

Because I spoke no German beyond "Wie gehtz, Fräulein," our lovemaking was virtually silent. The sounds of my heavy panting and what (I hoped) were "sweet nothings" from her floated away into the shadows of the room. When we became quiet, we heard talking from the next room. Ben was speaking Yiddish (ironic, I thought), and his girl was accepting it as some form of German.

When I tried to communicate with Ilse by speaking slowly, simple sentences in English, it seemed useless. But I was determined to communicate.

"How was your life under Adolf Hitler?" I asked her very slowly, again in English.

Ilse still didn't understand, but when she heard his name, it brought forth an avalanche of words ending in "Er hat magische augen! Ich liebe Hitler, meine fuhrer!"

I didn't understand her language either–something about "magic"–but I recognized three words: "I love Hitler." I couldn't speak. How could this sweet young girl love a monster? I had always heard Hitler was a mesmerizing speaker, and all she's ever known was life under the new Reich. Countless other

Germans loved Hitler. But hadn't she ever heard of the millions of Jews killed? I was no longer hot with desire. I was hot with shame.

"Ben!" I called out. "Ben, it's time to go."

Ben didn't answer. Gretchen sat up in bed, watching me as I pulled on my clothes and left the room.

"Warum?" she shouted after me. "Why?" she was asking, but I didn't answer.

I walked out of the house. The night air was cool and clean. I wasn't.

***

Long after the war was over, I learned that 2,621 enlisted men and 186 officers from the 8th Armored Division were killed in battle during the five months before VE Day. According to official records, the total number of American casualties in Europe during the entire war is estimated to have been more than 120,000. This figure does not include Americans killed in the Pacific theater, which would bring the overall total to a grisly 413,000 deaths. Maybe the number of wounded is available somewhere as well, but our combat soldiers endured unthinkable fear, anguish, and misery. Yet these Americans lost helped end the mass genocide in Europe. They are only a fraction of the nearly six million Jews who died in the Holocaust.

CHAPTER 34

HALLO, CZECHOSLOVAKIA

Summer 1945

O NE MORNING, AFTER showing a week of movies to a company of soldiers in a nearby town at the front, I loaded the film, the projector, and the folding screen into a jeep. The jeep driver helped me with the heavy generator. On our way back to SSO headquarters, we heard shouts from the road behind us,

"What the hell!" the jeep driver said.

The loud whoops and hollers, not understandable but joyful, were punctuated by horn blasts coming from a jeep speeding up close to our rear bumper. I turned around and saw four GIs waving bottles of wine wildly in the air.

"VJ DAY! VJ DAY!" they were shouting. "VJ Day! Japan surrendered! It's over! Ya-a-ay! The war in the Pacific is oh-vahhh!"

As their vehicle pulled up next to us, one of the guys stood up and tossed two bottles of wine to us. We waved as they sped away ahead, shouting the good news to whoever happened to be within earshot. My driver glanced at his wristwatch.

"August 15," he said over the noise from the jeep's motor. "This calls for a celebration."

I popped the cork off the bottle and passed the bottle to him. He took a healthy swig.

"Mazel tov!" he shouted as he handed the bottle back to me.

"Peace!" I drank. I did not know that American atom bombs had been dropped on Hiroshima and Nagasaki.

This must call for celebration everywhere, I thought. Then I wondered if we would not be shipped to the Far East after all. I soon learned the 8th Armored Division would not be sent to the Far East, and I assumed the possibility of going home could be in the not-too-distant future. As it turned out, that changed to the indefinite future. In other words, we would have to wait our turn. Fair enough. I also learned that the 8th would be sent as a "good will" occupational force to Czechoslovakia.

Czechoslovakia was lovely but achingly poor. My unit ended up in a pleasant rural town named Rokycany. The Czech people were very friendly. When they invited us into their homes, we learned the war had left them in need of everything except the barest of necessities. Actually, they were doing without in order to be hospitable. The coffee, brewed from roasted acorns, and the dark bread spread with lard were the most luxurious refreshments they could offer. We quickly responded by sharing our canned meat and butter, cigarettes, and sweets from our C-rations with our civilian hosts. Unlike the military rules in Germany, we were encouraged to socialize with the country's citizens. To GIs, that meant we could "fraternize."

When Dick and I heard that GIs were welcome at village dances, we went to the next one. The local people were dancing to Czech tunes, sort of like folk music but with a swingy beat. We saw American soldiers looking on, and a few had joined the dancers. So then Dick and I approached two young women standing at the edge of the dance floor and somewhat shyly pantomimed an invitation to dance with us. The girls spoke English well enough for us to socialize. They were friendly and pretty, so when the dancing was over, it seemed natural for us to ask if we could walk them home. The evening was so pleasant, Dick and I started seeing Vlasta and Marusa on a regular basis.

At a dance the following week, Marusa introduced me to a friend from Prague who had come to Rokycany for the weekend.

"This is Libuse Holubova," she said. "Libuse, this is my friend Howard. So now you waltz together, yes?"

Libuse was lovely—blonde and winsome, with a quiet smile. She looked into my eyes. "How . . ." she spoke slowly. "I Libuse. Hallo . . . you, Howdy."

"Hello," I said.

I couldn't speak a word of Czech, but Libuse smiled and held out her hand to me, and we danced. I tried a little sign language, but she just smiled. I held her close. It was nice, easy. When the music ended, I bowed and thanked her–in English, of course. She simply nodded, smiled again, and returned to the group of young women.

The music started again. The dancers paired up, side by side, in a large circle and began to move around the floor in a measured, stately fashion. It was beautiful to see them step and turn in time to the music. I felt a hand touching my shoulder. I turned. Libuse was standing there, smiling at me.

"Hallo, Howdy." (Obviously, she thought my name was Howdy. That was all right with me.) She held out her arms. "Mazurka?"

"Hello, Libuse. I don't know the dance."

Libuse took my arm and placed it around her waist. She held my other hand in hers and led me to join the dancers. As the orchestra began playing, the couples stepped forward in time with the music. It was a sort of folk dance, slow-moving and graceful. I tried to lead, following the dancers' footsteps, their patterns of twists and turns, as best I could, but it was too complicated for me. I was starting to sweat.

"I'm sorry, Libuse. I have to give up. Can we go outside and get some air?"

I guessed she didn't understand, so I led her off the floor and toward a door open to a courtyard. It was dark outside, but the light from the hall shone on us, and I could still see her face. She was beautiful.

"Hallo," she said again.

"Hallo," I repeated, thinking it might sound Czech-ish, but it didn't. "Hello," I said. "I guess 'hello' is all we're going to be able to say to each other."

"Hallo," she said. Then she cupped her hands to her ears. "I telephone work. Prague. Hallo, hallo." She laughed.

"Oh, you're a telephone operator? From Prague?"

"Yes, I work telephone. Hallo, hallo."

We both laughed and sat down on a bench. I put my arm around her shoulders. It seemed like the most natural thing to do. Libuse relaxed against me. Then I kissed her, just for a moment, and then again, much longer. That kiss was the sweetest thing I had known since my high school days, when we parked out at the country club in the moonlight. Now, here in a foreign country, I was kissing a girl whose music I hadn't heard, whose dances I didn't know, and whose language I couldn't understand. So we just sat quietly and held each other.

When the last dance was over, the hall emptied quickly. It was time to say good night.

"May I walk you home, Libuse?" I asked.

"I Libus-ka," she said, taking my hand.

"Libus-ka," I repeated it.

"Libus-ka," she said softly. "Love name."

"Love name," I repeated. "Yes."

"You, Howdy, go to Prague. So nice. Go to me in Prague."

I would have loved to have been able to accept Libuska's sweet suggestion to come to her in Prague, but that was impossible. Prague was occupied by the Russian military, and although the United States and Russia were allies in World War II, it was off limits to the American forces. If I had gone there and was caught, I would be AWOL and would be court-martialed. The penalty could be severe. I asked Marusa to explain the problem to Libuse.

Libuska came to Rokycany every weekend and stayed with Marusa, whose family was warm and hospitable. However, they were also very strict. So to be alone, Libuska and I went for long evening walks in the picturesque countryside. We talked as best we could, and after dark, we made sweet love in lush meadows, under the stars, or in the woods, by the light of the moon. It was an idyllic summer.

Suddenly, without warning, our division was ordered to move back to Germany. Saying goodbye to Libuska was sad. If the brief summer love we had seemed doomed, parting made it even worse. We gave each other our home addresses so we could keep in touch, but I think we both knew the chance of our seeing each other again was slight.

Our Special Services group ended up in Vilshofen, a town on the Danube River. Its waters may have been blue when Johann Strauss had composed his waltz, but when I saw it in Vilshofen, the river was a sad shade of gray. I was just twenty-one, perhaps younger than my years, and I was uncertain what my future would be. I did not realize fate would take its course.

***

Back in the States, I wrote to Libuska and sent her a small gift. She answered with a loving letter translated by a friend. After some months of writing to each other, another letter came directly from her translator. It was short, with no explanation except for the following words: "It will be better for Libuse, politically, if you do not correspond with her again." At that time, Prague was still under Soviet control, and the letter disturbed me. I feared for Libuska's safety and stopped writing. So did she.

Not long after that, I had a letter from Dick's friend, Vlasta, telling me she and her new husband had to flee their country, leaving everything behind.

"We are in a refugee camp," she wrote, "and our only hope is to immigrate."

She did not say to where they would immigrate or when, and I never heard from her again.

Libuska, c. 1945.

CHAPTER 35

FALLING IN LOVE AGAIN

France, 1945

FROM THE JANUARY night our Armored Division had landed in France to our miserable, freezing truck ride to Reims and our first night's sleep on the icy stone floor in the attic of the champagne baron's mansion, Dick and I knew we weren't "in Kansas anymore." In the grueling months our armored infantry division joined other armed forces, fighting the retreating Germans, Dick and I always stuck together. Czechoslovakia had been our first taste of freedom in Europe. We both felt the people there were most like the citizens of our homeland.

In Vilshofen, Dick and I continued our normal routine: showing movies, working on our musical, and, like all GIs, waiting for a word about when we would be going home. The word didn't come.

Then one day we learned new educational rehab centers had been set up by the U.S. government in other parts of Europe. Dick and I immediately applied, and miraculously, both of us were accepted, he to a music school in England and I to the newly created Biarritz American University in Southern France. We realized it was time for us to say, "So long for now." It wasn't easy.

"You know what?" I said to Dick. "Your musical is too good for the army anyway. We should save it for Broadway."

"Deal," agreed Dick, and we shook hands. We were very confident. (We were also very young.)

Before we parted ways, Dick Besoyan and I took a
boat trip on The Rhine River together (1945).

In 1859, Empress Eugenie, wife of Napoleon III, created an enormous rococo dwelling on the rocky shore of the Atlantic Ocean in Southern France. Situated on a half-moon sandy cove, the exquisite palace was destined, a half century later, to become The Grand Hôtel du Palais, catering to the rich and famous as well as the crowned heads of Europe. The town of Biarritz prospered and grew into one of the most popular vacation spots on the Atlantic coast.

Near the end of World War II, the elegant Hôtel du Palais became one of the dormitories for soldier students of the Biarritz American University, and I was one of the lucky ones to be quartered there. Of course, when the U.S. Army took over, all the fabulous art treasures and gilded furnishings were removed. We soldiers slept on army cots, four to a room, and although we were still in uniform, we were no longer required to wear our army caps once we began classes. Best of all, there were no more military duties.

The Hôtel du Palais, where students lived while studying at the University of Biarritz in France.

The University of Biarritz was wonderfully positioned right on the beach.

Me and an acting friend on a roof of the University of Biarritz.

With excellent instructors imported from the best U.S. educational institutions, virtually all the courses offered in those institutions were offered. I enrolled in the university's Fine Arts Department's classes in painting and theater production. I finished two oil paintings—one was a dark subterranean world with a foggy "River Styx" and a figure of a man climbing a narrow winding staircase up a rocky hillside to an immense pair of open doors. A blinding light pouring from the doors promised . . . what? The unknown? Freedom? Heaven? (I still don't know.)

My second painting was a portrait of a burly longshoreman.

That was as far as I got in the class, but as I began my next semester in theater classes, I devoted free time to my social life, dating Mary Bicknell, a WAC (Women's Army Corps), and a beautiful young French girl named Regine. Both girls were introduced to me by another GI student, surprisingly named Bill Barker. He was certain we were related. We were both from the South, but my dad was from Ohio, with no Southern relatives.

"So we are distant cousins," Bill insisted.

I let it go at that, and we did become friends, so Bill and his girlfriend, Birdie, double-dated with Mary and me.

I also started to spend more time in my classes in the Theater Department. They fired my interest. I liked my teachers, and I soon became involved with three plays: *The Night of January Sixteenth*, a modern drama, *Volpone*, a Renaissance comedy, and William Shakespeare's bloody *Richard III*. They were to be full productions, with sets and costumes executed by students, and presented in the local casino. I was walking around, intoxicated by my first real experience with a life I realized I really wanted—the world of entertainment.

Before World War II, in high school, that world was the movies. I idolized many beautiful stars, like tempestuous Rita Hayworth, luscious Loretta Young, and sultry Hedy Lamarr. There was a rumor that a famous movie star was coming to Biarritz to entertain the troops. Marlene Dietrich, the most enchanting movie star of all, arrived in Biarritz the following week.

For Dietrich's one-night performance, the empty main floor of the Bon Marche, an enormous retail center, had been set up as a concert hall with a performance platform and hundreds of folding chairs. It was packed with GIs, the overflow filling the multitiered balconies above.

When the lights went down and Dietrich appeared in the spotlight, a mighty roar of male voices filled the Bon Marche. The epitome of glamour, Dietrich raised her arms and spoke into a standing microphone.

"Hello, boys," her warm husky voice rang out to what must have been a thousand young men.

I was one of them. For just a moment, I was back in Holland. The beautiful woman standing on the stage in the spotlight was the beautiful woman in U.S. Army uniform who had waved to us from the jeep passing by that rainy day in Maastricht. Yes, she was—and I was seeing her again!

"Mar-lene! Mar-lene! Marrr-lene!" chanted the audience.

Blonde and beautiful, now in a black lace gown, microphone in her hand, Dietrich moved about, waving from the stage. "Hello, boys," she purred.

The music started, and Marlene sang. "Underneath the lamp post by the barracks gate . . ." Her smoky voice flowed out over the audience. "Every night you'll see her wait . . ."

Another roar. The words of Lily Marlene were familiar to almost everyone there, so when she raised her arms and said, "Come on, boys, sing it with me," the sound of hundreds of men singing was haunting and overwhelming. For at least an hour and a half, song after song followed—old favorites like "One For My Baby," "Makin' Whoopee," and "I Can't Give You Anything But Love" as well as a few songs in French and German. Then came the touching "Where Have All the Flowers Gone?" She closed with her raucous "See What the Boys in the Back Room Will Have."

Finally, she thanked us and brought the microphone close to her lips. "I understand you boys have heard I have legs?," she whispered.

"Yeah!" the guys yelled.

"Okay-ay, fellows!" She lifted her skirts above her ankles—applause!

"Higher!" everyone yelled. "Higher!"

She lifted her skirts to her knees.

"Higher!" A chorus of yells.

Then quite, quite slowly, she lifted the black lace above her knees and showed her beautiful legs 'as far as the law allows.' There was tumultuous applause and lots of laughter!

How does she top that? She turned to a small chair and picked up a saw—a common handsaw—and a violin bow. She sat down and placed the saw's handle between her knees and bent it gently. With the bow against its smooth edge, she produced quivering, violin-like music–another haunting melody, incongruous as it was beautiful. The audience went wild!

Encore after encore followed, and then in total silence, she sang the most romantic song of all–"Falling in Love Again."

The next day was Thanksgiving. The meal was served in our mess hall, the huge lobby of the Hôtel du Palais. Hundreds of soldiers were in two chow lines that snaked across the marble floor. The lines converged at the hot table where the cooks heaped metal trays with roasted turkey, sage stuffing, candied yams, and all the fixings. The smells were mouthwatering.

From my line, I looked across the room, and there was Marlene in the opposite line, smiling and chatting with the men. She wasn't wearing the lacy black gown she had worn in her show the night before. For Thanksgiving, she was in army uniform, cap and all. As the lines dovetailed at the hot table, I ended up facing her. I was speechless. With my heart throbbing, I made a small bow and an "after you" gesture.

"Thank you," she said, smiling at me, and we were served.

When Marlene and I sat down, all the men at the table were mesmerized. Marlene spoke with each one of us and charmed us all. I was a shy Southern boy, but after we finished the holiday dinner, I managed to ask if I could have a photo taken with her.

"Of course," she said. "But I think we should go out on the terrace. There is a beautiful view of the ocean."

She slipped her arm in mine, and we strolled out into the thin sunlight. The surf crashed against the rocks below, and the chilly air smelled of salt. As my friend focused his camera, I timidly reached for her hand. The glamorous Marlene turned to me and held out her arms. The sudden pressure of her hug surprised me, and the delicate sweetness of her hair made me want to not let her go. That's how I ended up with a picture of the two of us in a cheek-to-cheek embrace on a terrace, with the Bay of Biscayne in the background. Marlene Dietrich is the beauty hugging me, and I am the surprised young soldier.

Marlene Dietrich and me in Biarritz.

Marlene Dietrich on Thanksgiving Day in Biarritz, 1945.

Flash-forward ten years to an upper floor in Bloomingdale's, New York. A stunning lady lost control of her armload of Christmas gift wrappings. The bright, shiny rolls fell to the floor, bouncing in all directions. I picked them up and held them out to her. As she took them from me one by one, she looked directly into my eyes.

"Thank you so much," Miss Dietrich said in that low unforgettable voice.

I wanted to answer, "Marlene! Biarritz, Thanksgiving... Remember?" But I didn't. Could I expect her to remember me after all the young soldiers she must have hugged in World War II? *Not a chance*, I thought. "You're welcome" was all I could say.

Perhaps she smiled. I'd like to think so.

"Thank you," she said again.

Then we both turned away to go on with our shopping.

My next encounter with Marlene Dietrich was in the following summer on Fifth Avenue. In front of Tiffany's, I saw her walking toward me. Our eyes met so briefly, I really shouldn't consider it an encounter. As she passed, I turned and watched her walking on, her high heels tap, tap, tapping on the pavement up the avenue. It made my day.

One morning a few years later, I was walking near my apartment on Manhattan's Upper East Side. The sun was shining through the trees, and there was the snap of fall in the air. In front of a brownstone house just ahead of me, I saw a grandmotherly lady sitting on a low step and hugging her knees. She was wearing a housecoat and slippers, her blonde hair done up in curlers. She was talking to a small boy who played with a toy truck on the sidewalk at her feet.

As I passed her, she looked up, and I recognized the famous face—older now, of course, and without makeup—but she was still the lovely Marlene. (I can call her Marlene now if I choose to, can't I?) I smiled briefly, and she turned back to the child. I kept on walking.

CHAPTER 36

THE FRENCH CONNECTION

Biarritz, Spring 1946

BEN RODACK, THE budding comedian from the 8th Armored SSO, had also been selected to attend Biarritz American University. He loved being onstage, and with his background, he decided to enroll in the theater department. *Volpone*, the seventh-century comedy by Ben Johnson, was the second production scheduled, and Ben auditioned and snagged the role of the avaricious miser Corbaccio. I created his age makeup, and when he saw himself in a mirror, he laughed almost hysterically, freaking out. Fortunately, in the play, Ben was excellent and received praise for his performance as the wily old man.

Ben also had a talent for charming young women. Not the handsomest young man, Ben always seemed to be the first guy in our outfit to team up with a good-looking girl wherever we were, and Biarritz was no exception. Almost as soon as we had settled into our classes, Ben was dating Gracianne, a lively French girl who lived just blocks away from our quarters at the Hôtel du Palais. He had been coming in quite late at night, sometimes not at all.

I was still seeing Mary, the sweet young WAC. Unfortunately, she was still getting over her breakup with an officer in her old outfit and was not ready for hot romance. I'd also had a few dates with Regine, a beautiful French girl, but in spite of her neurotic air of mystery and sex appeal, she remained remote. Ben took pity on me.

"Howard, I want to introduce you to a fascinating woman," he said one morning after a date with his girlfriend. "Gracianne's mother is a knockout."

"Your girlfriend's mother—are you kidding? Why would I want to meet an old lady, even if she is a knockout?"

"She's not an old lady," Ben said, laughing. "Denyse must have been very young when she had Gracianne. She can't be older than thirty-nine or forty."

"Thirty-nine or forty! Ben, I just turned twenty-one! Will you please tell me what I would do with a forty-year-old French mother of a grown-up daughter?"

"No, but it could be fun to find out," Ben answered with a mischievous grin.

So I agreed to meet Baronne Denyse de Arlot de Saint Saud. (I believe her title had something to do with owning land.) I romanticized that there might be an estate somewhere in the country and that she and her daughter just liked to spend their summers in this elegant resort by the sea.

Ben was so sure The Baronne and I would enjoy each other's company, he arranged for Gracianne and her mother to join us for a late afternoon stroll.

Denyse was an extremely attractive woman. She had raven hair, dark eyes, and lovely skin. She spoke little English, but her speech was punctuated with warm bright smiles. She was certainly years older than I, and suddenly, I was intrigued with the possibility of becoming involved with this older woman.

At sunset, we stopped for aperitifs at a small sidewalk café on "la plage," the wide crescent of white sand on the bay where the French sunned themselves alongside American military. We watched the sun as it sunk below the horizon into the Atlantic beyond.

Mother and daughter lived in a small apartment nearby, and Ben had arranged for our stroll to end up there. After a glass or two of wine, we were invited to stay for supper. Gracianne spoke English well enough to entertain us, while Denyse prepared the meal—fried eggs, salad, and baguettes. (Meat was unavailable except occasionally on the black market.) Ben, always the comedian, kept the conversation bouncing in the air. I tried to do my share by talking about our drama classes and the upcoming play and Ben's role in it. At best, my contribution wasn't great.

Fortunately, the food and wine were. Soon after a demitasse, Ben and Gracianne slipped away into the bedroom and left Denyse and me alone. Talk was out of the question, so we just sat and smiled at each other. Then Denyse put an Edith Piaf record on her phonograph.

"Danse?" she asked.

I took her hand, and we danced. How does a simple dance together turn into a raging passion? Very easily, I discovered. We soon were holding each other close, and our hearts started to pound. As we danced, Denyse pressed her cheek against mine, and I could feel her warmth on my neck. When the song ended, she put another record on, and we danced again. Now both of us were breathing heavily. Before the music ended, we sank onto the couch. After a few moments of kissing, we made love feverishly and as silently as we could. My first affair with a much older woman had begun. If Denyse was a good teacher, I became a passionate student in the Gallic school of making love.

Not surprisingly, our foursome spent a lot of time together, most of our afternoons on the beach and evenings in small clubs, ending with erotic rendezvous in their apartment. Gracianne did not seem to mind my unlikely affair with her mother and appeared to be happy with Ben, who, as usual, kept us laughing. Denyse was blooming. I bloomed a bit myself.

Mary and Regine must have seen the four of us sunning ourselves on "la plage." Surprisingly, both of them asked me the same question: "How's it going with the black widow spider?"

Regine was slightly miffed. "Comme c'est va la veuve araignee noir?"

Some of my friends approved. Others thought I was nuts. I didn't think so. I was having lots of fun. "Cousin" Bill was delighted.

"Well, at least you're learning how the French do it" was his candid remark.

"Oui, monsieur." I smiled and nodded.

Portrait from later army days.

Actually, I was also spending more and more time in the theater workshops. In addition to turning Ben into an old man for his role in *Volpone*, I was hand-painting yards and yards of fabrics to resemble baroque embroidery for the Venetian costumes worn by the women, Columba and Canina, in the same play. Halloween was coming up, and a couple of us in the theater department decided to borrow something from the university's costume department to wear that night. First, I tried on the black tights Mosca (the mosquito) was to wear in *Volpone* the following week but quickly decided against it. What if a brawl broke out in a bar and the costume was ruined? When I found a U.S. Navy uniform, I quickly changed my mind. Remembering I had wanted to be a sailor in my first year of college in 1942, I was finally going to get my wish. For one night, I was the only "sailor" in a town of a thousand soldiers in olive-drab army uniforms! In every bar we entered, I was treated to free drinks and warm slaps on my back from the GIs.

"Hello, sailor!" they'd shout. "Where's your ship?" And when I'd mumble a port, they'd say, "Well, have a drink on me!" I guess I got pretty drunk, but I had a great Halloween!

***

Autumn turned into winter. While taking classes and working on theater productions, I learned a lot about stagecraft. I also learned that making love is not the same thing as being in love. With Denyse, there was tenderness—but only after the wildness. Whatever it was, physical attraction or a fascinating ego boost, it definitely wasn't love.

By spring, my points of time in military service were finally enough for discharge. The last time Denyse and I were together to say goodbye, she gave me a present, a bottle of cologne. I don't remember the name, but it was a good one.

"It is for . . ." She searched for words. ". . .pour le corps," Denyse said and rubbed her neck and shoulders with her hands. "For the body."

"Oui, the body," I said. "Pour le corps."

Then she gave me her photograph. "Take," she said.

"Thank you so much," I said. "It's lovely. Thank you for . . . for everything."

We embraced, with kisses on both cheeks.

"I will remember you, Denyse, always," I said. And I have.

CHAPTER 37

HOME SWEET HOME

April–May 1946

THE AMERICAN TROOP ship that brought me home was certainly better than the English carrier that had taken us to war. *HOME AGAIN!* I kissed the ground when I got off the gangplank. I stayed in New York, waiting for my honorable discharge from the U.S. Army. After three years of active duty, I had been promoted to Private, First Class. *Hot dawg!* I have to admit it was not a special achievement of mine. The entire personnel of the 8th Armored Infantry Division was raised one rank on discharge.

Before I left the big city, I took in a couple of Broadway shows. I was surprised and puzzled to find my cheeks were wet when John Raitt sang his big soliloquy in *Carousel*. Tears, I realized, I had not even cried when Aunt Maggie told me my parents had died. I was eight years old then, and now I was twenty-two. Fourteen tearless years! Why? At that moment in a New York theater, I did not know.

The next afternoon, I arrived at home on Main Street in Hattiesburg. My Aunt Amber was sitting in the swing on the front porch swing, waiting for me.

"Honeybunch!" Aunt Amber called when she saw me getting out of the taxi from the airport. She came to the steps, her arms outstretched.

"I'm home! Aunt Amber!" I hugged her tight and kissed both her cheeks the way I'd learned to do in Europe. "I'm home!"

"My darlin' angel! My apple pie, my dumplin' stew!" She hugged me back and cried just a little for a moment or two. "You look a little puny," she said. "Are you hungry?"

"No, ma'am, not really."

"Did they feed you good?"

"Yessum, they did, but not as good as you. Right now, I guess I'm just a little tired."   "Well, for goodness' sake, of course, you are. Now, I fixed up your old room for you, and you go right inside and lie down. I want to hear everything that's been happening since your last letter. This evenin' at supper, you can tell me all about everything."

"Yes'sum, I will, most everything, there is a lot to tell." I hugged her again. "I need to call Bishop to tell him I am home."

"I'll wake you up to call him before you eat," she said softly and led me inside.

Laying down on my old bed, my nap was peppered with bits and pieces of dreams. I woke up, and I began to think about my plans for a career in show business. Dick and I needed to finish our musical *At Your Service*. How can I explain to my beloved Aunt Amber I wanted to leave soon for California to work with my pal so we could go to New York and storm the "Great White Way"?

The next few days, I slept a lot. I ate a lot and I talked a lot. I was able to spend time with my brother and his family. I looked up some old friends from high school and learned my old girlfriend was married. Bettie Cile had already written to tell me she had some "unfinished business" to take care of. I guess that was what she was talking about. Well, we'd all moved in different directions.

My two and a half years in the Army made me happy to be home with my aunt. Our letters, important as they were, could not take the place of her hugs and home cooking, and I needed to reunite with my brother and his family. But I still couldn't get my hopes and dreams for a life in show business out of my mind.

So after a month, I packed my bag with my civilian clothes and left my comfortable nest with Aunt Amber. She had known of my hopes and dreams for a long time, and she sent me on my way with a tear or two, and probably an aching heart. I kissed her goodbye and boarded a westbound bus.

Me and my brother, Bishop, with our Aunt
Amber after our return from the war.

CHAPTER 38

GO, GREYHOUND

On The Road, May 1946

AS I WAS leaving Mississippi on the first leg of my trip to California, my mind was full of the past behind me and the road ahead. Crossing the state line into Louisiana, I was distracted by memories of two irresistible girls: Betty Jean Godbold, a dark-haired pixie from Baton Rouge whom I adored when she was in Hattiesburg, and Satchie Cooper, a red-haired vixen from Monroe, Louisiana, whom I fell for at a high school fraternity weekend in the Pelican State. Those were the days, I mused. I wondered where the two darling girls were now. As the bus rolled on westward past Camp Polk, memories of my infantry basic training blotted their faces out.

From my seat in the bus, the endless highway across the vast state of Texas was hypnotizing. As the trip to California was getting more and more boring, we pulled into a forlorn bus stop near the border of New Mexico. The bus driver got out to help a new passenger, a cute girl with a big suitcase. She was a vision in white—a snug white dress, a little white hat and shoes, even a pair of white gloves. As she got on and looked around, I smiled at her. She politely smiled back. Except for a young sailor and a girl in the seats behind me, the bus was practically empty, but I offered her the seat next to mine anyway and introduced myself. She thanked me, smiled, and sat down. She was wearing a flowery perfume.

"My name is Penny O'Day," she said, smiling again. Penny was more than cute. She was pretty.

"Nice name," I said. "Where are you heading?"

"I'm heading for Hollywood," she said, removing her gloves. "I'm going to be a movie star."

"Congratulations," I said, shaking her hand. "With your looks and a name like Penny O'Day, I bet you'll make it." I held her hand in mine.

"Why, thank you," Penny said, "and I bet you say that to all the girls." Penny was also a bright girl.

We talked about our hopes and dreams. When the desert sun seemed to drop suddenly behind the hills, a full moon took its place. The inside of the bus grew dark. As we ran out of things to talk about, I noticed the young couple behind us get up and move to the back of the bus. I took Penny's hand in mine again, and we moved to the back of the bus too. However, since this book is about older women, there is no reason to go into the details about a night of feverish kissing and frustrating caressing, a night that reached an incredible degree of heat.

Unfortunately, when we arrived in Los Angeles the next morning, Penny declined my invitation to spend a couple of days together, and so with a final kiss, we parted. Exhausted from two days on the bus and frustrated after striking out with Penny, I registered in a cheap hotel next to the bus station and called the only person I knew who lived in Hollywood.

I had met Julie Mitchum in Europe in World War II. She was one of those many young women with show business experience who, as Civilian Army Technicians (CATs), volunteered to go overseas during the war to provide entertainment for the troops. Julie may not have been so young, but she played piano and sang with a mellow, unforgettable style. CATs wore U.S. Army uniforms, but Julie had bedroom eyes and was all woman.

Anyone who went to the movies in the forties and fifties and sixties will remember Julie's brother, Robert Mitchum, who was nominated for an Oscar for Best Actor for his role in the movie *The Story of GI Joe*. With his tantalizing drowsy-eyed look, Mitchum starred in one hit after another and, with *The Big Sleep*, became a Hollywood legend.

Julie was not a famous movie star like her brother. However, she did appear in motion pictures as well. None of them were especially memorable, but she received praise for her work in *The High and Mighty*. Like her brother, Julie had sexy eyes with the lowered lids. She also had the Mitchum profile, the prominent nose, and the slightly receding chin like Bob, but her long eyelashes and sidelong looks were totally feminine.

Our wartime meeting had been brief, but she had given me her phone number. So I called her.

"Hello, Julie," I said when her husky voice answered. "This is Howard . . . uh, remember me?"   Silence.

"Barker," I said. "Howard Barker. U.S. Army. Private Howard Barker?"

"Oh, of course. Where'd we meet?"

"In a service club, Europe, right after the war. You gave me your phone number."

"I did? Well . . . how are you?"

"I'm fine. I'm in Los Angeles."

More silence.

"I'd like to see you. Could I possibly take you out for a drink? Maybe dinner?"

"No, Howard. I don't think that's a good idea. But why don't you come here for a drink? This evening, after dinner. Okay?" Then she gave me her address.

I had never been to LA before and had no idea how spread out the city would be. After an hour with many stops, the bus reached Julie's street. Walking past a row of modest houses, I came to hers, a small bungalow. A man's voice, accompanied by a piano, was singing something operatic. I stood on the empty porch for a few moments, looking through a screen door into the living room. Julie was at the piano, and the man, with arms outstretched, was singing at the top of his lungs.

When I rang the doorbell, Julie looked toward the door and beckoned me to come in. I did. As I started to speak, she put a finger to her lips and continued to play. Finally, the man stopped singing.

"Welcome to Hollywood!" Julie said and hugged me warmly. "This is my brother John. He has an audition tomorrow."

John smiled, excused himself, and left the room.

"He's all wrapped up in opera," Julie explained.

I was surprised not to find Julie in a huge gorgeous home, the kind I had seen in the movies and fan magazines. But her plain Los Angeles bungalow was unimpressive. Never mind. She was appealing and fascinating–the lowered lids, the seductive voice, and the sweet, sincere smile as she made us a drink. We talked–small talk, easy talk–about coming back to civilian life and her work.

"I have a few gigs coming up," Julie said simply. "I play clubs. Cocktail lounges, you know."

"My buddy and I plan to take the show we've written to New York and find a producer," I said.

"You're beautiful," Julie said, taking me by surprise.

"Don't say that," I said.

Julie just smiled.

"I don't like to be called . . . that . . . beautiful."

"Why, baby?" she said. "You are beautiful."

"I don't like it," I said. "Beautiful is for a woman. I'm a man."

"And a beautiful man, you are," she said through a smile. "It's okay to be a young man and be beautiful. Get over it, baby."

"And don't call me baby. That's what I was called when I was little. I hated it."

Julie just smiled again. This wasn't going well at all. "Okay. Let's not talk about it anymore," she said.

So we didn't, but we did talk, for a long time. We talked about our work in the war, about our short meeting after it was all over, and how good it was to get home again. Julie never mentioned her famous brother, Bob, and neither did I. I was thinking how it would be to make love to her, but that didn't happen. Julie was a sweet, wise woman who happened to have bedroom eyes. I've never forgotten Julie Mitchum.

Hollywood. No movie studios, no exciting parties, no glamorous stars. The bus ride through the darkened streets back to my hotel seemed interminable. The next morning, I boarded another Greyhound headed for San Francisco. Julie's eyes stayed with me all the way.

CHAPTER 39

THE CITY ACROSS THE BAY

San Francisco, 1946

S ITTING ALONE ON the long bus up the Pacific coast highway to San Francisco was beautiful but tiring. I had seen the old motion picture *San Francisco*, starring Jeanette McDonald, Clark Gable, and Spencer Tracy, which came to mind. It was an enthralling film about the city's destruction by fire. I was daydreaming as I suddenly visualized it as the movie had portrayed it, circa 1906. I was now passing through the great modern city. We stopped at the San Francisco station for only a short time for passengers to get off, and as we crossed the Bay Bridge and approached the small town of Alameda, my daydream quickly faded away. I soon realized I had seen a lot of California but nothing at all of San Francisco.

When I got to the modest Besoyan home near the bay where Dick had grown up, I knew I was in a place like the small town where I had grown up. And when Dick's mother, Madie, welcomed me and treated me like a second son, I felt at home.

In front of Dick's childhood home. I finally made it to California!

Richard–his mother preferred to call him that–had already taken a job over in San Francisco with the Savoy Light Company. He was playing leading comic roles in Gilbert and Sullivan operettas–Koko in *The Mikado* and Sir Joseph Porter, KCB, in *HMS Pinafore*. I had never seen Dick on a stage before and looked forward to seeing him perform in the shows.

Our first trip across the bridge into San Francisco was like my brief experience in Manhattan had been. The soaring buildings of the legendary city were exciting, and attending Dick's dress rehearsals of The Savoy Light Opera and meeting the performers backstage were special treats.

Dick also introduced me to the company's producer, Barry Breden, and fibbed a bit when he told his boss I was a set and costume designer. He also told Mr. Breden I had taught theatrical makeup in France and could also make stylized wigs, which was actually true. (I had learned both in Biarritz the year before at the Biarritz American University.) I must have made a good impression on Mr. Breden because he hired me, on the spot, to create stylized makeup and wigs for the leading actors in *The Mikado*. Dick and the other major performers were delighted with their wigs and "new faces." I was kept on the payroll to teach makeup for the rest of the company. I was surprised at the producer's confidence in me and grateful for the job.

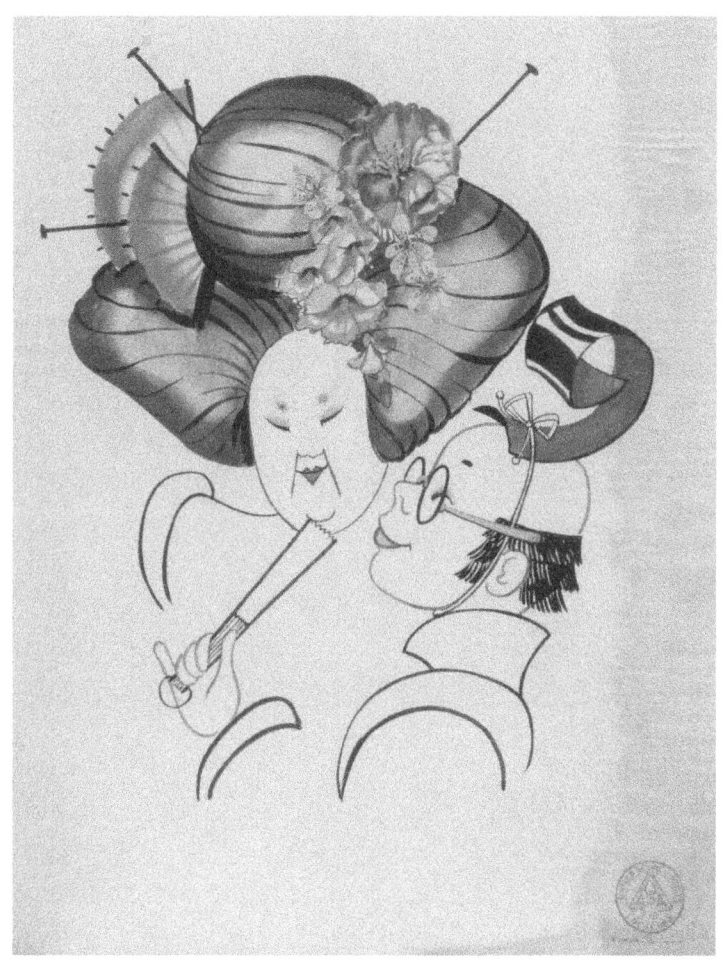

Mr. Breden also saw to it that Richard and I were invited to a gala weekend house party in San Francisco, hosted by Campbell McGregor, backer of the operetta company. McGregor, a wealthy widower living alone in a sumptuous mansion on Nob Hill, generously urged us to invite a guest for the weekend. I suddenly thought of Nell O'Mara, a classmate from Hattiesburg, who had moved to the West Coast. Nell was now living and working in a town near San Francisco. I had kept in touch with Nell sporadically since high school, but I telephoned her. She was as surprised to hear from me as I was when she had accepted the invitation. It was great to see Nell–blonde and beautiful, a perfect example of a "Southern belle." She charmed everyone. The weekend was marvelous–good food, good wine, and good company, for the most part wealthy San Franciscans.

One of the weekend guests was Juliette Miles Perkins, a widow from New York, who was probably in her late sixties, maybe even seventy, decades older than Nell, Dick, and me. Mrs. Perkins was a lovely, aristocratic woman, and she spoke with a gentle Southern accent. It wasn't an accent from my home state, more likely from Virginia or one of the Carolinas. Mrs. Perkins had dark hair, swept up in a pompadour, creamy white skin, a sweet smile, and kind eyes.

Juliette insisted on first names, and as we were seated together at dinner, we talked at length. She was gracious and asked about my life. I told her of my being an artist since childhood. I told her about the death of my parents, my war experiences, my plan to go to New York with Dick, and our hopes of finding a producer for our show. I told her of my ambition for a life in the theater and so on. Juliette was a good listener. In turn, Juliette told me many things about herself—her philosophy of life, her determination to see good in people, her loneliness, and that she was a widow. When she also told me that she was staying on as a guest of Mr. McGregor, I suspected she may have ideas of becoming the next Mrs. McGregor.

At breakfast the next morning, she asked me to look her up in New York. I was flattered and quite pleased. As we were saying goodbye, she put an envelope in my hand.

"It has my address and telephone number," she said. "Now don't forget to call me."

I promised I'd call, said goodbye, and kissed her soft white cheek. Back in Alameda, I opened the envelope. Under the monogram JMP, there was a handwritten note:

Dear Howard,

If you can find some small inspiration in these struggling lines and can feel what is in my heart today, I hope they may be the means of a small beginning to a great end. Thank you, my dear boy, for seeing something in me. I know you have the depths of understanding which should take you far. Live up to the best in you always.

The note ended with this:

By the Sea . . .
The cry of the surf as it falls on the sand
In answer to the winds that sigh in the pines
The flight of the shore birds that wing overhead
As I wait in the dusk on the wave-lapped shore
To greet in the mist which comes in o'er the land
The vision that creeps in my heart evermore

Your friend,
Juliette Miles Perkins

I showed Dick the poem. At first, he was noncommittal.

"I think it's a beautiful poem," I offered. "But I don't know what to make of it."

"Why don't you call her when we get to New York?" he asked with a sly smile on his face. "I think you'll find out."

"Richard," I said, "Juliette's an old lady."

"So . . ." was his unfinished reply.

Shortly after our San Francisco weekend, The Savoy Light Opera Company left San Francisco on a two-month tour of Southern California. While Dick was on tour, Madie and I found we had a lot of time together, and she often took me sightseeing. In San Francisco, we dodged the antique cable cars up and down the steep streets of the city and drove out to the Pacific Ocean for lunch. The Cliff House was a famous restaurant where movie stars wined and dined when they came up from Hollywood. Lining the walls were photographs of all my favorites. On our next trip into the city, Madie took me to dinner in Chinatown. It was my first taste of Chinese food, and I've loved it ever since. Another fascinating experience with Madie was our drive up north through Marin County into Muir Woods, where the ancient redwoods have flourished for centuries. I had always thought the stately long-leaf pines in Mississippi were tall, but compared to the Giant Sequoias, they are toothpicks.

Madie Besoyan on one of our many excursions.

In a short time, I grew fond of Madie, but I never thought of her as motherly. My mother–with her dark hair and eyes, her intense, sometimes emotional personality–was totally different from Richard's mother. Madie had a delightful sense of humor and an infectious laugh. As she was only in her forties and looking younger, with her bright blue eyes and light brown hair, she and I could easily have been mistaken for a couple. Nothing was further from the truth. The closest possible moment of intimacy between us might have been the night she had left her bra hanging on the back of a kitchen chair, and I pretended not to notice. To me, Madie was my best friend's mother.

I was beginning to feel the need of being with people my own age. I decided to catch up with Dick's operetta company in Los Angeles. I think Madie was probably ready to get rid of me for a bit of rest herself. So early the next morning, I hopped another Greyhound and headed south.

By late afternoon, I was watching a dress rehearsal of *HMS Pinafore* at the Patio Theater in Hollywood when I suddenly needed to go to the restroom. The door to the men's was propped open, and the cleaning staff was busy at work inside. Nobody was around, so I slipped into the ladies' room. Of course, there were no pissoirs, so I entered a toilet stall.

Apparently, a rehearsal break had been called, and just at that moment a torrent of women charged in. Instead of calling out to "the ladies" and exiting, I panicked and quickly crouched on top of the toilet stool to wait for them to do their business and leave. Then the door to my stall rattled and shook.

"Oh, it seems to be stuck!" a woman shouted to her friends. "But there's nobody in there. I looked under the door."

Whew, I thought. She couldn't see me perched up on the stool.

After listening to what seemed like an eternity of unmentionable ladies' room sounds as well as some gossip and unmentionable profanity, I figured the coast was clear and made my escape. Only a puzzled cleaning man saw me coming out. Never again was I ever in a ladies' restroom!

Madie Besoyan was a devoted Christian Scientist. I often went with her to the local Science Church on Sundays. She gave me two books: *Christian Science and Key to the Scriptures* by Mary Baker Eddy and Mrs. Eddy's biography as the church's Victorian founder. My upbringing had been traditional Methodist, and although I wasn't an actively religious person, I found the religion philosophically interesting. However, the restrictions against the use of alcohol, tobacco, and other stimulants were too stringent for me. I did continue to follow some of its principles, but I never fully embraced the religion.

Shortly before Dick and I were about to leave for New York, I had bad news from home. On a phone call from Bishop, he told me our Uncle Collin had died–flu and complications from pneumonia. It came as a shock because my uncle had always been in good health, and I immediately thought of my parents' death from the same cause.

"I don't think you should come home," Bishop went on. "He's gone. The cost of flying is too expensive. The funeral is the day after tomorrow anyway, and trains and buses would take too long. We have to be practical."

Sad news, I was thinking, *but my brother is right.*

"More news from home," Bishop went on. "This time, it's not bad."

"What are you talking about?" I interrupted him.

"Uncle Collin left us some money . . . for you and me and Aunt Amber. It's not a lot of money, about five hundred dollars for each of us. I don't know if there's something for anybody else. It's all the money Uncle Collin had when he died."

"Oh . . ." I didn't know what to say.

"Let me finish. Uncle Howard is setting up a bank account for you in New York at the home office of Chase, the bank where he works down here. Go there and identify yourself. The bank people will take care of everything. It'll help you to get started. Let me hear from you, boy." My brother sounded a little like Uncle Collin.

"Five hundred dollars! God bless Uncle Collin," I said. That seemed like a fortune to me. "All right, Bishop, I'll phone you too. Bye."

"Bye," he said.

CHAPTER 40

BROADWAY, HERE WE COME!

January 1947

DICK AND I bought our coach tickets to New York, we'd have to sleep sitting up all the way. It was a little like when we were on the troop train from San Antonio to Leesville, Louisiana, and the seats were just as hard. On the troop train, we had no idea where we were going. At least now we knew we were on our way to New York. That made all the difference.

Somewhere in one of the plains states between San Francisco and Chicago, Dick got up from his seat and handed me a folded piece of paper. I looked up to ask him what it was, but he was already walking away down the aisle. I unfolded the paper and read what he had written. I'm not revealing it here except for his last lines: "This is the only way I can tell you. If you would like to not be friends anymore, I'm sorry. I will understand." After a few minutes, he came back. He didn't say a word, and neither did I. I just folded the note in half and tore it up in little pieces. He watched me as I let them fall to the floor. I held out my hand. He took it, and we shook.

"Was that the bar car up ahead?" I asked. "Why don't we have a little drink to our future in New York?"

We did, and the train sped on.

Dick and I found a furnished room for rent on Riverside Drive. There were hundreds of beautiful old town houses and handsome apartment houses dating back to the days when an address on Riverside Drive meant you had "arrived." Now our room was affordable–ten dollars a week, five dollars each! Two unsophisticated youngsters had arrived. The unmerciful winds of early January, howling off the icy Hudson River, cut through our coats like razors and brought back memories of those January days when we had crossed France in the open troop trucks. Did we care? Not in the least. We were in NEW YORK CITY and starting our exciting life in show business!

I called Juliette Perkins, and she invited me to tea. She lived on Park Avenue in a beautiful apartment, furnished in exquisite taste. Conversation was easy, and of course, we discussed the party in San Francisco.

"It was lovely," Juliette said. "However, I . . ." She hesitated and looked around the room.

I waited for her to speak again.

"I have known Campbell a long time," Juliette said in her soft voice. "But I was not happy with his behavior the next evening."

I wondered what was coming.

"Howard," she said, "I think you know me well enough to know I am a lady."

"Yes, Juliette, of course, I do," I said.

"Well . . . what he proposed to me . . . was not marriage." She looked straight into my eyes.

"Maybe he was just terribly lonely," I said. "Maybe living alone, after losing his wife–"

"Maybe fiddlesticks!" she interrupted. "I knew Campbell's wife. She was a lady. When he held out his arms to me, I was shocked. I said, 'Goodnight, Campbell,' and left the room. I was out of that

house the next morning!" She paused for moment. "And that house! Did you evuh see such cluttah? Did you?" She pronounced the words. "Now I love things. Beautiful things. You can see I have many beautiful things myself. But Campbell's house was just too much. I could nevah, nevah live in that house. I simply can't stand cluttah!"

Then she laughed–peals of merry laughter. I knew Juliette had been troubled, but then I realized that now she was just fine.

"I understand, Juliette," I said. "I understand."

We ate small sandwiches and delicious cake and drank tea. We had a lovely afternoon, and she bid me goodbye.

My friendship with Juliette Miles Perkins was short and sweet, but I do treasure it. I wish I had known her better. Today, even as I transcribed the words of her poem, I realized this beautiful woman had a lot of love to give.

Miss Juliette Miles Perkins.

After studying a trade paper and haunting Broadway producers' offices for weeks, Dick and I actually got a chance to audition our show. While the producer and his staff watched, Dick played the score on the piano and sang the lyrics. I held up my sketches of the sets and costumes.

"Hey, good stuff. And call me Burt."

It would be nice if I remembered the producer's last name and even nicer if I could say Burt was ready to sign us up and produce *At Your Service* at once, but that wasn't the case.

"Boys," he said, "great show, but . . ."

The broad smiles on our faces began to fade.

"I'm already committed to another show. However, I can use your talents on that one. It'll be great," he went on. "Howard, I need designs for the show. I'll introduce you to the writers. They'll love you guys. Dick, you can play the piano and sing their songs for the backers' auditions. Don't worry, you'll get paid–after we open."

I designed costumes for the principal characters of the show and held them up as Dick played the piano and sang for a few auditions, but our relationship with Burt was almost as brief as his name. Nothing came of all our efforts, and all we got from Burt was "I'm sorry, guys. That's show biz." Then we ran out of money. We didn't know anyone, so we couldn't borrow. We couldn't move in with my cousin in Long Island. We couldn't go home. We had just enough for a few more days of food when Dick got a job waiting tables in a Howard Johnson's. His first paycheck was slow in arriving, and his tips covered only his subway fare and very little for food. I got a small art job, an illustration for the cover of a music catalog, but I also had to wait for my paycheck. Then one night Dick came in from work with a surprising announcement.

"Howard, I'm moving out."

I didn't understand what he meant. I guess I was speechless.

"I've met a guy at work, and I like him. He likes me too," Dick said quietly.

I understood what he meant. "Well . . . That's good . . . I guess," I said. "But what do you mean you're moving out?"

"He's got a small apartment downtown, and he's asked me to move in with him. It was a surprise for me. I know this seems sudden."

I didn't know what to say.

"The whole thing is sudden for me too–a new experience. Howard, I'm kind of like a babe in the woods, but I think this is right for me. And with my job at the restaurant, I'll just be able to pay my share of the rent." Dick stopped talking. His eyes were asking for understanding. "But if I move out, what are you going to do?" he asked.

"Well, actually, the guy I designed that music catalog cover for told me he has a large apartment and rents rooms to some college students. He even promised me some more art jobs. Don't worry, Dick. I'll be okay."

"So I guess we put show business on hold for a little while, huh?" he said.

"Yeah," I said. "Like the old saying, nobody promised us a rose garden."

"No. But we'll keep in touch?"

"Right," I said. "We'll keep in touch." But it wasn't the same.

In hopes of getting work modeling or as an extra on small productions,
I had some professional photos taken, but that never really took off.

CHAPTER 41

FIRE AND ICE

Greenwich Village, New York, 1947

MOVING THREE TIMES in three months–from a furnished room with Dick on Riverside Drive to sharing a large West Side apartment with a bunch of college kids and then moving into an almost empty basement apartment in Greenwich Village–was not as unnerving as it might sound. Actually, I was just enjoying the poor but freewheeling life of a Manhattan newcomer.

William Graham, an actor friend of Dick's from San Francisco who had recently arrived in New York and enrolled in a drama school, offered to share that basement apartment in The Village with me. For half the rent, it was a better deal than the overcrowded "college dorm." With the exception of my having to buy a new box spring and mattress, the two of us furnished the apartment with "odd and ends" of furniture and stuff left on the street plus discarded pieces from upstairs tenets. The result was not at all bad. In fact, it was pretty attractive. It also turned out to be practical. Our kitchen utensils were a donation from the superintendent's wife. Bill was very neat, and I was reasonably so. Bill knew how to cook, and I was able to do the basics like breakfast, snacks, and canned soups. We both had a sense of humor, which was a blessing. We entertained frequently. Some friends did potluck dinners with us, and we retaliated. We got along surprisingly well.

Autumn was coming in quickly, and there was a snap in the air. One of Bill's friends who lived in a Greenwich Village walk-up was giving a party for students of the Neighborhood Playhouse, and I was invited. As I started to climb the steps to the top floor, I looked up and saw a stunning creature on the landing above me. She had white skin, high cheekbones, bright red lips, and long black hair. She was wearing a full-length black cape, and she was looking down at me.

In a style reminiscent of Mae West, she crooned, "Hello, big boy. Why don't you come up and see me sometime?"

When I got to the top of the stairs, I saw her eyes–blue, blue eyes.

"I'm Paula," she said. "Who are you?"

"I'm enchanted," I replied like a smart-ass, but then I told her my name.

She flashed a smile at me as white as her eyes were blue. "You don't go to the Playhouse, do you?" It was almost an accusation.

"No, I don't. I'm a friend of Bill Graham's."

"Well, I'm just leaving." She flung her cape across her shoulder. "I'm at the Barbizon. Call me." She brushed past me and was halfway down the stairs before I called after her.

"What's the Barbizon?" I shouted.

She stopped for a moment. "The Barbizon," she said, looking over her shoulder. "You know, The Hotel for Women. It's on Lexington. Look it up."

"Then what's your last name?" I shouted to her back.

She turned and flashed a bright smile. "Oh, of course–Morgan. Paula Morgan, from Hollywood." She smiled again and was gone.

"Paula Morgan." When Bill said her name, she sounded like a movie star or a character in a book. "Paula's something else," he said, laughing. "Her father's in the movie business. He sent her here to learn to act."

"I liked her," I said and looked up Barbizon Hotel for Women in the phone book.

The next day, I made a date with Paula.

"Men are not allowed to visit young ladies in their hotel rooms," she said on the phone. "So when you get here, they'll direct you to the Visitors' Suite."

I had been waiting for nearly half an hour, sitting alone in the elegant room, when Paula made her "entrance."

"So sorry, darling. I was on the phone with Daddy," she said. "What would you like? A Coke? Maybe a sandwich?"

"No, I don't think so. Why don't we go for a walk?"

"A walk," she said. "A walk? Where?"

"Central Park. It's not far."

"That sounds divine," Paula said.

And that was the beginning of one of the most frustrating affairs in my life. The word *affair* was not exactly the right word to describe my relationship with Paula Morgan, but what had started that day with the walk in the park was exciting and frustrating. It was a perfect New York autumn day. Clear, and bright. We bought pretzels from a vendor, then hot dogs from another vendor. We lay in the grass and talked for hours. We played the game "If you were a tree, what would you be? If you were a bird, what would you be? If you were a song, which would you be?" and on and on. We were young. I was only twenty-two, and Paula couldn't have been more than a few years older.

At some point, lying on the grass late in the afternoon, we kissed. We kissed and kissed and kissed some more. We were totally unaware of the people around us. Maybe we just didn't care because everything seemed so wonderful. We strolled through the zoo and watched the seals. Instead of walking by the lake, we danced all the way to the carousel. We rode the plunging horses and tried to sing to along with the wheezing music of the calliope. We saw each other every day for a week, and every day I sat alone on the subway to The Village, rocking back and forth, eyes closed, with something like a hot baked potato inside my jeans.

Paula was an extrovert. She would exclaim, "I've never been so happy in all my life!" and throw her arms around me. She'd hug me so tightly, I could hardly breathe. Then she wouldn't see me for days.

"Darling, I do have classes, you know." Or "I'm working on a scene for Sandy. He's very demanding." Or "Daddy is in town this weekend. I've got to have lunch and dinner with him."

"Can't I meet him?" I would ask.

"I don't think that's a good idea," she would say.

"Why?" I asked. "Is your dad jealous of the young men you go out with?"

Paula's face became mask-like. Her frown appeared, and the tiny lines around her eyes seemed to deepen. "That's a horrible thing to say to me," she said. Her voice was low. "Horrible!" Then she smiled. "Oh, never mind. Daddy's brought some papers for me to sign. Important papers."

"Well, what about Sunday?"

"He's leaving for the coast Sunday night."

Then suddenly, Paula couldn't get enough of me. If I happened to be busy, she would become despondent.

"Are you involved with someone else?" she would demand dramatically. "Who is she?"

"No. I'm not. There's no one else. Don't be silly."

Paula could also be cruel. "You'd better watch out for that roommate of yours. He's queer as a goat, you know."

"I know." I had known about Bill when I agreed to share the apartment with him. But I wanted to get out of that crowded college-kids apartment, and Bill seemed like a nice guy. It worked out fine. We didn't impose our private lives on each other. We had an agreement—no casual surprise visitors or entertaining dates in the apartment. Besides, I planned to get my own place as soon as I could afford it.

The Barbizon was an elegant hotel, but it was strict. Younger women had a curfew—10:00 p.m. On Saturdays, it was eleven. Maybe the rules were required by out-of-town parents. But it did put a crimp in young physical appetites. We had to hug and kiss in movies and on park benches in the evenings, but whenever I "went too far," Paula would become quiet and pull away. Then just as suddenly, she would snap out of it and become her affectionate self again.

Fall turned into winter, and Paula's schooling became more demanding. Daddy came to New York more often. I got a job and started skiing with friends on weekends when I could afford it. When Paula and I did see each other, the magic had begun to fade. We both knew our romance wasn't going anywhere. Finally, the day came when we just didn't call each other anymore.

A few years later, I saw Paula in a movie, *David and Bathsheba*. She had a small part. It should have been larger. Paula was beautiful—high cheekbones, white skin, no tiny lines in her face, long black hair, blue eyes, and lips as red as the long red robes she was wearing as she kneeled at the crucifixion. I remember she was about to be stoned to death by an angry mob. Jesus said something like "Let anyone among you who is without sin cast the first stone." In the movie's credits, Paula was listed as "The Adulteress."

I suppose what we had wasn't love. Maybe it was just what Cole Porter's smart lyrics said—"It was great fun, but it was just one of those things."

CHAPTER 42

MON DIEU, SUIS LA
CALLEDON—CASSERON

Manhattan, 1947

IN 1947, AFTER our "army-conceived musical" was not optioned for Broadway, Dick and I still found it necessary to eat. Waiting on tables at Howard Johnson's provided food for him but not much else. Just as I was running out of money, I got a job in an East Side decorating firm named Reed and Stevenson. By coincidence, Capt. Robert Stevenson, U.S. Army, had been my teacher in the costume department at Biarritz University in France. As a fashion designer in New York, he had been known as Don Ten Eyck. As Captain Stevenson, he had been kind enough to suggest I get in touch if I was in New York. I was, I did, and voilà! Le job!

I found this photo from our war days, Capt. Robert Stevenson with
one of our customers, Madame Maynard, on the right and, on the left,
a friend from the Woman's Army Corps in France just after WWII.

On the parlor floor of a turn-of-the century town house, Reed and
Stevenson specialized in expensive wall decorations for occupants of the
sumptuous apartments and elegant town houses in the surrounding area. The
work staff consisted of four young men, including me, plus a delightful lady,
Mrs. Elinor Robbins. Elinor was a wealthy friend of Robert Stevenson. On the
shady side of forty, she was petite and attractive, bright and jolly, and the job
gave her something to do with her spare time. She had artistic talent, and she
enjoyed working with the four of us guys. Among other pieces of wall decor,
we created framed shadow boxes with antique lead soldiers marching in front
of architectural etchings of French palaces and chateaus. Elinor's specialty
was hand-painting the tiny figures with a tiny brush.

Elinor and I had one thing in common: we both adored Marlene Dietrich.
The huge photo poster of Dietrich put on the wall of our atelier by Elinor was
a daily reminder of my Thanksgiving dinner with the enchantress in Biarritz.
Looking down at us with her eyelids lowered, Marlene seemed to be saying,
"Okay, kids, keep your minds on business."

Here I am with Bob Freeman working at Reed and Stevenson and Elinor's poster of Marlene Dietrich hanging on the wall behind us.

A short time after I had started working at the shop, Elinor invited me to a masquerade party, a big charity ball at the Waldorf Astoria Hotel. She was all excited about it and planned our costumes.

"I'll be a circus ringmaster," she said. "Remember the Cecil Beaton photograph of Dietrich as a ringmaster? She wore a top hat, white tie, and tailcoat with short shorts to show off her gorgeous legs. I'll do the same. Of course, I won't look like Marlene, but I hope I'll be okay."

"You'll look great," I assured her.

Elinor grinned. "I'll carry a crop, and you'll be my trained horse," she said.

"Your trained horse? Ohhh . . . kay. Yeah, I can make a horse's head out of papier-mâché, black with a white mane, and I'll wear a black body suit. We'll be stunning."

My first masquerade ball! It was a glamorous, glittering evening. Hundreds of New York's socialites, preening in elaborate fancy dress, paraded past us, but Elinor and I won second prize!

Elinor and I dressed up for the masquerade ball.

Our work for Reed and Stevenson wasn't all mundane like cutting mats and framing prints. We were often asked to create unique pieces for special clients. For example, one of my projects, a custom job for a Broadway producer, was a gilt-framed shadow box containing a commemorative plate for *Life with Father*, the longest running hit in New York at that time. On the plate was a caricature of the play's stars, Dorothy Stickney and Howard Lindsey. I backed the plate with a gold-printed *Playbill* background and a pair of gold theater tickets. A golden cloth miniature proscenium curtain framed it all just inside the shadow box. My job was a hit with the producer.

Not only was Elinor a fun-loving person, but also, she loved to ski, and she often took us coworkers with her. We were virtually beginners, and she was our coach. Elinor's husband, Robby, didn't ski, so he was happy to stay home with their small son while his wife had four young men adoring her on the snowy slopes of Massachusetts, Vermont, and even New Hampshire. After work on Friday, the evening usually began with cocktails and dinner at the Robbins' handsome Madison Avenue apartment. Then with a thermos of martinis and a bag of sandwiches for a midnight snack on the road to one of those ski areas, we'd take off in her big car for a New England weekend.

After a great day of skiing on one of our trips, Elinor and I started flirting a little during cocktails and dinner. When dinner was over, our group headed up to bed. She dragged her leopard coat behind her up the chalet stairs. Halfway, she turned and looked back down at me with a smile a mile wide.

"Mon dieu, suis la calledon–casseron," Elinor said, giggling.

I didn't have a clue what her fractured French meant, but I followed her. At the top of the stairs, she turned, touched my cheek, and then entered her room and left the door open. I was tempted for a moment to go in, but something stopped me and made me continue walking farther down the hall to my own room and sleep by myself. The next morning at breakfast, our conversation was all about snow conditions. All of us had a great day of skiing ahead.

One day a friend of Elinor's named Bee-Gee dropped by Reed and Stevenson to say hello. She was a gorgeous woman who could have been Dietrich's double. Her prematurely white hair looked like platinum blonde and created a striking frame for her beautiful face. I was intrigued. At a young twenty-two, I was properly respectful of gray-haired ladies, but now this one was suddenly turning me on. Bee-Gee's smiles and direct eye contact made me think it might be possible for us to have more than just social chit-chat. Because this super good-looking lady was a close friend of Elinor's, my guess put her at twice my age. *But what the hell?* I thought. Denyse in Biarritz, was in her forties, and that affair had worked out just fine. The following day at work, Elinor came in with a broad smile.

"What did you say to Bee-Gee yesterday?" she asked.

"Nothing special," I said. "Just small talk."

"Well, you must have said something more interesting than that," she said. "She wants me to bring you by for cocktails tomorrow."

Bee-Gee lived on Park Avenue in an elegant apartment. The three of us had hors d'oeuvres and drinks and pleasant talk for an hour. Then it seemed to be over. Elinor and I rose to leave.

"Help me carry this out to the kitchen, will you, Howard?" Bee-Gee asked.

As I put the glasses in the sink, I felt her hands on my waist. When I turned around, she gave me a quick kiss on my lips.

"Can you come back later?" she asked. "After you put Elinor in a cab."

"You bet," I said. I was back in ten minutes.

"We don't have much time," she said. "I'm expecting someone."

"Then why did you ask me to come back?" I asked

"Because I want to see you," she said. "Alone. What about tomorrow?"

"Fine," I said. "What's wrong with tonight?"

"The man who pays for my apartment is dropping in tonight," she answered.

This situation was suddenly getting complicated.

"If he pays for your apartment, does he have a key?" I asked.

Bee-Gee admitted he did. "But that's all right. He always calls before he comes. And you can have your own key too."

"I don't think so," I said. "Look. I've got a little place in the Village. Why don't I make some dinner for us? It will be nice and private." What I was thinking was also *nice and safe.*

I prepared the only dish I knew how to make–"Newcomers Casserole," made with canned tuna, mushroom soup, and potato chips. All poor young newcomers to New York learned how to make it. I added a small can of green peas to 'jazz it up,' put it in the oven, and made a salad. Bee-Gee arrived on time.

"I brought a bottle of scotch," she said. "I didn't know if you had any."

"Great," I said. "Thanks."

I had just spent next to my last few bucks on a fifth of scotch, which I knew she liked. I didn't, and I never drank it. But that night, I did–maybe too much.

After dinner, Bee-Gee came out of the bathroom wearing just a black slip. She looked lovely. She smiled, got into bed, and patted the pillow next to hers. As I undressed, her eyes moved up and down my naked young body, and I jumped in bed. We moved closer together. On our second kiss, I was suddenly overwhelmed with a wave of nausea.

"Excuse me," I said, and I got up quickly, dashed for the bathroom, and threw up.

When I came out, weak and shaken, Bee-Gee was sitting up in bed.

"What's the matter, darling?" she asked.

"I don't know," I said. "I'm sick, really sick. I'm sorry." I sat on the side of the bed, holding my head. I was in bad shape.

"Do you think I should go?" she asked after a minute or two.

"Well, maybe you'd better," I said. "I'm so sorry."

She went. My head was swimming. I lay down. I was miserable. Maybe it was the scotch. Maybe it was the casserole. It could have been the combination. But I suspect it was none of the above. I suspect somehow it had something to do with my ingrained respect for gray-haired ladies and, just possibly, the realization you don't necessarily have to hop in bed with every attractive older woman who comes on to you.

Bee-Gee and I didn't try to rekindle the small fire we had started. There were a couple of phone calls, that's all. I did see her, however, just once more. It was winter. One night on Park Avenue I was leaning into a bitter wind near the Waldorf Astoria. I saw a familiar Dietrich-like figure standing alone, gazing into a shop window. Maybe Bee-Gee was just looking at the merchandise, but she seemed to be in a reverie. She hadn't seen me. I started to say hello, but instead, I turned and walked away.

CHAPTER 43

KENNEBUNKPORT PLAYHOUSE

NYC and Maine, 1948

MARCH COMES IN like a lion and goes out like a lamb–or so the old saying goes. This year, as it was going out like a lamb, I found myself involved with my first job in theater production.

I had looked up a lovely actress, Elizabeth Blake, whom I'd met when she was a CAT in wartime Europe. They were involved with entertainment units in the military service. (And yes, we had a minor romantic fling.) Liz was now a member of The Traveling Players, a small acting group, and they needed a set designer for their next play. At that time, I had not even heard of Oscar Wilde, the playwright, nor his brilliant Victorian comedy *The Importance of Being Earnest*, but I was wild to do the job, and I designed the set.

The group had precious little cash for the set and less for the designer. The result was a simple set, and it was built by the actors in the courtyard outside the basement apartment I shared with Bill Graham. It turned out that I also made food for the cast while they also rehearsed there. The actors were a talented bunch, and I'm sure the play, on the road, was delightful. I never saw it.

My second set design job was in New York, but it was also a small theater production. Another pretty actress I had met–Betty was a restaurant waitress–told me she was going to be in an Equity Library Theater showcase of *Hotel*

Universe, a drama by Phillip Barry. It had been well received years earlier on Broadway. When I told her I was a set designer, she introduced me to the play's director. He looked at some of my sketches and hired me to design the set.

"There is no payment," he said, "but hey, it's a showcase. theater producers will come and see your work. It could lead to a real job."

No producer saw my first "real job" on this showcase production, which was carrying a twenty-foot-long pipe with the young female stage manager from 44th street to 75th street on our young shoulders. The twenty-dollar prop budget couldn't cover the cost of a truck, and the modest production didn't lead to a real job, but I was asked to do another Equity Library showcase. The play was *Men in White*, Sidney Kingsley's drama about doctors. It had also been a success on Broadway in the thirties and a major motion picture. I was hoping that a producer or director would see my work and that it might lead to a job, any job, as a set designer. As it turned out, a director did see the show and located me backstage after the performance.

"I liked your sets," the director said, smiling as he shook my hand. "I know your budget was minuscule, but you solved the problem most effectively. I especially liked the malachite green wall color."

I was beaming, thanking him profusely, but I was almost in shock when he offered me a ten-week season at a summer theater in Maine.

"I think you'll do a good job," Mr. Fellows said, flashing another smile. "I always go on my intuition." Then my shock became a bit more complicated when he continued to hold my hand and said, "Tell me, do you think you'd sleep with your director?"

It took a moment for me to be able to answer. "I, uh, I think we should just wait and see," I said.

Mr. Fellows slowly let go of my hand. "Fair enough," he said with an easy laugh. "You've got the job either way." He never mentioned the subject again.

I arrived at the Kennebunkport Playhouse in Maine several weeks later. It was a charming little theater in a charming little town. The first play was to open soon, so I got right to work drawing plans for my first job as a professional set designer.

ROBERT C. CURRIER presents . . .

The Kennebunkport Playhouse

★

starring

THE GARRICK PLAYERS

EIGHTEENTH SEASON

The company of actors at the Kennebunkport Playhouse was typical of most summer theater companies—a leading man and leading lady, a "character" man and a "character woman," usually older actors who fill other adult roles. Young male and female actors may join the company when needed, and I learned that following the practice of many seasonal theaters, guest stars were imported for leading roles in certain plays. Those who came to The Playhouse that summer turned out to be delightful people and solid performers. Our company included a juvenile, a personable young man with a talent for comedy who assumed parts in a number of plays. Parts for young girls and young men were sometimes played by apprentices (aspiring students who worked in various jobs to earn their keep). In addition to working backstage and sometimes on, the apprentices would strike (take down) the set each week after the last performance on Saturday nights and help install the scenery for the following week's play. I supervised the work until the wee hours of Sunday mornings. The apprentices at Kennebunkport attended acting classes conducted by playwright Horton Foote, the director of a theater group from Washington, D.C.

Our company leading man was an actor-singer, Richard Eastham, and the leading lady was Barbara Joyce. Both had backgrounds on Broadway, and both played second leads when guest stars came to Kennebunkport. Still in her twenties and not yet a major star, Miss Joyce earned excellent notices when she played leads or "the other woman." I soon learned she also had an impressive array of New York radio and television credits. In addition to her sparkling talent, Barbara was lovely, and with her joyful personality, she was irresistible.

I had ten plays to design and draw plans for, with meetings and hours of shopping for set decor in the neighborhood stores and friendly Kennebunkport citizens' homes. As the resident set designer, I supervised the building of the scenery by the staff carpenter. With help from the apprentices, I also chose furniture and other decorations, down to the last detail, to make it ready for the director and actors to take over.

Myself dressing one of the sets.

I am sitting in the center of all the actors on my set
on Summer Theater in Kennebunkport.

The summer opened with *Petticoat Fever,* a romantic comedy that had been successful on Broadway some years earlier. The guest star was James Lanphier, a charming New York actor who played a love-deprived young fellow living alone in a cabin at a weather outpost in Alaska. Barbara Joyce played an adventurous young woman who arrived unexpectedly when her plane made a forced landing on the frozen tundra. Naturally, they fall in love– that is, the characters in the play, not Barbara and James. The two of them made an attractive, amusing couple. Audiences loved it. So did I.

I was involved with the following week's show when Sunday night, after the dress rehearsal, a chance encounter with Barbara led to fireworks of the most exciting kind: I slept with our leading lady.

Barbara Joyce's headshot.

CHAPTER 44

SUMMER AND SMOKE

Kennebunkport, Maine, 1947

H ER CABANA WAS warm and dark. It was hot outside in the summer sunshine, but we had closed the door and pulled down the window shade. Lying next to each other in the narrow bed, we were both breathing heavily. I touched her hair, damp and curling around her forehead.

"It's strange," I said, "I've always been involved with brunettes, not with blondes."

"Really?" she said, looking up at the ceiling.

"Well, maybe a few times. But almost always with dark-haired girls."

She looked at me and laughed.

"What?" I said. "What's funny?"

She sat up. "Well, you've done it again," she said and laughed again. "I'm not really a blonde." "You're not blonde?" I was astonished.

"No. I have naturally dark hair." She smiled a beautiful smile. "Peroxide can do amazing things, you know," she said.

"So . . ." I didn't know what else to say.

"So what do we do now?" she asked.

"We get to know each other," I said. "Blondes can do amazing things too, you know."

We kissed and made love again and then spent the rest of the afternoon talking–where we were from, where we had been, what we had done, what we wanted to do. By the time we had left the cabana, one of the ten small rooms clustered against the side of the Kennebunkport Playhouse, it was nearly six thirty and time for dinner. Several actors, leaving their cabanas with polite smiles on their faces, joined us as we headed for the company dining room. It was promising to be a marvelous summer.

When Lanphier returned a few weeks later to play John, the witch boy, in *Dark of the Moon*, a drama set in the Appalachian Mountains, he bewitched the audiences as well as the entire company. Barbara, his leading lady again, played Barbara Allen, the impetuous mountain girl who falls in love with this exotic, otherworldly creature. The mountain folk, reacting with fear and horror, turn against her for consorting with a witch, and they allow the town bully to "purify her" by violently raping her in a church ritual. The haunting drama ends on the mountainside with Barbara Allen dying in the witch boy's arms. Tearful audiences were enchanted with Barbara's touching performance. So was I.

Our summer stock company in Kennebunkport was also enchanted by Libby Holman, the guest star who had come to Maine to play the lead in a delightful Broadway chestnut *Here Today*. Holman was a smoke-voiced torch singer who had made headlines with the songs "Moanin' Low" and "Can't We Be Friends?" in *The Little Show* as well as "Something to Remember You By" and the unforgettable "Body and Soul."

Onstage in Kennebunkport in *Here Today*–with her svelte figure, jet-black hair, and outrageous sense of humor–Libby was an extremely appealing woman. She had an electric personality, and her performance in the farce was mercurial. Her comic timing was amazing, and her "business" (silent actions onstage) was unique. Audiences loved her.

Two elderly sisters came to matinees of each play at The Playhouse. Extremely conservative, they still enjoyed the racy comedy.

"Miss Holman was real funny, Bob," one sister confided to owner Currier.

"You betcha boots," the other sister piped up. "She was so funny, I almost laughed right out loud!"

Week Beginning
MON. AUG. 2
ROBERT C. CURRIER
Presents

LIBBY
HOLMAN
- in -

"HERE
TODAY"
By
George Oppenheimer
- with -

Robert Bardwell
James Lanphier
Barbara Joyce
Dick Eastham

Directed by
HUGH FELLOWS
Settings by
Howard Barker

I'd like to say Libby and I had a red-hot love affair in Kennebunkport, but nothing could be further from the truth. I didn't fall in love with Libby, but I did fall in love with her talent. Besides, I was smitten with Barbara Joyce, and I couldn't handle more than one affair at a time.

I often stood behind the last row of the theater, watching the plays to see how the actors worked in my sets. Barbara was a gifted actress and always seemed comfortable onstage, whatever show she was in. As Tracy Lord in Phillip Barrie's *The Philadelphia Story*, Barbara brought her own version of the comedic sophistication in the role that Katharine Hepburn (the original Tracy on Broadway and the motion picture) brought to it. Like Hepburn, Barbara could also be tender. She inhabited my set, the terrace of the wealthy Lord family's home, as if it were her own.

In the final moments of the play, Tracy stands looking through the French doors. Dexter, her ex-fiancé, dictates as Tracy makes an announcement to the one hundred wedding guests waiting in the Lord family living room offstage.

"Now if you will just be patient a few more minutes," Barbara spoke with real tears in her eyes, "there will be a wedding after all . . . as originally and most beautifully planned."

Then she turned to her leading man, and they kissed as the curtain came down. The audience was delighted.

Week Beginning MONDAY, JULY 12, 1948

Evenings at 8:30 --- Wednesday Matinee at 2:15

Robert C. Currier presents

"*The Philadelphia Story*"

A Comedy in Three Acts by
PHILIP BARRY

- with -

Barbara Joyce, Dick Eastham,
James Lanphier

Staged under the Personal Direction of
HUGH FELLOWS

Settings by Howard Barker
Lighting by Sven Peterson

Barbara Joyce

Even though she was occupied with her roles in seven of the plays that season and I with my own demanding work, we still found time to be together as often as possible. In addition to the delightful love affair, we got to know each other pretty well. I've always loved talent, and at times, I've mistaken that kind of love for the real thing. Without a doubt, I was attracted to Barbara's talent, but my feelings for her were turning into something much stronger.

Barbara was from Oakland, California. She told me she had married at an early age, against her parents' wishes, and was divorced a year later. She fled to New York, studied acting with the legendary Michael Chekhov School, and had a fling there with yet-to-be-famous fellow student Yul Brynner.

Her career took off, and after appearing in several Broadway plays interspersed with seasons of summer stock, she spent a year in Washington, acting and teaching with Horton Foote's theater group.

In my first season of summer stock in Kennebunkport, I was new to the intoxicating theater world. I may have been inexperienced next to Barbara and the other professionals, but I was happy and besotted with love. Our attachment was known by everyone. Some were amused, and some may have even envied us, but we were a popular twosome. There were a few other pairings-off, chiefly among the apprentices, as well as a couple of stormy relationships, one between two charming young women and the other between the theater's owner and the company juvenile. The company took everything in its stride.

The season rolled along, the plays came and went, and all of us played our parts. Even I, who had never been trained as an actor, had my chance. The director cast me in a small part, literally a walk-on, as the old doctor in *Life with Father*. With my age makeup, beard, and powdered gray hair, I looked very much like I had as the old pet shop owner in *Early to Bed*, the senior play back in high school.

My life in Kennebunkport was going beautifully until one late summer day. I was outside on the deck next to the scene shop, painting a flat for the next show, when I saw Barbara and a man walking toward her cabana. I was puzzled and then surprised as they both entered and closed her door. The two apprentices who were helping me with the scenery noticed my staring.

"That's Vincent Donehue," one of them said. "He's Barbara's boyfriend from our group in DC."

I watched as Barbara closed the door behind her and her visitor. I threw my brush into the water bucket and sat down on the edge of the deck. The apprentices went into the shop, but I couldn't take my eyes off Barbara's closed door. I was puzzled and angry.

What seemed like hours later, her door opened, and the two of them came out of her cabana. Mr. Donehue looked very serious, but Barbara was smiling. I was miserable. When I stood up, they saw me and walked over to the deck.

"Howard, this is Vincent Donehue," she said. "Vincent is director of the group in Washington."

We shook hands. I was not happy to meet him, and I probably showed it. He was cordial.

"I'll see you at dinner?" he said.

"Of course," Barbara answered. After he left, she hugged me and kissed me. "Darling," she said, "Vinnie and I had to talk."

"Oh, you did? Really?" I snapped. "For three hours?"

"You noticed?"

"I noticed."

"Howard, look at me. There's nothing between Vincent and me. There never has been, really. I do admire him tremendously, but that's all. He insists he's in love with me, but honestly, it's really just platonic. You have nothing to worry about."

After calming down, I accepted her explanation. The three of us had dinner together, and Vincent Donahue returned to Washington, D.C.

A few short weeks later, our summer season ended. Robert Currier, the theater owner, threw a farewell party for the company on the stage. It was a great evening, but now it was time for all of us to say goodbye and go our separate ways. I was faced with a serious problem: how could I say goodbye to Barbara Joyce?

CHAPTER 45

WASHINGTON MERRY-GO-ROUND

August 1948

A S IT HAPPENED, I didn't say goodbye to Barbara Joyce after all. We had our own "farewell party" in her cabana. Since there were no double beds in the cabanas, I later spent a restless night in my own single. When I woke up early in the morning, I went to knock on Barbara's door. It was open, and Barbara was packing. I watched her distribute things into suitcases for a minute or two.

"Why don't you spend a few days with me?" I blurted. "I mean, uh . . . in New York . . . before you go to Washington? I mean . . ." I gave up.

"I think that's a great idea," she said and hugged me.

I called Bill to break the news that I was bringing my girlfriend back to New York to spend a few days with me. Being a nice guy, he suggested he could move out while she was there.

"Three's a crowd," he said over the phone with a laugh. "I'll bunk with a friend. You'll have the place to yourselves."

Bill wasn't there when Barbara and I had arrived. I unlocked the door, and we went in. I looked around our basement apartment. Suddenly, the one room seemed so small.

Barbara must have said, "Nice." I was thinking, *But so small!*

We were opening our suitcases when Bill dropped in to welcome us. He and Barbara chatted about show business and seemed very much at ease.

"I think you'll have everything you need," Bill said. "Fresh towels, clean sheets, and I laid in a few groceries–things for breakfast and lunch." He started for the door. "Now you kids just settle in and . . . have fun."

"Thank you. I'll be out of your way in a few days," Barbara said to Bill. "I have to get back to Washington and get on with life."

Bill left, and we finished unpacking in silence. I couldn't think of anything to say. A love affair in summer stock is one thing. Figuring out the next step is another. I didn't know what to do with myself. Barbara did. She called a few agents, made some appointments, and made plans to be in and out, seeing people during her next few days in New York. We didn't talk very much. I don't think I realized it at the time, but Barbara must have sensed something was troubling me. (A woman's intuition can be a wonderful thing.)

"Why don't you call some of your friends and catch up with what's been going on around town the weeks you were gone?" she suggested. "They're probably wondering how your summer went."

Her advice worked. After talking to a few people, my outlook on life was one hundred percent brighter.

We were still in bed the next morning when Barbara called Horton Foote about getting back to Washington. She stopped talking and was listening.

"Darling," she said to me, holding her hand over the phone, "Horton told the institute about this wonderful set designer he'd met in summer stock–that's you–and if you're interested, there's a job for you teaching there this fall!"

Without thinking, I grabbed the phone. "Tell them I accept!" I shouted to Horton.

All three of us yelled, "Hooray!"

"This calls for a celebration," I said, pulling on my pants. "I'm going to the liquor store!"

Sometimes champagne can do wonderful things, and this time, it did. Barbara suggested she go to Washington first to find a place for us to live.

"I can stay with Angela," she said. "Maybe there's a place in her building. It's next door to Horton and Lillian's apartment."

Our few days together flew by, and Barbara took the train to DC. The following morning, she phoned me.

"I've rented a place for us in the house I told you about," Barbara announced cheerfully. "It's not the Ritz, but it's on a nice street with lots of huge trees. I think you'll like it. I'm all settled in our new home, on the same floor with Angie and Patsy, and I've called the phone company. We'll have our own phone when you get here."

I was on the train to Washington the next morning.

"Welcome to the Ritz Annex, darling," Barbara joked, standing with open arms and a wide smile in front of a large stone mansion.

I put down my bags and gave her a bear hug. The place she had rented was now a rooming house in a once-fashionable neighborhood. Still nice, it had seen better days.

"Well, it looks pretty grand to me," I said. "So this where Angie and Pat live?"

"Yes, and Bea Newport, another lovely actress from the group you'll meet later."

Inside, we climbed a grand–if somewhat scuffed-up–staircase. On the second floor, she opened a stained mahogany door and sang, "Be it ever so humble, there's no place like home."

I followed her into the L-shaped room, not large, but it had two good-sized windows, two chests of drawers, a small table with two chairs, and twin beds. As I plopped down on one, I couldn't help thinking a double bed would have been nicer.

"We share a bath down the hall with Bea and Patsy. That may sound a bit too cozy, but it works."

"That's okay," I said. "I'm used to sharing."

"Glad you like it, my love. I bought a hot plate for us." She touched the table. "We'll cook a lot of ground-round steak and make nonfattening salads."

"Sounds good to me," I said.

Looking back at that moment, I believe it was the first time I had said to myself, *This is really happening. Barbara and I are really going to live together in Washington, D.C.*

We settled in and soon began our teaching duties at the Institute of Contemporary Arts. Barbara held acting classes for beginning students, and Horton and Vinnie taught advanced groups. I, lacking any teaching experience, taught set design to both. I quickly realized the students' only interest was in acting, not sets. It wasn't easy, but I survived. So did the students.

Horton and Vincent were laying plans for the plays that Productions Inc. would be presenting during fall and winter. One was *Yes Is For a Very Young Man,* by Gertrude Stein, the American expatriate poet who lived in Paris. The second production would be a simplified version of William Shakespeare's *A Midsummer Night's Dream.* I read the plays and discussed my ideas with both Horton and Vinnie, the directors. We were a busy bunch, and the days were racing by.

These are some of the costumes I designed for *A Midsummer Night's Dream.*

This is Barbara as Hermia of *A Midsummer Night's Dream.*

Even though I was younger than Barbara and we didn't always agree on ideas about life, we loved each other and decided to get married. Angela Kennedy and her actor boyfriend, Charles Sladen, "stood up" for us in a judge's chambers for the simple but tender civil ceremony. The judge gave us a copy of it, spoke warmly to us, and offered his good wishes.

Horton Foote and his sweet wife, Lillian, hosted a small reception in their apartment next door. People from Washington we had met in Kennebunkport were invited. Barbara and I had our first dance to Billie Holiday singing "Lover Man" in her inimitable style on the stereo record player. We were toasted with champagne, and everyone wished us well, including Vincent Donehue (Yes, Vinnie wished us well too). We all drank, danced, ate, and drank some more.

Our wedding night wasn't all it had been cracked up to be. The next morning, I felt vaguely guilty, but I didn't mention it to my new wife. Later, I thought of other possibilities–the amount of alcohol I had imbibed, fatigue, or maybe a bit of the Madonna syndrome. I was young, in my early twenties, without as much adult experience as my new wife had. Our lovemaking slowed up a bit and wasn't as wild and free as it had been during our summer stock days in Maine. Sometimes it was a little tentative, as if we were unsure of our roles as a married couple–well, make that *I* was unsure. However, I thought, *Barbara and I are together, and that's all that matters!*

We plunged back into our work, enjoying it immensely, and had little time for much else. Besides teaching that winter, I designed sets and costumes for the two plays presented by Productions Incorporated. Horton directed them, and Vinnie Donahue costarred with Barbara. Both shows brought praise from the Washington critics.

Set sketches for *Yes Is For a Very Young Man*, 1948.

Their third presentation starred the sultry torch singer Libby Holman, known in the 1930s for her Broadway career as well as her recordings. She performed magnificently on an empty stage with a simple wooden stool as her only prop. Wearing a sequined long-sleeved blouse and a slinky black skirt, she was stunning. The skirt was, purposely, at least eighteen inches too long, but it gave Miss Holman many choices to use it to her advantage to express her humorous and serious sides. Libby created a special world of joy and humor, sadness and heartache. It was a great week, and her show was a complete success.

As I had once done for Betty Hutton's Service Club performance, I made a series of sketches of Libby and sent them to her. I received a gracious thank-you note but unfortunately no autographed photo.

"— don't do what I have done —"

HOWARD '52

"—fare thee well"   HOWARD '52

Spring and summer of 1949 were taken up with the Washington Theater Festival. Presented by Productions Inc., it was the first nonsegregated theater season of entertainment in the capital of the United States. The festival's special stage, a wood-framed canvas structure built outdoors in Meridian Hill Park, was designed by David Aarons, a Washington architect, who also taught at the Institute for Contemporary Arts. David's handsome creation faced a large natural amphitheater for audience seating.

The festival's plan of operation was the same as Kennebunkport Playhouse in Maine–a basic company of actors, a director, designer, and guest stars. Barbara was the featured actress, and I was the set designer. Our first production was Jean Giraudoux's *Amphytrion 38*, a sophisticated comedy set in ancient Greece. On Broadway, the original play won the Pulitzer Prize in 1939. It starred the famous acting couple Alfred Lunt and Lynne Fontanne and had a successful run of three hundred consecutive performances, impressive in those days.

Amphytrion set designs.

For our *Amphytrion*, the star was the legendary European actress Elizabeth Bergner. Miss Bergner, who began her acting career in Innsbruck at the age of fifteen, had been known as the greatest Shakespearean actor on the continent. She had also repeated her stage role of Rosalind opposite Laurence Olivier's Orlando in the 1936 film *As You Like It*, the first sound film version of Shakespeare's play and the first sound film of any Shakespeare play to be produced in England. *Amphytrion 38*, a spicy romantic play, is about a beautiful young married woman who succumbs to the "wicked wiles" of Zeus, king of the gods. I designed a unit set, the exterior of the wealthy couple's villa, which had to be redressed between acts to become a lush interior sitting room. Preproduction was chaotic. Putting up the scenery, dressing the set, and installing and focusing the lights took a full day and into the evening, one of the hottest in the city's history. Our production crew was sweating bullets, and the technical rehearsal did not begin until midnight.

Miss Bergner, who was seventy-four at the time, had been in costume and full makeup, sitting in her non–air-conditioned dressing room for six hours. When the stage manager called, "Places, please!" the beautiful but most patient lady came onstage and walked slowly to the edge of the apron. She stood very still and looked down at us—the producers, the director, the designer, and the entire crew, sitting to watch the rehearsal. Instead of throwing a temper tantrum, raving and ranting at us as some stars might have done, Miss Bergner just shook her head ruefully.

"You boys . . . you boys," she quietly repeated. Then she smiled—a sad little smile. "All right," she said in a firm business-like voice. "Let's get on with it."

The rehearsal, with its stops and starts, lasted until daybreak.

That night, the curtain opened, and Elizabeth Bergner performed magically. She became a dewy, delicate young beauty, Alcmene, whose ardor is intensified when Zeus "borrows" her youthful husband's body for a night of love. I stood in the wings and watched the enchanting actress every night.

After the final performance, the gracious star thanked the crew, one and all, and gave me an exquisite personal photo. On it, she had written, "To Howard, my handsome designer, Elizabeth Bergner." *Amphytrion 38* had been a tough but rewarding experience, and losing my heart to this gracious, beautiful woman was to be the easiest task of the entire season.

Elizabeth Bergner, from *Amphytrion 38*.

Other well-known performers graced our stage that summer, such as London's Estelle Winwood, who starred in Oscar Wilde's *The Importance of Being Earnest* as the formidable dowager, Lady Bracknell. Barbara, who shone as the haughty Gwendolyn Fairfax, was also featured in eight other of the festival's productions—a mix of Broadway comedies, dramas, and musicals. Devoted to her craft, she was well received by audiences and praised by the critics. Wearing thick-lensed glasses, Barbara was a comical standout as the adenoidal Lucy Smeeler in the zany musical comedy *On the Town*.

This was 1948, and one thing that made the Washington Theater Festival stand apart was that it was planned to be a nonsegregated theater audience in our nation's capital. One of my fondest memories is the day some children from the neighborhood showed up to "help" us with the sets for the show. It wasn't the best neighborhood, so it felt good to get them involved. I put two sweet young girls to work on a backdrop of Manhattan, sewing a cutout fabric skyline of the city I had pinned on a plain blue curtain. After some time, I noticed they had progressed only a few inches. On a closer look, I saw they were sewing with tiny stitches like fine embroidery.

"Sweethearts," I said, "you are doing a great job, but much bigger stitches will be fine, and we can hang the backdrop sooner, okay?"

"Who's he?" one little girl asked the other.

"Who's he?" she answered in a superior tone. "He's the New York designer!"

It was an exhausting summer for everyone in the company, but being part of such a unique event that ushered in a new era of nonsegregated theater audiences gave us all great satisfaction. Sadly, that fall, Productions Inc. went bankrupt and had to close its doors. With tearful hugs and kisses, the company's members departed and scattered in all directions.

CHAPTER 46

ALL IN THE FAMILY

Manhattan, Fall 1949

AFTER PRODUCTIONS INC. disbanded, Barbara and I moved back to New York. We found an apartment right away, just half a block off Times Square, in the heart of the theater district. The fourth-floor walk-up in a turn-of-the-century brownstone was on West 45th Street. It had a big living room, bedroom, kitchen, and bath and a small end-of-the-hall room we furnished for a possible overnight guest. It was a godsend to a young couple searching for jobs in show business. Its only drawback was that it was too expensive. Not counting the utilities, the rent was a hundred dollars a month.

"How will we ever pay it?" we asked each other. Well, with our weekly unemployment insurance checks and our savings, we managed to move in and settle down.

The cost of theater tickets was beyond our reach, but occasionally, we were able find discounted seats through the union Actors Equity, and we discovered an inexpensive little restaurant down the street just past Broadway. Working actors hung out there, and unemployed actors waited on tables. When we could afford a dinner out, you would find us at Johnny's.

Being with Barbara and living in the middle of the theater area was exciting for me. We were where we belonged, and anything was possible. We actually began to entertain–spaghetti suppers and cheap red wine or BYOB (bring your own bottle) gatherings of Barbara's theater pals in New York. Among them was an exotic actor named Yul Brynner. Yul had been Barbara's old flame when they were acting students of Madame Tamara Dakahanova at the fabled Michael Chekhov Drama School. Yul was a charismatic guy, warm and friendly, and he still had some hair in those days. That was before he shaved his head to star in *The King and I* and became famous. But we didn't see much of Yul after that.

Donehue and Foote had remained in Washington to shut down their company, Productions Inc., and arrived in New York a few months later. Vinnie became a regular at our gatherings, but Horton and Lillian moved on to a small town in New Hampshire. Horton wanted to concentrate his full time on his playwriting. His prodigious dedication to his craft through the ensuing years resulted in more than fifty plays produced on Broadway, off Broadway, and off-off Broadway during his writing career from 1940 to his death in 2008.

Jean Stapleton, an amusing young actress, was always the proverbial life of the party. She, of course, went on to quite a successful career on Broadway and in television, but in those days, we were starving artists. Of course, I will never forget–years later, after all of us had achieved a bit of success, Barbara, Jean, and I were guests for the weekend out at Vincent's summer cottage in Amagansett. Jean and I went out on a sailboat in the bay. I had learned how to sail in high school, but now I could not remember how to turn the boat around to get back to shore. As we kept sailing out farther, the boat eventually flipped over. At least I knew to pull in the sail for the boat to right itself, but we had to swim the boat to land. We soon realized we were in pretty shallow water and found ourselves laughing like fools at our stupid predicament. As we could see all our friends on the shore in the distance, we waved for help, but they just waved happily back. Eventually, they could see we were in need of rescuing, and thankfully, Jean was forgiving of my overconfidence.

Another dinner party attendee was William Alexander Kirkland, an older Broadway veteran who had become a Hollywood star in the 1930s. He became a new friend of ours when he directed several shows at the festival in Washington. Bill had been married to the stripper-author-superstar Gypsy Rose Lee and always had delicious stories to tell about the famous and near-famous in show business.

One morning Bill surprised me with a phone call. He wanted to talk to me about a project he felt might interest me. Any project at all would interest me, so I asked him to come right over for coffee.

"I've written a children's book, *Ellie the Elephant*," he said.

I thought, *Alexander Kirkland–theater and film star, director, man about town–has written a children's book entitled* Ellie the Elephant?

"You're an artist," he continued. "I want you to illustrate it. I think you'd do a great job. What do you say?"

"I say yes, when do I start?"

Bill read the manuscript for his book to me, and I liked it. We talked about the illustrations–realistic or cartoonish, simple or elaborate? I was thinking, *And what the about schedule? What about money?*

"Just do a few sketches you think will appeal to kids, and I'll present the roughs to publishers. We'll go fifty-fifty. Okay?"

"Deal," I said and started to work that night. A week later, I showed Bill my first few sketches.

"They're perfect," he said. "I mean it! I'll get back to you as soon as I have an answer."

A week passed–and then another week. I couldn't wait any longer. I called him.

"Howard, I'm sick!" Bill moaned. "I've peddled our book to publishers all over town. Those bastards don't know what they're missing. They all say the same thing–'Elephants are old hat.' One had the nerve to say it was unimaginative to call an elephant Ellie. No one wants our book!" he said. "And I guess I just don't know kids. I'm devastated. I give up!"

"I'm devastated too, Bill," I said. "More than you know." I was at loose ends again.

At that time, besides Barbara's friends, I didn't know anyone actually connected with the world of show business. However, crossing Broadway one day, I ran into Bert Lawrence, whom I had met when I first arrived in New York two years earlier when Fred Stewart, an acquaintance from my World War II days in Europe, had suggested I look up a couple in his theater group in New York.

"The Lawrences are members of my five o'clock theater group," he had said. "I think you'd enjoy knowing each other."

Warm and hospitable, Lee and Bert Lawrence were an ideal couple. She was petite, elfin, and effusive. He was magnetic. Both of them had a sense of humor. Fresh from college, they owned Lucid Art Productions, a new small company that produced short films with special effects and various backgrounds. Lee was the "creative," and Bert doubled as the producer and director. At that time, I was only a year younger than Lee and Bert, and although I was lacking in professional experience, Bert and Lee gave me my first break in the big city. I was an artist and needed a job, and Lucid Arts needed a designer for their shows.

I was hired to render paintings of various classic locations from around the world. My work was then photographed and then projected onto large screens as backgrounds for actors in silhouette.

Here are some of the sets I created for Lucid Arts Productions.

Bert and Lee were an attractive young couple, fun to be with. We became friends, and I enjoyed working with them until their company suddenly fell apart.

I was surprised to see Bert again but not surprised when he told me he had become a freelance film director. We stopped for a cup of coffee and chatted, and within minutes, he came through with a few art jobs for me. He needed storyboards, small sketches depicting a series of scenes to be filmed for TV commercials. At fifty cents a sketch, the jobs added up to around ten bucks apiece–not a lot, but at least I could look at myself in the mirror, shaving each morning.

The commercials Bert had been directing were for a film company owned by a gentleman named Herbert Kerkow. His clients were among New York's major advertising agencies, such as Dancer, Fitzgerald, and J. Walter Thompson. Shrewd in his business, Mr. Kerkow was easygoing and jovial, but he also "played his hand close to his chest." He was a warm person, and I liked him. In that respect, he reminded me of my father.

Mr. Kerkow and his lovely wife, Rosamund, were a sweet couple. She was pleasantly attractive and a bit motherly. Motherly? Well, yes, in some ways to me. If my parents had lived and my beautiful mother had worked in the office with my handsome father, I would say there was definitely a resemblance. Like my mother, Mrs. Kerkow had a sense of style and dressed accordingly. She was intelligent and serious-minded, but she also had a sense of humor that trickled into her conversations, and like my mother, Rosamund also had strong opinions and firm convictions. Neither she nor my mother could suffer fools gladly.

I always kept thinking that I should be doing something to further a career in theater, but summer stock was many months away, and my chances of designing sets on Broadway were next to zero. It did not boost my ego, and as always, Barbara kept busy making her rounds of agents' offices. Barbara's agent had me do headshots in hopes of maybe landing some acting work.

One afternoon Barbara came home with some good news. She had snagged a small part in a short educational film.

"It's called *Marriage for Moderns*," she said. "That's us, isn't it?"

"Sure is," I said, my reaction trying to sound positive. "That's great news."

"You bet it is, and you're going to play my husband," she said with a wide smile.

I was puzzled.

"When I told the director I was married, he said, 'That's fine. I'd like the scene to be realistic. Your own husband can play your husband.'"

"Sight unseen?" I was surprised. "He doesn't even know what I look like."

"It doesn't matter, sweetheart," Barbara said, "It's a short scene."

So we played ourselves. That was how I got my first—and probably my last—job acting in a movie. It was fun, and I got a hundred and fifty bucks for it (more than a month's rent)! Maybe that was an omen something was coming, not something, but someone was coming—Barbara's mother.

Bessie Joyce flew in from California for a visit. She loved our walk-up and was surprised we had found such a great little "hideaway" smack in the center of Manhattan. A chubby little lady with blue eyes, her strawberry-blonde hair cut in bangs, Bessie may have been a cute young thing in her day, but I believe she still fancied herself to be the cute young thing from "way back then."

Barbara's parents had never been to New York before, and her mother loved seeing the sights: Radio City Music Hall with the Rockettes, the Empire State Building, the Statue of Liberty, and even Central Park. Those points of interest may have almost become clichés to blasé New Yorkers, but to newcomers and first-timers, they are marvelous.

One day the three of us were strolling through Times Square, and Barbara's mother stepped on one of those iron gratings in the sidewalk. A blast of air from a passing subway train below us blew her white pleated skirt up around her shoulders.

"Oh, look! Marilyn Monroe!" she screamed, and without a trace of embarrassment, she burst into laughter as she pushed her skirt down to cover her undies.

Bessie was a good guest–witty, vivacious, and appreciative. How could I not adore her?

Not long after Bessie Joyce went back to California, I was called for a job. This one took me to a Lower East Side barn of a studio where I "created" small sets for four short musical films. They were to be shot by a producer-director for a jukebox film company called Neptune Productions. The production budget for *Songs, with Spice* was so low, I served as set designer, costumer, and prop man. Only one of the shorts had a really talented young performer named Alice Ghostley. Alice had an operatic voice and the soul of a comedienne. Her number was a slightly risqué song for a Wagnerian diva created by the equally talented composer-performer G. Wood. Dressed like a demented Valkyrie (without a horse), Alice was brilliant. The other three films were forgettable, which was just as well. I was paid the grand sum of four hundred dollars. I would not know that would translate into today's currency, but in 1950, it translated into four months' rent. At that time, I said "Hot dawg!"

New Year's Eve in New York in 1949 was like all New Year's Eves–an unforgettable night. The massive crowds in Times Square were overwhelming. We watched the glittering electric ball on top of the Times Tower descend on the countdown of the last ten seconds of 1949. The roar of the crowd celebrating the first minutes of 1949 was deafening. I enjoyed it all, and we kissed and shouted, "HAPPY NEW YEAR!" I couldn't help wondering what 1950 would have in store for us. My new wife and new friends were "naturalized" New Yorkers. Everyone one around me seemed to be older and more experienced than me. I was the new kid on the block, and I knew it.

CHAPTER 47

MOUNTAINHOME

The Pocono Mountains, Pennsylvania, 1950

BY JUNE, BOTH Barbara and I had secured jobs at the Pocono Playhouse in the mountains of Pennsylvania. We would be working together in summer theater again, this time for four months–through September. Barbara didn't have a role in the first play of the season, so I would be leaving her at home alone. My bags were packed.

"If you are thinking about any 'action' in Mountainhome, you'd better pick up some condoms," she said with a provocative smile. "My diaphragm is not in good shape."

We had not been "doing it" a lot lately, and when she hugged me and kissed me, I felt a little twinge down there, if you know where I mean. In Penn Station, I stopped in a drugstore and laid in a good supply.

On the train, instead of reading the first play I was to design, I sat looking out the window, daydreaming as I watched the green Pocono hills passing by. The seat next to me was occupied by a sweet-faced older woman who introduced herself.

"My name is Rebecca Brownstein," she said. "I'm on my way to Pocono Playhouse. Where are you going?"

"I am going to the same place to work as their set designer!"

When she learned this, she told me she was going to visit her friend Rowena Stevens, the owner of the playhouse. Then we fell into a friendly, easy conversation. At some point, Rebecca surprised me with a question.

"Do you have a lawyer?"

"No, I don't," I said. "Why do you ask?"

"Everybody should have a lawyer," she said simply with a smile.

"Why?" I asked just as simply.

She answered me with another question. "Do you have a will?"

"No, of course not. Why should I have a will?" *Nosy woman*, I said to myself.

"Because you will die," she said with a sweet smile.

Die? I thought. *Is she nuts?* "I don't plan to die anytime soon," I said as nicely as I could.

"We never know. Do we?" she mused with a small smile.

One of those quiet, comfortable moments that happens when conversation stops took me by surprise. *What's going on here?* I thought. *She's annoying, but I actually like this bold old woman.* Then she broke the silence.

"Many years ago, when I was very young–straight out of law school but had not yet admitted to the bar–I decided to test a New York City ordinance to see how strongly it was enforced. Early one morning a friend and I plopped ourselves down near a DON'T SIT ON THE GRASS sign on a large swath of green in Central Park. We sat there in the same spot, waiting until dark. No policeman, not even a park attendant, came near us! My little experiment may have been naive, but it had a strong influence on a young lawyer-to-be, and I became one of the first women lawyers to pass the bar in New York."

I guess it was my turn to speak, but when I didn't, Rebecca continued.

"Most young people never think about dying, but everyone should consider the future. A will is a good place to start," she said, and we chatted the rest of the way to Mountainhome.

Besides visiting her friend the playhouse owner, Rebecca was there to see the first play and her friend John O'Shaughnessy, the director. We talked again only briefly before she left for New York.

"Call me when you're back in the city," Rebecca said. "I'm looking forward to meeting your actress wife. And don't forget what I said about your will."

***

My first week at Pocono Playhouse was hectic, but because I had two seasons of summer stock behind me, I knew the drill, and everything fell neatly into place. Rowena Stevens ran a "tight ship." She was a lovely person, warm and friendly, but she was also a meticulous businesswoman. With John O'Shaughnessy, Rowena hired a first-rate company of actors from New York. The stage manager, Barney Owen, and the backstage personnel were experienced professionals. I was fortunate to have a good crew: my excellent carpenter, Munro Gabler, and the hardworking prop team, Tom and Betty Horne. The four attractive apprentices (two young men and two young women) appeared to be ready, willing, and able. The season was off to a good start.

Our first play was to be *Goodbye, My Fancy,* starring Nancy Carroll, a red-haired sweetheart from 1930s movies. On Miss Carroll's arrival, Rowena escorted her on a brief tour of the theater. The set for *Fancy* had been erected onstage but not yet dressed with furniture and props. The actress's reaction was sweetly positive, except for, as she put it, "just one small thing"–the color.

"But, Miss Carroll," I said, "I chose green because I knew you would look wonderful in green–under the lights, of course."

"Oh, I adore green," she said. "But it's too dark. I have to ask you to please repaint the set in a paler shade of green."

"It will be my pleasure," I crooned after a short moment.

The next day, at dress rehearsal, Miss Carroll was all smiles and gave me a quick hug.

"Thank you, Howard, for the new color," she said, "I love it!"

"My pleasure," I said.

My pleasure, of course, was simply that I never had even the slightest intention of repainting the set and never did. Miss Carroll didn't seem to notice the difference. The rehearsal went on without a hitch, and Nancy was a darling in *Goodbye, My Fancy*.

Barbara and I had a terrific reunion when she arrived. It was great being together, and I'll never forget that night of making carefree love again.

"You make me your slave!" Barbara cried out at exactly the right moment.

I had never heard those words from any girl before, and they were just what I needed to hear from her. Somehow I liked it. The next morning, I settled into work on the sets for the next play, and Barbara settled into the rehearsals.

The Velvet Glove was a comedy of manners, and the leading role, the Mother Superior in a convent, was portrayed by Lila Lee, an aging film star, still well-known in 1950. Although Barbara had been cast in dramatic roles on Broadway, in the supporting role of Mary Renshaw, she displayed a unique comic style in the Poconos.

Miss Lee's son, a young actor-writer, James Kirkwood, came up from Manhattan to see her. Lila, a proud mother, showed us his opening night telegram: "Good luck, Superior Mother. I'd love to get in the habit with you!" James became well-known himself with his semiautobiographical book, *There Must Be a Pony*, and Lila Lee demonstrated why she had been such a success in early motion pictures. She did a fine job with her *Velvet Glove*.

The set I created for *Velvet Glove*.

Zazu Pitts, a major star of silent film dramas, later became the dithery, handkerchief-twisting spinster of Hollywood's comedies in the 1930s and 1940s. In those days, she was then billed as the most outstanding comedienne in Hollywood.

In the Playhouse's production of the mystery-comedy *Post Road*, Miss Pitts starred as a comical detective. With her trademark wide-eyed glances and fluttering hands, she captivated the audiences. They fell in love with her, and so did I.

One day, at a midday rehearsal break, Miss Pitts surprised me and our stage manager, Barney Owen, by inviting the two of us to her cottage for lunch. We were very flattered and arrived on time. She welcomed us and began a lively conversation about nothing in particular. We listened politely for a while, wondering when lunch would be served and what it might be. She didn't seem concerned at all. Finally, she sighed and rose from her chair.

"Well," she said with the sweetest of smiles, "what would you gentleman like for lunch?"

We were puzzled and didn't know how to answer.

"I know. What about eggs?" she asked as if she'd just thought of it. "Will eggs be all right?"

"Fine," we said, both at the same time.

"Then eggs it will be," she said.

Within minutes, "Hollywood's most outstanding comedienne" served a feast–fried eggs on buttered toast with coffee. We ate in a hurry, thanked her profusely, and rushed back to the theater. We even made it to rehearsal on time, laughing all the way. You had to fall in love with Zazu Pitts. The only way to understand what I mean, you would have had to have been there.

After *Post Road*, the youthful movie star Lon McAllister proved to be a clever comedian in *The Poor Nut*, a collegiate comedy involving runners on track teams from Ohio State and Wisconsin competing for the championship. Starring opposite Lon, Barbara kept up with him as she played the comic athletic cheerleader out to win him as first prize.

On the spur of the moment, director O'Shaughnessy got the wild idea to have me be a student and dance the Charleston with Barbara in the show's hilarious party scene. We had a ball!

The following week, Barbara showed her gift for comedy again as the zany Deborah Pomfret in the outrageous farce *Clutterbuck* opposite Arthur Treacher, Hollywood's original favorite butler.

In 1936, Broadway's royal couple of sophisticated comedies, Alfred Lunt and Lynne Fontanne, appeared in Robert E. Sherwood's comedy-drama *Idiot's Delight*. I was twelve years old and had never heard of them nor the play. But three years later, at fifteen, I was enchanted when Norma Shearer, the reigning queen of Hollywood, tantalized Clark Gable in the film version.

Thirty-five years later, Clare Luce, the Broadway actress (not Claire Booth Luce, the daughter of *Time* magazine's Henry Luce), starred in the Playhouse's production of *Idiot's Delight*. Not only was our star funny, but also, she became heartbreaking as the phony platinum-haired Russian countess. Surviving by her wits, she is "traveling" in Europe with an unscrupulous munitions manufacturer.

Near the end of the play, when it turns into a serious drama–the start of World War II–Miss Luce gave one of the most sensitive and nakedly emotional performances I have ever seen on a stage. Something in her voice, her body, her whole being must have been drawn from her own life's experience to touch us so deeply. What a shame it was only for a summer theater and not recorded for posterity. She was yet another older woman I admired and was impressed with.

This is a drawing and the actual set that was created from it for the performance of *Idiot's Delight* with the beautiful Claire Luce.

Our last scheduled play was *The Apple of His Eye*, starring Edward Arnold. One of the busiest stage actors during his early career, Mr. Arnold followed with over forty movies in Hollywood. Barbara ended her run of comedies with a rare character role in this wholesome comedy about a gentleman farmer.

One of my best set designs of the summer was for a new play that Rowena added to the season. *The Vicious Circle* was written by Ouida Rathbone, wife of Basil Rathbone, the movies' famous English detective. I was disappointed when I learned that John O'Shaughnessy was not going to direct it. I had a small measure of satisfaction by painting a mural of six lavender monkeys frolicking in tropical foliage in an enormous mural on the set. I doubt if anyone realized the monkeys represented the six superficial characters in *The Vicious Circle*.

With "supervision" by Mr. Rathbone and a veteran leading lady, Lydia St. Clair, imported from France (as were her couturier gowns), the play, dubbed "a tryout for Broadway," had little chance of making it and was forgotten.

During the summer, Barbara appeared in eight of the twelve plays produced that season, and being Barbara, she was devoted to her craft. She knew her part thoroughly for each new play before rehearsing with the other actors. I often helped by "running lines" at night with her. She was devoted to me too, but between her shows, she was off payroll and often went back to New York for appointments.

Summer theater is great fun, but after thirteen weeks of make-believe, you have to go back home and come face-to-face with yourself in the real world.

Many of the sets I created for summer theater.

CHAPTER 48

THE REAL WORLD

NYC, Fall 1950

THE FORTY-FIFTH STREET walk-up was a good place to come home to, but the hustle and bustle of Manhattan was a far cry from the happy season of summer stock in the peaceful Pocono Mountains. The minute we opened the door, I realized it was not going to be easy to adjust getting up every morning without a workday to fill my time.

Barbara went out every day, making rounds to the casting agents, leaving her photos and new résumés, hoping for a part, large or small, in a play or a television show, even a radio program. She was very busy. I was not. There are no rounds to make for unemployed summer stock designers, and even with my share of the housework, I was at loose ends.

I got in touch with the few companies I had drawn storyboards for in the months before my stock job to let them know I was back in town. Even though I had confidence in my artistic ability, I didn't know of any other way I could make money in New York City. When there were no return calls, I began to brood.

Glancing out our kitchen window one morning, I saw a cat playing with a small green object on a rooftop below. Looking more closely, I could see the green object was a praying mantis, and the cat was actually fighting with the insect. The larger adversary, the adult cat, was cuffing the smaller one, a two-and-a-half-inch mantis, back and forth. When the cat smacked the mantis, it reared up on its hind legs and struck the cat on his nose with its sharp claws. Back and forth around the roof, the cat striking the mantis and the mantis getting up and striking back, the long bout continued. The cat obviously enjoyed the fight and was going to win.

Finally, the brave mantis lay still, dead, and broken into small pathetic pieces. The cat, bored with the lifeless insect, sat grooming itself. Then it looked up at a passing airplane, stretched, and walked away. At the time, I felt I identified with the mantis.

No grass grew under Barbara's feet. She finally secured an agent and started getting auditions for parts on TV shows. A number of television "soaps," daytime romantic dramas, were popular in those days, and they were bread and butter for actors. One afternoon she came home from an audition with a happy smile.

"I have an audition for a small part on *Search for Tomorrow*," she announced. "It's a soap at CBS. If I get it, I'll make a decent salary. We'll be on our way to easy street."

When Barbara read for the director the next day, she got the role, a running part. I was happy for her. Could I be happy and brood at the same time? Oh yes, I could and did. Now I really needed a job. I was beginning to feel my wife and I weren't quite sure of our roles as a married couple. Or maybe I wasn't quite sure. Wasn't the man supposed to be the breadwinner? Maybe I was too idealistic. I thought life was like the movies.

Fortunately, Kerkow and a couple of other film companies began to call me again to sketch storyboards for TV commercials. Nice–I was busy, but still, seventy-five cents a panel on a storyboard, made up of a dozen sketches, does not add up to much. During the next months, I made only a few hundred dollars. It paid the rent, but it was frustrating.

I don't remember much about the Christmas season that year. I'm sure we had a tree, probably a small one, but we weren't in the mood for the countdown of the crystal ball on the New York Times Tower and ringing in the New Year. When the crowd of thousands began to pour into Times Square, we took a subway to the East Side for a late movie. I don't remember the movie.

My one-year college education, as pleasant as it was, had not prepared me for work in any field. Though my limited experience designing sets in "little theaters" and summer stock was a good start, it was no guarantee of getting work in my chosen profession, the "thea-tah." Broadway was something of a private club. To join the golden ranks of set designers whose names were well-known, a young designer would have to be extra lucky. I don't believe in luck.

If I ever expected to be a professional set designer in the New York theater, I knew that first, I had to be a member of United Scenic Artists, Local 829.

In early January 1951, I called the union and asked about joining. I was told applicants had to pass an examination. The two-day test required knowledge of architectural periods and costume design as well as technical skills—theatrical drafting, set building, painting, and stage lighting. Even with my two seasons of summer stock, I was woefully unprepared. Anyhow, I put my name on the waiting list, and I was given the name of an older designer, a retired union member named Woodman Thompson, who taught the required subjects.

I attended classes in the teacher's home, a cluttered Victorian house perched on a hillside in Spuyten Duyvil, a town north of Manhattan, overlooking the Hudson River. Woodman Thompson was a fastidiously dressed, slightly Victorian gentleman, eccentric but pleasant, and I liked him. On my first day, I met several other would-be union members, among them a young man, Sy Tomashoff, and a delightful girl named Beulah Frankel. I became friendly with both of them and spent the next five months commuting by subway to Spuyten Duyvil.

After we finished the six-month course, my friends and I passed the tough examination with flying colors and joined United Scenic Artists, Local Union 829. Now all I needed was a JOB.

Television production was booming at that time, and I secured an interview with the Art Director of ABC TV, James McNaughton.

"You haven't mentioned where you got your training," Mr. McNaughton said to me as he looked at my sparse résumé. "Some of our designers graduated from Carnegie Tech."

"I'm afraid I didn't," I told him. "I went to the famous 'school of hard knocks.' But to pass the union exam, I did have a course with the retired set designer Woodman Thompson."

"I know Woodman. That's good enough for me," Mr. McNaughton said. "You're hired. And from now on, call me Jimmy."

Miracle of miracles! I became a full-fledged member of his staff of set designers just like that! Beulah Frankel and Sy Tomashoff, among several others from the prodigious Carnegie Institute of Technology, were on the ABC staff as well.

A gifted designer, Al Heschong was in charge of the department, which included Bob Bright, Jim Vance, Romaine Johnston, and Jim Trittipo, all Carnegie alumni. Don Gilman, a fine young easel painter, was an equally talented set designer, and Fred Stover, a "one martini at lunch" senior, could always be counted on for fatherly advice. George Corrin, Norman Davidson, and Tom Ford completed "our family."

My first assignment at ABC was *The Paul Whiteman Hour.* Mr. Whiteman was already known as "the King of Jazz." There wasn't much of a set. All I had to do was supervise the crew as they set up a tiered platform for Mr. Whiteman's orchestra each week, with the music stands and chairs in front of a velvet curtain. My job wasn't rocket science. Oh yes, I also supervised the scenic artists who painted a jazzy floor design in front of the orchestra platform. Before each broadcast, I attended the dress rehearsal, while Mr. Whiteman conducted his orchestra. He was a skilled, pleasant, and kind man.

Soon enough, I was trusted to design a few other one-set shows such as *At Issue, Back That Fact,* and *Take It from Me.* Then came *A Date with Judy,* an early sitcom. All were routine jobs. Never mind–it was the old story. I learned by doing and got paid (in those days) quite handsomely for it.

Months later, I faced my first real challenge when I took over *The Frances Langford–Don Ameche Show* from Romaine Johnston. The daily musical-variety hour with the two stars plus other performers and celebrity guests was great fun.

Frances Langford was well-known at the time from radio shows, movie musicals, and her tireless work with Bob Hope entertaining the U.S. troops overseas in World War II. Because their show toured the front lines in Europe before I was there in World War II, I never saw the famous stand-up comedian and the lovely Miss Langford. Mr. Hope has been quoted as saying the biggest laugh he ever heard was the time Frances was standing on a makeshift stage under the South Pacific palms.

"Hi, guys," she addressed several thousand applauding GIs. "I want to sing my favorite song for you–'I'm in the Mood for Love.'"

At that point, a young soldier stood up and shouted at the top of his lungs, "Fran, if love is what you're in the mood for, you've come to the right place!"

Don Ameche, an Academy Award–winning movie star in the 1930s and 1940s (over fifty motion pictures, both dramas and musicals), moved into television as Miss Langford's costar in a one-hour five-days-a-week show for ABC. The show opened across the boards five days a week, with Mr. Ameche singing a song and chit-chatting with Fran. Between their duets and solo production numbers, they introduced guests and other performers. I designed lavish (as the budget allowed) sets for Fran and Don.

There was also a daily fifteen-minute comedy segment in the show called *The Couple Next Door.* It always began with a young man and his wife already in action–talking, eating, or arguing, sometimes in bed–their tidy apartment set rolling onstage, on camera, in full view of the audience.

The Couple Next Door segment featured the budding star Jack Lemmon and his real-life wife, actress Cynthia Stone. The talented young actors were bright, witty, and attractive, and the studio audience loved them.

As most readers already know, Lemmon rose to fame from his early years as an amusing movie actor in light comedies, such as *Some Like It Hot*, opposite Marilyn Monroe, to a veteran of at least sixty films, comedies, and dramas. He won his first Academy Award for *Days of Wine and Roses*. Cynthia Stone went on to a successful career, starring in a half dozen TV series.

Creative lighting of sets was important, but special lighting for the actors performing in those sets required talent, education, and experience. Certain "tricks of the trade" could flatter actors and take years off their faces. I appreciated the lighting designers' work and learned a lot from them. Danny Franks, ace lighting designer on *The Langford–Ameche Show*, improved the look of everything and everybody. Fran and Don were both beautiful people who did not need his magic touch erasing wrinkles, but I can still hear Danny, almost sixty years later, call out to Fran onstage as the makeup man touched up her lips just seconds before showtime.

"Fran, look up and find your key light before you sing, sweetheart," Danny said through his mic in the control room. (Fran's key light was a single small spotlight from above, which sculpted the singer's roundish face, creating flattering, classic hollows and cheekbones.)

"Thanks, luv. You're a doll!" Fran called back, throwing Danny a kiss.

Danny Franks behind the camera back in the days at ABC.

"Okay," the director, Babette Henry, called from her mic in the control room. "Cue music."

"Welcome to *The Frances Langford–Don Ameche Show*! I'm Don." And the show began. At the end of the brief theme music, with applause from the studio audience, Mr. Ameche continued. "Welcome, all you lovely people! And now Fran will sing 'Who Cares?'" Don looked puzzled when everybody–the entire studio audience, the crew, and Fran–all broke into laughter.

"'Who Cares?' Don," Fran piped up, "It's not a question. It's the name of the song." Her voice, heard on the air by thousands of people listening, and we hoped were laughing too.

Me with Frances Langford and lighting designer Danny Franks, 1950.

The Langford–Ameche Show was on the air from noon to 1:00 p.m., Monday through Friday, and it was a lot of work, but I ate it up. As much as Barbara and I were enjoying our roles in the entertainment world, the roles in our private world were not as much fun.

Day by day, life on the home front was pleasant enough, but night by night, we seemed to be withdrawing into ourselves. I thought the problem would disappear. It didn't. It simply moved into the bedroom. In the first couple of years, making love had been spontaneous. But later, even though we were young, well, and in all other ways happy, our sex life was suffering. The old motto "Once a night is enough" had changed to "Once a week is enough" or "Once a month is well, uh . . . we need sleep." Now it had become "Almost never is not enough." I was frustrated and wondered if Barbara felt that way too. I never knew. Could it have been me? Maybe I just didn't know how to do the right thing. We didn't discuss it. Life plodded on.

I had been designing television shows for a year at ABC TV when rumors began to pop up about the company merging with UPT, a conglomerate that included Paramount Pictures. Not long afterward, the rumors became a fact. A reorganization of departments at ABC took place, and many employees were suddenly fired. I suppose "fired" is not the right word. "Laid off," even "let go," may sound nicer. But the result was a number of employees in the set design department were terminated. McNaughton was forced to let us go (shades of Major Rothenberg in World War II). Jimmy assured us it was nothing personal and hoped he could get us back "as soon as the dust settles." That was a nice thought, but without a paycheck, the sudden shock of being unemployed didn't improve my personal insecurity. While gritting my teeth, I tried to put on a cheerful face.

"Don't worry," I said to Barbara. "There's always storyboarding."

MUSICAL AMERICANA

of dance and song

including a dance story by
JEROME ROBBINS

produced and directed by
MARY HUNTER

music supervised and arranged by
BALDWIN BERGERSEN

BOSTON SINGING SCHOOL

Singing masters flourished in Colonial New England. They were stern and short of temper but with the aid of a faithful tuning fork could teach anyone the proper singing of a hymn.

"Fresh and joyous material."
Brooks Atkinson, New York Times

PAPA WAS A GOLDDIGGER

A traveling repertory company gets into a frontier saloon by mistake and there is a perfect 1849 setting for a lively Gold Rush ballet.

"Inventive arrangement of song, dance and drama native to America . . . in a joyous, sprightly mood."
Robert Coleman, N.Y. Daily Mirror

THE STATE OF THE NATION

Benjamin Franklin writes a letter from Paris to his children in Philadelphia appraising his homeland as he sees it from that distance. A fascinating chapter of Americana presented to special music by Baldwin Bergersen.

Here, at last, is the answer to a growing demand for a concert novelty—artistic, authentic, nostalgic, entertaining. "Musical Americana" is a glowing souvenir that will delight everyone.

LOWLANDS AWAY!

The jaunty music of the hornpipe invokes a set of sprightly nautical dances while a landlocked sailor sings of the sea in an unforgettable brace of American chanties.

"Sets a new style for the concert stage."
Brooklyn Eagle

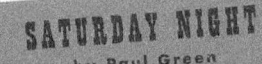

A nostalgic novelty culled from the memory book of American folklore.

SATURDAY NIGHT
by Paul Green

Paul Green, Pulitzer prizewinner, has provided a romantic setting in the Appalachian country in which a reluctant courtship culminates in marriage and a rousing square dance.

"Mr. Green has beautifully compounded it of evening leisure in the country. It would be hard to find more art and more homely touches compacted in so small an area."
Brooks Atkinson, New York Times

AND

Along with the storyboarding, I did many illustration jobs over the years along the way to help pay the bills. Above was a program for Mary Hunter's concert, and below are samples of sketches for comic books.

INK PLATE FROM HISTORICAL COMIC BOOK   1950

INK PLATE FOR ADVENTURE COMIC BOOK   1950

INK PLATE FROM ADVENTURE COMIC BOOK   1950

While I have written a little earlier that I didn't believe in luck, that "fickle lady" must have had a way of smiling on me when I least expected it because within a week, I had a phone call from Wolfgang Roth, a set designer I had never met before. Mr. Roth wanted to know if I could build a model of a set he was designing for a new production of George Gershwin's operatic masterpiece *Porgy and Bess*.

"Yes, I can," I answered, feigning confidence.

Of course, I did not know the show. The original production of *Porgy and Bess* had opened on Broadway in 1935. At that time, I was an eleven-year-old kid in Mississippi. Again, I learned by doing, and I made the model from his plans.

In addition to the model of Catfish Row, I redrafted Wolfie's plans and elevations. We got along famously and worked closely together for two full months on his project. One of his ideas was to use old newspapers to line the walls of the poverty-stricken characters' shacks in Catfish Row. I was reminded of the walls in the shacks my Uncle Collin had used to rent to poor black people in Hattiesburg. After all those years, those memories had stayed with me.

When my work on the models for the sets of *Porgy and Bess* was done, Roth left for London, where Blevins Davis and Robert Breen produced that first revival of the show. Naturally, I kept up with the show as best I could and learned it opened to warm acclaim at the Stool Theater in October 1952 and remained through the beginning of February 1953.

The cast for the production was headed by Leontyne Price as Bess, William Warfield as Porgy, and Cab Calloway as Sportin' Life, a role that was written with him in mind. The small role of Ruby was played by a young Maya Angelou. Afterword, it toured through Europe. Price and Warfield were married on the tour.

Financed by the U.S. Department of State, the production of *Porgy and Bess* came to Manhattan for a run at the Ziegfeld Theater. In 1954, the production went on the road again to Latin America, the Middle East, and back to Europe. During this tour, *Porgy and Bess* was presented for the first time at La Scala.

Notable also, a historic yet tense premiere took place in Moscow in December 1955. It was the first time an American theater group had been to the Soviet capital since the Bolshevik Revolution. An unofficial story has it that the set, shopworn from its many engagements on its travels, had to be replaced. The Russian set builders had problems reading the original plans, so they decided to construct the new set by using my model. If that was so, I'm glad the model had always accompanied the show on its travels in a protective carton.

Once again, I didn't have a job. Working as assistant to an established designer like Wolfgang Roth was one way a fledging like me could hope to break into the New York theater world. However, as Emily Dickinson once wrote, "Hope is the thing with feathers," and as it turned out, I didn't make it to Broadway. But I did make it through some pretty rocky months. In addition to some more storyboards and a few art jobs, I actually designed a couple of TV commercials. I also designed a cocktail lounge and painted a mural on one wall to look as if "tourists" were sitting under a striped awning of a Paris café, looking out at the Eiffel Tower. I even did an interior decoration job for–guess who? Vincent Donehue! Remember him?

Vincent, like the rest of the Washington contingent who migrated to the big city, had gone through some ups and downs too but, fortunately, was now a director in television. He called me and needed help with his studio apartment.

"At last, Howard, I have a little money to spend on myself–that is, where I live. I now have a regular income and want to live a more graciously. You've designed some beautiful rooms onstage, and I want you to do one for me to live in. Will you do it?"

"Of course, Vinnie. I'd love to," I said. "Let's do lunch and talk."

"I hope you'll give me a bargain with your fee," he said with a chuckle. "For old times' sake?"

I didn't really owe him, but I did take his girl away from him, so I made it a reasonable amount.

I took Vinnie with me to select everything–the furniture and accessories, his china, flatware, and glassware–so it would reflect his own taste. When I finished the job, he was ecstatic with the result, and he didn't flinch at the cost of it all. I think I was as pleased as he was. When I finished the job, without spending a fortune, Vinnie had a new home, still a one-room apartment with a kitchenette and bathroom but a place where he would be a gracious host to business associates as well as old friends. The walls were a soft shade of gray, matching velour draperies and slip-covered (sleepable) couches, a cocktail table, and comfortable chairs with occasional tables and lamps.

The large room now had a dining area with a table and chairs to seat ten and shelves for his book collection and his personal photos, including celebrities, and yes, Barbara and I were often invited to his dinners. His guests were always fun–interesting, sometimes fascinating, intelligent, talented, and attractive. If they were beautiful or handsome, sometimes surprising, they were never dull or boring, and only once, shocking. Well, nobody's perfect.

CHAPTER 49

DOROTHY AND THE VIKINGS

NYC, 1951

THE TITLE ABOVE could indicate that a Viking saga follows. In one sense, it does. Some months after Barbara and I had moved back to New York, Vincent Donehue introduced us to Dorothy Willard, one of the most fascinating but exasperating older women I have ever known. Of course, she was not a Viking, but she could have passed for one.

If Dorothy Willard was not beautiful, she certainly was arresting–easily six feet tall, with fair skin and flaming red hair. Her aquiline profile might bring to mind the prow of a Viking ship. She could have been a direct descendent of Eric the Red, a ruler of ancient Norway, and like Eric and all those other adventurous Vikings, she was strong-willed and confident, but here, the resemblance to the seafaring Scandinavians ended.

At the time we met, she was probably in her late seventies, maybe more. It's hard to say because her bright red hair owed its hue to frequent trips to Elizabeth Arden's beauty salon. The small cluster of curls on the top of her head was kept securely in place by a green grosgrain bow, and her manicured nails gleamed with vermillion lacquer. Dorothy wore long elegant dresses in a graceful ladylike manner, and she spoke in a musical if somewhat high-pitched voice, reminiscent of Eleanor Roosevelt.

As a young woman in Chicago society, Dorothy Willard was married to the scion of a famous multimillionaire family, and as hostess to his friends and important business associates, she met many interesting and influential people. She also traveled with her husband on his trips to foreign countries. Their wealth provided her with the means to purchase countless souvenirs of her travels, valuable artifacts, and antiques from all over the world that were destined to be stored in warehouses around New York City.

Years later, when Dorothy's husband died, she was entitled to his wealth, but in concern for the future, his wealthy family managed to have Dorothy's share tied up in trusts. This move allowed Dorothy to live in the manner to which she was accustomed, but it curtailed the amounts of money she spent on her habit of backing her favorite causes, notably a theatrical training school in its early days.

"Cyrus' family didn't approve of my keen interest in the theater," Dorothy once told me. "They didn't understand why most of my friends were theater people."

My guess was her husband's family understood how easily money slipped through Dorothy's hands and did not approve of the recipients.

Horton and Lillian Foote, Barbara and I, Vincent Donehue, and other "theater people" were often invited to Dorothy's impressively appointed duplex apartment in one of those fine old buildings on Central Park West. Dorothy was a gracious hostess, but at her dinner parties, she was often distracted by one of her own rambling stories, so much so, she rarely ate. She would lift a forkful of food to her mouth and then, continuing to talk, put it back on her plate. Trying to match Dorothy's slowness, her guests would listen politely to Dorothy's elaborate tales. As course after course would be brought in and taken away by her efficient maidservant, Olive, one's chances to eat comfortably were out of the question.

At a special dinner one evening, a lengthy story our hostess told was about her trip to Egypt in 1922. At that time, following archeologists' discoveries of royal tombs, thousands of tourists visited Egypt hoping to see and perhaps become owners of treasures buried with the pharaohs.

"In Cairo, we were introduced to an eminent Egyptologist by my friend Thelma, Lady Kier," Dorothy said, dropping the name of a royal family relative. "For years, the explorer Dr. Howard Carter had been searching for the tomb of Tutankhamun."

As her story unfolded with many colorful details, it sounded as if she had actually been there on the historic day Dr. Carter's crew cleared away the stones and debris covering the opening of a passage that led into the tomb itself. Her fork was poised in the air near her mouth, and Dorothy's guests' actions almost mimicked those of their hostess.

"The air was stale," Dorothy told us in hushed tones. "But the tomb itself smelled of exotic spices. It was filled with hundreds of golden treasures and fantastic artifacts. There was the solid gold coffin in the shape of the young pharaoh with his folded arms and painted face. In the dim light from the lantern, I saw one of its eyelids moving. It seemed to be winking."

At this point, all of us put down our forks and stopped eating.

"Of course, the eyelid wasn't actually winking at us. It was a small flake of gold hanging from the eye. In the still air of the tomb, our slightest movement caused it to flutter, and it gave the illusion of winking."

"Would Miss Willard like something more?" Olive asked quietly as she took Dorothy's plate of untouched food.

"No, thank you, Olive. You may serve dessert now."

In addition to her devotion to the theater, Dorothy Willard was consumed with the idea of creating a television series of dramatic programs depicting the lives of the Vikings. She was entranced by the Scandinavian sagas.

She saw herself as producer. To augment her previous knowledge of the Vikings and of other Norwegian, Swedish, and Danish bits of historical information, Dorothy researched sagas and created an outline for the series. Her plan was to have prominent writers originate the scripts and enlist the best directors and actors in the business to bring her dream to life as a series on national television.

This was when I became more closely involved with Dorothy and the Vikings. I accepted her commission to illustrate a presentation of the series to a TV network.

"I will ask Horton to write the first script," Dorothy told me at our first official production meeting. "Of course, Vincent will direct, and you will be Production Designer for the entire series."

I was pleased by her confidence in me and excited about the prospect.

"I'm sure Gadge will come on board too." Dorothy was referring to "Gadget Kazan," as he was known at The Actors Studio. Dorothy did know Mr. Kazan, and maybe he would have "come on board" if the series had become a reality.

I worked for months on color sketches of a number of Viking heroes and maidens in scenes described by Dorothy, all from the still-to-be-written scripts. I was fascinated by her ability to bring them to life in words. But I was also concerned that too much time was being taken with her lengthy dictation of memoranda and notes to her secretary, Iris. She had a way of putting things off with notes, statements, and telegrams, all seeming very important yet delaying the project itself.

Also, from time to time, work on the series would cease, and we would spend days in vast warehouses, with Iris making lists of antiques to be sold at auction. Ironically, even though Dorothy often needed cash, she would attend the auctions and buy back all the pieces she could not bear to part with.

Once, when we had been working diligently on the project, Dorothy announced we needed a break and asked Iris to call for a limo. The driver took us up the Westside Highway across the George Washington Bridge to Snedens Landing, where Dorothy's French-styled country cottage was perched on the face of the Palisades cliffs overlooking the majestic Hudson River. Dorothy handed me the key, and I unlocked the door.

Inside, all the rooms were furnished with antiques she had purchased on her travels through the years. I was surprised to see many of the pieces were still wrapped in brown paper while others were covered with sheets. It looked as if this sunlit cottage had never been occupied. As we walked from room to room, Dorothy's eyes scanned every piece in silence. I could not tell if she was enjoying the visit. For me, it was an eerie experience.

After she made a thorough inspection of each room, Dorothy led the way outside. We stood at the edge of the now overgrown garden, and I followed her gaze to the rocky terraces that climbed up the hillside. A gentle breeze lifted the ends of her scarf, blowing it away from her shoulders. After a few moments, she spoke.

"Yes," she said softly.

I just barely heard it. I couldn't know what she was feeling, yet that one word summoned up a number of emotions—sadness, loneliness, perhaps even despair. Then after one last look at the hillside, Dorothy turned abruptly and walked into the house.

We were silent while the limo took us back to Manhattan. I was thinking of a story Vincent had told me. Years before, when Dorothy purchased the cottage, he had been invited for a weekend and arrived to find Dorothy outside. He said she was dressed in summer white and wearing a wide-brimmed straw hat. Her sheer white scarf was blowing in the wind as she gestured wildly and shouted to a worker operating a backhoe high up on the hill.

"No, no, a little more to the left!" Vincent mimicked Dorothy's high-pitched voice. "To the LEFT! I want that stone just above the other stone—the larger one!"

Instead of Mother Nature, Dorothy was trying to create a mammoth pattern of boulders which would become a waterfall that would fill a pool below. Vincent said he had never seen the completed project.

On the day of our visit to the cottage, however, I saw the stones and boulders, but there was no waterfall. The pool was empty. Her obsession with perfection in everything as well as her desperate need to talk could bring about the death of her projects. I began to think that when it came to achieving her dreams, Dorothy was her own worst enemy.

At eight o'clock one morning, my doorbell chimed. I opened the door to a Western Union delivery man. It was a telegram from Dorothy: "IMPORTANT YOU COME TO MEETING TOMORROW STOP I TRUST YOU CAN BE HERE PROMPTLY AT TWO PM STOP PLEASE CONFIRM STOP."

The following day at 2:00 p.m., Olive let me in. I was expecting to meet a writer or director who had agreed to "come on board." Instead, Dorothy began a long narrative about new research on Gorm the Old–or was it Harald Bluetooth? (Both were Danish kings, 900–950 AD and 950–986 AD, respectively.)

"I will be dictating the changes for the files to Iris," she announced with gravity. "She will make a copy for you as soon as we're finished."

Time passed, week by week, month by month, and although I was fond of this exasperating woman, I thought that without knowing it, she was actually afraid of what might happen when the time would come to present her television project to a network. That time eventually came. There was no finished script, and no director had been hired, but Dorothy abruptly decided it was the moment to make the presentation. I never knew how it was accomplished, but an appointment was made with Gen. David Sarnoff, chairman of RCA and founder of NBC, the top executive in the world of television! Was the eccentric Dorothy Willard Superwoman after all?

We arrived at Rockefeller Center by limousine and proceeded to the Sarnoff Suite on an appropriately high floor. Dorothy was elegantly dressed, perhaps a little too elegantly, wearing an emerald green cape over a floor-length black dress, green gloves, and a wide-brimmed black hat. The startled receptionist led us into Mr. Sarnoff's office, introduced us, and placed our presentation package on his desk. Dorothy strode forward and shook hands with Mr. Sarnoff, and before we were seated, she began talking. For what seemed like an eternity, she never stopped.

Without interrupting her, General Sarnoff turned through the pages of my book of illustrations and listened politely to Dorothy's ramblings about Vikings, scripts, sets, costumes, Gadget Kazan, making television history, and the future of American culture. Intermittently needing to catch her breath, she punctuated her statements with the meaningless phrase "and so forth and so on," while Sarnoff maintained a stony silence.

Quietly, I died. I thought, and so did The Dorothy Willard Historical Scandinavian Television Series. However, as Mr. Sarnoff closed my book, he muttered something about being in touch, stood, and shook hands with Dorothy and me. We were escorted out of his office. We never heard from Mr. Sarnoff.

My professional work with Dorothy Willard was over, but because I liked her, I continued to see her for afternoon tea. However, under pressure from the estate to live more economically, Dorothy was forced to move from her spacious duplex on Central Park West to a small two-bedroom apartment in an undistinguished building on Lexington Avenue.

Olive, of course, was with her. Even in decidedly reduced circumstances, the two old ladies lived much as they had before. They were dependent on each other, and Dorothy still employed Iris to take notes and type them up for filing.

On my visits, Dorothy and I "talked shop"–theater and television–and she always wanted to know what shows Barbara and I were doing. At some point, Olive would appear from the tiny kitchen with a perfectly set silver tray of tea things and place them on a small table in front of her mistress.

"Would Miss Willard like anything else?" Olive would ask, just as she always had.

"No, thank you, Olive," Dorothy would answer softly as she poured the tea. "That will be all."

Not long after that, Dorothy Willard died of cancer. I never knew what had become of Olive and Iris. Gone were all of Dorothy's files, all but a few of her cherished possessions, and along with them, gone was my book of illustrations I had created of Vikings for her Scandinavian TV series. I suppose the estate had taken care of all that.

In one of her late-life shortages of funds, Dorothy put her beloved Snedens Landing country house on the market, and Mike Wallace, the famous journalist, bought it. I never knew how much time he had spent there, but when I read some years later that Mr. Wallace had sold it, I was prompted to write to him, hoping to hear a colorful story about his relationship with my eccentric friend.

Imagine my surprise when Mr. Wallace answered my letter with a direct phone call. I was not at home, yet the paragon of television journalism and a gentleman, to boot, left a long recorded message explaining why he and Dorothy Willard had never met. Too bad they didn't. I have a feeling it may have been amusing for them both. I've kept his voice mail to me, and I treasure it.

***

Years later, in 2013, a television series called *Vikings* made its debut on the History Channel. It was successful enough to be renewed to be seen in 2014. Since Gen. David Sarnoff died years ago, I doubt that the series has any connection with the meeting Dorothy and I had with him. But I believe it may well indicate that my friend, Dorothy Willard, was a woman who was brave enough to set her sights beyond the stars.

CHAPTER 50

IMAGES EMERGING

NYC 1952

D URING THESE YEARS of odd jobs and struggling to pay the rent, I managed to take some art classes. I had not picked up an artist's brush since my early efforts in Biarritz, and I found a teacher not far from our new apartment. His method was new to me. First, you swipe several complimentary colors on the canvas with a palette knife in a random pattern and then set it aside until the paint is totally dry. The next step is to brush the entire canvas with thinned black paint and, while it is still damp, rub several areas off with a cloth to reveal the colors underneath. When you find an image that appeals to you, let the black paint dry and finish your piece by laying on additional paint and, if needed, a few details. It could turn out to be an abstract or even an impressionist work of art.

It sounds like an odd technique, but in my first effort, I began to see something that looked a bit like two human figures, a man and a woman. As I developed it, adding colors and details carefully, the figures turned out to be a bearded man, actually a satyr, and a nude woman in a wild, whirling dance. The painting took a few sessions at the teacher's studio, but I was pleased with the result. I called it simply *The Dancers*. I went on to do another painting, which also turned out to be a mythical figure, a centaur poised to hurl a javelin. I named it *The Hunter.* Both paintings, rendered in earthy colors, could be classed as impressionistic.

My third painting was darker—a man dressed in colorful Arabic robes reclining in front of a silhouetted Moroccan village. The man had a blue face and was gazing at an egg lying on the ground near his feet. I decided to call it *The Enigma.* Curiously enough, much later, I discovered that an Arabic race unknown to me painted their faces blue. The egg was simply my idea and of no actual significance, but it is still one of my favorites. Next, I began a painting after deciding to give up the classes and to complete it on my own. At that point, it didn't occur to me that my artwork might be a reflection of my subconscious mind, my thoughts and feelings. It was a study of a kneeling naked man entangled in a long red rope that was being manipulated by three young female nudes. Much later, when I finished the painting, I named it *The Three Graces. The Three Fates* would have suited it better.

The Dancers.

The Hunter.

The Enigma.

The Three Graces.

This is a portrait of a singer friend of mine, Jane Romano.

My friend's wife posed for this painting, NOT in the nude.
She was quite surprised to see the final piece!

This painting was inspired by an early morning in Central Park.

I also painted my dear friend Dick Besoyan from a trip to Fire Island.

"Maybe I should join you and take some art classes too." Barbara suddenly surprised me one day with her suggestion.

"I had no idea you were interested in being an artist," I explained. "Would you really like to?"

"Well, no. But it might be fun—as a hobby. What do you think?"

"I think that would be fine. I would like that very much," I answered, thinking maybe this was a way for us to be closer.

Barbara joined the class and began a painting that looked as if it was going to be abstract. It was good to have my wife going to class with me. The following week, after she had added the thin black paint and revealed the underlying colors, she lost interest in it and decided to abandon the classes, her work unfinished. I guess I was disappointed, but I was not surprised.

CHAPTER 51

THE (TELEVISION) SHOW MUST GO ON

Manhattan, 1953

WITHOUT WARNING, OUR apartment landlord decided not to renew our lease. Barbara and I searched desperately for an affordable place in the neighborhood. There were some listed in the *New York Times* Apartments for Rent section, but everything was too expensive. Then Lady Luck smiled on us again–a second time in one year. Elizabeth Allan, an actress Barbara knew, was giving up her rent-controlled East Side apartment. It was in a good area on the eighth floor of a nice apartment building with a doorman. We had enough money for the deposit and the first month's rent, so we moved in. As it turns out, East 78th Street was close to my new job.

In January 1953, a successful set designer in television, Sointu Syrjala, was designing two shows at the same time, and he needed help. He had called United Scenic Artists, Local 829, to get an assistant, and I got the job. The salary was modest, but I needed a job and was hired. Mr. Syrjala was a quiet, gentle man, and I liked him. My work was, primarily, drafting his plans for NBC's highly acclaimed drama series *Robert Montgomery Presents*. The esteemed movie star had been wooed by NBC for some time, and besides presenting the broadcasts, Mr. Montgomery also appeared occasionally in the dramas.

Syrjala had a drafting table where I worked next to his personal desk in the living room of his East Side apartment. Regina, Syrjala's beautiful young wife, slept late and, wearing her Japanese robe, came into the room to have her first coffee and chat with us. Syrj obviously adored his wife, but Gina, being married to a quiet man, aimed much of her conversation at me. My work was mechanical, so I could do it and keep up with our conversation.

Syrj was given to having a martini with his lunch–warmed-up leftovers from what he had cooked the night before for their dinner. He invariably doused it with tomato sauce. I always went out for a quick lunch at a coffee shop down the street.

In addition to drafting, I also attended production meetings and hung out on the soundstage with my boss during rehearsals. During Syrj's summer vacation, he arranged for me to actually design the Montgomery shows and receive screen credit while he was away. Syrj was a generous man.

As much as I enjoyed my association with Syrjala, eventually, it came to an end. I was heartbroken when he let me go. The tenderhearted man actually apologized.

"I'm so sorry," he said. "But I'm down to just one show now, and I really don't need your help anymore. I hope you understand."

"I do, Syrj. Of course, I do. I learned so much from you."

"I'll miss you. Gina will miss you too," he said with a sly little smile. "She likes you, you know."

"Well, kiss her goodbye for me. Okay?"

"Will do," Syrj almost whispered, and we shook hands.

I had to give Barbara the news I was no longer working with Syrjala. "I'll get some freelance work," I assured her.

"Of course, you will," Barbara said, smiling. "And there's always our unemployment insurance."

I called the Kerkows. Fortunately for me, they had a training film coming up that needed storyboarding. It was a dry, technical U.S. government job, but in addition they actually had another film for me that involved a glamorous set to design.

"And surprise!" Kerk said. "You are going to direct it!"

I was in shock.

"With your artistic background, I think you are ready for the job."

I was overwhelmed. "That's great, Mr. Kerkow," I said. "When do we start?"

I believe whether or not I was ready or because the Kerkows missed having children and wanted to give me a chance to prove myself was moot. I accepted the gift–directing my first film–with childish enthusiasm!

The project was an industrial, a training film for Warner Brothers–not the famous movie Warner Brothers in Hollywood but for Warner's Foundations (bras and girdles). Unlike today's TV commercials with gorgeous models posing in provocative, sexy bras and panties, the 1950s women's underwear usually was shown on plaster mannequins. Though the Warner's film was for training within its company and not for commercial public television, we had to be discreet and extremely careful with the most tasteful photography when showing live models wearing bras and girdles.

He said he'd messenger the script over to me and told me to come in as soon as I finished it. "We'll break it down tomorrow," he said. "And it's time you start calling me Kerk. Everybody else does."

The next morning, over coffee, Kerk and I discussed the Warner script, page by page. I also started designing the main set to be built in Kerkow's modest studio.

A couple of weeks later, the AD yelled, "Quiet on the set! Scene twelve, take one!" and smacked the clapper. The shot was to be a full-figured model demonstrating the proper way to put on Warner's Full-Figure girdle. She was an attractive older model endowed with the full figure. On the set, our attractive gray-haired model tugged at the tight garment, but she couldn't maintain her balance.

"Cut!" I called. "Let's try it again." Someone had to support her, or she would simply topple over. I volunteered. But film footage of a man holding a pretty woman wearing a girdle would never pass the company's censors. I put my arms around the surprised lady and told the cameraman to go to a close-up of her hips. "Now you won't be seen on film in a man's arms while you're pulling on your girdle," I said. "It'll be just your hands." The clever cameraman, H'sin Min Chin, managed to get a close-up of the action, with me just out of frame when the lovely lady pulled on the elastic garment with ease. For the rest of the crew in the studio, we looked an outrageous sight, but we got the shot and had a good laugh! Although the Warner's Bra and Girdle industrial was a success, it was the first and last film I designed and directed.

In the meantime, Barbara had landed a decent role on *The Secret Storm*. The television series was a definite step above the radio version and others of its ilk. She enjoyed the work, and it paid well. As usual, when it went on hiatus for the summer months, its cast were out of work. Thankfully, Barbara "jobbed," appearing in plays here and there in summer stock. The times were tight, but once again, with unemployment, we met our expenses.

The dust must have settled at ABC because within a year, Jimmy McNaughton was able to rehire the designers who had been laid off. Happy to be back where I had actually begun my TV career, I did my duty designing and servicing one-set shows again, not the most challenging assignments on ABC's roster.

However, I was eventually rewarded with *The Mask*, a mystery crime series requiring multiple sets. Preproduction meetings went well, and line rehearsals were smooth, but when the temperamental director arrived late for the show's first dress rehearsal, he stormed off the set, shouting, "I can't shoot on this set. Do something about it before I set foot on this stage again!" I was flabbergasted. I didn't know what to do. The assistant director handed his boss a small envelope and then turned and spoke quietly to me.

"Take it easy, Howard. It'll be all right. You'll learn."

When that same director returned twenty minutes later, nothing had been changed on the set, but he was a pussycat.

"Okay, let's start from the top," he purred.

It was then that I realized the AD "had been there" and knew exactly what the director needed. I also learned that the director was a near genius on the job.

In those days, all television shows were in black and white. The scene shops at NBC and CBS painted their TV shows' sets in monotones of gray or sepia. Having been a set designer in movies on the West Coast, McNaughton insisted his staff learn the "gray scale" of colors too, and he instructed the ABC scene shop to paint our sets in realistic colors as well.

"In the not-too-distant future," Jimmy predicted, "television broadcasting will be only in color, and we must be ready for it."

Early in 1954, I graduated to a plum assignment, *The Voice of Firestone*, unfortunately still in black and white. The musical series featured Metropolitan Opera stars such as Risë Stevens, Eleanor Steber, Cesare Siepi, and Robert Rounseville. Each weekly one-hour broadcast was from ABC's huge main stage and required a different major set for each star's operatic performance.

The theme songs that opened and closed the broadcasts were composed by Harvey Firestone's wife. Her songs were melodic. Idabelle Firestone was not just the wife of the boss but also a very talented woman. Her theme songs were very emotional but melodic and appealing. As I sat with the director and choreographer in the control room, I watched and listened to the orchestra playing the opening theme, "In My Garden," before the dress rehearsal. It calmed my "opening night" nerves. I watched the entire show without speaking.

At that time, I had never been to the Met, so during the following months, I not only learned a lot about popular operas and the brilliant stars performing in them but also enjoyed designing the elaborate sets. My two favorite shows starred two youthful sopranos, Patrice Munsel and Roberta Peters. Still in their twenties, both were delightful performers who possessed unique voices.

Roberta Peters on the *Voice of Firestone* set performing "The Bohemian Girl."

Roberta Peters on another *Voice of Firestone* performing "La Traviata."

Roberta Peters singing "Indian Love Call" for *The Voice of Firestone* on ABC.

(Note: My children recently informed me that you can find these performances on YouTube, which I find remarkable and wonderful to see them again.)

Miss Munsel, the lyric soprano, chose Offenbach's "Barcarolle" from his *Tales of Hoffmann*. The director of the series suggested a Venetian canal scene, and she liked the idea.

"Per favore," the young diva trilled, "could I be in a gondola?"

My design for the Munsel broadcast included the gondola, moored on one of those candy-cane poles in front of a beautiful Venetian villa. In a wide-angle opening shot, Miss Munsel was discovered standing on a stone walk, where she strolled and sang the "Barcarolle." After her last note, she gave her hand to the handsome gondolier, stepped into his gondola, and was carried away.

To create a realistic reflection of the young diva in the gondola in the "canal," we set up an unframed mirror and tipped it at the proper angle under the television camera's lens to reflect the entire scene. The gondola, equipped with hidden wheels, and Patrice Munsel glided smoothly away on the "canal," and there wasn't a drop of water in the studio.

Patrice Munsel singing the "Barcarolle," approaching her requested Venetian gondola.

My other favorite Firestone production set was for the prima donna Roberta Peters. After she sang the series opening theme, the show began with a high-angle camera shot of Miss Peters standing on top of the world (a huge floor painting of the globe). When the camera panned away from Miss Peters to the area of France, it stopped on a small model of the Eiffel Tower. The shot then dissolved to Miss Peters as Mimi singing an aria from *La Bohème*. The following sequence was similar–a model of an American Indian totem pole dissolving to Miss Peters dressed in a "cowgirl" costume, singing her aria from *La Fanciulla del West*. Each of her following solos was introduced by similar shots of various points on the globe.

I designed *The Voice of Firestone* for a year–a total of fifty-two shows–and when I heard Mrs. Firestone's theme of "If I Could Tell You" for the last time, I still loved it, and I loved my job. My aunt Amber, who kept up with my comings and goings in TV, told me I was in "hog's heaven." She always asked about Barbara and was proud to tell people back home about "Howard's wife, the actress on the TV." Barbara was still on her soap, so she and I were both happily employed in what became known as the Golden Age of Television.

Me and Barbara on a visit with Aunt Amber. Even at
the picnic table, Barbara looked a movie star

Now having read about the ups and downs in the world of entertainment,
can you imagine the shock of being "laid off" again? Fired by ABC TV a
second time! Once more, Jimmy assured us it was no fault of ours, just one of
those upper-management decisions to cut costs. I appreciated his kindness,
but this time, the poor guy had no hope of rehiring us "when the dust settled."
I think that was when I realized there is no such thing as security in show
business. There are no permanent jobs. Making a living is precarious, and
you can only depend on your particular skill, your luck, or good fortune (or
perhaps all three). I had no knowledge or training for traditional professions,
so I had to "make it" on what talent I was born with. *Well*, I thought, *we still
have each other.*

We bought a car—that is, we managed to put a down payment on a small
English job, a Hillman Minx convertible, and on weekends, we drove to the
country, often to the ocean, which we both loved. We even talked of buying a
beach house. We didn't. To this day, I'm not sure what Barbara was thinking
about our celibate life, but I was still frustrated and unhappy about it. I guess I
simply refused to acknowledge how I felt and buried my feelings deep inside.
In any case, I did not complain or talk about it to my mate. Neither did she.
We were living together now almost as friends. But friends often have intimate,
even revealing talks. These were absent from our daily life. Nevertheless, we
hung on. I wrote another poem.

I know a place, a beach house,
by an ocean of heavenly blue
(past miles of sand, standing alone,
where we pick up shells and holding stones).
Sagging, windswept, sun bleached, and old,
the beach house looked strangely new.

We talked of it, the beach house,
on acres and acres of time—
time for laughter, leisure, and love,
drifting and soaring like gulls above
a garden growing bright poppies and roses
and climbing wisteria vines.

"Save that old chair for the beach house,
and this is still a good plate"
(things chipped and discarded in town
find a place they're wanted around,
bits and pieces from each of our years).
Let's go before it's too late.

It's growing lonely, the beach house—
waiting for us, empty, it lies
(a child wanders from room to room,
playing with flowers not yet bloomed).
As we sort out plans for living our lives,
hopes are fading—unborn butterflies.

We called our dream the beach house
but put off the dream in the air
(the beach needs walking, the garden tending—
the child needs bearing, the house needs living).
It's not very far to the beach house.
When will you meet me there?

When Barbara read it, she must have gotten the message. But it seemed
to me like she didn't know what to do either.

CHAPTER 52

THE PLOT THICKENS

NYC, 1954

BARBARA JOINED A small rehearsal group of actors she knew who got together a couple of evenings every week, even those who still had daytime jobs on "soaps" or plain business jobs.

"We work on scenes from plays," she told me. "Keeps us closer to theater technique, you know. TV is so different from acting onstage."

She was very enthusiastic and seemed to enjoy it very much. Usually, she would come home by ten o'clock. With her daytime work and the rehearsal group, we saw less of each other than before. Well, there were those five nights a week left. Should have been enough, I guess.

After a few weeks, Barbara began coming home later than usual. Sometimes I would already be in bed. I thought something was not right about the whole picture. One night I was sitting in our living room when she came in. It was much later than usual.

"How's it going?" I asked.

"Oh, fine," she said, sounding surprised. "We had a couple of new people. It's a little late. I thought you'd be asleep."

"Yes, it is late," I said. "And you can see I'm not asleep. Barbara, what's going on?"

"What do you mean, 'going on'?" she answered lightly as she walked into the bathroom.

I didn't answer until she came back. I was still getting up my courage. "Look, Barbara, I know things between us aren't as they should be," I said. "But I also know when something doesn't feel right. Is something happening I don't know about?"

She didn't answer.

"I mean something more than just rehearsing?"

"Yes," she answered in a soft voice.

"Are you involved with someone?"

"Yes." Almost a whisper.

"Do you love him?"

The silence in the room was deafening.

"No. I don't love him. It just happened."

We looked at each other for a moment. Then I walked into the bedroom and picked up my pillow and a blanket.

"What are you doing?" she asked.

"What am I doing? Barbara, if you think I'm going to sleep next to you tonight, you've got another 'think' coming."

I went into the small dining room, where we had a daybed. What I did wasn't a solution, but at least I could look at my face in the mirror when I shaved the next morning. Several painful weeks passed.

Then out of the blue, I got a call from Richard Besoyan.

"How's life treating you these days?" His cheery voice was a welcome relief.

"My professional life has been going well," I said. "But marriage to my lovely leading lady from summer stock is turning out to be a little more complicated," I went on, glad to be able to talk to someone about it. *Complicated* is not the word I should have used. I restated my answer. "Actually, Richard, my personal life is a mess."

He didn't comment on what I'd said. I was relieved. He told me he had moved up in the world from his old job waiting tables to teaching singing for actors at Stella Adler's Conservatory for Acting.

"I've got some really talented students, and I've decided to do a revival of Cole Porter's *Out of This World*." Dick sounded excited. "It's a fun show about a bunch of Greek gods who come down from Mount Olympus for a night's cavorting with humans on an island in the Aegean Sea. You might remember– it was an overblown flop on Broadway. But my version will be more intimate and simply staged, of course. I'll direct, and it will be in a small theater off Broadway. Would you like to design it?"

"Yes," I answered without thinking twice.

"The only thing that's holding me up is permission from one of the original libretto writers, a man named Reginald Lawrence. He holds the rights and hasn't answered my calls."

"Dick, I actually know Mr. Lawrence. What a coincidence," I said. "I took some classes on the GI Bill when I first got out of the Army, and I was in his playwriting class."

Dick was surprised. "Do you know him well enough to talk to him about the rights?" he asked.

"He was a nice guy," I said. "I could certainly try to get in touch with him."

And I did. He asked if I thought it would be a good production. I told him that I was going to design the show and that I thought highly of my friend's talent, and he gave his permission. The original production, with major stars, had been a failure, but our little show at the Actors' Playhouse in Greenwich Village proved that bigger is not always better.

Even though I no longer had a job at ABC, I accepted the "donation" of the yards and yards of sheer fabrics I used to create the revealing Grecian costumes for the members of the cast who were to play the muscular Greek gods and gorgeous goddesses. Bob Holloway, an eighteen-year-old chorus boy in the show, told me years later how much fun they had kidding around in their seminude togas and gowns.

"We would push the sequined pasties on each other's nipples and shout, 'Come in, Athens. This is Troy calling. Over!' We had a ball."

The kids were stunning, and they wore my brief costumes with reckless abandon. I should give credit to my teacher of costume design in Biarritz for the stylized wigs worn by the gods and goddesses. (I had learned from Captain Bob how to create the wigs of curled strips of brown wrapping paper and gluing them onto papier-mâché skullcaps. The finished products were then sprayed with silver and gold paint for an out-of-this-world look.)

I spent a lot of time in the Actors' Playhouse putting finishing touches on my set and costumes, so I got to know the talented young cast pretty well. Most of the actors in our *Out of This World* came from Dick's class at Stella Adler's studio.

Jane Romano, a natural young comedienne, was a standout as Juno, queen of the gods, without Charlotte Greenwood's famous high kicks on Broadway. Jane, only in her twenties, later understudied the mature Ethel Merman in *Gypsy* on Broadway. At first, it seemed to be a thankless job—Merman was known for never missing a performance. But one night the star actually didn't go on, and Jane took over. Half Merman's age, Jane was a knockout as Mama Rose! It led to a promising career for Jane.

Elizabeth Parrish was a delight in the leading romantic role in our *Out of This World* opposite Jim Eilers, actor-model and owner of the Showplace, a bar-cabaret in Greenwich Village. Ken McMillan, blessed with his athletic magnetism, made an appealing Greek god Mercury. He sang and danced with Barbara Loden, who played the beautiful resort hotel maid. Barbara had been a fashion model before studying acting with Stella Adler. After the good reviews of her performance in *Out of This World*, Miss Loden went on to become a celebrated triple threat: actress-writer-director. Her last appearance in New York was as a Marilyn Monroe–like character in *After the Fall*, a play written by her then husband Arthur Miller.

Strange how life can go on, more or less status quo, when you are busy with something you like. The show *Out of This World* sort of matched my current state of mind, and I was not oblivious to the charms of a lovely Greek actress, Paneota Lagodmos. Off-Broadway productions operate on meager budgets, and in addition to playing a goddess, "Poppi," as she was known to her friends, was making the costumes I designed. She and I worked closely together for weeks—costume fittings, rehearsals, all the way to opening night—and as the old saying goes, one thing led to another. "It" happened. I plunged into my first and last extramarital affair.

Poppi is the beautiful goddess standing the tallest with the Scales of Justice.

My adventure with an American Greek goddess in her modest Greenwich Village apartment was a magical experience, something I had desperately been missing. Poppi gave freely of herself to me, asking for nothing, and accepted me in return. It was marvelous. However, I also did share the affair with Poppi's high-strung cats. Those five wild animals were not hospitable to the new house guest. Each time we made love seemed to be a signal for them to exhibit their insane behavior. Strangely, it inspired a silly poem.

I hate those crazy cats
    Five yowling wild things,
    crouching, crawling, dancing,
    bouncing all around the room.
Annoying cats!
    Spitting, fighting, scratching,
    dashing, skidding, crazy things,
    flinging themselves across the floor.
Good Lord!
    The cross-eyed black one
    is climbing up the window curtains.
    Leaps and lands beside us on the bed.
I loathe those cats!
    Why can't they fall asleep
    while we are lying here?
    Oh well–all we can do is to laugh together.
Good night!

When winter brought a blanket of snow covering Manhattan, the winding road through Central Park became a comforting part of my nightly drive from Poppi's apartment downtown to mine and Barbara's apartment. As the first light of dawn sneaked over the low hills of Central Park, the early morning light made the pavement glisten as if it had been strewn with diamonds, and I felt sheer exaltation in the freedom of my body's release. Then it was I who slipped quietly into the apartment, trying not to wake Barbara, as I crawled into my couch in the dining room. Before giving in to sleep, a strange joy filled my heart.

As far as I know, Barbara was unaware of what was happening in the early stages of my affair, and even later, when she may have realized something was going on, she never brought up the subject.

I never knew Poppi's age. She could have been older than me–or possibly a bit younger. But perhaps because of her heritage, Poppi possessed the wisdom of the gods, and sensing my distress, she opened her heart to me at the time I needed it most. Eventually, we both realized the relationship was not going anywhere, and Poppi offered her friendship, which lasted longer than our affair.

CHAPTER 53

SINKING SHIP! MAN THE LIFEBOATS!

Manhattan, Summer 1955

WAS THE AFFAIR necessary? Who knows? It seemed to be, but neither Barbara nor I were truly in love with the ones we had done it with. My affair would seem to have been in retaliation to Barbara's. Often it is the man who is the first to cheat. I don't think it was because I was nobler or "holier than thou." As I remember, it simply was never discussed. I still believe we both wanted to make our marriage work.

Barbara surprised me one morning when she brought up the idea of moving. Although I was puzzled, I realized she must be suffering too.

"Maybe we could use a fresh start in a new home," Barbara said.

"That might be a good idea," I said. "But where would we move to?

"What do you think about a penthouse?"

"A penthouse?" My jaw must have dropped.

Tentatively, Barbara smiled. "Why not?" she said. "Wouldn't that be fun?"

"Yeah, we could use some fun." (At least now we were talking about us.) "All right," I said, "That sounds like a good idea. Let's find a penthouse. We could grow flowers on the terrace and eat out there too." I was starting to get excited again.

Barbara found the perfect place from an ad in the *Times*. On East 96th Street, overlooking Manhattan, it was not big–tiny entry, good-sized living room, one bedroom, small kitchen and bath–but really lovely. The terrace was L-shaped and enormous. From it, you could see a generous slice of Central Park. We could afford the rent. We moved in. We bought an umbrella table and chairs and planted flowers, bushes, and one little tree. We entertained friends at small alfresco dinners. Things were looking up.

Our gorgeous little apartment.

Many hours were spent on our lovely terrace, entertaining friends,
eating and drinking, gardening, and lounging in the sun.

Ironically, at this point, I had a call with a job offer in Hollywood. Al
Heschong, who was now head man of the CBS TV Art Department out there,
wanted me to join his group of set designers. I was momentarily tempted, but
with my resolve to make our marriage good again in our new home, I turned
it down. Good thing I did because believe it or not, we had also decided to
have a baby.

From the start, Barbara had told me she didn't want children. "I wish I
did," she had said the first time we talked about it. "But to be honest, I can't
say that I do."

Now though, she thought having a baby could be a good idea. We began
making unprotected love again and often. We assumed that was all you had

to do. Bingo—a baby! It was a good feeling. We thought it would be so simple. However, it wasn't.

After months of trying, there was no sign of a baby in our future. In those days, the in vitro method was unheard of, at least as far as we knew, and neither of us liked the idea of adoption. If we were not able to make a baby, we just didn't want to play the game. Consequently, making love seemed no longer in the cards. Barbara didn't seem to be interested, and my desire began to simply fade away.

Well, one good thing did happen. I got a new job, a freelance contract to design a weekly TV series, *The Vic Damone Show*. If you weren't around in the late fifties, you may not have heard of a handsome young singer of whom Frank Sinatra said had the "best set of pipes in the business." Mr. Damone was an excellent vocalist, and his phrasing was not unlike Sinatra's. He was an easygoing man, a gentleman, warm and extremely polite. He was great with guests and showed his appreciation to everyone on the crew. The show came along at a perfect time—good pay and good being busy again. I had the opportunity to design sets for musical numbers for Vic as well as production numbers for well-known guest stars throughout the run of the series. Among the many guest stars were Pier Angeli, the beautiful Italian film actress who became Vic's wife, comedian Buddy Hackett, movie star Shirley Jones, drummer Gene Krupa, and Paul Newman. The team of writers, led by a wisecracking elf named Selma Diamond, provided the show's comic moments, and producer Don Appell directed this delightful series. Tutti Camarata conducted the orchestra.

One of the sets for *The Vic Damone Show*, Vic performing front and center!

All signs for *The Vic Damone Show* were for it to be a big success. However, after the summer season, the show was not picked up for renewal. The "wrap" party was pleasant but not joyous. Vic bid the crew farewell with gifts and his sincere thanks and more personal gifts for myself and the director. His generosity was a surprise. He gave me a gold watch on which the following was engraved—"Thanks, love from Vito." Saying farewell to all, Vic went back to his recording career and national appearances.

Fortunately, my freelance work designing commercials kept me going. Even with that, the signs for my marriage were not good. Then to my surprise, Barbara suddenly took a big bold step: psychoanalysis, deep Freudian five-times-a-week psychoanalysis. After a short time into it, she felt good about it. Soul-searching seemed to help. We talked more. I felt good about that too and decided to follow her example. But instead of deep analysis, I took a different direction. I followed a suggestion from my old friend Dick Besoyan and called a psychotherapist he knew. With both Barbara and I in treatment, it was going to cost a lot of money, but we were able to pay for it, and we thought it might solve our problem.

I didn't lie on a couch for my first session with Dr. Noyes. I sat in a chair and looked around the room. It was comfortably furnished. One wall had floor-to-ceiling shelves filled with books. There were a few black-and-white photographs of outdoor scenes, no pictures of people. The doctor sat a few feet away. He seemed to be a young-to-middle-aged man and didn't exactly strike me as being what I had expected. I guess I thought all therapists would be older and wearing glasses. At first, neither of us spoke. It wasn't a bad silence. I just didn't know how to begin the conversation, so I waited for him to start it.

"Can you tell me what brought you here?" he asked.

"I . . . uh . . ." After taking a deep breath, I answered. "I don't know where to start."

"Why don't you just say what is on your mind?" Dr. Noyes said.

"Well . . ." I paused again.

After what seemed to be a long moment, I started talking without realizing exactly what I was saying. Words came pouring out of me. Like water through a broken dam, they wouldn't stop. At first, I talked about Barbara and me, from the time we had met through the recent years, and then I blurted out everything that had been more recently happening.

Surprising myself, I went all the way back to my childhood. I had not cried at the time of my parents' death or any time I could remember since, but now I was dissolved in tears and uncontrollable sobs. When I finally realized I had nothing more to say, I stopped and waited for Dr. Noyes to speak. He looked at me for a long moment. Then he told me that my session had lasted for three hours instead of the customary one.

"I didn't want to stop you," he said simply and smiled. "You had what we call a breakthrough. That was unusual, but sometimes it happens, and when it does, it's a good start. I suggest you see me twice a week as soon as you're ready."

"I'm ready, Doctor," I said, wiping my face on my sleeve. "I'm ready."

Dr. Noyes handed me a box of tissues. I felt like a huge bag of stones had been taken off my shoulders. When I left his office, I caught a cab and went to meet my wife at a cocktail party at Stella Adler's apartment.

Stella Adler often surrounded herself with colorful, delightful theater people, and to a young man enamored with the theater, being included was catnip. An invitation to her Fifth Avenue apartment was comparable to a royal command, and at some point in the time my wife and I were still trying to sort out the problems of our marriage, Stella invited us for cocktails. The party just happened to be on the day I had my first psychotherapy session.

Stella's cocktail party was in full swing when I had arrived, and Barbara was standing with a group of guests near the entry. When she saw me, she smiled, but she looked a little worried.

"Why are you so late, darling?" Barbara said. "You should have been here hours ago."

"You won't believe it," I said. "I had a breakthrough at the doctor's. He told me he didn't want to stop me. I was there for three hours."

Barbara looked at me, astonished at what I was saying. "Better have a drink," she said. "You might need one."

Stella came over and kissed me. "Welcome, Howard. You are late. Now have a drink and mingle," she said. "Mingle!"

I was a little excited, meeting all the theater people and artists who were Stella's guests. I did have a drink–several, in fact–as I mingled my way through the guests. Every time the butler came around with a tray of cocktails, I helped myself to another dry martini, and within an hour, I was unsteady on my feet. In fact, I was a little drunk. But I was a happy little drunk. When I saw my hostess chatting with an older woman seated in a large Louis XV chair, I approached them. Stella turned to me.

"Howard, darling," she said, linking my arm in hers, "I would like you to meet a good friend of mine, the distinguished psychoanalyst–"

Before she could say the woman's name, I fell on my knees in front of Stella's friend. "You are the most beautiful woman I have ever seen in my whole life!" I said, probably much too loudly. "I worship you."

The doctor may have said, "Pleased to meet you," or possibly nothing at all. I'll never know. My startled wife saw me kneeling and moved quickly to my side and put her hand on my shoulder.

"Excuse me," she said. "Howard, I think it's time for us to thank Stella for the wonderful party and be on our way."

Then she helped me get to my feet. I kissed the psychoanalyst's hand and Stella on both her lovely cheeks. Barbara led me to the door and out to the car. On the street, the cold night air hit me. I was really bombed.

"I don't think you should drive," Barbara said. "Give me the keys."

I happily surrendered them. As soon as we were in our apartment, I headed for the bathroom. I spent a good part of the night there, kneeling on the cool tiled floor and hugging the "porcelain altar." Dry martinis and psychotherapy don't go well together. I haven't had a drink of gin since.

CHAPTER 54

STELLA!

Manhattan, 1955

STELLA ADLER, A highly regarded theater actress and teacher, was a member of the legendary Group Theater, founded in 1931 by the eminent theater directors and producers Harold Clurman, Lee Strasberg, and Cheryl Crawford. Eventually, the Group included many major actors, writers, and directors, among them Elia Kazan of the Actors Studio and Miss Adler, whose acting career began when she was four years old. Later, she appeared in numerous Broadway productions. When she married writer-director Clurman, they became a famous theater couple like Guthrie McClintic and Katharine Cornell.

In 1940, Miss Adler created the Stella Adler Conservatory of Acting and molded the talents of many actors. Marlon Brando, Robert De Niro, Warren Beatty, Elaine Stritch, and Candice Bergen were among her pupils who were to become stars of stage and screen.

My friend Dick Besoyan was now teaching a singing course at the Stella Adler Conservatory for Acting and introduced me to Miss Adler. When Stella, a modern embodiment of the Victorian artist's "Gibson Girl," looked into my eyes, I was immediately enchanted.

Soon after, when the conservatory needed a designer for a class play, I was enlisted. As Stella watched me create the costumes from scraps of fabric and odds and ends of trimmings, she spoke to me softly.

"Hands of gold," she said, touching my cheek. "Howard, my dear, you have hands of gold."

That's all I needed. My infatuation with Stella Adler might have been nothing more than a young man's response to flattery from an older woman, a beautiful, flamboyant woman nearly twice his age. (I had just turned thirty.) If flattery from Stella fueled my infatuation, my feelings were no less real.

One day a telegram came—"I NEED YOU STOP CAN YOU PLEASE MEET ME TOMORROW AT BROOKS COSTUMES STOP YOU MUST HELP ME CHOOSE SOMETHING TO WEAR TO A MASQUERADE BALL STOP STELLA." Of course, I could. I came running. At the costumer's, we selected a dozen frocks, circa 1930s, for her to try on. Stella stood admiring herself in a three-way mirror. I stood admiring her.

"I think that's the one, Stella," I said.

"Do you really think it's all right?" she asked.

"It's perfect," I said. "You look great."

Dripping in bugle beads and fringe, Stella had become a dizzy young flapper ready to party all night in a thirties speakeasy.

Shortly after that evening, I took Stella to the opening night of Barbara's only New York theater appearance during our marriage. It was *A Stone for Danny Fisher*, a play based on the best-selling book by Harold Robbins. The harsh crime drama was performed by, among others, Zero Mostel, Phillip Pine, Bert Freed, Sydney Pollack, Barbara Joyce, Wolfe Barzell, Sylvia Miles, and Maurice Gosfield. Never in a million years would I have thought I would see my wife onstage with a schlump from my infantry basic training in World War II. But there he was, Maury Gosfield, playing a character known as Spit. He had a red nose, a rolling gait, and a very visible knife—in a play with my wife.

The reviews for the production were good, and the leading actors were singled out for praise. "Barbara Joyce gives what is probably the evening's most appealing performance as a love-hungry girl who begins by admiring refined speech patterns and ends by making friends with the bottle."

"Barbara was marvelous." Stella blessed my wife with a great review of her own. "She is a very wounding actress."

By that time, Dick had written another show, *Wake Up with Me*, a delightful musical comedy about department store mannequins who come to life every night after the store closes. (In the mid-fifties, display mannequins closely resembled humans.) Stella was set to play the leading role of a supersophisticated French mannequin whose big number was "I'm Madeleine

From Paris." She was delighted to be headed for Broadway again and willingly performed in backers' auditions for Dick. I was to design the sets and costumes.

Money was not coming in as quickly as Dick had expected. We were hoping an important radio interview would help. Dick, Stella, and I sat with the talk show host at his desk, a microphone in front of each of us. In response to the host's questions, Dick gave a synopsis of the show. Stella, charming as always, spoke about her role in a perfectly delightful French accent. When the host asked me to explain my position with the show to "our listeners," I suddenly visualized hundreds (maybe thousands) of people in the radio audience somewhere out there. I stared at my microphone and froze. I simply could not speak. The smart host knew how to handle the situation.

"There seems to be a problem with Howard's mic," he said. "Dick, help us out here."

Both Dick and Stella jumped in and covered for me, praising my talents until I found my voice. The interview was a success. I'm sure *Wake Up with Me* would have been a success too if it had made it to the stage. Unfortunately for all of us, it didn't. Production-backing money simply did not roll in, and the show was permanently shelved.

I saw Stella only once again somewhat later. She was walking arm in arm with a handsome young man on the beach at Fire Island. Stella looked gorgeous in a smart bathing suit, and her escort was in a brief bathing suit. Incongruously, Stella was wearing sheer pantyhose. Perhaps she thought they would help the look of her long, still lovely legs. The young man didn't need any help.

In addition to being a great beauty and a consummate theater actress, Stella Adler is rightly remembered as the foremost acting teacher of her time. Her teaching, highly praised, could sometimes be highly unconventional. In an explosive moment in the classroom, she had been known to rip open her blouse, expose her still-youthful breasts, and shout to her students, "Be daring!"

The forever beauty Stella Adler (photo courtesy
of the Adler Family Archives).

CHAPTER 55

THE GRAND TOUR

Abroad, 1955

FOR A WHILE, with the leavening of therapy, our life looked a little better. At least we were actually talking more. We spoke about going away someplace for a vacation. Barbara brightened up.

"My show is going on hiatus for a month," she said with a spark of excitement. "Would you like to go to Europe?"

"Europe?" I was surprised. "Well, it would sure be a lot different from when I was there in the war. Okay, let's do it."

Barbara called friends who had traveled abroad. She brought home travel folders and started making plans. She even made the plane and hotel reservations. I had not seen her looking this happy for a long time. London, Paris, Venice, Florence, Rome, and Madrid, with side trips to Stratford-upon-Avon, Versailles, Capri, Pompeii, and Majorca–an itinerary to dream about! And we did it all! God knows we saw wonderful places and enjoyed delicious food and wine throughout our trip. We even met some delightful people, like the friendly woman at the bar in London who slyly questioned Barbara about her bouffant skirt.

"What do you wear under it to make it stand out like that?" The lady and the rest of the bar customers had a good laugh when Barbara lifted her skirt and flounced it like a cancan dancer.

"We have a few beers next to the ice," said the friendly bartender. "I know you Americans like your beers cold." So we had a few beers.

Paris was so beautiful, we didn't mind that it was unseasonably chilly, but we took the subways or small black taxis to all the landmarks and the places we'd seen only in movies. At a "cave" restaurant called Le Grenouille, we shared a huge platter of succulent fried frog's legs, the signature dish. Yum!

Being in Paris brought back a jumble of memories of two days I had there as a soldier. After World War II ended, the city was in the throes of getting back to normal, and I got a weekend pass. Being an artist, I spent the whole first day at the Louvre, feasting my eyes on hundreds of paintings and sculptures. Walking through gallery after gallery alone, I kept wondering why I was feeling so frustrated. It was like being physically stimulated. At some point, it came to me. I'd had too much beauty in one dose with no one to share it with. I was having an attack of "visual indigestion."

In a bar that night, I met a very pretty girl. She was wearing a chic black dress and a string of pearls, and she accepted my offer to buy her a drink. She asked for "un seul eau d'minerale," and she said she knew a "small hotel nearby." This was my clue that she was a very pretty "lady of the evening." So I had my second and last wartime shack-up with a professional. I don't remember the girl's name or what the night cost me, but I do remember she never took off the string of pearls. Alone the next day, I bid a silent farewell to the City of Lights from the top of the Eiffel Tower. It was then that I realized Paris should never be experienced without someone you love.

Now, years later, Barbara and I were together to enjoy Paris but not quite making it. Of course, we enjoyed ourselves, but as usual, something was missing.

In Venice, the gondola ride was just as I had pictured it, and our gondolier's florid performance of "Be My Love" sounded remarkably like a solo by a Metropolitan Opera singer. Our hotel room was modest, but it had a huge terrace boasting a dreamlike view of Santa Maria del Popolo, directly across from us on the Grand Canal.

Barbara had done her homework perfectly. In addition to guiding us to all the regular tourist attractions, she found the way to Harry's American Bar, Ernest Hemingway's favorite watering hole. In his Venice novel *Across the River and Into the Trees*, the main character, Col. Richard Cantwell, drank Negroni cocktails at Harry's. No doubt Hemingway did too. So of course, Barbara and I ordered Negroni cocktails. As I remember it, there was a passage from the book where Colonel Cantwell asks if there was any fresh asparagus on the menu. The waiter apologized and told the colonel there was none at the market.

"Then I suppose my piss just won't have that special smell," the colonel muttered.

Another quote from the same book comes to mind–"You'll find everything on earth at Harry's except, possibly, happiness."

Rome was overwhelming. The Vatican was spectacular, and the first day we were there, its enormous plaza was filled with people.

"What is happening?" I asked an elderly couple carrying guide books and a camera.

"We were told that if the applause from the crowd was loud enough at noon, the Pope would appear," the wife said.

At a quarter to twelve, the enormous crowd began clapping wildly, and sure enough, precisely at noon, a tiny window on the top floor of the palace opened. Pope Pius XII leaned out and lifted his hands in silent blessing. The roar of the crowd was deafening.

Another day in Rome, Barbara called a producer she had met in New York. The proverbial Roman, he was charm itself and took us for a spin in his Alfa Romeo. Leaving the city, we sped along the ancient Appian Way toward Naples. The road was narrow and winding, and Barbara's friend floorboarded the gas pedal. When the speedometer needle passed one hundred and ten, Barbara clutched my arm in panic.

"Are you trying to kill us, you fool?" I yelled at the madman at the wheel. "Slow down!"

I had no intention of us becoming a statistic in an Italian morgue. The next day, on our own, we rented a small car and drove to Pompeii to see the ruins and then on to Capri. A rowboat ride to the Blue Grotto took us through a small opening in the island's rocky cliffside into a cave. A sapphire glow from the water around us lit up our faces with the metallic blue of a hummingbird's breast.

On our last day in Rome, we were guests of Rossano Brazzi. Rossano played the handsome lothario who melted Katharine Hepburn's heart–and broke it–in the touching film *Summertime*. Lydia Brazzi, Rossano's vivacious real-life wife, cooked veal scaloppini for our beach picnic. We spent a long and lazy afternoon with the gracious couple in Italy's golden sunshine, reclining on sandy blankets by the Mediterranean Sea.

Before heading home, we spent a couple of days in Madrid, where we feasted on Velasquez and El Greco in the Prado and small plates of tapas in a bar. We decided we couldn't leave Spain without seeing a bullfight. The sun was shining, music was spirited, and the crowd was cheering. The raging bull burst into the ring and charged the picadors on their horses. I thought the traditional planting of their sharp picks into the bull's shoulders was unnecessarily cruel. The angered bull tried, in vain, to retaliate by gouging at the horses' flanks. They were protected with heavy padding.

Blaring trumpets announced the handsome matador's entrance into the ring, with arms stretched above his head. As he strutted around the ring, he was greeted by wild cheering and loud applause. Flourishing his brilliant red cape, he avoided the charging bull and spun around to blow kisses to his rapt audience. After dozens of graceful passes, the matador faced the exhausted bull and drew his sword. The trumpets blasted, the matador plunged his sword into the bull's neck, and aficionados went crazy. I loved the music, but I felt sorry for the bull.

The last stop was the Spanish island of Majorca. The beach was a heavenly rest. Generally speaking, a month's vacation in Europe should bring a wealth of happy memories to savor after you return to your everyday lives. If the above pages sound like a fabulous travelogue, they were that and more. It was a great trip, and I wish I could say overall, it was a happy "honeymoon." It wasn't.

CHAPTER 56

HOME AGAIN, HOME AGAIN, JIGGETY JIG

NYC, 1955

AFTER WE RETURNED from Europe, exhausted but happy to be home. We continued our life, much the same as it had been–working, eating, sleeping, and going about our business day to day. Months passed. Some of the days were better than others, but that was it. There was no intimacy, not in the physical sense. We both were back in therapy but, as usual, didn't discuss our sessions. Then one day Barbara opened up.

"I have learned a lot about myself," she offered. "But I'm still me–the same little old me," she confessed with a rueful smile. She didn't elaborate.

"Off and on, I feel like I'm progressing," I offered. "I think I've learned a lot too, but I think I'm growing more and more dependent on my doctor."

"Would you like to know what I think? I think you are falling in love with your doctor." Her words tumbled out like a stack of children's building blocks. "And for all I know, your doctor may be in love with you too!"

"And I think you and your Freudian shrink are full of baloney," I said.

That was the end of her opening up. I can understand why Barbara said what she did. I was very fond of my doctor, but I wasn't falling in love with him. Maybe she was jealous of our friendship? I don't doubt there were other couples who were going through the same trouble as ours. If it seems I was putting all the blame on my wife, it was not intended. I'm sure we were both at fault.

Barbara's parents came for a visit. Bessie was her usual bubbly self, sweet and helpful in the apartment and appreciative for everything. Bob, a warm, quiet man, needed very little to make himself a happy camper. His one hope during their visit was to go to a game at Yankee Stadium.

"I've always wanted to see those Yankees in person," he told me. "Do you think there's a chance we could get tickets? I'll pay."

"Yes sir, to your question," I told him. "And no, sir, I won't let you pay. I'm taking you to see those Yankees play ball! You are our guest. We'll find out who they're playing and when, okay?"

Bob's smile was ear to ear. When Bob and I had our hot dogs and beers watching the Yanks win at the famous stadium, Bessie had a ladies' day, watching her daughter in front of the cameras in the television studio. We had a good visit with Mama Bess and Papa Bob, and they went home happy.

After a time, there was a change. It was not a good one. Occasionally, Barbara began coming home late from her job on her "soap." I knew the blocking rehearsals for the following day's broadcasts could run into overtime, but then it became more frequent. One night I decided again to wait up for her in the living room.

"You're still up?" Barbara asked. She seemed surprised.

I followed her into the bedroom. "Yes, I'm still up." My reply was difficult to finish, but I had to. "Barbara, what's going on?"

"Should there be something going on?" she asked, opening a dresser drawer. "What do you mean?" It was a scene almost identical to the one we had played a year and a half ago.

Now I couldn't stop myself. "Are you having another affair?" I asked as quietly as I could.

"Of course not," she answered. "Why would I at this point?" She took her pajamas and went into the bathroom.

"I don't know. Just a hunch," I said to the closed door.

A few days later, when I came home from work, I found a note on the stereo in the living room:

"I need to be alone for a while. I think it is better this way. I will still pick up my mail, but I will try to come when you are not here." It was signed simply–"Barbara."

My stomach turned upside down. Even after all we had been through, I couldn't believe this was happening. I went from room to room, searching for who-knows-what–something, a sign? Anything. There was nothing. She had said she would come to pick up her mail. I needed to talk to her, so I left a note for her.

Dear Barbara,

I hope you are all right and that this is doing something for you. It's strange, but it may be good for us both. I vary from feeling good about it to being miserably lonely. I hope you are not too alone–even though you say you want to be. Turn to somebody–your analyst or whoever you can allow to be close to you, please–and let your true feelings come through.

Howard

When I came home later that day, I found her answer written on the back of my note:

Dear Howard,

Thank you for the wonderful note. I think your attitude is both strong and wonderful–and I'm glad <u>all</u> your moments are not unhappy. I am doing well–relaxing a little bit and trying to be simple and just " follow my instincts." Thank you for paying my doctor bill.

Yours,
Barbara

A week later, while I was out, she came and took the rest of her clothes. Then I noticed she had taken a bed pillow and that the serigraph print of Georgia O'Keefe's *White Barn* painting was missing from where it had hung in our bedroom. I thought of the barn's stark white walls and black roof, the large open doors revealing nothing inside, just black emptiness. *Was that all she wanted from me?* I thought. *One pillow and a picture?*

The next day, I was coming home early, and from a distance, I saw Barbara coming out from our apartment house. I watched her, and I followed her. Yes, I followed her for two blocks. Then I saw her going into another apartment house down the street. She had found a place nearby. *She wants to stay near me,* I thought and wondered, *What next?*

A few days later, I found out. The doorbell rang. For a moment, I panicked. But when I opened the door, it was our cleaning lady.

"Mr. Barker, guess who I saw when I was coming here today." Her eyes were wide, and her voice was pitched two octaves higher than usual.

"I give up. Who?"

"Mrs. Barker! That's who." Then her voice dropped a notch. "And guess what–she was coming out of an apartment building down the street with a man."

Suddenly, I was overcome with a black anger. "Never mind, Bernice," I said. "Mrs. Barker doesn't live here anymore."

The next time Barbara came to our apartment, I happened to be at home. When I heard the key in the lock and the door opening, I walked out of the kitchen and confronted her. This time, she admitted she was involved with someone. She also told me she had given up her place down the street.

"So where are you living?" I asked. My anger was subsiding.

"I moved in with him. I couldn't afford to stay where I was on my own. It seemed like the best thing to do."

"So there's nothing left for us anymore, is there?" My anger was gone.

"I guess not," she said. On the way to the door, she placed her keys on the stereo. "I've left a change of address with the post office."

Now all I felt was resignation. I spent the next few days in a fog. Then I called Rebecca Brownstein, our friend and lawyer. I told her the whole story. She didn't seem surprised.

"What do I do now?" I asked.

"Ask Barbara to meet with you to talk," Rebecca said. "It won't be easy. Let Barbara ask you for the divorce. Be a gentleman. Tell her you'll pay for a trip to Mexico for her to get it. Be generous. Give her anything she wants–the apartment, the furniture, money, anything you have–but no alimony."

A couple of weeks later, my wife and I met at a little French restaurant. Barbara never mentioned alimony. She asked for nothing. Well, she did say she was worried about paying for her analysis. I offered her our savings. She accepted. Then and there, after nearly eight years of marriage, it was over.

While Barbara was in Juarez, I received a letter from my mother-in-law. At the time, I still loved Mama Bess, but I was surprised and a little shocked at what she had written.

Dear Son,

>*Over the years, I've come to think of you as a son. Of course, Bob did too. You were always so good to us. I'm thinking of the time Bob and I came to see you. You were so nice and took Bob to Yankee Stadium. He told me that was really the only thing he wanted to do in New York–see the Yankees play ball. And he said, "Mother, those were livin' days!"*

Of course, I'm very sorry about what's happening now, but I must say I'm not completely surprised. You know, we're none of us perfect, but I believe you may not have always been the right person for Barbara. I don't doubt you loved each other. But the time you took me and Barbara to Jones Beach and we were packing up to go home, I was trying to help with all the things we had brought. You stopped me (rather rudely, I thought). You said, "That's not right. I will do it." Then Barbara said, "Let him do it, or he'll just take it all out and pack it all over again the way he wants it—his way." Then you got mad at her, and you were so mean. I never heard anybody talk the way you did to your wife, who you're supposed to love. And that wasn't the only time you behaved like that while I was there with you and Barbara.

You know, Howard, you should have married a girl your own age, someone you could boss around, have had children with, and have everything your own way. You would have been happier.

All good wishes, Mama Bess.

On reflection, I can't help thinking about being brought up for the ten years with my aunt and my three uncles, who were my role models. They were just regular folks whom I loved and who loved me. But their behavior to one another—often rude, outspoken, and nearly cruel—may have been an influence on me. I am not making excuses for the way that I acted but maybe trying to explain why I turned out as I did. If I had understood myself better in my early adult life, I probably would have reacted differently. Who knows? I didn't.

After the divorce was final, Bessie wrote to me again.

Dear Son,

Your nice letter came today, and I will answer right away as I feel like a little visit. I hope we can always be friends, for in spite of my frankness, I still think of you (the real you) as one of the most likeable and charming persons I have ever met. And all this disharmony is like a bad dream. And now that I have discussed it with you, I no longer see it as real or anything with intelligence or power to disturb either of us—except to help us correct our mistakes.

Bessie went on to tell me of her own happy marriage. Her husband would be able to forgive anything "if I am just merry, He said he didn't care if I could cook or keep house if I was just rested and pleasant when he came home." There were several more pages of her "positive thinking." Her letter ended with,

"Do not forget, dear Howard, you are still very dear to us, and we wish nothing but the very best for you. Always with deep affection, Mama Bess."

CHAPTER 57

MOURNING BECOMES ELECTRIC

NYC, 1956

A MAJOR SIDE EFFECT of the failure of my marriage could be called The Garbo Disease–the "I vant to be alone" syndrome. For what seemed like months, I moped around my apartment. Maybe it was a mistake, keeping the penthouse, but it was the only tangible thing left from our marriage. I did little other than tend flowers, water shrubbery, and feel sorry for myself. Well, I did write a few maudlin poems. I called this one "Winter's Garden."

> I planted the tulip bulbs today,
> ten in each round tub,eight tubs in a row,
> lined up against the terrace wall
> just in time for the snow.
>
> Tonight I saw it falling
> through the white night sky,
> settling quietly on the table,
> shrouding the evergreen shrubs
> and masking the terrace.

Lights from the windows
cast long and ghostly shadows
across a carpet of frozen snow
as I watch, chilled to the bone,
standing in the open door.

If only you were here with me
To see this wintry miracle,
your doubting heart would melt
like the icy flakes of snow
that melt in my two warm hands.

Even though I had not wanted to talk to anyone nor had any interest in socializing, I finally decided it was time to connect with the outside world again. I started by trying to think of a few people who weren't close friends of my wife and mine. Out of nowhere, the smiling face of Lee Lawrence lit up like a light bulb over my head.

Having worked with Lee and Bert for almost two years until their business,and their marriage, went on the rocks, the Lawrences and I had lost track of each other. Maybe ten years had past, and with the breakup of my own marriage, the thought of seeing Lee cheered me up. I tracked her down, phoned her, and invited her to dinner. We had drinks outside on the terrace and talked. We watched the sun go down, I cooked, and during dinner, we brought each other up to date. I told her my wife had left me, and she told me about her divorce, her breakdown, and a number of months in a mental hospital. Her ex-husband had been given custody of their children. However, Lee finally managed to convince the doctors to put her into rehab, which led to discharge from the hospital. Then living in her own apartment, she was able to reclaim her children and begin a new life.

Now after dinner, as we sat quietly with our empty wineglasses, we were looking fondly across the room at each other. Neither of us spoke of what must have been on our minds—*Are you thinking what I'm thinking?* But Lee's twinkling eyes were inviting.

"It's all right," she said, smiling.

I wasted no time getting to the couch and taking her in my arms. What was, at first, tentative became wild and wonderful, and we quickly moved into the bedroom. Any inhibition I may have had about making love in a bedroom I had shared with my wife was gone with the wind.

For the following months, Lee and I had a joyous romance in my penthouse and her apartment in nearby Riverdale. Stevie and Jeremy, Lee's sweet preteen kids, seemed to accept my intimate friendship with their mother. We were very discreet, and maybe the boys just weren't aware of what was going on. The four of us went on a vacation to Provincetown on Cape Cod. I loved the boys, and they accepted me with warm affection. It was the kind of closeness that was new to me. I didn't realize it at the time, but our relationship was actually a loving rejuvenation of both our spirits, our self-respect, and our self-esteem. Sometimes the sun sets on love affairs, as it did eventually on ours.

However, almost as our affair had begun, the platonic friendship of earlier times reappeared. Lee and I were old friends, and our "friendship sun" rose again.

At some point during the changes of our deep feelings for each other, Lee sent me a note. It was written on an inter-office correspondence form from *The Today Show*:

Before the riches of the world,
I place a friend most true
To stand out like a flag unfurled
When you are feeling blue!
A true friend will stand
Through thick or thin
When your cup is full to the brim with joy
Or your outlook as black as sin
A true friend tells faults too–
And thus, through all life's phases,
Aids and comforts you.
So wherever you go and whatever your lot,
Dear Howard, remember this poem.
You will always have a special spot
Within my heart and home.

That's the kind of person Lee Lawrence has always been–open, kind, and loving. Life for both of us went on, but the pressure of Lee's television schedule (never enough sleep) coupled with being a single mother running a household as well as her erratic social life began to take its toll on this strong but sensitive young woman. Early one morning, I got a call from Lee's doctor from a hospital where she had been admitted after a crippling "accident." Dr. Loman told me she had been found unconscious in a cement courtyard on Manhattan's West Side. I rushed to the hospital. Dr. Loman told me Lee was still unconscious, her condition extremely serious.

"She has multiple injuries and broken bones. The worst is her totally smashed right foot. It will have to be amputated. Lee will be unable to walk for a long time."

Lee was a survivor. After her recuperation, she was able to be on her own again and chose a pleasant East Side apartment as her new home. Lee's hope was to have Stevie and Jeremy, who had been living with their father and his second family, come live with her again. This proved to be a challenge to all concerned. Separately, both sons left New York. My first thought was they didn't want to make a choice between their parents. I do believe the reason was both maturing young men just wanted to get on with their lives. Stevie moved to North California, where he was to marry and bring up a family. Jeremy settled in Los Angeles and pursued his acting career.

Lee's job at *The Today Show* being over, she devoted herself to a longtime favorite project: *The Little Prince*, a book by writer-poet and pioneering aviator, Antoine de Saint-Exupéry. In 1974, a U.S.-British motion picture had been produced and directed by the prolific director Stanley Donen, a veteran of twenty-seven movies, half of them musicals. The film, with songs by Frederick Loewe and Alan Jay Lerner, received good notices, but it was not a hit.

Lee's plan was to obtain the rights to produce a television special of the French classic. She wrote an impressively detailed treatment and got in touch with her considerable connections in show business. However, even with a genuine interest from the multitalented Gene Kelly, who would have played the aviator and directed the production, Lee's dream failed to materialize.

Even after her recovery and rehabilitation, Lee began to find her New York life too stressful.

"Just getting a taxi has become a major chore," she said to me one day, waving her cane in the air. "I don't think I can take it much longer."

She didn't. With help from friends she had made on her *Today* job, she managed to secure a less demanding government job and moved to Washington, D.C. After getting married again and adopting a dog, Lee settled down.

Lee Lawrence had been a busy girl. The full story of her life would fill a very large book. She didn't write it. She lived it.

Lee Lawrence.

Lee on one of her many travels.

CHAPTER 58

WILD OATS

Here and There, 1950s and 1960s

I THINK IT was Billy Crystal who once said, "A woman needs a reason to have sex. A man just needs a place." Perhaps Mr. Crystal was right, but in my case, reason did not play a substantial force. Ostensibly recovering from the divorce, I plunged into a series of flings, one-night stands, and affairs with a wide array of partners in a number of places. Whenever and wherever, my judgment simply plunged out the window. I was, I've been told, notorious in my choices.

At the time, a friend referred to me as a lothario. I looked up the word in *Webster's Dictionary*: "Lothario, a character in Rowe's play *The Fair Penitent*—a libertine, a roué, a fascinating deceiver of women." I was not familiar with the play, but I never thought of myself as a libertine or a roué, and I don't think I ever deceived a woman. Then I looked up the word *libertine*. The definition I liked best was "one unconfined, a man who indulges in his desires without constraint." With the release I had found during my psychotherapy at the time, I may have become a libertine without realizing it.

I "slept around" all over Manhattan—uptown and downtown. I made love in my penthouse on the East Side. I made love in a penthouse on the West Side. I met a lovely girl at a Fifth Avenue cocktail party, and we danced. We immediately started seeing each other. In her penthouse one evening, she excused herself and left the room. When she returned, wearing nothing but a black ribbon around her neck and ballet toe shoes on her feet, the darling girl danced into the room en pointe. Although she wasn't a ballerina, I was smitten. The affair continued longer than any other, but after months of fun and frolic, our affair cooled, and I was back into flings and one-night stands.

I indulged in a new hotel on Broadway, in an old-fashioned hotel in Toronto, and in an oceanfront Palm Beach mansion after strolling in the shallow surf under a full moon. I had one night in Greenwich Village with a charming English actress named Norah, the same name of the lady of the evening I had shacked up with in London back in World War II. Our night was a delight. But instead of surprising me with tea and toast the next morning, as the London Norah had done, the New York Norah joined me with coffee. Then she sat sideways on the john next to the sink and watched me shave with her razor.

"You know, you're cutting off the evil that's popping out all over your face," Norah said.

"What's evil about shaving in front of a lovely lady from London?" I asked.

"That's a line from the play about Victoria Regina. I played the queen."

Although making love and true love can be associated, it does not necessarily involve both those strong forces of nature at the same time, and likewise, loving women–younger or older–doesn't always mean you end up in the sack. Sometimes you do. Sometimes you don't. Nevertheless, considering all those wild oats I sowed, none of them ever turned out to be the love I was looking for.

CHAPTER 59

SKATING ON THIN ICE

Manhattan, 1956

W HAT DOES A thirty-two-year-old bachelor do when his divorce is final? Well, if the weather out on his penthouse terrace is freezing, he floods the terrace with water and creates an ice-skating rink. It was a crazy idea, but that's what I did, and then I invited friends over for a spin on the ice. One of those friends was C. Robert Holloway.

Bob (as he was known in those days) was a bright, talented young man from the chorus of the off-Broadway musical *Out of This World*. Bob was also wildly ambitious and impatient to make his mark in the theater. He and his friend, a young composer named Jack Holmes, had conjured up a delightful musical revue with the lighter-than-air title *Balloons*. The show had songs by Jack and sketches by Bob and three other young (then) unknowns–Sheldon Harnick, Murray Grand, and G. Wood.

The comedian Paul Lynde, well-known from Leonard Sillman's musical revue *New Faces of 1952* on Broadway, was set to star and direct. Alice Ghostley, the eccentric comedienne with an operatic voice whose hilarious "Boston Beguine" was a high point in Mr. Sillman's revue, was set to costar. Bob had asked me to design the sets and costumes and be coproducer.

C. Robert Holloway as a young man.

The ice rink on my terrace seemed to be a perfect spot to stage a preproduction publicity stunt for Bob's revue *Balloons*. The *New York Times* agreed to send a photographer to cover the event. Actress Eileen Brennan and I donned skates and faked performing an ice dance, while comedian John Myhers, wrapped in a blanket, sat shivering next to the ice and pretended to coach us. The photographer did his job, and the photo appeared in the *The New York Times* theater section the next day. I was overjoyed, but the owner of the apartment building was not. The following morning, my doorbell rang.

"Look, Mr. Barker," the building manager said when I let him in, "I know what's been going on since your wife left you." There was a slight leer in his voice. "You and your friends have some pretty wild times up here on the eighteenth floor, but I figured, who would ever know?"

"Well, I really don't–" I started to defend myself, but the manager interrupted me.

"Then the building owner sees the article in the *Times* with a photo of you and a girl ice-skating on his roof! Come on! Whatta you think?" He stopped and chuckled. "Look, I told the landlord you are a nice guy, an excellent tenant who always pays his rent on time. I said I'd take care of everything. I asked him to overlook it and to give you another chance."

"Thank you. Thank you so much. I really appreciate it," I said, shaking his hand. "You'll have two front-row seats to *Balloons* on opening night. I promise."

With a slightly puzzled smile, the manager left, and I went inside to have coffee with Eileen. That afternoon, I turned a hot water hose on the terrace, and within one hour, the ice rink was down the drain.

The picture that ran in the *New York Times* article on February 14, 1958.

So what happened to *Balloons*? Well, instead of flying high, it went down the drain too. After eight months of backers' auditions in living rooms of wealthy prospective investors, we had raised only five hundred dollars. That investment was from my lawyer, Rebecca Brownstein, who had agreed to be our show's attorney. Back then, five hundred bucks might pay the cast for a week, but to open the show off Broadway, we would have needed more than ten times as much. Although I was sure it would have been a hit, our *Balloons* floated away into oblivion. So did the sweet times I had spent with Eileen. Both events elicited a sense of failure and regret.

During the summer months, I lived on that terrace, sunning, gardening, and entertaining. One July evening sixty-odd guests sat on straw mats under rented palm trees, drinking rum punch out of coconuts and eating roasted turkey (instead of roast pig) at my Hawaiian luau. Girls came in sarongs or hula skirts, and most of the guys wore flowered shirts. Those who didn't had to strip to the waist, and I placed leis of flowers around their necks. The party was a blast. Next morning, the sun rose over the palm trees and found me and two boozy friends lying on the straw mats next to the punch bowl, slurping the remains of the rum punch. There were no more big parties after that.

CHAPTER 60

WAKE UP AND SMELL THE GERANIUMS

Manhattan, Winter 1957

FLOYD CURTIS, AN actor and old friend I had known for years, invited me to visit the set for the television series in which he was appearing. No matter how many movie sets or television shows I work on or visit, a warm feeling of excitement always comes over me when I walk into a soundstage. Floyd introduced me to Patty Duke, its young star, and she charmed me instantly. The rest of the cast was warm and friendly. The actress who played Patty's mother was tall and beautiful, and she had a bright, easy smile.

"I'm Jeanne Baron," she said, shaking my hand. "I'm from Los Angeles, but I'll be here in New York for the run of the series."

Floyd and I watched the rehearsal, and Jeanne joined us for dinner at a cozy restaurant near the studio. We sat chatting for what seemed a little too long with no attention from the waiter. Jeanne focused on one standing nearby.

"If that sucker doesn't take our orders in one minute," she said sweetly, "I'll tell him what he can do with this menu." She rolled it up just as the waiter sauntered over to our table.

"May I get the lady and gentlemen something from the bar?" the waiter crooned. He got Jeanne's message clearly when she ordered "a vodka martini, straight up, with a twist, and it had better be ice cold." He also got her bright but firm, wide smile.

Right then, I learned Jeanne was a tough cookie, but there was also a lively sweetness that shone through and an instant attraction between us. It was one of those "your place or mine" moments, and we took advantage of it. I also learned Jeanne was an expert at making love.

Jeanne's days in the studio were long, and mine were even longer, so we usually saw each other only on weekends. These, we spent together in her place or mine. We both liked to eat, and we both liked to cook, usually with a martini or a glass of wine in hand. We must have gone to movies and the theater too, but I can't remember anything we saw. Our tastes were simple, and we indulged ourselves. When winter came, Jean learned I liked ice-skating in Central Park, so she immediately bought a pair of skates.

"Okay, sport," she said into the phone the next time I called her for a date. "Grab your skates and meet me at the rink. You're gonna teach me how to do it." Now we had another thing we liked to do.

One night, after an hour on the ice, we decided we'd had enough fresh air and headed for her apartment. Cocktails were followed by a delicious dinner and a delicious evening in bed. In the middle of the night, something awakened me. I looked out of the window and saw that the first snow of the season was falling. The silence of the moment was broken by Jean's voice.

"Isn't it beautiful?" she said.

I turned over and saw she was propped up on a pillow and gazing out at the snowflakes. "Have you been awake long?" I asked.

"No, not really," she said dreamily. "It started just a little while ago. It's so pretty. We don't have snow in LA, you know."

"No, I guess you don't," I said.

We shared a few tender moments until I suddenly sprang upright.

"Oh my god!" I shouted.

"What's the matter, darling?" Jean asked.

"My geraniums!" I said.

"Your geraniums?" It didn't sound exactly like a question.

"You know, all those pots on my terrace," I said. "They'll freeze!" Now I was out of the bed, standing stark naked at the window, staring at the steady snow falling outside.

"They'll freeze. So what?" Her tone was matter of fact.

I stumbled. "They'll die," I said as if to a child. "Jeanne, where are my shorts?"

"On the floor, lover, where you dropped them," she said. "At the foot of the bed, remember?"

There was an icicle hanging on each syllable.

I found my shorts and put them on. "I can't let my plants die," I said a little too loudly. "I've got to get them inside!" I explained, pulling on my pants.

"You mean to tell me you're leaving my bed and driving all the way up to 96th Street to take some pots of geraniums inside?" She was incredulous.

"Yes, Jeanne," I said as I buttoned my shirt, grabbed my jacket in the living room, and headed for the door.

"Well, sweetheart, why don't you just do that!" she shouted after me. "Good night!"

The next time I saw Miss Baron was in Long Beach, California. I was twenty-five years older, married, and the father of three children. I had been hired by Cynthia Baer, my old friend and coproducer from *Little Mary Sunshine* days, to design the costumes for *Bittersweet*, the Noel Coward musical starring Shirley Jones. It was good to be working with Cynthia again, and Miss Jones was a darling woman. When Shirley learned I had been booked into a ho-hum hotel, she was not pleased.

"You must be with all the rest of us on the *Queen Mary*," she insisted.

I was immediately moved into the vintage luxury ocean liner. The ship had been converted into a world-class hotel and was now moored permanently in Long Beach harbor. My stateroom was sumptuous! I was most grateful.

BITTERSWEET   L·B·C·L·O

MADAME SARI LINDEN   ACT II SCENES   Howard Barker

BITTERSWEET   L·B·C·L·O

LADY SHAYNE   ACT I SCENE I   Howard Barker

Here are three of the costumes I designed for Shirley Jones in *Bittersweet*.

At the first rehearsal of the show, who should I see? Jeanne Baron! She was as surprised to see an old flame as I was, and she greeted me with genuine delight. Neither of us brought up the winter night when we had last seen each other. Jeanne looked lovely. She was playing Shirley Jones' aunt in the show, but ironically, Jeanne was actually younger than Miss Jones. However, as they sometimes say, "That's show business." Jeanne was also pleased when I came backstage on opening night.

"You were marvelous!" I said and presented her with my bouquet of long-stemmed red roses. "I wanted to bring you geraniums. But I couldn't find them anywhere. Will these do?"

Jeanne's look was unforgettable. Her response was perfect. "Darling, they are beautiful," she said, flashing her great smile, "and yes, they will do."

The always lovely Jeanne Baron.

CHAPTER 61

MR. DEMILLE, I'M READY FOR MY CLOSE-UP

NYC, 1957

I WAS INVITED to another one of Stella Adler's cocktail parties, and once again, I arrived late. This time, I did not drink martinis, and this time, only a few people were still there. One of Stella's guests was the silent-film star Gloria Swanson.

Gloria Swanson started her film career in 1914 in *His New Job*, starring and directed by Charlie Chaplin. She appeared in seventy-two movies and many shorts and television shows and won the Golden Globe for Best Actress for her starring role as Norma Desmond, the silent-film star in the motion picture *Sunset Boulevard*. Miss Swanson may still hold the title of Queen at a court of the most glamorous movie stars of all time.

Although I had never seen her early movies, I was captivated by this enchanting actress. Now only in her late sixties, Miss Swanson was a stunning woman. Her skin was pale and lovely, her eyes were sparkling, and her smile was incandescent. Holding the ever-present red carnation, she was utterly charming. We were introduced, and she linked her arm in mine.

"Please call me Gloria," she said. "Shall we go out on the terrace? The park is so beautiful at this time of year."

It was a scene right out of a movie. As we strolled among the flowers and plants on Stella's terrace, I soon discovered Gloria and I shared an interest in gardening.

"I live in a tiny penthouse near here," I told her. "My terrace is actually larger than my whole apartment, and I really love taking care of my plants."

We were deep in conversation when Stella came out from the living room.

"What in the world do you two find so interesting to talk about out here?" Stella asked, ever so slightly annoyed.

"Fertilizer," Miss Swanson replied.

"Fertilizer?" questioned our hostess, her eyes wide.

"Yes, my dear, fertilizer," Gloria answered sweetly, flashing that blinding, clinched-teeth smile.

Stella turned and withdrew to her living room.

Flash-forward ten years to 1967. Surprisingly, I found myself sitting with Miss Swanson in her living room with a group of filmmakers discussing plans for a testimonial celebration for her. Like Stella Adler, Gloria Swanson was hypnotizing. As ideas for the event were presented, she listened and made suggestions while holding us in the palms of her expressive hands. The celebration was to be held at the Astoria Film Studios in Queens, where Miss Swanson's silent movies had been filmed back in the 1920s. My job was to decorate a mammoth soundstage for the gala evening. As a set designer in movies and TV, I had worked on that stage before, but to decorate such an enormous barn-size space for a memorial dinner was daunting. A date was set for a final meeting, and we disbanded.

After many hours of thinking, I came up with a plan. I decided to have giant blowups of photos from all of Miss Swanson's films made and hang them high around the periphery of the unlit stage. The lighting designer would illuminate the photos with spotlights so they would stand out in the darkness. For one end of the stage, I designed marquee-like signs framed by electric lights that would hang in space and spell out the titles of her major movies. The marquees were to hang in the dark, surrounding a twenty-four-foot-long hot-pink neon replica of the Gloria Swanson signature.

On the big night, spotlights shone down on the round tables seating the hundreds of guests at dinner. On cue, the electric light marquees flashed on, and as Miss Swanson made her entrance, the neon signature lit up high above her head.

"Ladies and gentlemen—Miss Gloria Swanson!" announced the emcee to the guests' applause.

Escorted by a handsome escort, the diminutive star made her way to her table of dignitaries on the stage platform. An orchestra played for dining and dancing.

There were speeches, and Miss Swanson was presented with a commemorative plaque for her long and illustrious career. All the guests were given a large autographed caricature of Miss Swanson, drawn by the star herself. In her gracious speech of appreciation, Gloria thanked me for my part in making the evening memorable. Madeleine Arentoft, my new young wife from Denmark, was there with me and a group of our friends from the entertainment world. All in all, it was a gala, an unforgettable event.

CHAPTER 62

HAPPY EASTER EGG

Hollywood, 1958

WELL, IF YOU'VE read this far, you might as well know about my one-night stand with Martha Raye. Of course, if you happen to be a young reader, you may not have even heard of Martha Raye. The comedienne was famous for her big mouth and for entertaining audiences with her outrageous behavior in the many movies she made in the 1930s, 1940s, and 1950s.

Sometime in my late thirties, I was in Los Angeles designing a TV commercial. Having nothing to do for the weekend, I decided to look up James Lanphier, the actor whom I knew from summer stock ten years earlier. Jim was now living in Hollywood.

"Why don't you come over for dinner this evening?" he suggested. "We'll have a drink, and I'll whip up something light. And around midnight, I'll take you to a small party to dye Easter eggs."

Dye Easter eggs? At midnight? Could that be a code word for a special kind of fun in La-la land? "Sounds good to me," I said with a small smirk to the telephone.

"You look just the same as you did ten years ago," I said when Jimmy opened the door. "Hollywood must agree with you."

"Same to you, baby," he said. "New York must agree with you."

I hadn't been called baby since I left Mississippi, but now in Hollywood, where everyone calls everyone else "baby," I didn't mind. We talked shop and had a few drinks, I vodka, he scotch and milk.

"Easier on the tummy," he said.

Somewhat later after dinner, we drove to the party. On the way, I asked who was going to be there.

"Martha Raye and a bunch of other actors," he said. "It should be great fun."

Sure, I thought. *Martha Raye and a bunch of Hollywood actors dyeing Easter eggs at midnight?* Again, my imagination went into overdrive, and all kinds of scenes raced through my head.

When we arrived at the party, it was in full swing. There were only a few actors there, none of whom I'd ever seen before. Loud music was coming from a stereo somewhere, but nobody was dancing on the tables. Indeed, Martha Raye was there, and she was dyeing Easter eggs! Jimmy kissed her on both cheeks, and she kissed him on the mouth.

"Martha, meet my friend," he said. "Howard's from New York."

"Hi, Howard!" Miss Raye shouted over the loud music. "Call me Maggie! I'm gonna make you a very special Easter egg!"

She did, and it was a very beautiful one. Pleasant conversation with a few drinks and a midnight supper–the party was a totally innocent experience. I think the most salacious thing that had happened that night was Maggie telling about her first appearance in show business, when she joined her parents' vaudeville act at the age of three. Tough and boisterous on film, Maggie was sweet and tender in person, very warm, very funny, and very down-to-earth. She was Martha Raye.

After I came back to New York, I kept that Easter egg she had made for me as long as I dared. When I finally ate it, the egg and the memory of Maggie at the party was all there was to my "one-night stand" with Martha Raye.

When I was twelve years old, I saw Martha Raye in her first movie, *Rhythm on the Range*, a musical western starring Bing Crosby, Frances Farmer, and Bob Burns. Over the years, I saw Miss Raye in a number of the twenty-nine films in which she sang, danced, and clowned her way to stardom. With such great performers as Jimmy Durante, W. C. Fields, Joe E. Brown, Abbott and Costello, and Bob Hope, Miss Raye carved out an impressive niche in the world of movie musicals and comedies.

In 1947, Martha Raye played a wealthy woman in Charlie Chaplin's last motion picture, *Monsieur Verdoux*. Acting opposite one of the greatest performers in motion picture history, Miss Raye had been chosen personally by the star and director of the movie–Mr. Chaplin himself.

The irrepressible, rambunctious star performed on early television when that medium was very young. On *The Martha Raye Show* (1954–1956), she was the lead, and her awkward boyfriend was portrayed by retired boxer Rocky Graziano. Among her many appearances on other television shows in the fifties, sixties, and seventies and as late as the mid-eighties, Miss Raye was seen on *The Love Boat*, *Murder She Wrote*, *The Judy Garland Show*, *The Carol Burnett Show*, *The Jackie Gleason Show*, and *The Andy Williams Show*. She has two stars on the Hollywood Walk of Fame, one for motion pictures and another for television.

She may have been boisterous and brassy and known for her big mouth, but Martha Raye also had a big heart. She joined the USO soon after the United States entered World War II, and for entertaining the troops tirelessly in Vietnam and subsequent wars, she was named Woman of the Year. She was an Honorary Colonel in the Marines and an Honorary Lieutenant Colonel in the U.S. Army. Among dozens of other awards, she received the Presidential Medal of Freedom.

Martha Raye was seventy-eight when she died of pneumonia in Los Angeles. In appreciation of her work with the USO, special consideration was given to bury her in Arlington National Cemetery. But at her own request, she was ultimately buried in Fort Bragg, North Carolina. Martha is the only woman buried in the Special Forces Cemetery there, and she was given full military honors.

As a U.S. Army veteran of World War II, once stationed in Fort Bragg, I salute Martha Raye with my deepest gratitude and sincere affection.

CHAPTER 63

THE MILLINER AND I

NYC, 1958

THE SHOWPLACE, A bar in Greenwich Village, was primarily a hangout for young theater people. The upstairs cabaret had an adequate platform for performers and a baby grand but not enough space for anything else, such as sets for Richard Besoyan's new musical revue *In Your Hat*. Therefore, my costume designs for the show, especially the hats, would actually become more significant.

Nicholas Giangrande, a window display director at Lord & Taylor and a good friend of mine, told me he would be able to supply the hats and jewelry for the show from the store for program credit. Nick introduced me to Ingrid Schieder, the extremely attractive millinery department head at L&T. It proved to be a good deal for everyone.

Mrs. Schieder, who bore a striking resemblance to a dark-haired Marlene Dietrich, had quickly risen through the ranks from hat model to buyer to department head. Soon after we met, she spoke candidly about her present position.

"My department has increased hat sales by at least fifty percent," she told me. "I could have done it sooner if the managers had taken my suggestions. It amazes me how stupid they could be." She went on, "I have been in this country just five years. I know my German heritage means I'm supposed to be aggressive, but I am ambitious and simply trying to get ahead."

"Being German doesn't necessarily mean you have to be aggressive," I said. "Nick told me you've been compared to Marlene Dietrich and Greta Garbo. Both of those dames were ambitious, and they surely got ahead."

"I'm only half German," Ingrid explained, calming down. "My father was German, but my mother was Swedish like Garbo, so I guess I have something in common with both women."

"Not only that," I went on. "Like both of them, you're beautiful too." As Ingrid softened a little, I kept on going. "I've heard Ernest Hemingway's nickname for Marlene was the 'kraut,' but I believe he was in love with her at the time."

I was looking directly into her eyes. Working closely with Ingrid became a pleasure. In fact, it was more than a pleasure. By the time *In Your Hat* opened, we had become intimately involved.

Richard's little revue had a talented cast of actor-singers. Two actresses, Barbara Sharma and Eileen Brennan, gave memorable performances. Barbara, a titian-haired Kewpie doll, sang "Cuckoo" to a bird while she danced in ballerina toe shoes. Eileen Brennan, a lovely showbiz soprano, sang contralto as an inebriated opera diva, sipping from a liquor flask she had removed from her walking stick.

Jane Romano (Juno in *Dick's Out of This World*), with her boisterous singing and comical sketches, was a standout. Karen Anders's nice but naughty renditions of Dick's songs brought down the house. Handsome baritone Bill Graham and the appealing Ken McMillan, also from *Out of This World*, appealed to all audiences. Owner of the Showplace Jim Paul Eilers kept a close eye on all of the proceedings.

In Your Hat was a success. It was popular with the regular clientele of the Showplace and their friends as well as friends and families of the cast. Also, Greenwich Village citizens and word of mouth did the trick for a decent run.

The second act, entitled "Gems From Little Mary Sunshine: A New Musical about an Old Operetta," was delightful and attracted most of the attention. Dick decided to expand it and turn it into a full-length musical. (Who knew this idea would turn into an off-Broadway hit that would run for three years?)

Whirlwind romances with women, even with older women, can be tempestuous. They can happen so quickly, and all that seems important is to be together. Ingrid and I were constantly together. Her apartment was near Lord & Taylor, and mine was not far away. We met for lunch frequently, and our dinner dates invariably turned into sleepovers at her place or mine. Weekends often meant a drive to Connecticut to visit Ingrid's family transplanted from Germany.

Ingrid had two sons from a former marriage. They were living with Ingrid's sister and brother-in-law in a small house Ingrid had bought in New London so she could be with her children from Friday night through Sunday as well as all holidays.

If Ingrid was an ambitious businesswoman, her sister, Gertie, was just the opposite—a zaftig, happy hausfrau—and Peter was her jovial, pipe-smoking husband. The two boys—Tomas, eleven, and Stefan, twelve—were great kids. They were sweet kids too, and it was easy for me to become attached to them.

Ingrid's children always wore lederhosen on the weekends, and
I had bought myself a pair when I was in Germany, so I figured
I should wear mine and fit right in on our weekend visits.

I spent many happy weekends with Ingrid and her family before it began to dawn on me that I wasn't quite ready to settle down to a tranquil life with a readymade family. I knew there were more wild oats to be sown. The original fireworks of our affair burned out. I felt like a louse, but Ingrid firmly assured me she wasn't heartbroken.

"Our relationship was never serious, Howard. We were really just good friends."

Nevertheless, the good friends stopped seeing each other.

CHAPTER 64

LITTLE MARY SUNSHINE

Greenwich Village East, 1958

WHILE *IN YOUR Hat* was still running, Richard had been working for months on the mammoth task of converting the second act into his new full-length musical *Little Mary Sunshine*. Now it was done, and Dick had wisely set his sights on off-Broadway. Two of his acquaintances, Cynthia Baer and Bob Chambers, both young theater aficionados, came on board to produce the show. As I had done for *Out of This World*, I was to design the sets and costumes for *Little Mary*.

One day Dick and I met for lunch, and we had not even finished our martinis when Dick asked me to coproduce the show.

"Backers' auditions are underway," Dick told me. "But it's slow going. Cynthia and Bob are doing a good job, but we have a long way to go. Frankly, pal, I really need your help."

"What'll Cynthia and Bob think about all this?" I asked.

"I'm the silent senior partner, and that means on all major issues, what I say goes."

I liked the idea of being part of management, and I accepted his offer to be a coproducer.

"You can handle the advertising too. You'll be good at that," he said. "I've met an ad agency woman named Gladys Bentley. I like her a lot. Why don't you give her a call?"

Right after lunch, I did. "My name is Howard Barker," I said. "I'm coproducing Richard Besoyan's new show. Dick asked me to call you."

A gravelly voice said, "I'll see you at my office tomorrow at noon. We'll have coffee and talk."

At twelve o'clock sharp the next day, I was there.

"I'm Gladys Bentley," said the woman sitting behind a large desk and sticking out her hand. "Call me Gladys and sit down." Gladys had a firm handshake, a tip-off of a strong woman. She poured two cups of coffee and handed me one. "When I started out, I was young and ambitious," she said. "I was a feisty, redheaded newspaper reporter, all over the place. Now I'm a one-woman advertising agency."

Gladys was actually a tough, fast-mouthed, gray-haired dame, and she was no beauty. In fact, to borrow one of my Aunt Amber's expressions, she was "as plain as a mud fence." Gladys and I liked each other instantly.

Gladys turned out to be a sweetheart, and we worked well together. We coauthored the ad copy—Gladys dealt with the newspapers, and I handled the artwork. Actually, all the artwork except for one thing.

"Howard, Dick tells me you are a terrific set designer and a good all-around artist," Gladys said and paused. "Do you know Dick's friend, Don Cornelius?"

I shook my head. "But I've heard of him."

"Well, Don has come up with a sketch Dick thinks is a great caricature of his Little Mary." She took a drawing from her desk drawer and handed it to me. "Dick's mad about it," she said. "He wants it to be in all the ads for the show. Wha'dya think?"

I studied the sketch—the wide smile, luscious but sweet, with turned-up corners, the eyes, bold and bright, and a tumbling mass of curls falling away from the girl's face. "I love it. Actually, it's a caricature of Eileen Brennan, the actress who'll be playing Little Mary."

From that moment on, Don's caricature appeared in virtually every ad as well as on the posters.

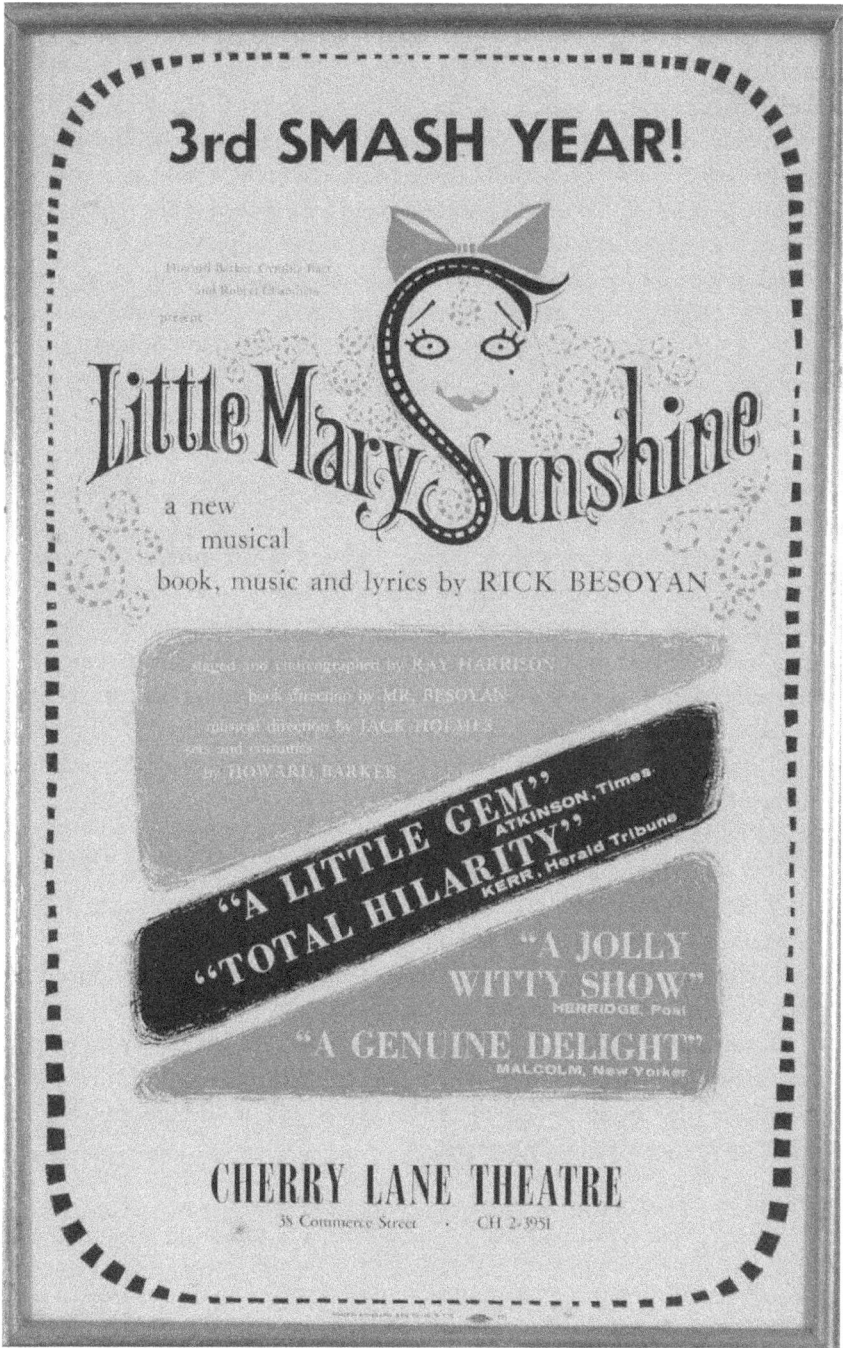

Raising the twenty thousand dollars to put on the show was an enormous undertaking. It took almost a year of backers' auditions with actors whom we could not afford to pay but were promised roles in the show. The three largest investments at that time were five hundred dollars each–Richard's mother's, Gladys Bentley's, and mine. The smallest was twenty-five dollars, and there were many of those, mostly from money-strapped friends who wanted to wish us well. My terrace, without the ice rink, made the *Times* again when my apartment, inside and out, was photographed for a spread in the paper's home section. Show business, even off Broadway, thrives on publicity.

Jules Wallach, a carpenter I knew, owned a construction shop, and he agreed to build the sets as an investment in the show. With some assistance from our actors, I started painting the sets in the shop and finished the job after they were moved into the theater. Installing the sets and lights was a backbreaking task, again done primarily by the same young men and the lighting designer, Jim Gore. With help from the ladies ensemble, more than thirty period costumes were executed by Poppi Lagodmos, my Greek goddess from *Out of This World*.

The week before we were to open, a myriad of last-minute set problems had to be faced. Ed Royce, the indefatigable stage manager, worked day and night, with assistance from his magic pills, a cocktail or two, and me. Opening night was upon us, and we were exhausted, but finally, everything was ready–almost everything, that is. While Ed was behind the set speaking to the actors, I walked on the empty stage carrying a bucket of paint and a long-handled roller with a paint tray. As I was about to pour the paint into the tray, Ed appeared.

"Whatta you think you're doing?" he shouted.

"I'm just gonna paint the stage floor, you know, grass green."

"Like hell you are!" he shouted. "Get that shit outta here before I throw it at you!" This was my friendly stage manager blowing up.

"Calm down, Ed," I spoke like I was talking to a child. "I'll be done in no time. The show doesn't start for another hour."

"Calm down?!" He was turning purple. "Opening night curtain goes up an hour earlier! I've just called five! We go up in five fucking minutes! Now move!"

I wasn't the producer anymore. I was just the set designer. I moved. I picked up my stuff and disappeared.

Myself and the other two producers, Cynthia Baer and
Bob Chambers, in front of the Orpheum Theater during
opening night of *Little Mary Sunshine*, 1959.

At seven o'clock, November 19, 1959, when the house lights dimmed in
the Orpheum Theater on Lower Second Avenue, a spotlight came up on
producer Cynthia Baer in front of the red velvet curtain. She was wearing
an old-fashioned gingham frock and carrying a lighted taper. The audience
quieted down.

"Hello," she said, and as she moved across the stage, she simulated lighting
the old-fashioned fake footlights, one by one. "I would like to take you back to
a time when the world was more simple than ours is today," she announced.
"For instance, good meant good, bad meant bad, virtue was all, and justice,
well, justice always triumphed."

The audience tittered.

"At least, we like to think it was that way. But before we begin, the company
wishes to express its appreciation to everyone who made this production
possible, especially"–she checked her notes–"Johann Strauss, Rudolf Friml,
and Victor Herbert."

There was polite laughter from the audience.

"And now it gives us great pleasure to present a saga of Colorado, *LITTLE
MARY SUNSHINE!*"

The audience burst into applause.

Earlier, Richard and I had sent each other opening night telegrams quoting a line from an old movie when a couple of theater producers were watching their show—"Well, Max, it looks like we've got a hit on our hands," one of them said to the other—and now standing in the back of the theater, the two of us shook hands and hoped.

The sound of spirited whistling came from the lobby behind us, and a line of scarlet-jacketed Forest Rangers—the men's chorus, led by their captain—marched down the center aisle. There was more applause as they ascended the steps onto the stage, and marking time as the house lights went down and the curtain went up, the Rangers burst out singing their marching song, "Stout-hearted Men." Big applause! The expanded full-length musical *Little Mary Sunshine* was born.

I never knew where the money came from to pay for the opening night party at Sardi's, but the entire company, families, and friends were there. As the reviews in the city's six newspapers were read aloud, we listened to the critics' raves about Richard's spoof of the operettas of Johann Strauss, Franz Lehár, and Rudolf Friml. The *New York Times* and the *Herald Tribune* had sent their "second string" critics, Louis Calta and Judith Crist, to cover the opening, and they loved it. We were a smash hit! We celebrated—drinking, eating, drinking, laughing and crying, drinking—until Vincent Sardi had to turn off the lights to get us out.

The next morning, with only $2.50 in the till, there was a long line outside the box office. People of all ages flocked to the theater for tickets, and Rick (as he was now suddenly known) became the toast of the town. Magazines published articles about the miracle of his "overnight success." Radio interviews blossomed (television interviews were rare in those days).

The following Saturday, both the *Times*' and the *Tribune*'s first-string critics, Brooks Atkinson and Walter Kerr, attended the show and came out in the Sunday editions with glowing reviews. I loved Kerr's. "Total hilarity: Watch what happens when Eileen Brennan, walking as if she had an adorably broken toe, lowers her eyes at the precise instant that all the Forest Rangers raise their voices to the heavens in 'Look for a Sky of Blue.'" Eileen, who played Little Mary, charmed the critics and instantly became the darling of off-Broadway.

To celebrate the show's successful launching, Gladys Bentley invited Rick and the show's three producers to lunch at the expensive new restaurant The Four Seasons. Maybe I forgot to mention Gladys was generous too.

Gladys Bentley and I created over a thousand ads, large and small, for the major newspapers and magazines such as the *New Yorker*. What started as purely a business relationship turned into a true affection as Gladys and I became personal friends. We took in movies and shows together, gossiped together, and philosophized together.

Eventually, we even shared stories of our personal experiences. Gladys learned about my on-and-off romance with Eileen and then surprised me with an account of her ongoing affair with her dentist, a married man. Gladys wept with the admission.

"The bastard is driving me crazy!" she sobbed.

Only one other time did my tough old friend reveal her vulnerability. We were in a heated argument about placing an ad, and I questioned the size of it, the cost of it, and whether it was even a good ad or not.

"What the hell do you know about advertising anyway?" Gladys snapped.

"Maybe not much, but don't be such a bitch about it!" I shot back.

"You can't talk like that to me!" She burst into tears like a schoolgirl ignored at the prom.

I was flabbergasted. "Gladys, I'm sorry," I said.

"Never mind," she mumbled, drying her eyes. "Let's get on with it."

Even after *Little Mary Sunshine* closed, we made it a point to see each other over lunch or for dinner. However, without a common interest, we eventually lost touch.

A few years later, I was shocked to learn Gladys had been found dead her bedroom, apparently of a heart attack. Remembering the days we worked and played together, I think of her good work, her spontaneous laugh, and her surprising sweetness. I miss my old friend Gladys Bentley very much.

Like the uptown shows, *Little Mary Sunshine* had its own press agent. Bob Ullman, a pleasant, energetic guy, set up interviews with *Time, Life, Newsweek, The Theater, Mademoiselle, Dance Magazine,* and *Rogue.* The writer-composer-director Rick Besoyan and actress-singer Eileen Brennan were highly praised, and so were the first-time coproducers Barker, Baer, and Chambers. At those interviews, Rick spoke of his background in Gilbert and Sullivan operettas but also of his love of the Jeanette MacDonald and Nelson Eddy movies and those of Buster Keaton, W. C. Fields, and the Marx Brothers. When Miss Brennan was asked where she got her inspiration for Little Mary, a lovely, gentle heroine with a backbone of steel, her answer was simple.

"I drew from my mother, Snow White, and Jeanette MacDonald–all three of them, in just about equal parts."

Eileen Brennan as Little Mary Sunshine, 1959.

"Young Ladies from the Eastchester Finishing
School" in *Little Mary Sunshine*, 1959.

Young Ladies with the Forest Rangers.

Me and the ladies of *Little Mary* posing for a photoshoot.

Richard Charles Hoh as Colonel Oscar Fairfax dancing with the ladies. Richard and I eventually became personal friends, traveling together in Europe and visiting each other long after *Little Mary* closed. He was an incredible painter and did many portraits over the years. Our friendship continued, with us visiting each other as recently as last year, he at the ripe age of ninety-two and myself at ninety-four. Unfortunately, he just passed away this year, so I am glad I was able to see him one last time.

Here is Richard and I on our European travels together.

Richard would visit for holidays. Here we are much later in life.

This was a portrait of me Richard Charles had painted in our earlier days.

CHAPTER 65

LITTLE MARY SUNSHINE: THE MOVIE?

Manhattan, 1960

WITH THE RAVE reviews and lines of theatergoers buying tickets for our hit, I started to fantasize about a movie, a musical movie, based on *Little Mary Sunshine* (my fantasy included the idea that the screenplay would be written by me). That fantasy began to become partially real the day I finally sat down at the typewriter. To escape the distraction of fun and friends, I holed up in a Catskill Mountains hideaway owned by a friend of mine, a French cameraman named Joe Brun. After a couple of weeks of nonstop writing, alone in Joe's cabin, I had what I thought was a pretty good draft. Joe loved it and wanted to direct the movie and shoot it too. Joe and I flew out to Colorado to scout possible locations for the movie's exteriors in the glorious Rocky Mountains. With a guest ranch as our base, we spent a couple of weeks in and around Estes Park on horseback, photographing some of the most gorgeous scenery imaginable. As soon as we got back to New York, I called my ex-wife's agent, Archer King.

"Are you still on good terms with Sue Mengers?" I asked.

"Sure," he said. "But since she became the hottest agent on the coast, we don't chat often. Why do you ask? You still want to get into the movies?"

"No, thank you," I said. "That was your idea, and it didn't work. No, this time, I want to sell my screenplay for *Little Mary Sunshine*, preferably to MGM. They used to make the big musicals. I thought Mengers might know how to get to the right people."

"Yeah, you're right," Archer said. "Good idea!" Archer smelled money, and we sent her a "treatment" along with my screenplay and the location photos.

Within days, I was surprised to find myself sitting with Sue Mengers on the thickly carpeted floor in her Park Avenue office.

"Let's be comfortable, Howard," she had said, explaining her preference. "And please call me Sue." She was charming. I was excited. "What do you think about Bob Redford for Captain Jim?" Sue asked.

Now I was speechless. *The number-one male movie star, Robert Redford, as Captain Jim of the Colorado Forest Rangers? Is she kidding? Had she even read my screenplay?*

"Well, I think Redford is great."

Sue waited, and I blurted, "But can he sing?"

"I don't know," she answered. "As I remember from the show, he has only sung a couple of songs. They could dub him."

"Right," I said. "Actually, I've already asked Rick to write another song, a solo for Captain Jim. Any leading man would insist on that."

"Right," Sue agreed. "Okay, I'll set it up for you to take meetings with reps for new properties at MGM and a couple of other studios on the coast. We'll see if *Little Mary* will fly. Call my secretary tomorrow for the list of names and numbers."

I got to my feet, and being a Southern gentleman, I felt I should help her up and extended my hand. With a bright smile and a shake of her head, she looked into my eyes and declined.

"Call me the minute you get back. Good luck, Howard."

Looking back on that meeting, I remember being a mite chagrined that Miss Mengers never even mentioned Archer's old call to her about me being a good bet as a young leading man. C'est la vie.

Two weeks later, I was sitting with wunderkind Marty Meyerson, a minor Vice President in charge of new properties at MGM. Marty's office was appropriately lush. I was trying to sink deeply into the soft couch like Marty, who was lounging on it next to me. Life on the West Coast moves at a slower pace than it does in New York.

"I understand your little show was a big hit in New York," Marty said. "How long did it run?"

"It's still running," I said.

"Great!" Marty growled. "How's business?"

"Business is great."

"Great," Marty echoed.

"I mean, we're selling out." I couldn't say "great" again.

Marty could. "Great! Now where do we go from here?" *Could it be he's interested?*

"I would like you to make a big movie of *Little Mary Sunshine*," I said as simply as I could.

"Great. *Little Mary*," Marty said. I didn't know if he meant "great" or if he was asking a question. Then he did. "Is it a kiddie show?"

"No, people of all ages love it. It's a comedy about music. It's a spoof."

"Spoof. Ah, I see." Plainly, Marty didn't. "*Little Mary Sunshine*? Not a kiddie show?"

"No," I answered quickly. "Little Mary is a sort of nickname for the leading lady. It doesn't mean anything, really. I realize our show is an off-Broadway production." I said, "And of course, it would need to be opened up for a big movie, with stars playing all the major roles." No reply from Marty, so I tossed another ball in the air. "Sue suggested Robert Redford for Captain Jim."

"Great!" Marty sat up. "Who's Captain Jim?"

"The male lead," I think Marty understood. There was no comment, so I went on. "My screenplay opens in the year 1910, with a high-angle shot of an old-fashioned train chugging through the mountains in Colorado. The Rocky Mountains."

"Your screenplay?" Marty looked into my eyes for the first time. "You wrote the screenplay?"

"Yes. I wrote it," I said confidently. "I've cowritten a musical with Besoyan before." I decided not to mention the show was never produced.

"Now this screenplay opens in 1910?" Marty actually showed some interest. "So how do you make it work?"

"Work?" I parroted him, looking directly into his eyes.

"To bring your show up to date. Like that English musical based on a stage musical too, called, uh, what was it called? You remember, a bunch of actors putting on a show–*The Boy Friend*. It was like one of those old movies with Garland and Rooney, only English. The Brits made it more human. It was all about their problems. They cut out some of the songs and stuff, and it was funny."

"Well, *Little Mary Sunshine* is funny. So I say you just shoot it, songs and all, like *Annie Get Your Gun* and *The Unsinkable Molly Brown*. They were funny, and they were period musicals. What about *The Sound of Music*? It was one of the best of all time and a period musical. That worked. They didn't bring it up to date." Marty listened politely.

"Anyway," I continued, "in my screenplay, we are on the train. Yellow Feather, the Indian villain, silently saunters down the aisle and plops himself down on the seat next to two girls, two beautiful young girls. I want Joe Namath to play Yellow Feather. He's a football star, but he could look like an Indian."

Nothing from Marty.

"The girls–their first song is 'Young Ladies From Eastchester Finishing School'–are on vacation in the mountains."

The phone on Marty's desk rang. Marty sat up.

"Let me tell you about the other stars I have in mind," I said. "Eileen–"

The phone kept ringing.

"Eileen Bren–" I tried to continue. "Eileen–"

"I've got to take this call," Marty said, springing up from the couch.

"Brennan, the original Little Mary" came out of my mouth.

Marty cut me off with a dramatic wave of his hand. "We'll talk next week," he said and warmly shook my hand. "Ciao, baby."

I never heard from Marty again. I actually met with producers and reps at a couple of other studios. Those meetings were amazingly similar and just as disappointing as my meeting with Marty. I got out of Hollywood as quickly as I could.

During its three-year run, there were many replacements in the cast of *Little Mary Sunshine*. After a year as Little Mary, Eileen Brennan moved uptown to take over Anne Bancroft's role as the devoted teacher Annie Sullivan in *The Miracle Worker*. In 1961, she went with the play on a National tour. Then she starred as another teacher, Anna Leonowens, in the New York City Center production of *The King and I*. In early 1964, Eileen created the role of Irene Mulloy, the milliner in Jerry Herman's *Hello, Dolly!*, starring Carol Channing, on Broadway.

Marian Mercer had become our new leading lady, and everybody fell in love with Little Mary all over again. Richard Charles Hoh, who originally played General. Oscar Fairfax, replaced William Graham as Captain. "Big Jim" Warrington. Richard also sang "Colorado Love Call" with two more lovely Little Marys, Margaret Hall and Joleen Fodor, who brought their own special charms to the role, making four Little Marys in the show's happy three-year run.

L'envoie–with performances in light opera companies, little theater groups, colleges, and high schools, Little Mary has sung her heart out countless times in every state in the union, including Alaska and Hawaii. In addition to Los Angeles, Boston, London, and Australia, productions of the show have graced stages in many foreign countries such as Chile, Columbia, Czechoslovakia, Hong Kong, Hungary, Iceland, the Philippines, Poland, South Africa, and Uruguay. According to royalties sent to the Richard Besoyan Residuary Trust, Rick's recorded songs have continued to be heard in more than thirty

"Select fabrics now, Senors," the tailor said. "Shorts finished at 4:00 p.m., okay?"

"Okay," Bob said, laughing. "Good service."

The tailor smiled and bowed.

"Si, Senor," I said. "Muy bueno."

When we went water-skiing the next morning in Acapulco Bay, I was wearing the best-fitting swim shorts I've ever had.

Not long after our trip I painted a portrait of the Shuler family at the beach.

CHAPTER 67

HOORAY FOR HOLLYWOOD

Beverly Hills, 1963

E VEN AT THE "ripe old age" of thirty-eight, I still had stardust in my eyes. My childhood dream of meeting movie stars came true on another trip to the West Coast with the Schulers. Pat's parents lived in a charming pink Spanish-styled stucco cottage in Malibu, and to be close to them while we were in Los Angeles, Bob rented a modern beach house on the ocean. He had hoped we could start raising backing for *Chrysanthemum* through some of his and Pat's acquaintances and business friends in Hollywood. Of course, I didn't know a soul out there, so I spent all my spare time by their swimming pool.

When Bob and Pat were guests of bigwigs in the motion picture world, I was included. With them, I was invited to a cocktail party in the spectacular home of a movie producer, Rock Hunter. That evening, I met superstars Rosalind Russell and Rock Hudson! I couldn't help myself from wondering if Hudson was Hunter's namesake.

At a gala party another evening, I danced the twist with Mitzi Gaynor. The darling girl, a good seven years younger than I, was already a bona fide movie star. Famous for her talents as a dancer-singer in the musical comedy films *Les Girls* and *There's No Business Like Show Business*, she had also won an Academy Award for Best Actress for her role opposite the Italian star Rossano Brazzi in the film version of *South Pacific*.

After our energetic dance that evening, Mitzi breathlessly gasped, "Thank you, Mr. Twister."

"No, thank you, Mitzi. Now I can say I've danced with a movie star!"

She gave me a quick hug and disappeared.

Many years later, I watched Miss Gaynor's TV special on PBS. In between the spectacular clips of her dancing and singing in lavish Las Vegas productions, she was interviewed by the show's moderator. In a light moment, Mitzi reminisced about a phone call from the legendary star Marlene Dietrich, who had seen the TV special.

Perfectly mimicking Marlene, Mitzi cooed, "Dawling, I loved your act, but you are so much better vehn you are amusing."

Now back to that gala night forty years ago. Standing with Bob and Pat, I pointed to a stunning lady in a blue evening gown across the floor from us.

"She could pass for a young Loretta Young," I said.

"Pass?" Bob questioned me, laughing. "That is Loretta Young."

"But I saw Loretta Young in *Ramona* when I was twelve years old," I said. "That was a long time ago!" I couldn't believe my eyes.

"She started in movies when she was sixteen," Patrice said, steering me across the room. "Wouldn't you like to meet her?"

I was speechless.

"Shall we dance?" Miss Young asked. "But not the Twist," she said with that dazzling smile.

All I could do was smile back and hold out my arms, and we danced–smoothly, effortlessly–and I never stepped on her toes, not even the hem of her gown.

"Are you enjoying your visit here?" Loretta asked.

"More than you can imagine," I answered and held her lightly as we circled the dance floor.

She snuggled close, and for a few minutes, I was in heaven. She was more beautiful than she had been thirty years earlier, when she starred with Tyrone Power in the movie *Second Honeymoon*. I was all of thirteen and must have had a schoolboy crush on both of them–Miss Young, with her limpid eyes and luscious lips, and Mr. Power, with his black eyebrows.

The following afternoon, we had tea with Miss Young in her palatial home. Even in the bright daylight, she lived up to her name, and she was as lovely as she had been the night before.

Now at the age of thirty-eight, I had traveled with an opera diva, danced with movie stars in Hollywood, and was going to coproduce a show on Broadway. This was the life I had dreamed of, but after ten days in Tinseltown, the *Chrysanthemum* producers had not raised a cent for their Broadway debut.

CHAPTER 68

CHRYSANTHEMUM

NYC, 1963

B ACK IN MANHATTAN, Bob and I sat down with up-and-coming Barbra Streisand after seeing her act at the Blue Angel. In her dressing room, Miss Streisand was quietly enthusiastic about playing the lead in our show, but she was no dummy. Of course, she wanted approval of director, choreographer, etc., etc. At that time, we had neither a director nor a choreographer. So no Barbara Streisand.

On Bob's suggestion, I went to Boston to see Tammy Grimes in a pre-Broadway engagement of *High Spirits*, the musical version of Noel Coward's comedy *Blithe Spirit*. After Miss Grimes' remarkable performance, I went backstage to her dressing room. When I explained my mission, telling her all about our plans for a production of *Chrysanthemum* on Broadway, I ended up asking if she would consider starring in it.

"*Chrysanthemum*," she cooed. "Charming name for a musical. Yes, I'd love to if I'm available. And if we could get Gower Champion to direct and choreograph." Tammy was smart.

"Naturally, we'd love that too. Champion is on top of our list. As soon as we settle with him to join our team, we'll let you know."

I was so pleased with Tammy's reaction, I sent her the script and flowers immediately. In return, I got this note from Miss Grimes.

Dear Howard,

Twenty Chrysanthemums–mon dieu, Mr. Barker, c'est merveilleux. I'm going to do the same. Enclosed is a 3-minute sketch of a chrys–etc., etc., etc. Couldn't we change the name to *Rose*? They're so much easier to draw. I'm always so happy I can act and don't have to be a painter. Wonderful to have seen you. It was sweet of you to come to Boston. Settle with Gower, and I'll be there.

Love, Tammy G.

I was so surprised and delighted by Miss Grimes' colorful pastel of a chrysanthemum, I sent my profuse thanks and promised to frame her artwork. Another note from Miss G. in Boston:

Dear Howard,

I suggest you buy a mat and a 15th-century piece of something and cover the "mum." I thought I did thank you for the flowers. They are still in full bloom and most beautiful. I shall try a more impressive "mum" and send it to you soon. So good to hear from you.

Love, Tammy G.

I remembered Tammy mentioning roses and promptly sent her a bouquet. My thoughts were beginning to bloom–could this be the beginning of a fun romance?

She wrote, "Howard B., You are too much. When we got home, they were absolutely beautiful–such a fantastic color and your dear note. Thank you and love – Tammy G."

Bob sent the script and the score to Mr. Champion. He responded through a secretary that he was too tied up with negotiations with David Merrick to direct *Hello, Dolly!* All our further efforts with Gower Champion failed, but we didn't want to lose Tammy G. We hoped to hold on to her with another top director-choreographer. I called our lawyer, Benjamin Aslan, a show business veteran, for his advice. Ben also represented Jerome Robbins, the world-renowned director and choreographer, and he suggested we offer the show to Robbins. That, to me, was unthinkable. Two unknown producers with an unheard-of property having the balls to approach such a theater master–unthinkable!

"Why not?" Ben said. "Jerry's human. What have you got to lose?"

We sent the script and score to Mr. Robbins and started chewing our nails. After two weeks, no answer was forthcoming. We were disappointed and frustrated. Bob told me (realistically) that if Jerry Robbins didn't read "C" right away and we didn't have something to report to Tammy and the authors, we would lose Tammy and the production.

"I called Ben today, who told me Jerry hasn't even cracked the script open. If we can't get to him directly," he said, "then I think we should request the material back and submit it to other directors pronto."

At that point, I had to agree with Bob, and we learned from Ben that Robbins had other projects that were demanding his involvement. We had to assume he wasn't interested. What I thought seemed like a great idea (and possibly a sweet relationship with Tammy) was over. We would have to find another Chrysanthemum.

Kaye Ballard, the comedienne from the musical *The Golden Apple*, came to mind. Warmly received by the press for her standout number "A Lazy Afternoon," Ballard seemed like a good choice. Bob and I went to see her cabaret appearance in the Empire Room at the Plaza Hotel. We were blown away! She seemed to be exactly what we now needed–a good-looking comedienne, tough but sweet, with a great voice for a Broadway musical comedy. We met Kaye in her suite after the show. When we outlined our plans for a Broadway production of *Chrysanthemum*, she was very interested. (Wisely, we never mentioned Barbara Streisand or Tammy Grimes.)

"We think you'd be perfect as our leading lady," I said.

"Chrysanthemum is gorgeous, warm, and funny," Bob chimed in. "You can handle that, I'll bet."

"You can bet your ass I can, you silver-tongued devil." Kaye hugged him. "When do we start?"

"As soon as we raise the backing," Bob answered. "I wish I could tell you how long that will take."

I took a deep breath and spoke up. "We believe if we can get a major record company to do a show album for a hunk of backing, the investors will climb on the bandwagon."

"Goddard Lieberson at Columbia is a friend of mine," said Kaye. "Goddard and I are like THAT", She said and held up her clasped hands. "In a couple of weeks both of us will be in London. I'll speak to him over lunch. It'll be easier then."

"Kaye, you're the greatest!" Bob said.

"The greatest!" I chimed in.

Suddenly, Kaye looked at me, then at Bob. "You know, I'd love to do your show. I'm tired of getting great reviews and doing great with audiences here and in London. Really GREAT! Now dammit, I want some respect in this 'dumby' world. I want *Chrysanthemum* to be a hit."

Bob and I wanted it to be a hit too, and a hit with Kaye Ballard sounded just fine with us.

I put together a new presentation portfolio with Kaye's impressive résumé and some glamorous professional headshots. I cabled Kaye in London to tell her my friend Arnold Goland, the orchestrator who had done the *Little Mary Sunshine* cast album, said he could get us a deal from a music publisher to pick up the tab for a demo record of Kaye doing songs from *Chrysanthemum*. Kaye wrote me from London that she didn't want to do the demo. She thought it would take away her stature if she made it.

"I want people to think of me as a STAR," she said. So we made the demo without her.

I wrote Kaye and told her that we did the demo–five numbers with a seven-piece orchestral ensemble and three singers–and it turned out fine.

"I'm sorry you didn't want to do the record," I said. "It was a major disappointment to the publisher who backed the deal as well as to Bob and me. Bob said it seemed as if you have lost interest. I assured him you have been terribly busy and you're still with us. I don't think I convinced him."

Kaye wrote back, "I have not lost one bit of interest! Never. Bob must never think that. I love you and Bob and *Chrysanthemum*. So now let's get it on!"

I believe she was sincere, but as it happens in life–it also happens in the world of theater–there are no guarantees. She did speak to her friend Mr. Lieberson in London, who told her he was very interested in hearing the score, but he did not come through with a show album and a hunk of backing. Our happy time with the delightful Kaye Ballard was destined to lose its glow. Kaye left for a gig in New Orleans and went on with her career to more engagements and, shortly, to movies and television.

Bob and I set our sights in another direction. Bob's wife, Patrice Munsel, had recently broken all box-office records with Lehár's *The Merry Widow* at Lincoln Center. Coincidentally, Bob had a phone call from Frank Hale, the producer of the Royal Poinciana Playhouse in Palm Beach, about the possibility of Patrice appearing in the operetta at his theater. Flying by the seat of his pants, Bob told Mr. Hale that Pat was interested in doing a new musical from London that was being readied for Broadway, and she suggested *Chrysanthemum*. This led to Mr. Hale's offer to foot the bill for a pre-Broadway tryout of anything Patrice

Munsel would star in at his theater–for a participation deal, of course. There was one hitch. Pat didn't feel comfortable about doing the show on Broadway.

"You know, what you boys really need is a comedienne," she said. "A comedienne who can sing too. I'm a singer who can do comedy. There is a difference." But even as she said it, Pat saw us deflate, and she relented. "All right. If it will get you a first-class production at the Royal Poinciana, I'll do it. It will be fun for me, and it could be your out-of-town tryout."

Bob and I found a director and a choreographer, not famous, but highly talented, and I started to work designing the sets and costumes. Finally, we relaxed and had fun producing.

Below are sketches of some costumes I designed for *Chrysanthemum*

MARY ANN
1-8

CHRYSANTHEMUM
1-7

Howard Bender

Many weeks later, the Royal Poinciana curtain went up on our production of *Chrysanthemum*. All the aging dowagers, the millionaires we were courting, staged their own show. Dressed in evening gowns, adorned with glittering diamonds, they paraded up and down the aisles on the arms of their handsome young men until they were ready to sit down. Then the show went on—two hours late!

Singing the delightful score, playing the comedy and looking gorgeous, Patrice Munsel was a knockout. Much applause! Many encores! It was a great night for all. The next morning, an investment prospectus with a huge pom-pom chrysanthemum was hand-delivered to each and every member of the wealthy opening night audience. Bob and I were rubbing our hands and waiting for the phone calls...

There were no calls. Not one! No investments were forthcoming. Sadder but wiser, the would-be Broadway producers of *Chrysanthemum* left Palm Beach, their tails between their legs. End of story.

CHAPTER 69

YOU LOVELY ISLAND

Puerto Rico, 1964

I WAS SITTING at a table in the immense nightclub at the new Americana Hotel in San Juan, happy to be surrounded by a group of "the beautiful people"–famous individuals who had been invited to lend glamour to the hotel's grand opening. Neither famous nor even well-known, I was glad just to have been invited by my friends, the beautiful Patrice Munsel and her beautiful husband, Robert Schuler. The beautiful movie and TV star Eva Gabor was at our table with her beautiful husband of the moment, Richard Brown. Across from me was the aging but still beautiful Mama Jolie Gabor and her beautiful but aging husband, Count Edmond de Syvigeny. The other two beautiful Gabor sisters, Zsa Zsa and Magda, were conspicuous by their absence.

Cocktails and hors d'oeuvres had been served to the several hundred formally dressed people in the audience. When the emcee managed to quiet down the crowd, he began introducing important people around the room. The Governor of Puerto Rico and other dignitaries stood and received hearty applause. Then the emcee announced the Metropolitan Opera star Patrice Munsel, and Pat stood and received a huge applause. The Gabors at our table, Eva and Mama Jolie, were announced, and they stood, waved, and received a large applause. Applause for Robert Schuler was somewhat smaller but substantial. When Howard Barker was introduced and I stood up, there was a scattered but polite clapping of hands from a very puzzled audience. I sat down.

After the first course of dinner was served, the room darkened, and a spotlight lit up an arch-shaped opening on the stage.

There was a loud drumroll, and the emcee's voice rang out, "Ladies and gentlemen, we are proud and happy to present . . . Senorita Maria Alba!"

To the wail of a trumpet and the strumming of a guitar, the clatter of castanets was heard. A striking woman in red appeared in the arch and stood motionless, acknowledging the applause. Her traditional flamenco dress was formfitting to her hips and then burst into a mass of ruffles stopping just above her ankles in front and ending in a train behind her. Her jet-black hair was pulled back tightly into a bun at the nape of her neck, framing her pale face. Her mouth was a slash of red, the color of the rose in her hair. Trumpets screamed, and with her clattering castanets held high, the dancer moved forward to face the audience.

With stamping heels matching the clatter of her castanets, Senorita Alba began tracing a pattern across the floor. She moved slowly at first and then faster, twisting and turning to the insistent rhythm of the music. The castanets, now held low behind her back, echoed the stamping of her heels. I couldn't take my eyes off her.

Flamenco! Proud, fiery, sensual! Senorita Alba circled the floor slowly and then faster and faster, with the ruffled train of her skirt flaring in the air behind her. Lowering her head, she performed a series of complicated steps and turns, and then she threw back her head and spun around with her eyes flashing. At the height of her dancing, her hair came undone and flew wildly about her head and shoulders. Tossing it in the air behind her and stamping her feet to the music, she made her way across the floor back to the arch, stopped for a moment, and was gone. Wild applause brought her back for a bow. She rose from a deep curtsy, surveyed the room with a smile and flashing eyes, and disappeared. I was mesmerized. I don't remember much about the rest of the program, but I knew I would never forget Senorita Alba.

The next morning, when I glanced out of my hotel room window, I saw what looked like a brightly colored bird flitting under the palms in the courtyard below. On second look, I realized it wasn't a bird at all. The bright colors moving under the branches of the waving palms was Maria Alba's caftan blowing in the wind as she crossed the patio to the coffee shop.

That evening, the Schulers, the Gabors, and I were invited to the governor's mansion. Maria Alba was there among the guests, and at dinner, I was surprised, pleased, and a bit overwhelmed to be seated next to her. Miss Alba was very quiet during the meal, but at coffee, we finally made small talk.

"Do you travel a lot in your work?" I asked.

"Yes, I do," she said in a low accented voice. "I am now on tour with my company of dancers, but after it is over, I will return to New York."

I asked if I could call her. She declined, saying her schedule was uncertain.

"Perhaps I can call you," she said. "When I return."

I assumed it was a graceful farewell, but I gave her my card.

Here we are at dinner together, Maria Alba in the foreground,
Patrice Munsel on my right, and Patrice's husband, Bob
Schuler, at the head of the table with the Gabor sisters.

A few weeks later, I answered my phone and recognized her voice.

"This is Maria Alba. I said perhaps I would call," she said. Of course, I remembered the accent.

"I'm so glad you did. Does this mean I will get to see you again?" I asked, hoping it didn't sound like pleading.

"Yes," she replied.

At a small West Side restaurant, we had a quiet dinner. In the course of our conversation, Miss Alba told me she was born in Spain, a descendent of the Duchess of Alba.

"The painting of my ancestor is called *The Naked Maja*. It is by the Spanish artist Goya." She also told me her early life had been spent poverty-stricken in China. "We had to trap rabbits in the fields to survive," she said. "It was a very difficult childhood."

She was a little vague as to how she had become a flamenco dancer, but I was so enchanted, I really didn't care. I told her a little about myself, and she listened quietly. I dropped her off at her apartment with a little good night kiss on the cheek and told her I'd like to call her again.

Our next dinner ended much the same way, but when I brought her home this time, I was invited inside her apartment for a few minutes. It was a large studio in an older building. High ceilings with big windows, it was modestly furnished in no particular style, the kind of place where the owner didn't spend a lot of time. I learned she had her own company of flamenco dancers and often toured with them.

"A dancer's life can be hard," she told me. "Securing enough engagements in New York is hard. I must also teach to make a modest living."

I shared some of my own experiences, the ups and downs of being a set designer in the big city. No nightcap but coffee was offered, which I declined. As I was leaving, she offered both cheeks for good night. Again, I declined, but there was a warm reaction to my quick good night kiss on her lips.

The third time I saw Maria was different. The door was slightly ajar when I rang the bell.

"The door is open!" she called. "Come in."

I followed her voice. A second door in the living room was also ajar. I pushed it open and found her in a large bathtub under a mound of bubbles.

"Would you like to join me?" she asked.

I answered by untying my shoes and stripping off my clothes.

"I have just come from rehearsing," she said, smiling. "This helps me to relax. Would you like to scrub my back?"

I slid into the tub. This was a first for me, but Miss Alba seemed very easy about the whole thing. Our legs were touching, and I felt my excitement rising. Then our toes started to explore.

"Maria . . ." I said.

"No, no," she said. "Don't talk. Just relax."

The hot water was relaxing, but I was too stimulated.

"I'm sorry. I can't relax," I said.

Maria smiled, stood up, and reached for a towel. "Get up," she said. "I'll dry you."

She did, and then I dried her. She led me into the bedroom.

The following weeks were an erotic adventure. Dinners always ended with cognac and then crazy love in her apartment or mine. There were breakfasts— or maybe just coffee–with me rushing off to work and she to rehearsals. It was all exciting and so much fun.

One night it was different. We were having an after-dinner brandy in her apartment when the doorbell rang.

"Are you expecting anyone?" I asked.

"Come in!" Maria called out.

A young woman, blonde and very attractive, came in.

"This is Anna, my friend from upstairs," Maria said. "She is one of us. She is a ballet dancer."

Soon, we were sipping brandy. Anna was very friendly, and conversation was easy. When Maria became openly affectionate with me, Anna showed no signs of leaving. The brandy began having its effect, and without much encouragement, the three of us fell into bed.

It was another first for me. I suppose it should have been confusing, but strangely enough, it wasn't. Anna seemed to be happy holding Maria's hand and stroking her hair, while I was totally occupied with my part of the encounter. When I awoke in the morning, Anna was gone, and Maria was making coffee. Nothing was ever said about the evening before.

Maria invited me to watch a rehearsal of her company at a dance studio on the West Side. Her dancers, four women and three men, mostly young Latinos, were excellent. She also had a few students. I asked Maria when I could see her perform in New York.

"New York is very difficult," she said. "Getting a decent concert hall, unless one is rich or famous, is impossible. I have made a few appearances here and there, only one recently in the Kaufman. It was reviewed by Walter Terry in the *Herald Tribune*."

She showed me a full page from the Sunday entertainment section. I read his review and quote his words of praise here: "To be engaged by the same theater at the midway point of a debut program is a tribute which show folk dream about but rarely get. It happened, however, where a wildly enthusiastic audience, jamming the theater to the extent the fire laws permit, screamed itself hoarse over Maria Alba . . . she dances as one possessed. The fires aren't banked . . . the sensual fury of Miss Alba . . . she projected an unleashed, doom-crazy, savage, but somehow proud sexuality which fairly knocked the beholder into the aisles." The glowing article featured a large full-length photograph of Maria in costume.

"I have an idea," I said. "A friend of mine, Robert Holloway, is an agent who books talent for the *Ed Sullivan Show*. Your company would be a natural for it."

Maria was very pleased. An audition was arranged. Maria worked hard, rehearsing her company relentlessly. Hours were spent starching and ironing costumes, making sure every ruffle was perfect. I couldn't attend the audition, but Maria told me it had gone extremely well. When the agent called to say she did not get the job, Maria's disappointment was profound. She plunged back into rehearsals and fortunately secured another concert tour in Central America.

The night before Maria was to leave New York, we were having dinner at our favorite little West Side restaurant. It was very quiet, and so were we. At some point, Maria said she had something to say to me. She spoke in the same low voice as usual, but now there was no Spanish accent. I was speechless. I put down my fork.

"My name is not Maria Alba," she said. "I'm not from Spain, I never trapped rabbits in China, and I don't have black hair. I'm more of a mousy blonde."

"But . . ." I was staring at her. "You're a flamenco dancer."

"Yes, I am. All the rest is true. I love flamenco. I love my work. I love you. But I'm not in love with you. You already know that, don't you?"

"Well, yes, but . . ." I was stammering.

"But that's all right. You may love me too, but you're not in love with me either, right?"

"Well . . ." I didn't get any further.

"So all right," she said. "We've had a wonderful time, and now I'm going away. The tour will be a long one. Maybe you'll see me again. Maybe you won't. Time will tell." She stood up. She gave me a quick kiss and walked out of the restaurant.

I never knew Maria's real name. But I know this for certain—I'll never forget the dedicated artist, the exciting, fiery flamenco dancer, the warm, beautiful woman I loved for a time and never expected to see again.

CHAPTER 70

TIMES, THEY ARE A-CHANGIN'

NYC, 1960

MY LAST BIG show was the Lucky Strike Hit Parade when I took over for Paul Barnes. I was chosen to design the Hit Parade's Christmas Special, staged in one of the largest film studios in New York City, featuring falling snow scenes and horse-drawn sleighs of singing stars and dancers performing in seasonal costumes. But the Golden Age of Television was in the midst of its decline in New York, and many designers had fled to Hollywood, where jobs were opening up. I had not fled to the West Coast, so I looked to the busy world of filmed TV commercials for my bread and butter.

I designed sets for a number of small production companies until I found a welcome mat at the door of MPO Productions, one of the largest commercial companies in New York. For several years, when television commercials lasted for thirty (sometimes even sixty) seconds instead of today's twenty-, fifteen-, and ten-second spots, I designed sets for hundreds of products from A to Z. In the Clio Awards for Advertising Excellence Worldwide, I was awarded three times for my set designs—not as glamorous as Hollywood's Academy Awards but awards just the same.

At some point, stars from Broadway, Hollywood, and television began to appear regularly in TV commercials. These were commercials like those mentioned above, but the fame and personality of the celebrities guaranteed attention from the viewer. The first one of these I had designed was a special set for an older famous celebrity, a motion picture queen–Joan Crawford, who did a public service spot and thanked me later with a personally signed note.

Hollywood, Broadway and TV star Angela Lansbury and Met Opera diva Beverly Sills praised products and services in my sets representing their living rooms. I was flattered when both ladies told me they wished I had designed their own living rooms.

This was the living room set I had designed for Angela Lansbury.

Jane Russell, whose impressive breasts were stars in a classic Western movie *The Outlaw*, lauded the merits of 'Cross-Your-Heart bras' in my commercial set as well. Lauren Bacall, Carol Channing, and Phyllis Diller touted products in my sets. The delightfully outspoken Whoopi Goldberg was probably the gentlest, most cooperative actress of all to grace my set for a TV commercial. I was excited to have international movie greats like Catherine Denueve (a car commercial), Sophia Loren (a food product), and Lynn Redgrave (a diet drink). They may have rivaled their "American cousins" when they performed in my sets too.

Not all actresses for commercials were older. A number of years ago, I designed a spot starring the very youthful, very popular singer with multicolored hair Cyndi Lauper. She must have been very young at the time because when I saw her recently on Anderson Cooper's TV program discussing her work on the Broadway hit *Kinky Boots*, the darling blonde Miss Lauper (just a touch of pink in her hair) looked as young as she did years ago.

A number of entertainment's comedy greats–Bill Cosby, Rodney Dangerfield, and Tony Randall–sold products in my sets as well. The famous

English rock star George Michael did a thirty-second Coke commercial in my version of his all-white London apartment, directed by a fellow Brit, Stephen Frears, who, long since, has become a respected director of feature films. When John McEnroe became an international star on tennis courts around the world, he was filmed for a thirty-second razor blade spot. McEnroe shaved. I designed his bathroom.

The complete list of famous entertainers who appeared in my sets is too long to include here, but virtually every one of them was pleasant to work with. They were down-to-earth, punctual, cooperative artists who did their job without complaints or unprofessional behavior.

As I remember commercials that featured movie stars in those days, I think of Ronald Reagan. When he decided to announce his candidacy to run for President of the United States on national television, I was chosen to design the set representing his study. On the morning of the shoot, Mr. Reagan arrived at the studio on time with a cheery "Good morning" to all. After only one "walkthrough" for the director's staging, a lighting adjustment, and a sound test, filming began, and the teleprompter rolled. Mr. Reagan started speaking, seated at his desk, and then continued as he moved about the set with ease and finished his twenty-five-minute speech without stopping.

"Was that okay?" Mr. Reagan asked the director.

"That was very good, sir," was the answer. "Would you like to take another shot at it?"

"Not unless you need it. If you're happy with it, I am too," Mr. Reagan said. Then he approached each member of the crew individually, shook hands, and said, "Thank you."

I wasn't a Republican, but I admired Ronald Reagan for his poise and his professionalism. The man was cool.

I designed sets from small to large, like the enormous cruise ship set where the Radio City Music Hall Rockettes were to show off their high kicks for a commercial. Among the most lavish sets of all I had done were Hess Truck's Christmas commercials in the sixties and seventies. Silvercup Studios' mammoth soundstages in Long Island City were filled every holiday season with enormous snow-covered mountains and small villages featuring each year's new toy truck available for purchase by collectors.

Some sketches from the Hess Christmas commercials.

In the fifties, I was hired to design and build commercial film sets for the opening of Lincoln Center. We tried to imagine a futuristic world utilizing modern home products and furniture of the time.

I had many résumés over the years. I have
always kept them for posterity's sake.

HOWARD BARKER

PRODUCTION DESIGNER • ART DIRECTOR • MOTION PICTURES • TELEVISION

MOTION PICTURES:

"Carolina Skeletons". NBC-TV, John Erman, Director.
"Clinton and Nadine". HBO/ITC/Donald March,
Jerry Schatzberg, Director.
"Romancing the Stone". (New York sequences), 20th
Century-Fox. Robert Zemeckis, Director.
"Paternity". Paramount (New York sequences),
Paramount David Steinberg, Director.
"Dreams Don't Die". ABC-TV. Robert Young, Director.
"Sojourner Truth". CBS-TV. Peter Levin, Director.
"Stop Thief". CBS-TV. William Claxton, Director.
"Days In My Father's House". ASA FILM/MPO, filmed in
Denmark. David Nagata, Director.
"Come Spy With Me". MPO. Filmed in Jamaica, West
Indies. Marshal Stone, Director.

TELEVISION: CBS, NBC, ABC.

Over two hundred productions, including - "Free To
Be... A Family" - An ABC US/SOVIET satellite
Spacebridge between the U.S.A. and the U.S.S.R.
Marlo Thomas and Dalrymple Productions. Gary
Halvorsen, Director.

COMMERCIALS: Hundreds of Products from A to Z.

Celebrity spots:
Elizabeth Ashley, Lauren Bacall, Shari Belafonte, Sid
Caesar, Dick Cavett, Carol Channing, Bill Cosby, Joan
Crawford, Rodney Dangerfield, Catherine Deneuvre,
Phyllis Diller, James Garner, Mariette Hartley, Sophia
Loren, John McEnroe, Carl Mauldin, Tony Randall, Lynne
Redgrave, Jason Robards, The Rockettes, Dr. Ruth,
Beverly Sills, Sarah Vaughn, Nancy Walker, Nancy
Wilson, and oh yes, Ronald Reagan.

DIRECTORS: For commercials includes, alphabetically:

David Anspaugh, Bob Brooks, Barbara Campbell, Peter
Corbett, Melissa Costello, Stephen Frears, Jim
Gartner, David Griffith, Brian Loftus, N. Lee Lacy,
Domenick Rossetti, Lee Smith, Dickson Sorensen, Ron
Travisano, Bruce Van Dusen and Roger Vadim.

ADDITIONAL INFORMATION, PORTFOLIO, CASSETTE REELS ON REQUEST

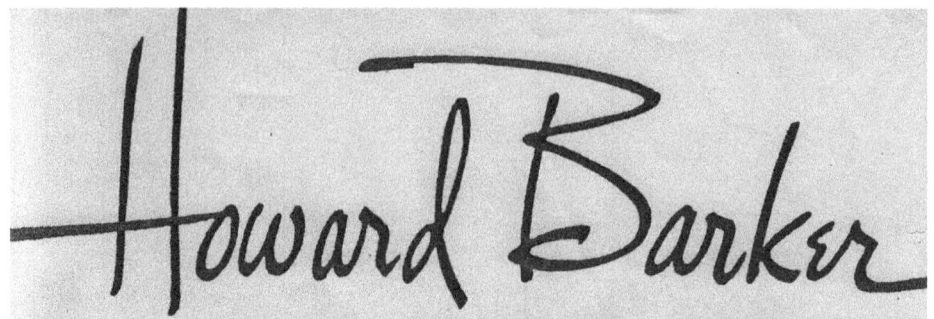

SET DESIGN: TV, FILM, THEATER

MOTION PICTURES:

Romancing The Stone 20th Century Fox. Production Designer in New York. Locations and Interiors.

Paternity Paramount. Production Designer in New York. Locations and Interiors.

Dreams Don't Die ABC/TV. Production Designer, Locations and Interiors.

Dream House CBS/TV. Production Designer, Locations and Interiors.

Sojourner Truth CBS/TV. Production Designer, Locations and Interiors.

Stop, Thief CBS/TV. Production Designer, Locations and Interiors.

Days In My Father's House Production Designer in Denmark. Sets and Locations.

Come Spy With Me Production Designer in Jamaica, West Indies. Locations and Interiors.

TELEVISION:

CBS, NBC, ABC. Production Designer, over two-hundred studio productions.

COMMERCIALS:

Hundreds of them, including "celebrity spot" sets for Lauren Bacall, Bill Blass, Bob and Ray, Sid Caesar, Dick Cavett, Carol Channing, James Coco, Bill Cosby, Joan Crawford, Rodney Dangerfield, Catherine Deneuvre, Phyllis Diller, Lola Falana, James Garner, Mariette Hartley, Geoffrey Holder, Angelica Huston, Lauren Hutton, Jack Jones, Reggie Jackson, Sophia Loren, John Madden, John McEnroe, Carl Maldin, Robert Morse, Joe Namath, Patricia Neal, Marie Osmond, Clara Peller, Tony Randall, Sally Jessy Raphael, Lynne Redgrave, Jason Robards, Cliff Robertson, The Rockettes, Jane Russell, Dr. Ruth, Beverly Sills, Leslie Uggams, Verushka, Sarah Vaughn, Nancy Walker and Nancy Wilson. Oh yes, George McGovern and Ronald Reagan.

36 SHERMAN AVE. DOBBS FERRY, N.Y. 10522 914·693·5461

One of the top advertising agency producers for which I had designed TV commercials was Catherine Ames. A modest lady, Catherine spoke softly in production meetings, but she "carried a big stick." She was a true professional who knew how to get the work done with a minimum of hysteria in an often hysterical business. In the advertising agency world, she was a star.

Catherine Ames was also a pretty woman. She dressed in an elegant, conservative style. She was sweet, in the best sense of the word, and she liked me. Obviously, I liked her. As we left a production meeting one day, Catherine stopped me at the elevator.

"You've told me you like growing flowers on your apartment terrace," she said. "If you're free for lunch, I'd like to show you my terrace and ask your advice."

"Well, sure," I said. "You mean today? Now?"

"Why not? I live just a few blocks away. I'll make sandwiches, we can have a glass of wine, and we could be back in time for the shoot."

Catherine's apartment was also on the East Side in an older building like mine. It was charming, tastefully furnished, and the terrace, like mine, was filled with pots of flowering shrubs and small trees. Comfortable outdoor furniture indicated Catherine enjoyed being outdoors too.

"You may have guessed, Howard," she said with a sweet smile, "I had more in mind than lunch and advice about my plants."

"Oh? Uh, I mean, okay."

"Actually, I just wanted your thoughts on what color I should choose for the study," Catherine said. "Everything's beige. I'm really so tired of beige, and I have some paint color swatches."

I admit for a moment, I was a little bit disappointed. "Well, let's have a look," I said in her foyer. "Maybe we can have our sandwiches in there."

We decided on a soft gray-green, and then we had lunch on her terrace.

As we were leaving, I stopped in and looked at an interesting silver plate on the small table. I picked it up. In the center was a white ceramic disk with a black line drawing of a bull.

"Taurus," I said. "It's a beautiful plate. I'm a Taurus. May 14, 1924."

"Really?" Catherine said. "So was my husband. May 15, 1918. He died five years ago. I miss him."

"Of course, you do. I can understand," I said, meaning it. "Well, I guess we'd better get back to the studio."

Catherine took the plate, studied it for a moment, and then handed it back to me. "Howard, would you like to have it?" she asked.

Surprised, I shook my head. "No, it must be very precious to you."

"It is, but I want you to have it," Catherine said softly. "Please take it."

Today, forty-something years later, the silver Taurus plate sits honorably on a living room table under a painting of the Barker family. Thank you, Catherine, with my love.

CHAPTER 71

FLY ME TO THE MOON

Jamaica, West Indies, January 1966

DESIGNING COMMERCIALS AS well as several full-length feature films had made it possible for me to afford to find my way back to the theater world with *Little Mary Sunshine* in 1959 and *Madame Aphrodite* off Broadway. Then came Tad Mosel's *Who's Happy Now?* and eventually Besoyan's *Babes in the Wood*. I could thank all those production companies, but the list would be too long and probably too boring. However, MPO pops into my head first. When Arnold Kaiser, the company's boss, asked me to work full-time at MPO, my answer was simple: "Why?"

"It will give you a regular paycheck for your work" was his simple answer. "And you'll have a private office."

My reply was somewhat cocky. "I work all the time and can choose my jobs. I already have a private office at home, where I can sketch all night if I need to."

"Okay," Arnold said. "What if I offer you the two feature films we are going to shoot?"

"When do I start?" I asked.

"Now." Arnold extended his hand, and I shook it.

The movie crew of *Come Spy With Me* was sitting on the moonlit terrace of a glamorous hotel in Ocho Rios, Jamaica, West Indies. They were having drinks when I had arrived from New York. It could have been a romantic scene, except there were no women. None were to be involved in filming the establishing shots, which were scheduled for the next morning.

"Come sit down, old pal!" the cameraman yelled a little too loudly. "Ya gotta have some of this rum punch!" He'd obviously had a few too many. After I joined them, I did too.

The shoot was a picnic. What else could it be? My day always started with an early morning swim with the director, Marshall Stone (hotshot creator of commercials for MPO), breakfasts of fresh island fruits and omelets, and days of filming in a tropical paradise with a beautiful cast. It was heaven-sent for a feature film's production designer.

The leading lady in *Come Spy With Me* was an appealing young actress, Andrea Dromm, well-known for a series of National Airlines commercials, all of which ended with her looking directly into the camera and announcing, "My name is Sue Anne. Fly me!" She wasn't a flight attendant in our movie, but she was very appealing. As I remember, the only other female involved with the production was a tough Englishwoman, coincidentally named Sue, who wasn't an actress in the film. Appropriately titled, Sue was our Production Manager. She managed her job with an iron hand, especially when she managed the Jamaican crew. They were tough too but warmhearted and happy workers (especially on ganja). My job was to select locations with the director and supervise converting them to look like sets for filming. It was sometimes challenging but fun.

Our leading man was a handsome Hollywood actor, Troy Donahue, just a few years past his prime but pleasant, hardworking, and a really nice guy. The villain was played by Albert Dekker, also past his prime but an excellent actor who had starred in *Doctor Cyclops*, a bizarre film about a mad scientist. Mr. Dekker seemed to need his own form of stimulation. None of us knew what he was disappearing to do, but he would always return to set and proved to be effective as our villain.

Shooting progressed without any major problems. The New York crew members were excellent, and the experienced native Jamaican members were the hardest working guys I've ever met on a movie. They were driven hard by Sue, who seemed to know how to handle the local Jamaicans, but they just laughed and, fortunately, knew how to handle her too.

Shooting continued for a total of thirty hectic days in sets ranging from the villain's hideout in a deep underground cave to the explosion of his yacht in the bay. None were as fascinating as the day I had gone to rent a vintage Rolls-Royce for the villain. We were told the only Rolls on the island was owned by an elderly lady, an Englishwoman, living on a mountain near the small town of Mandeville. It wasn't far from our hotel, so the prop man and I drove there to have lunch and rent the limousine. The only restaurant in Mandeville was a tiny intimate establishment where a scattering of older British types were lunching quietly. I thought immediately of Celia Johnson and Trevor Howard in the romantic English movie *Brief Encounter*.

When we had arrived at the elderly lady's home, screeching peacocks were sauntering about the grounds. The lady herself was in her garden. She was wearing a picture hat and a long dress, and she carried a basket filled with flowers (another English movie, but which one?). She approached us tentatively and answered my request with a puzzled smile.

"You see, I'm not in the automobile-renting business," she said with a gracious smile. "My car is up on blocks. But if you would like to see it, you may."

She led us to the garage. The Rolls was in perfect condition.

"I don't use it anymore," she continued. "Petrol is too expensive, so I do my shopping in a small runabout." When she saw my admiration, the lady was pleased. "However, I will lend my car to your motion picture company on one condition. My chauffer is to be the only person to drive it, and he will be paid exactly what you would pay an actor." We struck a deal, and filming continued.

My then fiancée, Eileen Brennan, flew down for a little R and R. Instead of a happy holiday, her visit became a nightmare. Exposed to Jamaica's blazing sunshine, Eileen's pale Irish skin turned beet red. She spent the next two days nursing the severe sunburn in our darkened bedroom. The third day, she departed for a chilly New York City.

The shoot went smoothly, and the principal company members, with drinks in hand, watched "the dailies" every evening and loved them. There was lots of backslapping and "Good show" and "Here's to ya" all around.

The last scene of the movie was to be shot in a Jamaican bar. For the set, I designed a bamboo hut, which we built in a grove of palm trees next to the hotel's terrace. After the final shot was done, my set became a real bar for the wrap party. Food was prepared by the hotel. Lots of booze was courtesy of MPO. Ganja weed was supplied by our Jamaican crew. The Calypso music brought out the hidden talents of Jimmy, our shy prop master. He literally swept the leading lady off her feet, and together, they performed the wildest dance this side of Montego Bay.

The filmed footage of *Come Spy With Me* was edited at MPO back in New York. It was beautiful to look at, but the editors could not make head nor tail of it. When it was cut together, the finished movie had to be released with a voiceover narration for it to be understood.

CHAPTER 72

FOREIGN MOVIE

Manhattan, Spring 1966

M Y SECOND FILM for MPO, *Days in My Father's House,* was to be shot in Denmark. I had given up my tiny penthouse for a large apartment on Central Park West, and while I was away in Jamaica, a trio of generous friends–Dick Hoh, Floyd Curtis, and Ed Royce–packed up all my stuff (painless farewell to the past) and supervised the move for me. Boys, I am forever grateful.

Still surrounded by packing boxes, I invited Bob Gilston, the producer of the Danish-American movie, to have dinner with me and Eileen Brennan. It was a sultry summer night. All the apartment windows were open wide, and "La Bohème" was playing, rather too loudly, on the stereo. Eileen was freshening up in the bedroom and singing at the top of her lungs along with the opera. I was in the kitchen when I heard a man's loud voice from the apartment below.

"Cut out that fucking noise up there!" he yelled.

I went into the bedroom, and Eileen was leaning out the window.

"It's not fucking noise!" she yelled back, looking down. "It's grand opera!"

"I don't care what the fuck it is!" shouted the man. "I've called the super. Now I'm calling the police!"

"Call whoever you like!" Eileen shouted back at him and slammed the window shut. But she did turn down the volume and stop singing.

We went into the living room, where Bob was sitting.

"Let's have another glass of wine," he said. "And during dinner, I'll tell you all about the movie. *Days in My Father's House* is not a comedy. It is about an American and his romance with a Danish girl. It will be filmed in Denmark."

The dinner was pleasant, and the rest of the evening went fine. As he was saying good night, Bob turned to Eileen.

"Howard will be away in Denmark for over two months, you know. Your man just might wander, and those Danish girls are something else. They can be mighty appealing."

"Don't you worry," Eileen said. "So can I."

"Well, you'd better watch out."

That night, my fiancée and I had a passionate farewell. Eileen's remark stuck with me, but Bob's last words were prophetic.

CHAPTER 73

SOMETHING ELSE

Summer 1966

DENMARK ITSELF WAS enchanting. A small, incredibly beautiful country made up of many islands and one peninsula attached to Germany, it's one of those "you have to see it to believe it" places. The gently rolling countryside is filled with farms, thatched-roofed cottages, and real stone castles with moats, notably Elsinore, where Hamlet lived, loved, and died.

The cities are fascinating, the largest being cosmopolitan Copenhagen, the capital. Strøget, the Walking Street, winds through its center, where throngs of Danes as well as other people from many countries walk, sit, eat, and drink, enjoying the day. Strøget ends near Nyhavn, with its canal filled with working fishing boats, houseboats, and motor-driven barges for throngs of tourists. The famous statue the Little Mermaid, sitting on her rock near the shore of Kattegat, is one of their favorite sights. The hotels, the shops, the restaurants, and the sidewalk cafés are filled, especially in the tourist season, with people eating *smørrebrød* (open-faced sandwiches) accompanied with *ool og* snaps (beer and aquavit), a lunch favorite. The Danes are a happy, hospitable people.

One day I walked all around Copenhagen with my camera, taking pictures, just enchanted with the city.

I had been working day and night on the film since arriving at ASA Film Studio in Kongens Lyngby, a quaint little town near Copenhagen. I was sketching sets, drafting plans, meeting with David Nagata, the director of *Days in My Father's House*. Togo Esben, my assistant, was equally busy with a myriad of pressing details. Togo was an amusing Dane who dressed very formally in suit and tie every day. In explaining his odd given name, he said, "My parents were crazy." My set decorator, also Danish, had his first beer of the day first thing in the morning in the studio commissary before hitting the antique shops (yet he still took his work seriously and did an excellent job).

One day I stopped by the production office to see Bob Gilston, our American producer. A beautiful girl was sitting opposite him.

"Sorry, Bob," I said. "Nothing important. I'll come back later."

"No, stay, Howard," he said, turning to his visitor. "Madeleine Arentoft, this is Howard Barker. He's our set designer for the movie."

I looked into the most beautiful eyes I had ever seen. The girl was more stunning than any movie star–Marlene Dietrich included.

"Hello," she said in a sweet low voice and held out her hand.

I took it and didn't want to let go. *Everyone in Denmark shakes hands*, I thought. *I like the custom.* "It's so good to meet you, Madeleine. Uh, I guess I'll be seeing you tomorrow on the shoot."

As I backed out of the room, I couldn't take my eyes away from hers. She was smiling.

David wanted more extras for the party scene, and he had asked me to fill in. "All you have to do is dance with a pretty girl and fake conversation," Dave said. "Can you handle that?"

"I have, lots of times," I answered.

My dance partner did not turn out to be Madeleine Arentoft. Dave paired me up with a very pretty Chinese girl who didn't speak English very well. The scene got off to a late start with long and boring delays between shots. At midnight, I found myself in an empty room with the party extras. I sat on the floor next to Madeleine.

"Hello again," I said. "I'm sorry. No speak Danish."

"I speak English," she said.

"Oh, good. Have you been in many movies?" I asked.

"No, not really," she said. "But I did appear in a TV commercial once. I'm a model. Sometimes I get a call like this. It's fun, and the money helps."

I commented on her lovely English accent.

"Thank you. We must learn your language in school," Madeleine said. "And I was an au pair girl in London for a time. That helped. We also learned French and German. Very few people in the world 'have' to learn Danish. We are such a small country. Have you designed a great many movie sets?"

"Only one feature before this one," I said. "Not a very good one, actually, and you wouldn't have seen it anyway. It's still being edited. They're trying to make some sense out of it."

Between scene takes, Madeleine and I sat together, picking up where we had left off. There was a lot of talk, and I loved the sound of her voice. By dawn, I learned, among other things, that she had been a fashion model in Copenhagen since she was fifteen. She had also been modeling in Israel for a while and in Paris for a year.

"I worked for Christian Dior," Madeleine said rather proudly. (I was impressed.)

She mentioned she was twenty-four and a single mother. I told her I was forty-two, had been married when I was too young, and was now engaged to be married again.

"I'll be going back to New York when we wrap," I told her.

"What do you wrap?" she asked.

"Wrap means when the shooting is finished," I explained.

I thought she was delightful and asked her if she'd like to have dinner with me. She told me she was leaving the next day for two weeks on a modeling tour.

"Why don't you call me when I return?" she said, smiling. "That would be nice."

When she gave me her phone number, I was still wishing she had been my dancing partner in the party scene.

A few weeks later, Madeleine and I were having dinner in a *hyggeligt* ("cozy" in Danish) little restaurant on a canal in Copenhagen. Conversation was easy. I loved her voice and the way she talked. I liked her very much. That dinner was followed by others—and then there was an evening that ended at her place.

Madeleine lived on a nice street with the odd name of Sneppevej. Her apartment was small but furnished with a warm mix of modern and antique furniture. There were some plants and a few pictures. It was *hyggeligt* too, and I felt perfectly at home. There was no sign of her child. When I asked about him, she told me her son was with her mother.

"Thomas is a little over a year old. He will be moving in with me soon."

We had coffee and a cognac, and we talked some more. Then we had another cognac. The stereo was playing American songs. The atmosphere was romantic, and Frank Sinatra was singing "Strangers in the Night," the pop hit at that time.

Exchanging glances, wondering in the night
What were the chances we'd be sharing love before the night was through?

By then, I believed we were both attracted to each other. The words of the song were potent.   *Something in your eyes was so inviting*
Something in your smile was so inviting
Something in my heart told me I must have you

Without any other encouragement, I followed the words of the song and held out my arms. We danced closely for a few moments, and then we kissed. We stopped dancing and kissed some more. The record played again and again and all through the night. If you don't know the rest of the lyrics, look them up, and the song will tell you everything that happened.

One morning, not long after, I woke up to the smell of brewing coffee and the sound of a shower. Madeleine had an early modeling call, and I should be getting up to go to work. My feet were cold, sticking out from under the *dyne* (that's Danish for "comforter"). When I looked down at the end of the bed, I saw a little red-haired boy. His two blue eyes were looking straight at mine. Thomas. He looked like a baby *nisse* (that's Danish for "elf"). I didn't speak

Danish, so I wiggled my toes. Thomas laughed. I was still wiggling my toes, and Thomas was still laughing when Madeleine brought me a cup of coffee. Not all women look beautiful when they wake up. Madeleine was beautiful.

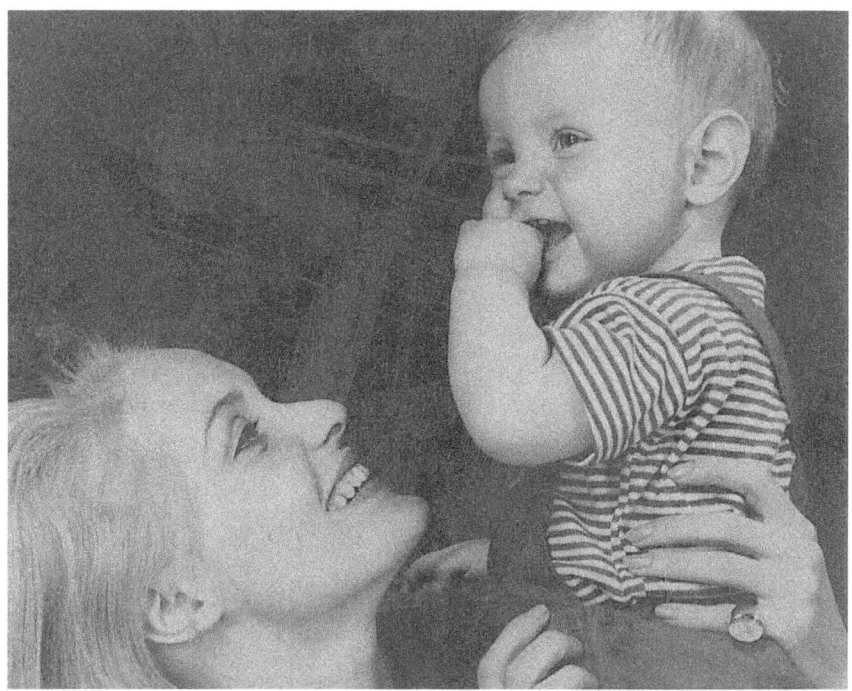

"I have to hurry," she said. "I must dress and take my son to my mother on my way to work. You may call me, if you like, this evening."

Some days later, I met Madeleine's mother, Pia, and her father, Geovanni. Then I met her brother, Rene, and Rene's wife, Vipse. They were all warm and friendly, and except for her father, they spoke English pretty well. Geovanni and I managed to communicate with smiles, gestures, and good intentions. This felt like the start of something good, and it turned out to be just that.

Weeks passed, and the filming of *Days in My Father's House* wound up with a flurry of details. Props were returned to dealers, the sets were struck, and stacks of paperwork had to be finished. Madeleine was busy with her modeling work, but we still found time to be together.

These were some modeling photos of Madeleine Arentoft.

Somehow I had conveniently forgotten to mention that my fiancée was coming to Copenhagen when the movie wrapped. To be honest, I was not ready for her arrival, and I wasn't at all sure how I was going to handle it.

When I finally told Madeleine, it was morning, and we were at my place, a guesthouse that belonged to the mother of Hanne Borchsenius, the leading lady of our movie. Instead of being alarmed or angry when I broke the news, Madeleine was calm and seemed to be realistic. I said nothing.

"You will go back to the United States and get married," she said quietly. "I will be sad for a little time, and then I will forget you."

I didn't know what to say.

"I have been waiting for the right time to give you a small present," Madeleine said as she opened her purse. "I guess this is it."

The present was an antique brass matchbox. It was beautiful. I had nothing to give her. I felt completely foolish. It was a sad farewell.

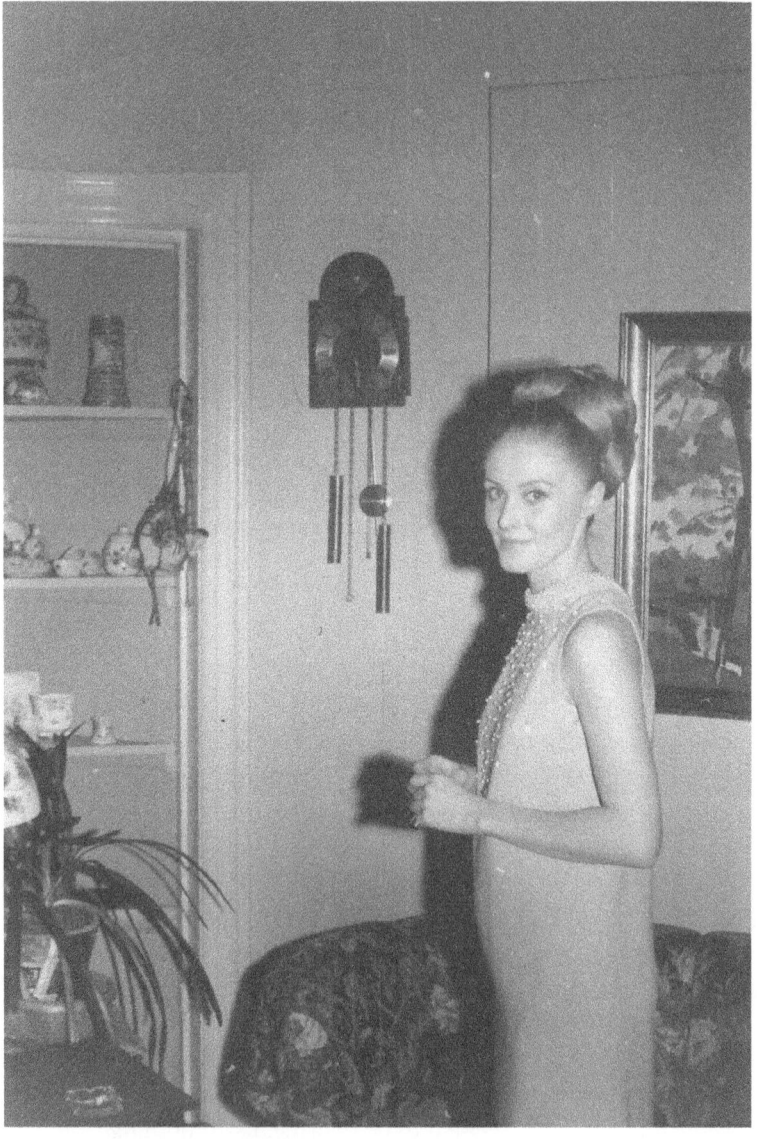

CHAPTER 74

STORMY WEATHER

Autumn 1966

EILEEN'S ARRIVAL IN Copenhagen was not joyous. She had not slept well on the flight from New York and stayed in bed most of the day to catch up. Conversation at dinner was strained. I was feeling guilty as hell, and Eileen seemed to be in low spirits too. That night, we had too much wine. The old adage "In vino veritas" could not have been truer.

Before we went to bed, we both confessed to having had affairs. I don't remember who admitted it first, but it didn't make much difference. I told her about Madeleine, and she told me about Mario. Another old adage, "Honest confession is good for the soul," was not true for us. We both were still miserable.

"What's this?" Eileen asked, picking up the little brass box from the night table where it had lain since Madeleine gave it to me.

"That? Oh." I hesitated for a moment. "It's a little present Madeleine gave me to remember her by," I muttered. "It's an antique matchbox."

Eileen put it back on the table and took something from her purse. "Mario gave this to remember him by. Turn it over." On the frog's underside, there was a set of sizeable male sex organs. "Well, she gave you her box," she said. "And you can see what he gave me." No wonder our reunion was glum.

In happier days, Eileen and I had planned a pleasant driving trip from Denmark to Italy. Now that trip seemed futile. However, the next morning, with aching heads and butterflies in our stomachs, we piled our suitcases in the trunk of my rented Volkswagen and headed south. The silence was grim. Because the engagement was in big trouble, the trip had turned into the "bumpy road to Rome."

Our mood didn't get any better as we made our way through the picture-postcard countryside of Germany. We stopped in a quaint village and went into an ancient church. In the darkened sanctuary, the rays from an afternoon sun turned the stained glass windows into glowing jewels. The pews were empty, but soft organ music came from somewhere in the shadows. It was a moving moment. Actually, I prayed for guidance. I imagine Eileen may have prayed for guidance too.

As we drove on through the hypnotizing, scenic perfection of Deutschland's mountainsides, dotted with black and white cows posing for tourists, my mind began to wander. What was I thinking?

I remembered that at some point during the last eight years, my old "friend" Ingrid Scheider had moved back to Germany and was living in a suburb near Munich. Sometimes, I have found, opening a closed door works, and sometimes it doesn't. Wondering if it would be nice to say hello to the "kraut" again, I decided to give it a try. I phoned Ingrid. (Yes, I still had her phone number.) I told her that Eileen and I were approaching Munich on our way to Rome.

"How nice," Ingrid said pleasantly. "Why don't you stop and say hello?" As always, she was hospitable. "If you would like to take a break from driving, you are welcome to have some dinner and spend the night in the guesthouse."

I thanked her profusely.

"My brother, Jurgen Goslar, is here. Jurgen is Germany's answer to Robert Redford. He and Eileen can compare notes during dinner. I will look forward to seeing you both. You and I can compare a few notes too."

When Ingrid opened the door, she looked the same as always—lovely. Her home was lovely too. (What else did I expect?) Her brother was handsome but not a reddish blond like Redford. Jurgen had a shock of raven hair and was charm itself. During dinner, he invited Eileen and me to visit him the next day at the film studio where he was directing a new movie. It was a tempting, but we declined.

"We really must get up early and get on the road," I explained.

Jurgen and Eileen hit it off nicely, and when they were settled in the living room with coffee, I helped Ingrid clear the table. Her remark on the phone about comparing notes came back to me. In the kitchen, she surprised me with her question.

"You are not happy, are you?"

"No," I answered. "Does it show?"

"Well, you don't look like a happily engaged man."

"Your perception is faultless. I'm not."

Venice, with its winding canals filled with gondolas, stirred up bittersweet memories of a visit twelve years earlier with my ex-wife. I blotted out those thoughts as best I could and tried to enjoy the surrounding beauty. Eileen and I explored the narrow "streets" and fed the hungry pigeons that haunted the magnificent Piazza San Marco. But I believe neither of us were able to ignore the truth and the pain in our hearts.

In Florence, Michelangelo's immense statue of David was, in the purest sense of the word, awesome. Both Eileen and I were overwhelmed. At the end of the first day in this incredible city, Eileen suddenly decided she needed to telephone the man she had been seeing in Hollywood. I left her alone in our pension to make her call and went for a walk. When I came back, her face was wet with tears.

"Mario's mother is dying," she said. "His family lives in a little town south of Rome. He's flying over to be with her. I have to go to him."

We said very little on what seemed to be an endless drive from Florence to Rome.

The Eternal City was spread before us like a comforting blanket. We walked for hours through throngs of tourists dodging honking cars and noisy Vespas in the ancient streets. The monumental fountains in the sunny plazas welcomed us to come sit, relax, and be happy. We were not able to accept their offer. Looking into store windows to kill time, we paused outside a shop near the foot of the Spanish Steps. The shop's window was filled with a display of frothy garments. Eileen surprised me with a bright smile.

"Want to buy me a goodbye gift?" she said, opening the door of the shop.

Anger began to rise up inside me. *Are you for real?* I thought. *Do you think I'm going to buy some fancy underwear for you to wear with your new man?* It never occurred to me she might be trying to induce me to beg her to forget him and make up with me. I still don't know.

A smiling saleslady welcomed us as we entered the shop. Racks on the counters and glass cases were filled with enough ravishing garments for a convention of honeymoon couples.

"Like it?" Eileen asked as she held a lacy negligee against herself in front of a full-length mirror.

"Don't you have enough underwear?" was my ungallant reply.

"Obviously, you've never kept a woman before," she said, suddenly dropping the negligee on the counter.

She stormed out of the shop, and I followed her across the street. I caught up with her, and we climbed the famous steps to our little hotel at the top.

After sharing a fitful night in our room, we parted. The goodbyes were tearful. *Just like in a movie*, I thought. *But this isn't a movie. This is real life all over again.*

For a while, I was despondent. Then I guess I was relieved. Finally, I called some old friends, Max and Peggy Gunther, a couple I had met on an earlier trip to Italy. They invited me to come to dinner. As I drove to their villa near Rome, I tried to sort out my feelings.

The Gunthers listened quietly to my story until I told them I wanted to call Madeleine.

"I don't think that's a good idea," Peggy said. "Why don't you send her a telegram? Tell her the engagement is off and you are driving back to Copenhagen alone."

Max agreed with her. "That way, Madeleine can collect her feelings," he said. "You'll know what to do when you are together again."

I took their advice and sent the telegram. That afternoon, I went for a walk in some old ruins nearby. Among the shards of broken pottery, I found a small clay amphora, perhaps made for wine in the times gone bye. The jug was slightly chipped, but otherwise, it was in good condition. To hold something so old, made by human hands, was strangely comforting.

"Take it back to Madeleine," Peggy suggested. "A little peace offering."

Early the next morning, I waved goodbye to the Gunthers and hit the road.

CHAPTER 75

BACK TO THE FUTURE

Copenhagen, 1966

WITH MY ANCIENT wine bottle and a passenger, Jorge Mara, a pleasant fellow I had met through Max and Peggy, I was on my way back to Denmark. Jorge shared the driving and kept me amused with his excellent impersonations of Fred Astaire and Cary Grant, his idols from American movies.

We drove up the Italian coast into France and on to Paris, his destination. With only one night's rest stop in Paris, the trip to Copenhagen took me less time than the sad drive to Rome. At that time, I had no idea what Madeleine would say to me or even if she would want to see me at all.

When I finally arrived at the door of her apartment, Madeleine was happy to see me, and I was very happy to see her. She listened quietly as I told her what had happened, and she never mentioned it again.

As weeks went by, I got to know Madeleine's family and little Thomas better. I even entertained thoughts of staying in Denmark and getting into the busy film business there. Eventually, however, when winter came and reality set in, I decided I really needed to go home. I asked Madeleine to come to New York for the Christmas holidays.

"I cannot," she answered. "I must be with my family at Christmas. But I will fly over to see you for a New Year celebration." She arrived December 30th.

I have to admit New Year's Eve was a near disaster. Hanne Borchsenius, the leading lady of the Danish movie, and her new husband, producer Bob Gilston, had come to New York to do a new play called *Come Live with Me*. She would be starring with the comedian Soupy Sales. Hanne invited us to the opening of the Philadelphia tryout the next night–New Year's Eve!

We'd hoped for a fun-filled evening. It was not exactly that. The play wasn't bad, and Soupy invited the Gilstons, Madeleine and me out afterward to celebrate the New Year. It was a frigid night. No taxis were to be found. We followed Soupy, walking to restaurant, after restaurant, after restaurant. Scanning menus posted outside, Soupy declared each of them "not good enough" (read: too expensive).

"Let's go back to the hotel and order in," he suggested. "See you there!" Then he disappeared around a corner.

We walked back to the hotel and called room service. It was closed. We were tired.

"Welcome to Philadelphia," I said.

"I think I'll call Mor and Far and wish them Happy New Year," Madeleine announced.

"At this hour?" I said, surprised.

"Why not? It's already tomorrow morning in Copenhagen. They'll be happy to hear from us. Happy New Year, *lille skat*." Madeleine used the Danish term of endearment. As she dialed her parents, she kissed me.

"Happy New Year, darling," I said and kissed her back. "Tell them we're getting married."

Madeleine nearly dropped the phone. The next few minutes of joyous three-way Danish conversation are not possible for me to translate here.

Then Pia spoke with her delightfully accented English. "I left my family long ago in Austria to marry Geovanni. Now it is the same. Young people must do what they must do. It is right," she assured us. "I know you will be very happy. Just be sure to bring your first baby to visit the grandparents."

Then Geovanni's voice came over the phone, loud and clear. "Skol, skater (plural of *skat*)," he shouted. "Vi elsker jer (We love you)!"

Finally, we turned out the light, went to bed, and celebrated Happy New Year.

CHAPTER 76

HERE I GO AGAIN . . .

New York, 1967

I'VE ALWAYS WONDERED why Madeleine married me. She could have married that wealthy Danish shipping magnate who courted her or the attractive but eccentric young entrepreneur who skipped in and out of the country, always one step ahead of the Danish income tax bureau. Or she could have married the even younger, more dependable sheep farmer or perhaps the less dependable handsome actor, but she didn't. The lovely Madeleine Arentoft married me.

Whenever I asked her, sometimes she answered, "For your money." But of course, we both knew I wasn't rich. Another time, she might answer, "I thought you would be a good father to Thomas." Finally, she would simply declare, "Because I loved you."

Certainly, we were attracted to each other, but I believe the real reason she married me was something else—something she had told me once in a quiet moment.

"After the first day we met in the film studio and after we sat on the floor and talked until the wee hours of the morning, I told my mother I thought I had met the man I was going to marry."

I think Madeleine knew what she wanted, and I did too. I had finally met the woman who loved me and whom I could love. I didn't consciously know it at the time, but eventually, I realized it was the only way I would survive.

Pat and Bob Schuler adored Madeleine, and so did my cousin Ruth. When I told her we were going to marry, Ruth insisted it would be in her home. I was happy to agree. Ruth secured the services of a Unitarian minister. The ceremony was intimate but very beautiful. There were two pedestals of flower arrangements in their living room near the French doors leading to the garden. Since it was January, the doors were closed, but even in winter, the view was lovely.

Madeleine selected the music for her descent on the stairs, a violin passage from Vivaldi's *Four Seasons*–"Winter." Pia and Geovanni could not attend, so Bob Gilston gave Madeleine away. Robert Schuler served as my best man, and Patrice was Madeleine's matron of honor. Ruth and Russell were the witnesses. Their daughter Cynthia, and her husband Angelo Pagano, were the only guests. It was a simple wedding, just what we wanted.

Following the ceremony, the Schulers gave us a festive reception at Malmaison, their palatial home nearby. They had coerced an actor friend of mine, Floyd Curtis, to slip them my address book, and everyone I knew in New York was invited. Most of them made their way out to Long Island for the celebration. All my friends fell in love with Madeleine too. To paraphrase Julius Caesar, "Veni, vidi, vici." She came, she saw, she conquered.

Champagne flowed and dinner was served. The Schulers had located a baker who made a traditional Danish wedding cake two feet high–marzipan tiers layered in a cone shape, decked with miniature Danish flags, and topped with a replica of the Danish royal crown. It was an unforgettable evening.

Our happy wedding day, Pat and Bob Schuler by our side and producer
Bob Gilston on the far right, who had introduced Madeleine and me.

We were lucky to find a baker who knew how to make the special Danish wedding cake since Madeleine's family could not be there for the wedding.

To clear our heads the next morning, my bride and I drank ice water from the champagne bucket that had been placed on our night table. After breakfast in bed, we drove back to the city, and I went to work.

A few days later, Madeleine flew to Copenhagen to pick up baby Thomas and to say, "Farvel saa laenge" to her family and Denmark. What she had thought would be a quick trip became a frustrating month of waiting to obtain the necessary papers for her and my new son to immigrate to New York.

When an exhausted Madeleine and a screaming Thomas finally arrived at Idlewild (pre-JFK), I hugged and kissed them both and thrust a toy, a small gray mouse, into Thomas's little hands. He immediately calmed down and went to sleep. We taxied into Manhattan, which seemed to be all aglitter just for the three of us to begin our life together in my apartment at the El Dorado on Central Park West.

To borrow the words sung by the hero of the musical *Candide* when he reaches the fabled city, El Dorado, "We'll build our house . . . and make our garden grow!"

CHAPTER 77

TAKIN' A CHANCE ON LOVE

Central Park West, 1967

MADELEINE'S LIFE IN "the New World," as she called it, was alternately joyous and sometimes difficult, but it was always a fascinating learning experience for us both. Considering we had known each other for such a short time, it was a blessing how compatible Madeleine and I were. However, it took years for her to admit how homesick she had been in those early days of our marriage.

"Why didn't you complain?" I asked. "I would have understood."

"I had no time to complain," Madeleine told me. "I was too busy being a mother and trying to be a good 'home wife.' I didn't even know how to cook."

My young bride had not only left her homeland, her family, and her friends, but also turned her back on her career as a model, yet she swore she never missed the modeling.

As to her learning to cook, she later explained, "I spent a lot of time with Betty Crocker in those early days when I was a new bride, nursing India and then Mia into all hours of the night." That tattered old cookbook is still sitting with the others on our kitchen shelf.

I reveled in our new lives. On Sunday mornings, Thomas and I walked a few blocks down West 91st Street to Broadway to buy the *Times*. Going on two and already showing his *nisse* nature, Thomas would run ahead of me and hide in a doorway. When I got there, he would jump out and shout a loud "BOO!" to scare me. I loved it. Eventually, I learned all children loved to play "boo!" As a father, I was a neophyte.

As far as cooking went, Madeleine would go to the market daily, like all good housewives in Denmark had done for centuries (they didn't have refrigerators with built-in freezers), and come home with mysterious bony cuts of meat and a few chicken backs or any "special" of the day. If I suggested something else, she would look at me with alarm.

"Everything is too expensive," she would say.

I tried gently, I hope, to let her know we could afford better pieces of meat like steak now and then, or a whole chicken or some fish, and explained we could even freeze leftovers for another meal. I had cooked for myself during the ten years of being a bachelor after my divorce.

"Okay." Madeleine brightened. "You cook two nights a week, and I'll cook two nights. We will go out for dinner on Friday nights and eat leftovers on the weekend."

We tried out Madeleine's plan, and it worked—sort of.

Summer was still at its hottest, and my wife and I were expecting a baby. In those days, we didn't know if we were having a boy or a girl. We had decided on Peter, my favorite name for a boy, but we had not selected a name for a girl. Grandmother-to-be Pia arrived from Copenhagen to take care of Thomas while Madeleine would be in the hospital and to help with the new baby while I was at work in the film studios during the day. We were sure Pia would have some good ideas for a name if the baby turned out to be a girl.

Here is Madeleine, very pregnant, with little
Thomas and Madeleine's mother, Pia.

On August 4, the day after Madeleine's twenty-sixth birthday, our daughter was born. Now we were a family of four. Our baby looked for the world like an adorable little doll, but she had no hair! Pia, now "Mormor" (Danish for "mother's mother"), assured us new hair would grow in soon.

"What will be her name?" Mormor Pia asked.

I had assumed she would favor a Danish name. Pia would have been fine with me, but she didn't have any suggestions.

"Are not there many beautiful Southern names for girls?" she asked.

"Oh, sure, like Elizabeth Ann and Mary Jean and Daisy Nell?" I reeled off some names of girls I knew. "I don't think so."

"What about the old Southern names?" Pia asked. "What would they be?"

"Amber," said Madeleine. "That was Howard's aunt on his mother's side. I like the name Amber."

"I loved my aunt's name, but Amber Barker has a hard sound to me," I said. "Some old-fashioned Southern names were soft and pretty, but some were odd, like Melanie, Tallulah, India."

"In-dia. I like that name. In-dia Bar-ker." Pia said it slowly. "Was it used a lot in the old days?"

"Well, I suppose so," I said. "India Wilkes was Scarlett O'Hara's rival in *Gone with the Wind.* Maybe not so many in modern times, but a woman named India Edwards was a well-known Secretary of the Treasury–you know, in Washington."

Pia looked pleased. "In-dia" rolled off her tongue.

"But no middle names," Madeleine said. "I have two middle names, Yvette and Smaru. She does not get either one of those. Thomas has no middle name. I made sure of that," she added with a firm voice. "Our children will have no middle names." Madeleine was never fond of her middle names, and so for this, I agreed to her odd request.

At the end of the week, the nurse came in with discharge papers and asked for the baby's name.

"Her name is India," Madeleine said.

The nurse blanched. "You can't be serious," she said. "You can't name that sweet baby India. That's awful! She'll be laughed at the rest of her life. Well now what's her middle name?"

"No middle name. India is her name," Madeleine said, looking the nurse straight in the eye. "And that is the end of it."

When our baby daughter was christened India Barker in the Lutheran church nearby on Central Park West, nobody laughed. A month later, we saw she was sprouting some blonde peach fuzz for hair. We tried taping a pink bow on the top of her head. The bow fell off. Then we all laughed.

There was a sandbox in the park across the street from our apartment where, winter and summer, my wife took the kids for fresh air. It was there that Madeleine had made her first friend, Diane Groman. Diane's little son, Paul, was Thomas's first playmate. Not counting all the pee-pee trips back to our apartment, Madeleine and Diane spent many hours in that playground, and they became close friends for life.

Fortunately, I was busy in my work, one interesting job after another, but Madeleine's life was one diaper after another, one bottle after another, day after day, and we needed a break. Remembering my earlier trip to Puerto Rico with Bob and Patrice, I was sure a belated honeymoon for us there would do the trick.

Our hotel in tropical San Juan and dining out on exotic food every night was about the biggest contrast possible to our daily life in New York. However, with two small kids, daily life in Puerto Rico can be remarkably similar to daily life in New York: one diaper after another, one bottle after another, day after day . . . Well, you get the idea.

There were diversions. For example, on our first day, I had to drag tough little Thomas, kicking and screaming, from the kiddie pool and take him out of the broiling sun. When we were back in the hotel room, we had a surprise. Madeleine's jewelry case had been stolen. She didn't have a lot of expensive pieces, just a few family jewels and sentimental things, but all were gone, even my gold watch from Vic Damone.

But then there was a good surprise on that vacation. At nine months, India took her first steps, laughing and toddling all the way across our hotel room. We flew back to New York refreshed and happy. To keep up with Thomas, India was soon running everywhere. Within a year, she started to talk, coming up with childish malaprops like "Laggedy Gann" for her Raggedy Ann doll and "hangbag" for her mother's handbag.

CHAPTER 78

OUT OF THE BLUE

Central Park West, late 1967

"HELLO, HOWARD," SHE said on the phone. "Guess who."

"Barbara! I recognize your voice." I was really surprised, but not with panic. "What's new?" came out in my normal voice.

"I'm in New York, on my way to Israel. I thought we might meet somewhere for a drink and see how ten years has treated us."

I wasn't expecting that. "Hold on for a moment. I want to tell my wife who's calling." When I had explained, Madeleine didn't seem surprised.

"Tell her we'd like her to come here for a cocktail," Madeleine said. "I've already met your ex-fiancée. I'd love to meet your ex-wife."

When Barbara arrived, Madeleine was nursing India, and we all settled down for a pleasant, civilized chat. Barbara also met our little son, Thomas, and after his brief hello, he was put to bed. Our first cocktail led to a second. Madeleine invited Barbara to stay for dinner, but she pleasantly declined, saying she was a vegetarian.

"That's all right," my wife assured her. "You'll have a baked potato and some vegetables."

An hour or so later, at coffee, my wife excused herself and got up from the table. "Why don't you two go on talking?" she said. "I'm exhausted. I have to go to bed."

Barbara and I did go on talking for quite a long time. I learned Barbara had continued her checkered career in theater and television, and after our divorce was final, she had married the man she left me for, the actor William Windom. That came as something of a surprise. I told her I had known Windom fifteen years earlier when we both were in the army. We both had been allowed to use the time taking theater classes at Biarritz American University in Southern France until our turn came up to be returned to the United States for discharge.

"It's ironic, isn't it?" I went on. "Bill was an acting student. He had the lead in Shakespeare's *Richard III*, and I painted baroque designs on the cape he wore as the king. In the coronation scene, he climbed up out of the orchestra pit, and as he walked to the throne, the enormous cape spread all the way across the entire stage, left and right, to the wings. It was an impressive entrance."

"So, you knew Bill," she said quietly. "Amazing."

"Only slightly. We weren't buddies."

"Neither were we, it turned out," she said, sounding a little like a confession. "He dumped me."

She told me the rest of her story. After a few years of marriage, Barbara and her husband had been divorced. She left Hollywood and moved to Puerto Vallarta. While living there, she was cast in the movie that was shooting, *The Night of the Iguana*, with Richard Burton and Ava Gardner. She left Mexico and began traveling, searching, perhaps, for a number of things, most importantly, I think, for truth–truth and peace. I believe her quest was over when she had discovered the Bahá'í faith and embraced it. I don't know how many years it took her to find it, but that evening before she left, she told me she was on her way to Israel to visit the Holy Land.

CHAPTER 79

RECHERCHÉ LE TEMPS PERDUE

NYC, 1967

O NE SNOWY FEBRUARY morning I woke up thinking of my old skiing days. I guess it was only natural. I also thought of Elinor Robbins, the woman who was responsible for many happy ski trips to the mountains here in the east. I was also thinking it would be nice to get in touch with her after ten years.

"Elinor is a fun lady I used to know when I was new in New York," I said to Madeleine.

My wife was too busy changing a diaper to answer. Without considering what time it was, I picked up the telephone and dialed.

"Hello," a sleepy Elinor answered.

"A voice from the past," I began.

"Uh, hello?" Elinor said.

"This is Howard, Howard Barker," I said to the silence on the other end. "Elinor, I live just across the park from you. How are you?"

"Well, hello, Howard," she said, suddenly cheerful. "I'm fine. How are you after all these years?

"I'm fine. I'm married now, and we have three children—a little boy and two little girls. One's still a baby. I'd love to see you and show off my family. If you're free this afternoon, why don't you and Robbie come over for cocktails and I'll tell you all about it? Bring your son too."

"Davey is away in college, Howard. Robbie isn't well and . . ." She paused.

"I'm sorry, Elinor. Is he all right?"

"Well, he's okay . . ."

"Elinor, say hello for me, and if you feel all right about it, why don't you come on over for just a little visit? Five-ish, okay? We'll toast old times."

"Okay," Elinor said. "I'll be there."

Elinor arrived with a wide smile and her typical joie de vivre. She looked great and had not lost her artistic touch from our days working together at Reed and Stevenson. She was carrying a mobile of dangling red paper hearts, a valentine she had made for our children. I made martinis, and Madeleine served hors d'oeuvres.

Elinor and I reminisced about our ski trips, the first one to Pittsfield, Massachusetts, where I, with the other two guys, tried to ski down the bunny hill of frozen snow. I fell and slid on ice all the way to the bottom on my face.

"Madeleine, your husband's cheeks looked like raw hamburger."

My smiling wife listened politely.

"We dragged him to the first aid hut, and they painted his face with some kind of clear emulsion," Elinor went on. "It stopped the bleeding, and he was fine."

"And then there was the time we got lost in a snowstorm at midnight in Vermont," I said. "Elinor drove around a traffic circle five times, not knowing which exit to take. Finally, we spotted a snow-covered sign.

"'Hop out of the car, Howard, and see what that sign says. Your pals in the back seat are asleep.'

"I brushed the snow away and called back to Elinor, 'It says TURN RIGHT ANY TIME!', I shouted.

"Elinor fell into a fit of laughter and turned right. It seemed funny–at the time. We arrived at our farmhouse lodging at 2:00 a.m. After thawing out by the still-live coals in the fireplace, we got a good night's sleep. The next two days skiing were great. Elinor was a good teacher, and we neophytes were good students. Remember the time in New Hampshire we skied in the White Mountains?" I asked Elinor. "I thought I could take the trail down from the top. I tumbled practically all the way down."

"I remember." She laughed. "When you finally hit bottom, you looked like the abominable snowman."

Madeleine, obviously, was thinking we were insane.

I didn't mention that night long ago when we all were going to bed after drinks and wine with dinner that I politely declined Elinor's open door offer as she disappeared into her bedroom: "Mon dieu, suis la, calledon–casseron."

The sun had set on Central Park West, and our baby daughter, India, had fallen asleep in her mother's arms. Madeleine, perhaps just a little puzzled, seemed pleased to have met this jolly old lady friend of mine. Martinis, hors d'oeuvres, and laughter made the afternoon fly by, and Elinor stood up to say farewell.

"Mon dieu," she said, kissing Madeleine and me on both cheeks and heading for the door. At the elevator, she turned and waved to us as she sang out in her fractured French, "Suis la calledon–casseron!"

CHAPTER 80

NOW WE ARE FIVE

Central Park West, Fall 1969

I T'S SURPRISING HOW time flies when you're having fun. Married life is full of surprises mixed with routine. Life provides both. Our days and nights were busy–mine fortunately filled with career work, Madeleine's with children and housework–and most of time, both of us were exhausted. More than once, we fell asleep in expensive Broadway theater seats trying to watch loud musicals. (Now what was *Little Johnny Johnston* all about?)

There were some wide-awake high points too. One was when we met Dr. Benjamin Spock. Millard Lampell, writer of the screenplay for *Days in My Father's House*, had invited us to dinner, and the author of Dr. Spock's *Baby and Child Care* was there. With two young kids and a baby on the way, my wife and I were excited to meet the doctor. Madeleine spoke for both of us.

"Dr. Spock, your book is like a bible to me," she said. "I couldn't do without it."

The affable doctor replied with genuinely warm thanks. If we had known in advance, we'd have brought the book with us and asked him to autograph it.

Less than three months later, our second daughter was born, and once again, we could not agree on a name for our new baby. We had trouble with the nurse.

469

"You had nine months to make up your minds." She sounded exasperated. "Wasn't that enough time?"

We brought our newborn home with "Baby Girl Barker" written on her birth certificate. Madeleine wanted to call her Pia, and I agreed, but Madeleine's mother, who had come from Denmark again to help out, did not want her new granddaughter to be named after her. I asked her why.

"One Pia in the family is enough," she said, and that was the end of it.

Madeleine suggested Amber, as she'd done when India was born.

"Howard's Aunt Amber brought him and his brother, Bishop, up from the time their parents died until the children were grown," said Madeleine. "And I still like the name Amber."

I should have kept my mouth shut, but I still disagreed. "I've always liked my aunt's name too," I said. "But somehow, to me, it doesn't seem to fit our little baby." I was hoping to come up with a name all three of us would like or at least a name we could agree on. "What about Mia? It rhymes with Pia. It's close but still different."

Pia liked the name. At that point, Madeleine agreed.

"Well, Mia does sound like Pia," Madeleine said. "That's close enough for me."

Mia was a delight. Her beautiful pixie face always lit up with impish smiles like her brother, and like her sister, India, Mia showed her independence early. She crawled early, stood early, and walked early, and just after her first birthday, she scorned diapers and potty-trained herself.

Our two-bedroom, two-bath apartment was quite large, but as months passed, Madeleine and I could see it would be better if we had a separate bedroom for the two girls. Then Thomas, at six, would have his own room. I realized we could achieve that by dividing our huge dining room in half with a new wall. That idea had to be abandoned when the landlord wouldn't allow alterations.

"What about Faye Dunaway's alteration upstairs?" I demanded to know. "The famous movie actress is remodeling her apartment to accommodate the Italian star Marcello Mastroianni."

"Miss Dunaway is an exception" was the building manager's answer. Before I could sputter my reaction, he went on. "She has removed a wall between the adjoining apartment and hers and is paying double for the two rentals." My jaw must have dropped. "She's also signed an agreement to replace the wall if she moves out." Case closed.

Once, we had seen Faye Dunaway and Marcello Mastroianni sitting tight-lipped on a sofa in the El Dorado's lobby. Shortly afterward, during a rare power failure, all four banks of the El Dorado's elevators were out of order. My wife and Mr. Mastroianni almost bumped into each other on the stairway somewhere between the first and eighteenth floors. Madeleine told me they had smiled and nodded to each other like all the other apartment dwellers on the stairways had done.

As time went on and the cost of city living increased, including the looming possibility of private schools for our three children, a move to the suburbs seemed like the answer. Thomas's little friend's bike was stolen at the public school next door, another negative adding to the equation.

"How does a city girl from Copenhagen feel about becoming a housewife and mom in suburbia?" I asked Madeleine.

"I'm already a housewife and mom," she answered. "What would be different in suburbia?"

"It would be nicer for the children," I replied. "Maybe you'd like it too."

For me, to get up an hour earlier in the morning and take a train into the city for my work in the studios suddenly seemed daunting, but we started house-hunting in Long Island and New Jersey.

I had visions of a rambling farmhouse sitting on a hillside acre or two, with trees and stone outcroppings, overlooking a peaceful valley. Man, was I dreaming! We looked at dozens of houses, even one resembling my dream, but after the better part of a year searching in Long Island and New Jersey, they were way out of our price range. Without realizing Westchester County is the most expensive place in the United States to live, we turned our attention north of the city to the coastal towns on Long Island Sound, of course. Poor

Madeleine! After getting used to life in what she had called "the New World," like me, she had to learn about real estate. We kept on searching.

Finally, a year and a half later, we found a house we liked and, more importantly, we could afford–a pleasant five-bedroom colonial in a small town on the Hudson River, less than an hour north of New York. It was on a quiet avenue facing a golf course, walking distance from Main Street's shops and a supermarket. There was even a small movie theater, the Pickwick Theater. Years later, when designing the sets for Dick Besoyan's off-Broadway musical comedy *Babes in the Wood*, we actually did a week's tryout at the Pickwick before opening in New York. As a freelance set designer, I was worried about being able to make the mortgage payments on buying a house.

The astute real-estate agent asked, "In New York, did you always pay your rent on time?"

"Yes, I had to," I answered.

Her point well made, we bought our new home on 36 Sherman Avenue in Dobbs Ferry, New York.

Our glorious home of nearly forty-four years, 36 Sherman Avenue, home of many great memories.

On moving day, we left the city under black clouds and arrived at our new empty house and no moving van. We used a neighbor's phone to call the movers. They had used our truck with our load for a small job in Long Island. Our load would not arrive until the next day. By nightfall, the truck had not shown up. Mary, an angel from next door, appeared with a small mattress. Our three little ones slept on it. Madeleine and I slept on the floor.

Moving day. I am not sure if you can see the little naked
ones running around in the background on the stairs!

Twenty-four hours later, the truck arrived with all our earthly goods during a rainstorm. I sat on a stool in the kitchen, holding my floor plans of the house, drinking vodka, and directing the movers where to put the furniture, room by room. The last piece was unloaded at three o'clock in the morning.

When the sun came out the following day, the Barker family ventured outside into the fresh rain-washed air. Our next-door neighbors, Mary and Jack Degnan, welcomed us to Dobbs Ferry. Mary lifted her youngest daughter and set her down on our side of the fence. Mia and Maureen, both two years old, stood looking at each other for a moment. Then without saying a word, they joined hands and toddled away on a walk around our new backyard. Forty years later, they're still friends.

CHAPTER 81

WIENER BLUT

1960s–1980s

MADELEINE'S MOTHER WAS a remarkable woman. Pia Permoser was born and grew up in Austria, in Sauerbrun, Burgenland, a small mountain town not far from Vienna. The Permosers were very poor, and as a young girl, Pia was obliged to go from house to house selling her homemade embroidery to make ends meet–a sad story, but even sadder was when Pia got home at night, her two brothers would have eaten what little food there had been for supper.

When a dashing Dane, a magician named Geovanni Arentoft, came to town with a small variety show, the Permoser family attended the performance. Geovanni was quite taken with pretty Pia and offered her a job as his assistant. Swept off her feet, Pia said farewell to her mother and father and traveled throughout Austria, Germany, and Denmark with the show. Pia's brothers, Joseph and Wilmar, did not approve of the situation. In fact, they threatened to come and kill Geovanni if he did not do the right thing by their sister. Geovanni and Pia were married soon afterward.

I don't know Pia's mother tongue well enough to say, "Like mother, like daughter," but I do know enough to say that it was also hard for both of them to say "Auf wiedersehen" and "Farvel saa laenge" to their families. I'm sure the young fräulein Pia was as homesick as her daughter had been when I spirited Madeleine and baby Thomas away to "the New World."

In many summers and winters over the next twenty years, we flew to Copenhagen with our kids to see Madeleine's mother and father. We always spent time with her younger brother, Rene, his wife, Vipse, and their kids, Leslie and Lasse, as well as others of Madeleine's relatives. It was very good for Madeleine and our kids to keep in touch with their Danish roots, and I became a member of a large loving family of Danes. I cherish every minute of it.

On one of our trips to København (Danish for Copenhagen), Madeleine and I drove out to a suburb called Hellerup to show me and our three kids where she had lived when they were children.

"It was a beautiful house, and I would like for you to see it," Madeleine said. "It had a curving stairway in the entry hall."

She was right. The house was beautiful. It was two stories high and sat on a generous corner lot.

"Let's ring the doorbell," I suggested. "Maybe the owners will let us go inside."

We were very near speechless when the door opened and an Asian man in a monk's robe stood smiling at us. When Madeleine explained in Danish who we were, he welcomed us to come in. We entered what was now a Tibetan monastery!

"We are honored to have His Holiness, the Dalai Lama, here on a rare visit," the smiling monk said. "I will ask if he will grant you an audience."

Within minutes, all nine of us were climbing the curving stairway as Madeleine, Yvonne, and Renee had done when they went to bed each night as children years before. Then we were ushered into an empty room where we were asked to stand and wait. Presently, two young monks entered ahead of a third, who, by his appearance, could only be the Dalai Lama himself. As he stopped and faced us, a little dog, probably a Shih Tzu, trotted in and looked at the line of visitors. Our four-year-old Mia and the pup spotted each other at the same moment, and Mia scooped him up in her arms. The adults froze. One of the young monks stepped forward, took the Shih Tzu, and silently left the room. With a benevolent smile, the holy man looked at each of us and spoke a few words as he placed a circle of red cotton cord around our necks. And the audience was over.

We will never know what His Holiness had said, but we knew we had been blessed by the Dalai Lama himself. The monk who had escorted us up the curving staircase told us the red cords would bring us good luck if we wore them, without taking them off, for one month. We went down the curving staircase and left the monastery. It had been a strange but somehow enriching experience. Mia and I were the only ones in the family who wore our red cords, even while showering, for one whole month.

***

My dear mother-in-law, Pia, had a keen sense of humor, and with the slightest provocation, she could go into gales of laughter over some silly incident, dissolving into tears and ending up with a red nose. Pia and Geovanni were also delightful companions on our trips to the Spanish island of Majorca to visit Madeleine's sister Yvonne and her children, Sandra and Ilan. Pia provided many light moments. No afternoon at the beach would go by without Pia's conspiring suggestion.

"Howard, it is quite warm. Don't you think it is time for a little tonic with gin?"

If I said, "Isn't it a bit early?" she would politely agree.

"But, Howard," she would continue with her hand on my arm, "it would be so fresh."

I will never forget the time we were celebrating Yvonne's fiftieth birthday at a small nightclub in Palma de Majorca. When the musicians ensemble struck up a waltz, I asked Pia to dance. Being Austrian, Pia was a natural-born dancer, and I loved to waltz too, so I whirled her out onto the tiny dance floor of the club.

"Wein, wein, nur du aleine," Pia sang in her throaty mezzo as we spun around and around. As other couples politely left the floor to make room for our gyrations, she was dancing and singing, "I'm in love with Vien-na. I'm in love with Vien-na."

Finally, to a friendly applause, we had to give up and go back to our table laughing, and I hope Pia's memories of that night were as happy as mine. Strauss waltzes have always created a sense of nostalgia for the Belle Époque in Vienna, a time and place I had never known before.

One winter Pia came alone to visit us in Dobbs Ferry. The ground was coated with a heavy blanket of snow, and Pia decided to try Madeleine's cross-country skis on the golf course across the street in front of our house. Pia wanted to go alone, so I decided to watch her schuss down the gentle slope. Halfway to the bottom, she fell and lay motionless in the snow. *Is she hurt?* I wondered. *Should I rush out to help her?* After a moment, I saw her move, twisting her body and rising awkwardly to her feet. She stood still for a few moments. Then looking around, she picked up the skis, which had come off, and trudged slowly up the hill.

As she approached the front door, I called out, "Are you all right, Pia? What happened?"

"I cannot," she said. Tears were rolling down her cheeks. "I cannot ski."

"Of course, you can," I assured her. "It was only a little fall. You're just out of practice."

"No," she answered. "I was a good skier long ago." She jabbed the skis into the snow and came inside, wiping the tears away. "I am foolish. I'm too old."

"No, Pia, you're not. You're fine." I handed her a tissue. "Here, blow your nose."

She did and smiled. I gave her a quick hug and a wink.

"Now just for old times' sake," I said, "don't you think it's time for some tonic and a little gin?"

Pia smiled. Then she laughed. "Yes, Hovard—it would be so fresh!"

I could not have asked for a more wonderful mother-in-law. Pia was sweet, generous, and loving, always grateful and happy to see us when we came to Denmark on a visit. Geovanni was a good father-in-law, a charming man, and I was very fond of him. But I reserved my adoration for Pia.

Pia and I on one of her visits to America.

CHAPTER 82

THANKSGIVING

San Luis Obispo, 1989

IN THE LATE 1980s, my brother and I discovered we had a long-lost aunt, my father's only sister, eighty-nine years old and living in San Luis Obispo, California. As a young man, in Ohio, my father had broken up with his fiancée. When she returned the engagement ring, he impulsively gave it to his teenage sister. A few years later, during World War I, when my father was stationed in South Mississippi, he fell in love with our future mother and requested his sister return the diamond ring so he could propose marriage. Hurt and disillusioned, she returned the ring and vowed never speak to him again.

"Clarence was an Indian giver," Amber said to Bishop and me as we dug into a piece of her apple cobbler. "My own brother gave my diamond ring to a Southern belle."

"Now slow down, Aunt Helen," Bishop said. "How did all this come about?"

"How could he do such a thing?" I said. "Why would he?"

"He was in love with your mother!" she said, the words spilling out in exasperation. "He had asked her to marry him. I was so hurt when he wrote, asking me to send him the ring. That was back in 1918," Aunt Helen explained in a gentler tone with moist eyes. They never spoke again.

My Aunt Helen as an older child, with my father
on the far right, and grandparents.

Now, nearly eighty years later, after a phone call and several letters back
and forth, my brother and I flew to San Luis Obispo to have Thanksgiving
dinner with our newfound Aunt Helen. Bishop had arrived the day before,
carrying a large cooler containing a smoked turkey, stuffing, and "all the
fixin's." I came a day later because I wanted to have Thanksgiving with my
wife and children.

At San Luis's tiny airport, my brother and Aunt Helen were standing next
to a long white vintage Chrysler. She welcomed me with open arms.

"I told your brother we weren't having his turkey until you got here," she
said. I knew I was going to like Aunt Helen.

As we sat down at her dining room table, Bishop placed a small tape
recorder next to his plate and switched it on.

"Bishop, I'm not sure Aunt Helen is comfortable with your recording our
conversation right off the bat," I said. "Why don't we wait 'til later?"

My brother paid no attention to me. "Now the first thing I remember—"
he said, about to plunge into our history.

"Hold on, Bishop," Aunt Helen interrupted him. "Are you sure that thing
is on?"

When he assured her it was, she started talking and didn't stop for three
days. It was tough to get a word in edgewise, but we all had our turn. As we
enjoyed Bishop's smoke-roasted turkey and all the "fixin's," we exchanged
stories about our lives. Aunt Helen had lost her son to cancer, and her husband,
Marvin, had died some years later.

When she learned my brother and I had a happy childhood and what a good man and a good father her brother had been, she told us she forgave him "in her heart." She said she could now make peace with herself about their estrangement. Happily, it was a cathartic experience for our aunt and an emotionally charged experience for all three of us.

Aunt Helen lived alone in a modest Spanish-styled bungalow. It was furnished simply with plain, practical furniture and a minimal amount of decor. Other than her great kitchen stove and a very large television set (she loved to watch football games), her only luxury was her 1964 Chrysler New Yorker, which she drove, sometimes too fast, until she was over ninety.

"When I was young, I loved to dance, but Marvin loved to bowl," she said. "So when he'd go bowling, I'd go dancing at the Grange. Oh yes, we both had our fun."

Bishop and I made many trips west to see our aunt, some together and some with our wives. Many more letters were exchanged, and many tender feelings passed between us all. Aunt Helen kept up with world events, and she was a teetotaler. She did not tolerate alcohol in her house. When Bishop was there, he had to hide his beer in a cooler behind his bed. On my visits, I disguised my martinis with cubes of ice in water glasses (no olives). Tillie Peaker, one of Aunt Helen's older friends, was more easygoing. A wiry little woman who still smoked, Tilly would invite me for cocktails each time I came out to San Luis Obispo. Tillie outlived Aunt Helen.

After two strokes, Aunt Helen had to be moved into a nursing home. She was confined to a wheelchair, and when she tried to speak, her impatient stream of words were incoherent. One day I sat with her, urging her to eat.

"Have some broth, Aunt Helen," I said, holding a spoon to her lips. "It's really delicious."

She looked me straight in the eye and shook her head stubbornly. "I'd rather have a good cup of coffee," she said clearly. It was one of the last things she said to me.

The mysteries of the human brain are profound. She died shortly afterward at the age of ninety-two. I inherited her '64 Caddie and a small oil painting of ocean waves crashing onto the Pacific shore. Aunt Helen was a tough old bird. She may not have always been lovable, but I loved her.

Me, Aunt Helen, and Bishop.

CHAPTER 83

INTERMEZZO

Restaurant Row, NYC, 2011

"THAT WAS A long lunch," my wife said when I threw my keys on the kitchen counter.

"It was a great one!" I said. "And you'll never guess who I had lunch with."

"You told me you were taking Vida Licata to Joe Allen's today," Madeleine said. "You wanted to thank her for putting us in her Variety column, NY to LA. But was it such a great lunch? You've got a smile on your face a mile wide."

"The lunch was okay, but let me explain why the wide smile." Then I told her the whole story.

As soon as we sat down at the restaurant, Vida checked out the room to see if anyone she knew was having lunch too (you know Vida).

"Look, there's Maggie," Vida said.

"Who?" I asked.

"Maggie, Margaret Whiting, over in the corner. She just sat down."

"So it is," I said. "Do you know her?"

"Sure," said Vida. "Known her for years. Maggie's a friend of the Golands too. Arnold did the arrangement for 'Wheel of Hurt,' Maggie's last big hit."

"Really? Arnold's a genius," I added, glancing across the crowded room. "Too bad Miss Whiting didn't record some of Nancy's songs." I said, "You know, Como's version of 'Where You're Concerned' was sweet, but I'd love to hear what Whiting would have done with it. Her phrasing is so incredible."

"Yeah," Vida agreed. "You know, before Nancy married Arnold, she was a good singer herself–"

"She still is," I interrupted. "Did she ever sing 'I Suppose' for you? It will break your heart. I've always thought she wrote that after she and Arnold got back together, you know, after Nancy took off with that guy. When I asked her about why she wrote the song, she just laughed and said, 'Are you kidding? Forget it.'" I looked over at Miss Whiting. "Should we ask Miss Whiting to join us?" I suggested.

Without answering, Vida immediately went over to her friend's table, sat down, and started chatting.

I had loved Margaret Whiting's records since high school–"That Old Black Magic" and "Time After Time"–and later, "Moonlight in Vermont" and "It Might As Well Be Spring" became her signature songs. Strange how her singing just flows through your head. It's her special sound–husky but crystal clear. She always touches my heart. As soon as I saw Vida walking back toward our table, arm in arm with Margaret, I stood up and held the chairs for the both of them.

"Margaret, Howard Barker. Howard, Margaret Whiting," Vida introduced us simply.

By this time in my life, I've met and worked with quite a few celebrities, but once stagestruck, always stagestruck, and today, as I sat across the table from Margaret Whiting, I was fascinated and touched in a different way. I have no idea what we had for lunch, but I ate and drank Miss Whiting's every word and gesture like a hungry man. She spoke and laughed freely, she was constantly moving, gently touching her hair and cheeks, her arms, and her ample breasts. She was sweet and boisterous at the same time, bold and funny, warm and outspoken, and thoroughly entertaining.

Finally, it was time to leave. I had not planned on such a gala lunch, but I was quick to ask for the check.

"I'm heading east," I said. "Can I drop anyone off?"

"I'm walking back to the office," Vida said. "I can use the exercise."

"Well, Howard, I'll join you," Margaret said and took my hand. "I'm over on First, near United Nations."

Heading east on 50th street, the cab hit heavy traffic. I didn't mind. Margaret kept the conversation bouncing–and my heart too–all the way across town.

"I'll show you where to let me off," Margaret said.

As she leaned on me to speak to the cabbie, I was enveloped in the scent of her perfume. When we got to her apartment building–much too soon for me—she leaned on me again, thanked me with a quick kiss, wished me luck, and said goodbye.

Daughter of the celebrated composer Richard Whiting, Margaret was a recording artist, stage and screen actress, nightclub performer, and a brilliant star of the pop music world. I loved to hear Margaret Whiting sing. But for me, Maggie had another special talent. She could make me smile a mile wide.

CHAPTER 84

STAPLETON REDUX

Manhattan, 1990

I HAD NOT kept in touch with Jean Stapleton as years passed, but I did follow her career as it blossomed and grew. In the fifties and early sixties, she delighted Broadway audiences in the original Broadway musicals *Damn Yankees, Funny Girl*, and *Bells Are Ringing*. From early television series, including *Robert Montgomery Presents* and *The Philco-Goodyear Television Playhouse*, all the way through the nineties, Jean starred and costarred in numerous familiar TV productions, much too numerous for me to list here. However, you may remember her as Ray's imperious aunt in *Everybody Loves Raymond* and Miles's grandmother in *Murphy Brown*.

Of course, Miss Stapleton will always be best known for her portrayal of Edith Bunker, the long-suffering, lovable "dingbat" wife of Archie Bunker (played by Carroll O'Conner) in the eight-year classic sitcom *All in the Family* during the seventies. I always thought Edith proved to be the smartest one in the entire Bunker clan.

In 1982, I had the pleasure of designing a sequence in *First Lady of the World*, starring Jean Stapleton as Eleanor Roosevelt, a feature movie made for television by Sony Pictures. My job was to prepare the location and to supervise the period scenes that were to be filmed when the First Lady, Mrs.

Roosevelt, occupied Val-Kill, a small two-story cottage on the Roosevelt estate at Hyde Park. The exteriors on the grounds by the water were simple, but the long-unused interiors of the cottage needed refurbishing, which would take several days of work with my crew.

Another scene to be filmed was at Franklin Roosevelt's gravesite in Hyde Park. The actual tombstone on the estate bore Franklin's and Eleanor's names. Since Jean, as Eleanor, would be standing there, very much alive, a simulated facing with only Franklin's name on it would be necessary. I designed one and had it temporarily installed on the face of the stone for the shot. That was it.

After Miss Stapleton arrived for the filming, the director, John Erman, invited me to join them for dinner at the historic Rhinebeck Inn the night before shooting began. When I sat down next to Jean, I surprised her with a single long-stemmed red rose.

"Oh my, Howard, Thank you!" she said with a merry laugh as we recalled our sailing disaster in Amagansett Bay twenty years earlier.

Mr. Erman was surprised that Jean and I knew each other. It made the dinner a special one for me.

It was some years later before I actually saw *First Lady of the World*, and I was overwhelmed and deeply touched by Jean's portrayal of the brilliant and unpretentious Mrs. Roosevelt. I wished I had been responsible for the look of the whole movie, not just the limited portion that was mine. Whoever was production designer for the rest of *First Lady* did a brilliant job. I also greatly admired John Erman's intelligent and sensitive direction. His creative work on the film was admirable. I crossed paths with John years later on *Carolina Skeletons*, which I was able to design in its entirety. I learned a great deal from him.

Jean Stapleton and I were to meet again but not on a movie. This time, it was on a ship deep in the jungles of Brazil. Having visited several Caribbean islands, Madeleine and I were on an American Theater Wing cruise making its way up the Amazon River to Manaus, a bustling port city a thousand miles into the interior of Brazil. The only people we knew onboard were Patrice Munsel and her husband, Bob Schuler. Pat was one of the stars who provided the ship's entertainment. Madeleine and I were having lunch on deck when I saw Jean looking, in vain, for an empty chair. She stopped at our table and asked if she could join us.

"Please do, Miss Stapleton," I said.

Jean put down her tray, smiled, and thanked me. "Is that . . . you, uh . . . Howard?"

"Yes, Jean. It's me, and this is my wife, Madeleine."

"Oh my goodness!" She burst out laughing. "What are you doing on a ship in the middle of Brazil?"

"Cruising, the same as you are," I answered. "Except you are performing in the ship's big show, and we are just passengers on for the ride."

During lunch, we reminisced about her *First Lady of the World* and laughed again about our disastrous dunking in Amagansett Bay at Vincent Donehue's beach house years ago.

"I miss him, Vincent," she said. "Don't you?

"Yes, but it was a long time ago," I said. My wife listened politely.

"And do you ever see Barbara?" Jean asked.

"Years ago, she came to see us once," Madeleine answered. "After our first daughter was born."

"Barbara came for a drink and stayed for dinner," I added. "She told us she was on her way to Israel and visit Jerusalem. Later, she wrote me after she settled down. She actually lives on an island in the Caribbean."

The surprise lunch on deck with my old friend Jean was a delight. The last night of our cruise, Madeleine and I were at Manaus's historic opera house for the gala performance by the group of stars from the ship. Sandy Duncan, Broadway's Peter Pan, sang and danced with her husband, Don Correia. Mary Louise Wilson presented excerpts from her one-woman show channeling the amusing, eccentric Diana Vreeland, editor-in-chief of *Vogue* and special consultant of the Metropolitan Museum's Costume Institute. Tenor Cris Groenendaal, star of Broadway's long-running *Phantom of the Opera*, sang selections from the musical, accompanied by his wife, Broadway orchestra conductor Sue Anderson. The Academy Award–winning movie actress Patricia Neal read from *As I Am*, her outrageous, sometimes shocking autobiography. From English stage and film, Lynn Redgrave and her mother, Rachel Kempson, performed a delightful music hall number. In the eleven-o'clock slot, our friend Patrice Munsel surprised everyone by singing "My Funny Valentine" instead of an operatic aria. She delivered it Broadway style, looking directly at her husband, Bob, who was sitting in the audience with Madeleine and me.

Jean Stapleton was the final performer. Dragging an enormous gilded harp to center stage, she sat down in a tiny golden ballroom chair and proceeded to carefully adjust the harp's tuning knobs. Then without plucking a single string on the harp, Jean smiled sweetly at the audience and launched into a hilarious monologue about nothing important or relative to the show. It brought down the house. When she stood up to take a bow, the audience kept her bowing with their applause until she dragged her harp off the stage. Jean immediately reappeared (without her harp) to more applause, but instead of offering some sort of encore, she raised her arms and looked offstage. The rest of the performers then came out and joined Jean, singing that theater anthem "There's No Business Like Show Business."

In 2002, Madeleine and I went to Lincoln Center to see Jean star in Horton Foote's *The Carpetbagger's Children*. After the final curtain, Jean greeted us warmly backstage in her dressing room. Of course, we told her how much we enjoyed her performance.

"Isn't Horton's play wonderful?" Jean said, shifting attention from herself to our mutual friend. "And Hallie is so touching, isn't she? Horton would be so proud of his daughter."

"I'm sure he would," Madeleine agreed.

"And didn't I read somewhere," I asked, "in the reviews, I think, the play is like his homage to Chekhov's *Three Sisters*?"

"Yes," Jean said, laughing. "I liked to call him Anton Foote. But now tell me about yourselves and your children." As always, Jean was gracious and a joy to behold.

By 2004, Jean Stapleton had appeared in at least sixty productions onstage, television, and motion pictures. She and her husband of thirty years, William Putch, director of Totem Pole Playhouse, had two children: John, actor-writer-director, and Pamela, television producer.

Jean died on May 13, 2013, of natural causes in New York City. She was ninety. New York theater marquees were dimmed one minute on June 5 at 8:00 p.m. in a tribute to her memory.

Photo courtesy of the Stapleton family.

CHAPTER 85

SABA FLASHBACK

Dobbs Ferry, 2004

S OMETIME IN 1980, I received a letter from Barbara "just to say hello" and to see how my life was going. She also told me that she'd had a number of exhibitions of her paintings and that they were selling well to tourists.

That was about all I had heard from her until thirty years later, when a friend of hers, a man named Bill Froelich, called from New York and asked if he could drive out to see me in Dobbs Ferry.

"Barbara told me she hoped she had not ruined your life. She just wanted to find out if you are okay."

I gave him directions and told him to come on out. When Mr. Froelich arrived, I showed him our beautiful backyard and gave him a tour inside our home and showed him pictures of my wife and our three grown-up children.

"Barbara didn't ruin my life," I assured him as we chatted over coffee. "And please give her my very best."

He gave me his email address and invited me and my wife to be his guests anytime at his home in Saba, a small island in the Caribbean.

A few months later, we were thinking of a Caribbean vacation, and Madeleine suggested we go to Sint Maarten and stop off in Saba to see my ex.

I agreed. We had not seen Barbara since that time in 1967, when she came for a drink and stayed all evening. (Well, Madeleine did invite her to stay for dinner.)

The island of Saba is actually a tiny mountain, lush and green, near Sint Maarten. With no apparent beaches, it rises steeply out of the sea. The pilot of our prop plane, steering directly toward the side of the mountain, seemed determined to be searching for an open spot to make a crash landing. At the last minute, he banked left and swerved around it like a deranged seagull! Just ahead of us was a level plateau and the shortest landing strip I had ever seen.

When Bill and Barbara met us at Saba's one tiny landing terminal shack, they were both grinning. We all hugged.

"You look a lot older," Barbara said, laughing.

"So do you," I answered, and then we all laughed. "What did you expect after forty years?"

"I want to show you my studio, and I'll make us some lunch," she said as we piled into Bill's tiny car.

The motor wouldn't turn over. Madeleine and I got out and pushed, Bill steered, and Barbara coached from the back seat. Fortunately, the car wasn't parked on a steep hill, so we were soon on our way.

Barbara's studio, where she lived, was a modest one-room dwelling in The Bottom, an area near the water at the foot of the mountain. Her house was divided into several open areas–a work area with a large easel and small tables filled with paints and brushes, a sitting-sleeping area, and, behind a shelving unit, a kitchen area with a door to the bathroom.

Some of her paintings–colorful, impressionistic–were on the walls. Others were rolled up in an immense shelved cabinet. There was a bed, piled with brightly colored throw pillows, that also served as a sofa.

"It's small, but it's all I need," Barbara said cheerfully. "I'd like you to have a painting of mine. What sort of thing would you like?"

"Um, let us think about that," I said. "In the meantime, why don't we take you and Bill out for lunch?"

"Oh, that would be great." Barbara sounded relieved. "I just remembered I ate the last can of tuna yesterday."

We had a very tasty island lunch at a nearby restaurant and then headed up to the Windward Side at the top of the mountain. On its peak, Bill's home, surrounded by trees, sat in the middle of a good-sized piece of property. It was known as the Pyramid House for a very good reason. It was a shingle-covered pyramid with gabled windows all around and had spectacular views of the ocean. The four of us walked through the woods and looked at some of Bill's unique sculptures, all constructed of stones.

In the garden, there was a swimming pool and a meditation circle made of large stones. Bill invited me to join him ("It's very good for agitation"), and we walked slowly and silently, around and around, to the center of the circle and then slowly back in the opposite direction out to the starting point. I had not been agitated, but if I had, I'm sure it would have been calming.

For a good part of the next day, we sat on the patio talking about old times. When Barbara mentioned she was relieved to see she had not ruined my life by leaving me, Madeleine spoke up.

"Does Howard look like a man whose life has been ruined?" she asked.

There was no immediate reply. We took a few snapshots by Bill's fountain, and the two women got along just fine. I suspect it may have been because they were both Leos. Barbara was born on August 2, and Madeleine on August 3 (but twenty years apart, of course).

At some point, Barbara brought up her own marriage and divorce. Apparently, she didn't remember she had told us about it thirty-odd years earlier.

"What happened?" I asked. (I thought I should?)

"Bill dumped me," she said simply, and changed the subject.

I shot a few moments with my video camera of Barbara and Madeleine talking until Barbara said, "Turn that thing off." With a rush of tenderness, I did as I was told.

A couple of years after our visit, we received a gift from Barbara—a painting she had done of an azure sea, waves crashing against black rocks, the sun, and a lone cloud in a lavender sky. I called her with our thanks.

"It is a beautiful painting," I told her. "It's hanging in our living room. And like you, we love the ocean. Barbara, I'm so glad we had a chance to see each other again."

"Yes," she said simply. "So am I."

Barbara's painting she gave to Madeleine and me.

The last time I spoke to Barbara was on the phone again in 2009. I had a call from the Saba Hospital near her home. I was told by a nurse that I could speak to Miss Joyce, but "she is very weak."

However, when she said hello and talked to me, she sounded strong and cheerful.

"After all, you know, we can't go on living forever," she said with a laugh. "I'm just curious to find out what's going to happen next."

I hope she did, and I hope she will remember what I said. "I love you, Barbara. I'll never forget you."

I received this email from Barbara's close friend, the owner of the gallery on Saba who represents Barbara's work:

Howard,
Happy Holidays.
    Barbara had only a few requests as part of being a Bahá'í
for her funeral:

She was to have a casket made of hardwood, she was to be wrapped in a silk shroud, a Bahá'í ring was to be placed on her finger, and her money was to be given to Bahá'í USA. As for the funeral we planned, a woman from Saint Maarten who is Bahá'í joined us for the funeral and read the obligatory Prayer for the Dead over her grave. My husband and I picked several Bahá'í prayers that were read, and we included a brief description of the Bahá'í tenets for those attending who were unfamiliar with the faith. Several read their own eulogies. A group who sings in a local church played and sang as people gathered for the beginning of the ceremony. Barbara was carried then from the gazebo where we had gathered to the nearby cemetery where she was buried. We then gathered at the nearby house of a friend who served refreshments. It was all beautiful. We miss her.

Please know how much fun we had showing those great pictures you sent of Barbara onstage. That really brought her so much in her last days.

Hugs, Judy

Barbara later in life in Saba.

CHAPTER 86

LITTLE MARY WHO?

Los Angeles, 2013

Eileen and I traveling through Europe.

THE MERCURIAL ACTRESS Eileen Brennan was years younger than I am and technically should not appear in a book entitled *I've Always Loved Older Women*. Never mind. As you may have noticed, Eileen has already appeared in several earlier chapters, and because she made an unforgettable contribution to my life, I would like to continue the rest of her story here.

Back in 1982, when I was packing for a trip to California for a commercial film job, Madeleine suggested I look up my old fiancée, Eileen.

"You really should, you know, even if you two are history," Madeleine said. "Remember the time when her husband once came here, house-hunting? They were thinking of moving east?"

"Yes, I do remember, I was working and he came and you made lunch for him. You told him where to look for houses and he took your advice combing the area with a local agent, without any luck. Apparently, he felt anything they would like was all too expensive. Anyway, now they are divorced, and she has two boys she is raising in California. I will give her a call when I am out there."

As it turned out, I never met Mr. Lampson. But while I was in Hollywood, I visited Eileen on the set of her TV series, a spinoff from the motion picture *Private Benjamin*. (She had won a Golden Globe Award for her role as the tough, cranky Capt. Doreen Lewis in the movie and an Emmy for the series.) It had been fifteen years or so since we had seen each other, and it was good to see her again. They were on a lunch break, and Eileen introduced me to Lorna Patterson, the TV Private Benjamin.

"My old boyfriend, Howard," she said. "Isn't he a hunk?"

I was taken by surprise to hear that label pinned on me, especially by Eileen. I quickly changed the subject before Lorna could answer. "I'd like to invite you and my old girlfriend to lunch," I said. "You must know a good place nearby. We can be very affectionate, and everybody can be jealous of me with two such beautiful women."

"I have to meet with the director," Lorna said with a smile. "You two go on without me. I'm sure both of you have some catching up to do."

Indeed, we did. At lunch, Eileen told me about her two young sons, Sam and Patrick Lampson, and I showed her snapshots of my children–Thomas, India, and Mia–with Madeleine. We reminisced about the past. A lot of water had flowed under the bridge. The sparks that caught fire between us on Bob Holloway's ill-fated revue, *Balloons*, had died down and flared up several times in the passing twenty-odd years. Her career bloomed with Besoyan's off-Broadway hit *Little Mary Sunshine* as well as the original *Hello, Dolly!* and others on Broadway. Both our careers took off as we found "other fish to fry" (another of my Aunt Amber's expressions) and after we dropped our engagement for good.

How ironic it was, just after that Eileen worked on the film *Divorce American Style*. After a brief stint as an original cast member in Rowan and Martin's *Laugh In*, Eileen's movie career continued with films like *The Last Picture Show* and the Oscar-winning *The Sting*, starring Robert Redford and Paul Newman. Shortly afterward, she was cast in *Private Benjamin*, which brought her an Academy Award nomination.

As I recall, Eileen and I never discussed her arrival in Copenhagen and the disastrous driving trip to Italy, where the romance ended with our final goodbyes in Rome. Considering our stormy track record, it was probably just as well. The Hollywood lunch turned out to be a very pleasant one, and the visit ended on a happy note.

One evening not long after that, Eileen was in a horrible accident. Outside a restaurant in Studio City, when she was saying good night to her friend Goldie Hawn, she was hit by a speeding car. Her injuries were so severe, her condition was critical. When I visited her months later, she was still in a wheelchair, convalescing.

"I woke up two days later in the hospital," Eileen told me. "I don't have any recollection of what happened. I just know what I read in the papers. My legs were broken. Every bone in the left side of my face was crushed."

Eileen's rehabilitation was long and difficult. Nevertheless, in time, she was able to overcome the accident and all that was involved and continue her successful career, appearing on television and in motion pictures. We made a point to keep in touch over the years, I am happy to say with respect and affection. Yet unfortunately in July, 2013, Eileen Brennan died of cancer in her home in Burbank, California.

In her own way, the always beautiful Eileen Brennan.

CHAPTER 87

MUNSEL, MERRY DIVA OF THE MET

NYC, 2011

IN THE MAGAZINE *Opera News*, Brian Kellow wrote about an evening dinner tribute to Patrice Munsel, former Metropolitan Opera star:

> ON APRIL 10, I attended a tribute to another native of Spokane, Washington–PATRICE MUNSEL, who was receiving the NATIONAL ARTS CLUB's Medal of Honor for lifetime achievement. The NAC is a singular organization, the kind of place where you can see stalwarts of what I think of as the real Golden Age of New York show business gather several nights a week. They were out in force to pay homage to Munsel, who was decked out in [a] gold-and-white sparkling pantsuit and a coffee-table–sized yellow topaz ring, and she seemed delighted with the unveiling of her portrait by Joel Spector. In her touching acceptance speech, she said, "What I really wanted to do was be an opera star. I did not want to be an opera singer." She spoke of the joy of being in front of an audience–"There's nothing else like it. It's the glory of being able to take what God gave

you and pass it around." Then she did just that by singing an amazingly fresh rendition of "Send In the Clowns"–talent, charm, and vocal savvy all intact.

My wife, Madeleine, and I attended that tribute at the National Arts Club, and not only was it a marvelously entertaining evening, but also, everything Mr. Kellow had said about Patrice Munsel was true, especially his last line about "Send In the Clowns." As far as I could see, there wasn't a dry eye in the house. I daresay her performance was the most touching and the highlight of the evening's offerings. Only the absence of Bob, her husband, and Rhett, her firstborn son, both no longer with us, could be cause for sadness. But neither of them would have wanted that on such an evening of joy. Being long-standing friends of Patrice and Bob, we were at their table with her children and her grandchildren. Once again, time spent in their company was a great pleasure and fun. Pat was a true embodiment of my title above: "MUNSEL, MERRY DIVA OF THE MET." Patrice had that rarest of talents–meeting adversity with good humor and flashing a wide smile.

Patrice Munsel passed away just a few years ago after her
dear husband and my good friend, Bob Schuler.

CHAPTER 88

FOREVER AMBER

1932–present

S O MUCH FOR famous leading ladies. The time has come for me to face a fact I have ignored for most of my life. My most important leading lady wasn't famous at all. She wasn't beautiful, at least not in the conventional way. She wasn't sexy and exciting. She wasn't a talented actress, singer, or dancer or an artist of any kind. She was my mother's elder sister, my Aunt Amber, who raised me. She was strong yet had a vulnerable vitality, had a sense of humor, and was warm and loving to me and my brother. These qualities were not always apparent to everyone, but they were always there, to be appreciated by the right audience.

When I was still a little boy, Aunt Amber surprised her family when she got a job downtown in McLeod's Department Store on Main Street. I'm pretty sure my mother admired her sister, and she must have thought I'd profit by visiting Aunt Amber at her work. I was impressed with the way my aunt waited on customers.

In those days, most people paid cash for purchases, and the sales clerks at McLeod's would insert the money into small metal cylinders hanging from overhead cables. By pulling down a wooden handle, the clerk would send the carriers up to a balcony at the end of the store. There, a cashier would ring up the purchase and send the receipt and change, if any, back down to the clerk.

Imagine my childish delight when, with a mischievous wink to me, Aunt Amber would send the carrier with the customer's money flying away on the cables. It looked like so much fun. My aunt was good at her job, chatting with her customers while she wrapped up their purchases. I was so proud of her. She couldn't have made a lot of money at McLeod's, but somehow she managed to save enough to buy herself a small car, a secondhand Model A Ford. She learned to drive and no longer had to ask Uncle Collin or Uncle Grady to take her to work. My uncles may have been surprised and a little annoyed by their sister's show of independence.

I was eight years old when my parents died, and Aunt Amber took over the formidable job of caring for me and my thirteen-year-old brother. Considering that my aunt was an unmarried woman with little education and no experience as a mother, it must have been a tremendous adjustment for her to assume that role, and yet she did it without hesitation and with no complaint. Running the house for her three unmarried brothers, Aunt Amber now had two needy kids to care for and had to quit her job at McLeod's. It wasn't long before she had to give up her car, a bitter loss of her independence.

One day, when I found a small toy bus on the front porch, I was puzzled. "How do you think it got there?" I asked Aunt Amber

"I figured my little sugar lump needed a new toy," she said with a loving hug.

She cared for "her two boys," my brother and me, as if she had given birth to us.

I never actually thought of Aunt Amber as taking my mother's place, but in truth, that is what she did. In addition to caring for my daily needs, she encouraged me in many other ways. When I showed an early interest in "picture drawing," she praised my talent. Later, when I was just thirteen, she insisted I be allowed to take lessons from Miss Nannie Donovan, the only art teacher in Hattiesburg. After a few months of copying Miss Nannie's fruit and flower postcards, I executed my first original, a charcoal and water-color sketch: *Mallard Ducks Migrating.* Aunt Amber had it framed and entered it in an exhibition sponsored by the Utopian Club, a local organization for women. I won a special award. I don't recall what it was, but I was proud of it. The ducks still hang in my office after eighty years.

My award-winning drawing from age thirteen, 1936.

My aunt was sweet and gentle with my brother and me, but with her own brothers, she could be outspoken, even caustic. She often carried this trait over into her daily life and never failed to say whatever was on her mind, peppered with old-fashioned Southern expressions. Now, nearly eighty years later, I still hear her colorful language coming back to me almost every day.

"You can put that in your pipe and smoke it," Aunt Amber would say if she wanted to drive home a statement just spoken. To "badmouth" an acquaintance she didn't like, she spoke scornfully–"Speak of the devil, and his imps will appear!" Or, of course, there was always "Other fish to fry!"

Aunt Amber was frugal. Never having had a nickel to spare, she spent as little money as possible, watching carefully where it went. When she visited other family members, she seemed overly careful if not a bit distrustful. Even at my brother, Bishop's, home, his wife, Irene, couldn't understand why Aunt Amber kept her purse tucked under her arm.

"Now, Aunt Amber, make yourself at home," Irene would say. "Let me take your hat and your pocketbook."

"No, thank you," Aunt Amber would answer with a smile. "I'll just keep it right here with me."

I never knew how my aunt and uncles could afford to send me away to college in Alabama, but they did. I'm afraid their only reward from me were my letters about needing spending money, joining a fraternity, and going to campus dances every weekend. (Oh yes, I also learned to drink bootleg whiskey, but I didn't mention that in my letters.) Aunt Amber always wrote to me during my one year in Auburn. Recently, I found an old letter she had written after getting my request for some new socks! She sent them, along with a few dollars she had saved from her boarding house earnings.

Aunt Amber also wrote to me faithfully the three years I was in military service in World War II. "I miss my honeybunch," she would write, always ending her letters with "I love you." I always answered, ending my letters with the same words: "I love you." However, before and after the war, I'm afraid I never said those words to her person to person. When I left home to follow my dream of being in show business, my sweet Aunt Amber never tried to stop me. She always encouraged me. Maybe it was because she never had the opportunity to follow her own dreams.

My aunt liked to read, but to the best of my knowledge, the only book she ever read besides the Bible was *Gone With the Wind*. However, she loved newspapers. She read the *Hattiesburg American* every day, and occasionally, she scanned the *Times Picayune* from New Orleans. She liked to clip recipes and articles.

"I'll save them 'til later," she would say, placing the papers in neat stacks around her bedroom.

She actually did save the clippings and filled her dresser drawers with them. The stacks of newspapers grew bigger and bigger until her room looked as if it were furnished with them. Bishop warned her of the fire hazard she was creating, but she refused to throw the papers away.

"I want to try some of the recipes, and I'll catch up with the articles" was always her answer.

One day, while she was out of the house, Bishop took stacks of her newspapers into the backyard and made a huge bonfire of them. When Aunt Amber came home and found what he'd done, she was furious. When he tried to reason with her, she burst into tears and became inconsolable, almost as she had been when Grandmother's house burned years ago. I don't think Bishop ever entered her bedroom again. She may have forgiven him for what he did, but I'm certain she didn't forget it.

Since both Aunt Amber and my brother Bishop have long since passed away, it's impossible for me to know if he thought of Aunt Amber as a mother figure or if, in his heart, he accepted her as such. He must have, whether he realized or not, because he always acted as a loving son would have. Bishop was the one who cared for our aunt while I pursued my career in New York, Hollywood, Jamaica, or Denmark. When our aunt was no longer able to run her little boarding house, Bishop moved her to a new home and provided her with what she needed. He grocery-shopped for her and bought her carefully chosen canned goods.

"Be sure to check the numbers on the bottom of each can," Aunt Amber insisted. "They might be the code for the ones that are poison!"

In her later life, when our aunt became senile, Bishop responded to her phone calls every day, and sometimes she would wake him up at night.

"They are outside in their car right now," Aunt Amber would say on the phone. "And they will come in and beat me up."

Then Bishop would get dressed and go to her, look at her bruises, and realize she must have bumped into the furniture or, worse, fallen. He would wait for her to quiet down or go to sleep.

About that time in 1966, I was working on the movie in Denmark when I heard my name on the PA system. "Trans-atlantic telephone call for Howard Barker."

It was startling. I was in a meeting, showing my set sketches to the director and producers. "Excuse me, gentlemen," I managed to say. I knew a trans-atlantic call had to be urgent.

"Bad news." My brother's voice came through as clearly as if he was next door. "Aunt Amber died."

I didn't speak.

Then he continued. "She'd not been well, you know. She'd been having lots of problems . . ."

"I know, but . . ."

"Well, she was in her eighties . . . and she'd been getting weaker. The doctor told me she had developed pneumonia. I took her to the hospital." He stopped for a moment. "She died in her sleep."

I think I was in shock because all I managed to say was "Bishop, I've got to call you back." My voice was unsteady.

"Anything wrong, Howard?" the producer asked.

"Yes, Bob," I said, putting down the phone slowly. "Death in the family."

"We'll finish this after lunch, okay, Bent?" Bob said to Bent Christianson, the Danish producer. "Howard, let's go into my office. Who died?" he asked as we left the room.

"My aunt Amber," I said. "She raised me and my brother. She . . . she was like a mother to me." The words surprised me as soon as they came out of my mouth. It was the first time I realized that I thought of her that way.

"Then you'll have to go home for her funeral, Howard."

"How can I, Bob? It's too expensive, we're shooting, and I . . ." I was searching for excuses. I didn't want to go home. The thought was overwhelming.

"I'll pay for it. We'll manage without you for a few days. Don't worry about it. You must go."

The next morning, I was on a plane to New York. Seven or eight hours later, I landed, took a cab to my apartment, showered, changed into a suit, and caught another plane to New Orleans. Bishop was waiting for me. He had driven two hours to the airport, and he drove two hours back to Hattiesburg. The following day at Hulett's Funeral Home, we met the few of our relatives who were still living and some friends who had known Aunt Amber.

Then it was time for me to approach the open casket. In it, surrounded by satin and lace, a tiny pink lady was lying as if she had just fallen asleep. Dressed in a pretty frock, her white hair set in meticulous waves, her hands folded on her breast, she looked nothing like my Aunt Amber. My aunt's hair wasn't white. For as long as I can remember, she had always dyed it dark brown and arranged it softly around her face, with a bun in the back. Somebody had picked out a dress like none I'd ever seen my aunt wear. She favored cotton house dresses and sort of shapeless cardigan sweaters, And Aunt Amber never had time to fold her hands on her breast. She was always too busy—cooking, cleaning, and taking care of a houseful of boarders and two nephews or maybe occasionally reading a newspaper.

But now it was my Aunt Amber—Aunt Amber, lying peacefully in her casket. As I stood looking at her, I was glad I had made the trip to see her for the last time.

After the funeral, I caught the next plane back to Denmark. On the eight-hour flight, I had plenty of time to think about my life with Aunt Amber and my life away from her—more than twice the number of years I had lived with my parents before they died. I realize now, Aunt Amber was the one who really did take my mother's place. She was truly my one and only real "leading lady." Now, even if it's too late, I'm saying as clearly as I can . . . Aunt Amber, I love you.

CHAPTER 89

I HOLD THESE TRUTHS . . .

MADELEINE AND I, proud parents, watching our three children grow, loving them through all the highs and lows in the ongoing journey of life, has been a wonderful experience I wish everyone could have. Thomas, India, and Mia are so different. As they have matured, with their different psyches, living their different lifestyles and with unique mates, I believe all three have comfortably settled into being their own special selves.

Thomas, after graduating from the Culinary Institute of America, worked as a chef for a time in New York restaurants before becoming manager of prepared foods for a major company. He now has his own business as a personal chef in Napa Valley, California. He is married to Finny Lee, an Asian beauty, who is also a miraculous computer analyst.

India, a business major, is in the business of managing an office building in Connecticut. She is married to Jay Liddell, manager of a nearby branch of a prodigious national investment company. India and Jay have two wonderful sons: teenager Christopher and pre-teen Patrick. Both are creative, good athletes, talented artists, and good kids whom I know will become real gentlemen.

Our youngest daughter, Mia, went into "the family business" and became a director of photography of documentaries and small productions. Her husband, Todd Seidman, also in the business, is now a clever set designer/ art director on commercials himself. Mia and Todd have a wonderful young daughter, Pearl. Pearl is a constant reader, talented, and artistic, and we are so proud of her, along with our two grandsons.

If you've heard the advice "Live your life in the moment," believe me, when you are around young children, you live in the moment. With our grandkids, there is no past or future. Everything is now–period.

Madeleine, my wonderful wife, went back to school and got a Bachelor's Degree in Social Work and worked for twenty-five years in a tough, but rewarding job in foster care helping troubled children. Now she's helping me take care of myself.

Here we are all together as a family at Madeleine's seventy-fifth birthday with my dear nephew John Craig Barker, my brother Bishop's youngest son.

CHAPTER 90

I'VE ALWAYS LOVED OLDER WOMEN

In Mississippi, it was a tradition on Mother's Day for children to wear a carnation to Sunday school and church–a red carnation if your mother was still living and a white carnation if she was not. So in our childhood on Mother's Day, my brother and I wore white carnations pinned to our shirts, just over the heart.

Now every time I smell carnations, the scent–something like cloves–takes me back to those Mother's Days. Even though I refused to go to my parents' funeral, I've been to others through the years, and funeral flowers always seems to be redolent of carnations, those spicy, sweet carnations. I have always loved the smell.

Many of the memories about my mother have grown dim since she and my father died nearly eight decades ago, and yet some things stand out as clear as crystal. My mother was beautiful–dark eyes, fair skin, and raven hair. I remember in particular one dress she wore–black with white spiderweb designs all over it. I think it was velvet because it was soft when I pressed my cheek against it. Mama spoke with a strong, sweet voice. She loved to sit at our new baby grand piano, playing and singing, "Tiptoe through the tulips to my window. You will find me there, singing, 'Tiptoe through the tulips with me.'"

As important as fathers are to their children, a mother's love is a very special kind of love. Over the years, while making my way through life and its precarious jungle of adventures, I may have been, unknowingly, reaching out to older women for the mother I had lost when I was a child. But when I fell in love with Madeleine, seventeen years younger than I am, I no longer needed those attachments to older women. Finally, I had found a partner who not only offered me the love I was searching for but also was the one I could love too. You might call it my finally, midlife, coming-of-age.

When Madeleine and I first spoke about marriage, I reminded her of the gap between our ages. "After all, I'm forty-two, and you're only twenty-five. That's okay for now, but what about when I'm old?"

"I promise to push you in a wheelchair when that becomes necessary," she said with a sweet laugh. "What's seventeen years if you love each other?"

Well, I'm still not in that wheelchair, and we're still in love.

The Sinatra record we played more than fifty years ago in Copenhagen ended with these words: "Ever since that night, we've been together, lovers at first sight, in love forever. It turned out so right for strangers in the night." It has always been our song.

Madeleine and I have a silly little game we play sometimes in the morning when we wake up. We speak French and only French to each other for as long as we can until one gives up. One morning, when I brought tea up to our bedroom, Madeleine woke up, said, "Bonjour," and closed her eyes again.

"Bonjour, ma petite chou-chou. Apres tea," I said. Then giving up my fractured French, I spoke in English but with the best wicked French accent I could muster, "I weel meck mad loff to you."

"Do whatever you want with me," she said without opening her eyes. "Just don't wake me up!"

Madeleine could have answered in flawless French, but she didn't. Even if she had, I wouldn't have understood her anyway. I guess I won? Maybe it was a tie.

***

One last little story to end this memoir: Not long ago, on our wedding anniversary, Madeleine gave me a greeting card picturing a couple standing on a lush green lawn. Inside, the woman was saying to the man, "We have the greenest grass!" Under that, my wife wrote, "Howard, nobody's grass is as green as <u>ours</u>. Thank you for fifty years with the greenest grass. Love from your wife, Madeleine."

It doesn't get any better than that.

Madeleine and I renewed our vows at her Dobbs Ferry Lutheran
Church on our fiftieth anniversary–January 8, 2017.

EPILOGUE

TO QUOTE ROBERT K. Massie, author of the book *Catherine the Great: Portrait of a Woman*, "You never finish a book, even after it goes to press—et cetera, et cetera." Mr. Massie was so right! Now I would like to just keep on writing.

ACKNOWLEDGMENTS

I WANT TO THANK everyone who has been so helpful and supportive during the writing of this book. The book would never have been completed without my editor, my daughter Mia, who has spent endless hours with me working on the book, for which I am eternally grateful. My daughter India also has put so much time into the book, scanning the multitude of photos and printing and sending versions of the book to me numerous times.

My son-in-law Todd worked his wonders on the computer, bringing my ideas for the cover into a reality as well as doctoring a few photos that needed some special attention. Actually, come to think of it, Todd also helped retrieve the entire book when we thought I had deleted it on the computer!

I am greatly indebted to my dear friend C. Robert Holloway, who was kind enough to read the memoir earlier on and give his feedback as well as guide me in the world of self-publishing. Thank you to my dear niece Cathy Shearer for hunting down the Hattiesburg artist Donna Woods as well as the old photos of my Uncle Ledger.

The incredible portrait of me on the back of the book was painted a few years ago by my extremely kind and talented cousin Cynthia Pagano. The amount of time and consideration she put into achieving an ageless version of me is a testament to her craftsmanship.

Finally, I will always have to give my greatest appreciation to my wife, Madeleine, for her patience over the years as I wrote and rewrote my memoir. To Madeleine and all my family and friends, thank you for your love and support as this book has meant so much to me.

IMAGE CREDITS AND ACKNOWLEDGMENTS

Illustrations of Hattiesburg buildings courtesy of Donna Kirkland Woods of Southern Art (donnalovesart@hotmail.com)

Portrait of Howard Barker by Cynthia Pagano (www.cynthiaharris-pagano.com)

Stella Adler photo courtesy of the Adler family archives

Betty Boop image courtesy of King Features Syndicate/Fleischer Studios Inc.

Patrice Munsel image courtesy of Walter McBride Photography

Musical Americana brochure courtesy of Columbia Artists

Marlene Dietrich photos approved by son John D. Riva

Jean Stapleton headshot courtesy of the Stapleton family

New York Times penthouse ice rink photo courtesy of Redux Pictures

Cover art courtesy of Todd Seidman, son-in-love

Barker obituaries and wedding announcements courtesy of *Hattiesburg American* newspaper

CPSIA information can be obtained
at www.ICGtesting.com
Printed in the USA
BVHW030553050719
552677BV00002B/25/P